MYTH, CULT AND SYMBOLS IN ŚĀKTA HINDUISM

MYTH, CULT AND SYMBOLS IN ŚĀKTA HINDUISM

A Study of the Indian Mother Goddess

BY

WENDELL CHARLES BEANE

LEIDEN
E. J. BRILL
1977

ISBN 90 04 04814 6

PRINTED IN BELGIUM

To
DeAnna, Songhay, and Mark

CONTENTS

PREFACE

Durgā-Kālī is the theistic manifestation of a widespread concept in Indian religion called *Śakti*, or the religion of "Power". As the "Goddess" (*Devī*) she is regarded as both Mother of Timelessness and Life and Arbitress of Time and Death.

This work proposes to deal with our chosen divinity with respect to three broad yet distinctive categories of religious understanding: cosmology, rituology, and eschatology. It is felt that the use of such traditional categories need not pose any serious general problems; the more specific responsibility does consist, however, in pointing out the peculiar meaning which such terms or systems tend to have in their own cultural-religious environment. The choice of these categories derives from our discovery that there exists in the religious thought and practice connected with this goddess a remarkable homologous relationship of myth, cult, and symbols. The grist of our thesis, then, is that the foregoing phenomena constitute an integration of structures that provide an almost unique opportunity for significant religious understanding.

There have been many treatments of varying aspects of the worship of Durgā-Kālī. However, there has apparently been no attempt made, heretofore, to examine this religious phenomenon as a potentially unified structure of thought and expression. Here we are undertaking such a task, focusing upon this goddess as the prototypical image par excellence in the religious tradition of Śākta Hinduism.

We are aware, then, that, nominally, Durgā-Kālī is merely one manifestation of the *Śakti* phenomenon. To be sure, other nominal and formal types do exist and may have their own ritual peculiarities according to regional differences and religious temperaments. It is more important to recognize, nonetheless, that there are certain distinctive features in the larger Indian religious tradition that enhance the feasibility of our study (*vide* Chapter I). For now, at any rate, let us mention one positive contributive factor in all this: that certain basic mythological conceptions elaborated, probably, by a "Great Traditional" (Smārta-) Brāhman elite — often in creative religio-political tension with popular and/or tribalistic ideas and forms — have facilitated our avoidance of phenomenal chaos. Historically, therefore, what may have seemed only a chaos of ideas and forms was gradually understood amidst non-religious pressures and religious yearnings to be potentially capable of vital "convergences" for the ultimate purpose of creating a cosmos of religious meaning. Not barring real non-religious contexts, after all, it is still the *religious* meaning with which we are so intimately concerned.

Furthermore, for ourselves, the feasibility of this task is borne out by our own investigations into three crucial aspects of the problem. Their aspectual convergence thus concerns itself with mythic structure (i.e., Kālī as Śaktic Creatrix), cultic structure (i.e., Kālī Pūjā), and eschatonic structure (i.e., Kali Yuga).

We are especially indebted to many scholars, not the least of whom is Sir John Woodroffe whose copious studies and translations of several, especially Tantric, texts from the Sanskrit are indispensable to this endeavour. The suggested presence of a multi-structural unity, such as we propose, owes much to two distinguished scholars, the late Jean Przyluski and Mircea Eliade (now at Chicago). Przyluski intimated the direction of our thesis in philological terms in an original article in the *Indian Historical Quarterly*, in 1938. He demonstrated highly probable religio-linguistic affinities between such nominals as *kālī*, *kāla*, *kalki* and other derivatives. Although apparently overcaptivated by cross-cultural generalizations on mostly linguistic grounds, Przyluski's influence upon us continues; that is, we continue to profit from the *intra-cultural* implications of his basic findings for a better understanding of how language influences religion and culture and vice-versa. Przyluski, of course, did not (neither was it probably his intention to) indicate the relevance of the cultic aspect of the entire problem. Anyone who starts out to study the relationship between religious symbols and human culture without the guidance of Mircea Eliade's works deprives himself of the luxury of a deeper understanding from the very beginning. It is Eliade who maintained in an article in the *Eranos-Jahrbuch*, in 1951, that there was a structurally justifiable association between the notions of *kāla* (Time), the goddess Kālī, and the Kali Yuga.

Here we shall attempt to show that, at least as a tristructural religious manifestation, the entire phenomenon deserves further examination, historically and phenomenologically. Yet there is also a need to emphasize a third *methodological* component which comes to bear particularly upon the role of the *cultus* : the *pūjā* as an essentially integrative religious complex. This means that a structurological cultic dimension is most vital to the total religious orientation.

In approaching our overall study, therefore, we intend to apply a triangulation of methods to the religious phenomenon. In a word, our aim is to render a reasonably comprehensive historical, phenomenological, and structural exposition and interpretation of Durgā-Kālī as part of the Indian "mother-goddess complex" but especially as it is manifested in Bengal. The myths, rites, and festivities in homage to the Goddess occurring in that region of India are already recognized as constituting a veritable stronghold of her adoration. Nevertheless, it is because of the nodal role which certain structuralist criteria tend to play in our presentation that functional-symbolistic correspondences can be made between other regional manifestations of such worship derived from various field studies.

Broadly speaking, our thesis has some retrospective historical significance in terms of the general Motif of the Feminine per se as a cultural-historical reality which characterized parts of the world outside India. The full inter-cultural significance of our study in the light of contemporary (especially American) re-evaluations of the role of woman in modern society cannot now be estimated. At any rate, just as that problem offers no easy solution, it would also seem that no one method of approach could ever hope to encompass the endless potentiality of meanings hidden in the *Worship* of the Feminine (Principle). In the case of a general mother-goddess motif admirable attempts from various field perspectives have been made by such scholars as E. O. James, Erich Neumann, Sibylle von Cles-Reden, S. K. Dikshit, and others. With regard to a specific female personification of the Divine of India, there are the works of P. Ghosha, V. R. R. Dikshitar, Ernest A. Payne, Vasudeva S. Agrawala, and others.

Both of these kinds of treatments (general and specific)[1] tend to display the following disadvantages, not necessarily in themselves, but in the light of our own objectives. In the former cases, however invaluable, the works of these authors reveal clearly the tendency to adopt a delimited methodological approach or ideological stress. Their main difficulty, however, consists in their range and scope as compared to the depth of their relevance in terms of *religious* understanding. In the latter types of monographic accounts the problem is not so much that of depth of religious understanding but rather range and scope even having to do with a *specific*, religiously understood

---

[1] *Vide* the Bibliography.

phenomenon. Ghosha, for example, renders an indispensable, though still only a liturgical, journal of goddess adoration. Dikshitar's work is essentially a literary-historical approach to his subject but suggests no real themic unity. Payne's presentation is conveniently historical, but the author blurs the religious significance of his work by insisting upon the "impermanence" of Śaktism; in his treatment, therefore, religious creativity is ultimately subjected to historical eventuality. Agrawala's work, though precious, is primarily a commentative translation of one major textual glorification of the Goddess. Through this and other articles, however, Agrawala's contribution to our understanding of how several of the cultic motifs are related to classical modes of Indian thought remains substantial.

What the foregoing scholars have attempted as legitimate aspects of a particular religious phenomenon, we would undertake from a more *totalistic* perspective. Certainly, this objective does not preclude our awareness, methodologically, that the proposed unified approach, itself, can never encompass the whole of Indian religious experience and expression. At best, our study would turn out to be but an aspect, too, of that country's broader religious panorama. The ongoing significance of this thesis, nonetheless, will reside in the fact that it contributes to a better understanding of that very larger Indian ocean of religious life.

In the pages that follow our "Methodological Concerns", then, we shall be discussing the philosophically abstract and personalistically concrete aspects of the Durgā-Kālī complex. This will be accomplished largely within a framework of Tantric and Puranic notions of Cosmic (sacred) Time and Terrestrial (sacred) Space. As the dynamics of Sacred History are juxtaposed with the movements of historical times and events in a specific methodological understanding of religion's inexhaustible potentialities, at least two things should become clearly known. First, that Durgā-Kālī as a theistic manifestation can indeed be understood, despite bizarreness of form and changes in historical-cultural milieu. Secondly, that Durgā-Kālī reflects, also, a universal ontological malaise which can be aptly correlated with "experiences that arise from an irresistible human desire to transcend time and history" (Eliade). Thus in a very real rense this study might be said to amount to a theoretical and practical inquiry into the soteriological dynamics of an Indian religion.

The author wishes to acknowledge and to thank the following persons, especially Professors Mircea Eliade, Joseph M. Kitagawa,

Charles H. Long, and Edward C. Dimock, Jr., of the University of Chicago. These scholars are important for the guidance and encouragement they gave during my graduate years and in the formation of this study. Further research was made possible by a post-doctoral fellowship granted by the American Institute of Indian Studies in 1974. It is not feasible to mention, yet gratitude is felt for what seems, all those innumerable templeguides, museum curators, university librarians and personal friends who were so gracious to Mrs. Beane and me while in India.

Among Indian scholars particular thanks are due to Professor S. C. Dube of the Indian Institute of Advanced Study for making library facilities available and arranging consulations with several scholars there. Those scholars are Professors L. P. Singh, S. K. Ghosh, S. Miri, and, especially, S. C. Malik, who read the entire manuscript and made helpful critical observations. Additional thanks should go to Professors D. C. Sircar, and V. Raghavan, as well as B. M. Pande, member of the Archaeological Survey of India, in New Delhi. From such wonderful minds East and West, significant understanding and inspiration were gained concerning many of those inimitable "things Indian".

W. C. Beane

INTRODUCTION

USES OF THE LITERATURE

The literary texts relevant to the thought and worship of the divinity, Durgā-Kālī, are vast and complex indeed. The principal reason is that this goddess, as the focus par excellence of a major religious denomination of Hinduism (i.e., the Śāktas), can be adequately understood only against the broader, and seemingly abysmal, background of Tantric belief and practice. About this general vogue [1] as a religio-cultural expression there is hardly a dearth of literary material. Thus the Tantric current also provides a dynamic vehicle for for certain aspects of other forms of religious development such as Buddhism and Jainism. No attempt shall be made, therefore, to use *all* of the literature probably related to the goddess under study (if, indeed, that were possible!). To be sure, it constitutes no mean task to undertake the present study even with the religious texts that are in fact available to us.

Our primary purpose, nonetheless, is to make an attempt to set the goddess Durgā-Kālī in some form of structural relief; that is, to make her more intelligible to readers whose conceptual orientation may have barred an adequate understanding and reasonable appreciation of her, specifically, as well as of non-Occidental religious expressions in general. Yet it is also to demonstrate that when one focuses upon the goddess Durgā-Kālī as the prototypical image of the worship of Feminine Power (i.e., *Śakti*), one gains also a better perspective not only of the Tantric vogue itself, but hopefully the larger Indian ocean of religious experience.

The vastness and complexity of the religious texts are, again, created by the relevance of many *puraṇas* (or ancient traditions) to the study of our divinity. The two principal texts most often quoted in glorification of the goddess are the Mārkaṇḍeya Purāṇa and the Devī-Bhāgavata Purāṇa. Not to be excluded is another type of epic poetry (*itihāsa*) such as found in the Mahābhārata. To these must be

---

[1] The single word "vogue" does much to suggest the nature of Tantrism as a religio-*cultural* force. *Vide* Mircea Eliade, *Yoga : Immortality and Freedom* (New York : Pantheon Books, Inc., 1958), p. 200. For the phenomenon of Tantrism in relation to the Śāktas, *vide infra*, "Historical and Traditional Origins".

added the classical Vedic texts, especially the Ṛg and the Atharva Vedas, in addition to other sources, for example, the Brāhmaṇas and the Upaniṣads. All these and others become pertinent in our search to indicate significant lines of historic-mythic continuity and change between what are probably earlier and later phases of religious literary creativity in Indian thought.

Scholars are aware, of course, that there is a host of Tantras not easily available either in Oriental or in Western languages. The reasons are clear and decisive. On the one hand, there is the sheer immensity of materials that would constitute an all-inclusive bibliography of primary and secondary texts. On the other hand, apart from the need for additional contributions by philologists and Indologists, other possibly relevant texts or sources remain difficult to obtain, being either no longer published or else zealously guarded by private hands. Agehananda Bharati (in *The Tantric Tradition*) tells us quite candidly that "a complete tantric bibliography would make up a book of about seven hundred pages"[2]. Numerous illustrative excerpts and quotations from some of these "other" scriptures are included, however, in a few of our primary sources.

We must hasten to mention here another collective source for the goddess, Durgā-Kālī—that is, various Śākta Upaniṣads. Also of particular significance for our study is the theistic denominational affiliation between the goddess and the god, Śiva. In this regard, it is interesting to notice that Sinha commences his book *Shakta Monism : The Cult of Shakti* [3] with a discussion of Śiva (the Destroyer) in Hinduism. We intend in this study to consider the historical and religious sectarian relations, if any, between these two divinities, Durgā-Kālī and Śiva. For now, at any rate, we merely point out that, besides Śākta tantras, there are also Śaiva tantras.

Such being the case, there appears to be at once an implicit broadening of the range of texts to be considered. Usually such Śākta and Śaivite tantras are classified as *Āgama* and *Nigama*, respectively. The former term typifies the revelation by Śiva to the goddess (e.g., Devī/Durgā/Kālī, etc.); the latter term typifying a revelation by the goddess to the god, Śiva. Their common traditional structure is that of a dialogue between the two divinities. We shall have more to say

---

[2] Agehananda Bharati, *The Tantric Tradition* (London : Hillary House Publishers, Ltd., 1965), p. 303.

[3] Jadunath Sinha, *Shakta Monism : The Cult of Shakti* (1st ed.; Calcutta : Sinha Publishing House, 1966).

of this remarkable theological relationship as the work proceeds. What we wish to emphasize now is that, though literature characteristic of both aspects of the traditional form will be used here, our study will aim primarily at a strategic phenomenological *literary* reduction in favour of the more distinctively Śākta texts. Our main objective, then, is to explicate the "realm" of the goddess, Durgā-Kālī, in myth, cult, and symbols. Her specific relationship with Śiva, as her mystic spouse, will be taken into account, nonetheless, but in the light of our ultimate purposes.

We should mention at this time two important things which have tremendously facilitated our work. The first observation, which has become a source of methodological consolation in this study, is the phenomenon of mythological repetition of words and *motifs* in many of our sources. Account is to be taken, nevertheless, of mythological "variants" and legendary "cycles" in keeping with the centrality of *structure* [4] in our phenomenology of symbols. At any rate, our work suffers no detraction in breadth and depth in terms of what is available to us for presenting a reasonably comprehensive picture of how the goddess has been symbolized and worshipped by her devotees. The factor of recurrence of ideas and themes, then, is immediately pertinent to our need to be eclectic in the treatment of such materials. Moreover, this is illustrated symbologically in our subsequent discussion of a few of our methodological concerns. We, therefore, point out certain underlying literary *motifs* which may also be correlated with historico-religious processes that have shaped Indian culture. Some of them are the following : (1) the *daivāsuram* theme : an idea which has long dominated the imagination of Indian thinkers and enthusiasts. This feature does much to confirm the existence of continuity and change in the conceptual and practical relations between an earlier Vedo-Brāhmaṇic period and a later Tantric-Purāṇic phase of religious contemplation. (2) The idea of *exoteric/esoteric* participation in the Divine : here one has to consider the presence of a series of mythic and initiatic homologations expressed in thought and action that revolve around the goddess, Durgā-Kālī, as the divine *Śakti*. (3) There is also the motif of *imitatio dei*, which involves in our specific context erotic or sexual acts and gestures conceived as having soteriological value. Finally, there appears an extremely fascinating phenomenon which we might call the *multi-morphic motif*. Under this may be

[4] *Vide* Chapter I.

subsumed a host of phenomenal ideas and forms of an iconographic, cultic, and theogonic nature. All the foregoing shall be illustrated textually and morphologically in the chapters ahead.

Our work is again facilitated by the availability of textual translations, commentaries, and interpretations concerning the Tantric and Purāṇic materials, especially by such persons as Agrawala, Avalon (i.e., Woodroffe), Ghosha, Sastri and Ayyangar, and others. The finest enumeration and explication of the Tantric literary deposit and its influence appears to be the work of Mircea Eliade and Agehananda Bharati. A magnificently helpful general source happens to be Volume IV of the *Cultural Heritage of India.*

We should not bring this literary introduction to a close without some remarks about a few texts that are particularly useful for Chapters III-V of this work.

Vastness and complexity apart, a key text for the cosmological dimension of this study is the Kāma-Kalā-Vilāsa. Briefly, let us say that this text contains an exposition of the unfoldment of the transcendent, noumenal goddess into the immanent, phenomenal multiforms of human experience. For our particular purposes, however, this source needs to be supplemented by other primary texts such as the Varnamālā (Garland of Letters) and other *māhātmyas* to the goddess.

With regard to the more prominent texts, it is convenient to bear in mind the following elements. First, the role of the goddess as Śaktic Creatrix tends, on the one hand, to be merely "affirmed" in one text; and, on the other hand, to be actually "portrayed" in another text. For example, this is the case with the Devī-Māhātmya portion of the Mārkaṇḍeya Purāṇa as well as the Devī-Bhāgavata Purāṇa, respectively.

Another factor is that the principal texts to be employed tend to betray singular, varying, if not, overlapping conceptualizations of the degree of sovereignty that the goddess has. These conceptualizations may take the form of (a) a type of Vedantic or Upaniṣadic monism, (b) a *deva-asura* type of dualism, or even (c) an amazing but discernible multiunism. This last mode is exemplified in the Devī-Māhātmya, to be sure, wherein the goddess is all at once the Mahāmāyic Ground and Cause of the World *and* the "Created" and Anthropomorphic Focus of the Energies (*tejas*) of the Gods.

A final textual observation has to do with the historico-phenomenological intentionality of certain cosmologically usable texts. Such texts, it seems, may well have been designed for purposes probably related to a *ritual milieu* and/or more didactic ends. Didactically, for instance, a "hidden" mythic-intentional or mythic-tendentious quality and affinity are apparently shared by Uṣas of the Kālikā Purāṇa, Umā of the Kena Upaniṣad, and Devī of the Saundaryalaharī.

The distinctively rituological aspect of our study finds a well-known source in the Mahānirvāṇa Tantra. Bharati tells us that this work is regarded as supremely important among the Śāktas of Eastern Bengal. This Tantra is, again, considered an invaluable text for Hindu tantric *dīkṣa* (particularly Chapter X of the work). Other elements of ritual worship are to be found in additional texts that are, fortunately, available to us. Among such texts are the Kūlārṇava Tantra and at least two other works on laya-yoga : the Ṣaṭcakranirūpaṇa (Investigations into the Six Bodily Centers) and the Pādukāpañcaka (the Fivefold Footstool). Concerning the so-called "left-handed" form of worship of Durgā-Kālī, especially, there is the Karpūrādi-Stotra, which is considered to be the most characteristic Tantra of its kind. Other helpful texts will be mentioned in passing as the work proceeds. Incidentally, the commentaries on ritual are quite adequate indeed, we believe, to effect a rituo-structural analysis of the goddess as Sacred Object. Moreover, when we make use of the phrase, "stratifications of symbolic significance", the reference is to comparative levels of thought and worship that concern popular or elite strata; or, again, the exoteric and esoteric modes of cultic liberation.

In the eschatological area of our study a few of the texts tend to reveal a peculiar metaphysical co-emphasis; that is, an implicit Ground of Being (*Urgrund*) is so often assumed in the texts, irrespective of the intended focus of cosmogonic power under the form of a particular deity. Again, in much of the mythological imagery germane to the activity of the goddess, cosmogony and eschatology are but dual aspects of a single *event*—the revelation of the cosmos as capable of absolute staticity and relative dynamicity. Cosmos and chaos tend to be so thoroughly intertwined that this fact alone draws special attention to what happens in that milieu where myth *and* ritual betray a similar kind of cohesive bond.

Moreover, it is in the eschatological dimension that we discern another characteristic which has significance for much of Hindu religious thought. It is the presence of an interdenominational adherence (mainly, the Vaiṣṇavite, Śaivite, and Śaktic sects) to a common Weltanschauung, specifically regarding the cyclical "Ages of the World". For example, since *Mahāpralāya* comes to all creatures and beings, the texts are, therefore, more conspicuously ecumenical in terms of the content and imagery of cosmic dissolution. Thus the Viṣṇu Purāṇa and other texts seem to provide rather synoptic pictorializations of apocalyptic events. Devotees of the goddess, Durgā-Kālī, of course, view her as *the* ojbect of soteriological adoration and advantage, all the more needed to nullify, even more, to transcend the ravages of time and history.

In general, let us say that a certain creative use of the foregoing literary treasures will be reflected in our study. However that creativity need not become a source of intellectual distortion — what with the guides we have — but, hopefully, a means to a better understanding of the divinity and the culture we have chosen. Towards this end we intend to study Durgā-Kālī within and against the dynamic background of sacred tradition and secular history.

CHAPTER ONE

METHODOLOGICAL CONCERNS

History and Religious Hermeneutics

Within the realm of the scholarly enterprise there are many obstacles — historical, cultural, and social — which confront the investigator in his search to understand other peoples. Such barriers to effective inquiry have led researchers in several fields to expect various kinds and degrees of epistemological results in their work. Broadly speaking, one quite optimistic view of what it is to understand another culture, or another religion, places unlimited confidence in either the rational comprehension or the intuitive perception of the individual. These common extremist attitudes have oftentimes been characterized in turn as positivism or romanticism. Another outlook tends to place its confidence in a limited access to a true picture of what is usually "foreign", but always understood at a second remove. Still another perspective — that which we share — cherishes the possibility that the scholar is capable of bringing multiple talents and sensibilities to his study, while facing the burden of what Joachim Wach calls "hermeneutic circularity".[1]

The process is thrust upon us in part by the need to "relook", in depth, at particular religions often in their recurrent manifestations throughout time and space. However, the task has a far more formidable source. It is the fact that the historian of religions has to face, continually, a seemingly unmanageable abundance of data accumulated about religions by ethnologists, anthropologists, archaeologists, and other culture-historians. It has thus become a constant challenge within the History of Religions field even to attempt to keep abreast with developments in all areas.[2]

---

[1] Joachim Wach, "The Meaning and Task of the History of Religions (Religionswissenschaft)", *The History of Religions: Essays on the Problem of Understanding*, ed. Joseph M. Kitagawa (Essays in Divinity Series", Vol. I; Chicago: University of Chicago Press, 1967), p. 6. (Kitagawa's book will be cited hereafter as *History of Religions: Understanding*).

[2] Cf. Mircea Eliade, *The Quest: History and Meaning in Religion* (Chicago: University of Chicago Press, 1969), p. 1.

In the light of this, perhaps the most important thing to remember about a methodology is its necessarily provisional character. This would seem to apply whether one were thinking in terms of a theoretical or a practical methodology.[3] Accretion of knowledge alone, nonetheless, suggests that a given method of approach to any *human* phenomenon should never be conceived as the perpetually obvious "other side" of the equation of understanding. This remains true whether one proposes to study either an historic reality or, indeed, a transhistoric (ultimate) reality. It is the latter term which, we feel, designates the fundamental perspective that has to do with religion. It is the human response to an Ultimate Reality,[4] then, that is the essence of the religious phenomenon.

In a very critical sense our reference to the tentativeness of methodologies has special relevance for the Social Sciences in general. It would therefore apply to any particular notion of reality, whether that reality be conceived, for example, as social, economic, political, or other.[5]

With regard to discussions in theory and method within the discipline of the History of Religions, it has, of course, been recognized that we have at least to do with "history" and "religion". Holding these two basic aspects of the field in wholesome and creative tension continues to be one of the major elements of the hermeneutical task. For not only are we at times tempted simply to reduce the one to the other; but the legitimate possibilities of each may also be subjected

---

[3] Cf. J. M. Bochenski, *The Methods of Contemporary Thought* (Torchbook ed.; New York : Harper and Row, Publishers, 1968), pp. 9f.

[4] Cf. Joachim Wach, *The Comparative Study of Religions*, ed. Joseph M. Kitagawa (New York : Columbia University Press, 1958), pp. 30-36; also Kitagawa, *History of Religions : Understanding*, pp. 40ff. Although religion has been variously defined (*vide* Julian Huxley, *Religion Without Revelation* [Mentor Books; New York : New American Library, 1957], pp. 93ff.), we continue to appreciate the Wach-Kitagawa definitive development in terms of both ultimacy and relatedness. Echoing G. van der Leeuw and others, a synthetic usage (i.e., "Ultimate Power") is apparent in Winston L. King, *Introduction to Religion : A Phenomenological Approach* (2d ed. rev.; New York : Harper and Row, Publishers, 1968), pp. 13ff. Cf. Mircea Eliade, on a "sacred thing", in *Patterns in Comparative Religion*, trans. Rosemary Sheed (Meridian Books; Cleveland : The World Publishing Co., 1963), p. 158.

[5] *Vide*, for example, the reconstructive and revaluative discussion in one field in I. C. Jarvie, *The Revolution in Anthropology* (Gateway ed.; Chicago : Henry Regnery Co., 1969).

to procedures bordering on methodological *purism*.[6] We need only to recall Max Muller's original linguistic claim to have found "the key which was to open all doors". Muller was convinced that only a "master key" could accomplish such a task. To be sure, we need also to remember another scholar's still instructive observation on this very point, which was that "critics are today almost unanimous in recognizing that a [single] key which one uses for all locks is certainly a false key".[7]

Approaches to the study of history per se have not been without similar problems.[8] It has been especially true, however, with regard to varying field-approaches to the study of religion.[9] Thus, for example, we are accustomed to hear, among other interesting terms, those such as historicism, phenomenologicalism (or phenomenology), and structuralism. In the case of all such usages and procedures the essential difficulty would seem to reside not in our words so much as in our scholars. Rather than the familiar phrase "omnipotence of thought", it appears to be specifically a question of "omniscience of method". At any rate, the fact remains that such tendencies have sometimes too easily become the romantic "isms" of one school or another. They, therefore, serve no longer as adequate methodological *tools* [10] or means, particularly, for understanding *religion*. Ultimately, such methods tend to become ends in themselves which do not inform but confuse, tend to blur rather than clarify. Indeed, within a largely rationalistic

---

[6] Max Gluckman, ed., *Closed Systems and Open Minds*: *The Limits of Naivety in Social Anthropology* (Chicago: Aldine Publishing Co., 1964), esp. pp. 13-19, 158-261, discusses this matter in terms that may deserve ongoing attention. His views on a positive but "deliberate naivety" in social anthropology and in all sciences are not necessarily to be understood as supporting the kind of purism criticized here. Gluckman's evaluation emphasizes mainly the search for legitimate confines concerning a single field-approach to a specific problem. Gluckman, then, admits that "if the aspects which one thinks are relatively independent are in fact interrelated, then confining one's study to a particular aspect leads nowhere in terms of understanding reality" (*ibid.*, p. 161). In the latter case the scholar would seem also to support some "deliberate *non*-naivety" (anaivety).

[7] H. Pinard de la Boullaye, *L'Étude comparée des religions* (Paris: Gabriel Beauchesne, 1922), I, 324, note 1.

[8] Cf. Edward H. Carr, *What is History?* (Vintage Books ed.; New York: Random House, 1967).

[9] Cf. Jan de Vries, *The Study of Religion*: *A Historical Approach*, trans. with an introduction by Kees W. Bolle (New York: Harcourt, Brace and World, Inc., 1967).

[10] Cf. J. Milton Yinger, *Religion, Society, and the Individual* (New York: The Macmillan Co., 1965), pp. 5ff.

modern milieu, the meaning of religion in the study of religions has tended to be reduced, for example, to anthropological, sociological, psychological, or other "realities".

These remarks are important because we intend to apply those very terms (i.e., historical, phenomenological, structural) in our effort to suggest a way of understanding better the goddess Durga-Kali as a religious symbol. Yet in our own application of those terms we are aware that in the intellectual process a methodology becomes a type of yoke. It is a paradox. For the very construction of any kind of method implies, first of all, a limitation. But then a method can also be an instrument for helping the scholar to by-pass or supersede certain existing difficulties of the intellectual inquiry. Hence no matter how many descriptive adjectives may be employed, it should be remembered that, ideally, underlying all the enthusiasm for methodological techniques is the quest for a profounder understanding of man.

Generally, therefore, in this study of a major religious symbol of the Hindu faith, our uses of the term "historical" will tend to be more dynamic than deterministic.[11] Here and there, moreover, one may find evidence of a continuing existential appreciation of the data of religious experience. For we regard this as central to both a philosophical interpretation of religion and a religious interpretation of history. It should be said, nonetheless, that history is not here conceived as simply a record of the absolute spontaneity of human thoughts, words, and deeds. For it appears from various field studies that there may well be determinism in the most effervescent spontaneity,[12] as well as dynamism in the most rampant determinism.[13] Yet, on the

---

[11] Cf. Ernest A. Payne, *The Śāktas* (Calcutta: Wesley Publishing House, 1933). The work, though invaluable to our study, understands the Śākta "reality", unfortunately, as determined largely by the eventualities of history (*vide* our Preface, p. xii).

[12] Cf. Emil Durkheim, *The Elementary Forms of the Religious Life*, trans. Joseph Ward Swain (Paperback ed.; New York: The Free Press, 1965), esp. pp.245-251. The point is, *paradoxically*, that, apart from the often unappreciated idea of "a new being" (*ibid.*, p. 249, bottom), the individual *is* in a sense "dominated and carried away [in the collectivity] by some sort of external power".

[13] While one should not exaggerate the point, it is interesting to note that even Freud had his moments when "death" as the "aim of life" was tempered by an apparently genuine egoic freedom. We owe this insight to R. S. Woodworth, *Contemporary Schools of Psychology* (3d ed.; New York: The Ronald Press Co., 1964), pp. 285f. See Sigmund Freud's own work, "Analysis Terminable and Interminable", in *Complete Psychological Works*, ed. James Strachey (London: Hogarth Press, 1953-), XXIII, 216-253, esp. p. 240. (Though the example seems to serve our purpose, we are not convinced, unlike Woodworth, that Freud makes any commitment in the text).

whole, we continue to lend decisive weight to the idea of human freedom and creativity as integral to religion in essence and manifestation. Our insistence upon this derives principally from the fact that historical determinism forever tends to court the notion of inevitability (which, incidentally, betrays its ultimately romantic origins). We are more impressed with a view of human nature which emphasizes an "occasionalistic" factor in the intercourse between history and religion, man and nature, or history and culture.[14]

The crucial object is to recognize that the concern of the historian of religions can never be limited to notions of "what happened" to man. Just as relevant and important — perhaps even more so — remain these factors : (1) to discover what *man* has "caused" to happen as meaningful event,[15] and (2) to discern how he has religiously understood his own being and salvation in relation to otherwise "uncaused", if not merely given, natural-historical phenomena.[16] Thus the historical-mindedness reflected in this study will go hand in hand with an attempt to take adequate account of the nature of religion as *sui generis* and, therefore, not bound by the methods of historicism, or even historiography.[17] That distinctively religious dimension involves the quest to penetrate to the heart of the religious phenomenon, while at the same time recognizing its potentially inexhaustible character and meaning.

Yet, even if we begin to have confidence that we can understand something of man's religious response to life's given phenomena, what is "history" to the historian of religions in methodological

---

[14] Cf. "A Historico-Cultural Hypothesis", in Mircea Eliade, *Myths, Dreams, and Mysteries*, trans. Philip Mairet (Torchbook ed. ; New York : Harper and Row, Publishers, 1967), pp. 176-179, esp. p. 178.

[15] Cf. Mircea Eliade, *The Sacred and the Profane*, trans. Willard Trask (New York and Evanston : Harper and Row, 1961), pp. 20-65.

[16] Cf. King, *Introduction to Religion*, pp. 51-77.

[17] Of course, historicism is not necessarily synonymous with historiography, the latter being capable of "levels" of undertaking (*vide*, for instance, Phil L. Snyder's edition of essays and letters of Carl L. Becker, esp. the section, "What is Historiography" ? in *Detachment and the Writing of History* [Paperback ed. ; New York : Cornell University Press, 1967], pp. 65-78, esp. pp. 75f.). The technical issues involved in historicism are too complex to be encompassed by this document. For now (contrary to Carr, *What is History?* "Causation in History", pp. 119n-120n) we are not inclined to believe that the historicistic/historical-minded distinction is merely a matter of "pedantic" vocabulary; for such terms have real significance when they refer to reductionist attitudes by certain scholars towards the specifically religious phenomenon. Cf. Eliade, *The Quest*, pp. 50-53 *et passim*; Mircea Eliade, *Images and Symbols* (New York : Sheed and Ward, 1961), pp. 27-33, 171n.

terms? We have already said that historians per se have had their share of hermeneutical headaches about the matter. It is important that we mention this problem at the outset—for it *is* a problem common to all scholars concerned with history. The History of Religions, as a discipline, continues to reappraise itself from within [18] and to endure criticism from without.[19] On the one hand, there are those who expect historians of religions to act as mere chroniclers of religions; and, on the other, those who continue to remain suspicious of our role as phenomenologists of religions as compared with theologians of a particular religious faith.

With regard, then, to the attitude of the historian of religions to the "historical", it serves our purposes well to call attention to what appears, after all, to be the finest and most succinct statement on the meaning of "history" in the History of Religions.

> The *history* of religions is not necessarily the *historiography* of religions. For in writing the history of one or another religion or of a given religious phenomenon (sacrifice among the Semites, the myth of Herakles, and so on) we are not always able to show everything "that happened" in a chronological perspective; we can do so, of course, if the documents permit, but we are not obliged to practice *historiography* in order to claim that we are writing the history of religions. The polyvalence of the term "history" [20] has made it easy for scholars to misunderstand one another here; actually it is the philosophical and general meaning of "history" that best suits our particular discipline. To practice that discipline is to study religious facts as such, that is, on their specific plane of manifestation. [21] This specific plane of manifestation is always *historical*, concrete, existential, even if the religious facts manifested are not always wholly reducible to history. [22]

Another related aspect of the problem of history and religious hermeneutics has to do with man's *religious* place in society. The issue as to whether society should be regarded as the content and/or context

---

[18] Cf. Charles H, Long, "Archaism and Hermeneutics", in Kitagawa, *History of Religions : Understanding*, pp. 67-87; Mircea Eliade, "The History of Religions in Retrospect : 1912 and After", in *The Quest*, pp. 12-36.

[19] Cf. Robert Luyster, "The Study of Myth : Two Approaches", in *The Journal of Bible and Religion*, XXXIV, No. 3 (July, 1966), 240.

[20] Cf. Johan Huizinga, "A Definition of the Concept of History", in Raymond Klibansky and H. J. Paton, eds., *Philosophy and History*, The Ernst Cassirer Festschrift (Torchbook ed.; New York : Harper and Row, Publishers, 1963), pp. 1-10.

[21] Cf. Eliade, *The Quest*, pp. 4-8.

[22] Mircea Eliade, *Shamanism : Archaic Techniques of Ecstasy* (New York : Pantheon Books Inc., 1964), p. xvi.

of man's religious life still continues.[23] Our main concern right now, however, is not to question either man's historicity or his socialization. It is, rather, to criticize a certain kind of understanding of "where man is" once he discovers the pervasive ambivalence of the structures of his existence in the world. "All the definitions given up till now of the religious phenomenon have one thing in common: each has its own way of showing that the sacred and the religious life are the opposite of the profane and the secular life. But as soon as you start to fix limits to the notion of the sacred you come upon difficulties ... both theoretical and practical".[24] The crux of the matter seems to reside not only in "where to look for the evidence" and assemble it, but also in how to grasp the meaning of such phenomena. "The central and the most arduous problem", therefore, "remains, obviously, that of interpretation". But "do those who are making use of ... symbols take all their theoretical implications into account".[25]

The question would appear, essentially, to turn about the following reciprocal issues: (a) the interpretation of the structures of man's religious response to symbols in his social world — as part of a specific culture; and (b) the interpretation of the functions of symbols in relation to man's religious world—as grounded in myth. The resolution of this hermeneutical paradox has not always adequately concerned enough anthropologists or historians of religions, both of whose work is so intimately involved with much common data. The problem continues to be a specific source of methodological tension within the

---

23 Many issues are articulated by various scholars in Louis Schneider, ed., *Religion, Culture, and Society* (New York, London, and Sydney: John Wiley and Sons, Inc., 1964); *vide* Part III, pp. 51-181, *ibid.*, and Part V, pp. 374-588, *ibid. vide* also, "A Sociological Theory of Religion", in Yinger, *Religion, Society, and the Individual*, pp. 49-72. In the classical Durkheimian conception a kind of co-inherence of content and context seems to occur. Cf. Gustav Mensching's articles in Schneider, *Religion, Culture, and Society*, pp. 254-261, 269-273. Joachim Wach (*Sociology of Religion* [Chicago: University of Chicago Press, 1957], p. 156, note 241) assures us that "lack of conformity, skepticism, and heresy as well as schism [are] already in primitive society". Cf. Robert Redfield, *The Primitive World and Its Transformations* (Paperback ed.; New York: Cornell University Press, 1966), pp. 88, 114-118. Even the "charismatic" leader, however, needs to be accepted *as such* by his society or group; *vide* Max Weber, *On Charisma and Institution Building*, ed. S. N. Eisenstadt (Chicago and London: University of Chicago Press, 1968), p. 20. For a general religio-cultural perspective, *vide* Paul Tillich, *Theology of Culture*, ed. Robert C. Kimball (Galaxy Books; New York: Oxford University Press, 1964), pp. 42f., 47ff.

24 Eliade, *Patterns in Comparative Religion*, p. 1.

25 Eliade, *Images and Symbols*, p. 24.

History of Religions.[26] But it has also become in recent times a source of recurrent controversy between the two fields.[27] In the most specific disciplinary terms the matter concerns the tension between structural-functional anthropology and structural-symbolistic religion. Now it is certainly not within our competency to discuss the peculiar methodological problems and prospects integral to structural-functional approaches in the field of Anthropology.[28] Our main concern is to insist upon the legitimacy of speaking in terms of, first, a structuralist dimension in historial-religious studies without malice to either history or society; and second, of the distinctive significance of methodologically integrating the "characteristic structures" or the "essence of religion"[29] for the purpose of generalizing upon certain paradigmatic religious structures in the life of man.[30]

Actually, the phenomenon of distinguishable, however complementary, "wings" within any one academic discipline is not in itself unusual. We shall have cause to notice, for instance, the nervous persuasion that one anthropologist reveals towards another (Lévi-Strauss) with regard to the latter's revised form of structural analysis (*infra*, pp. 43f., n. 88). Edmund Leach, we believe, typifies much of the restlessness among scholars who are continuing to search for ways of understanding "social structure" in more effective anthropological terms. Historians of religions, too, have their share of the responsibility

---

[26] This "methodological schizophrenia" is at least candidly recognized within the field. See Joseph M. Kitagawa, "Primitive, Classical, and Modern Religions", in his *History of Religions : Understanding*, pp. 42f.

[27] For example, what was obviously intended to be a terse *coup de grâce* to a preeminent scholar in the field and, perhaps, to the History of Religions itself as an "historical" discipline was launched by Edmund Leach (*The New York Review of Books*, October 20, 1966, pp. 28-31). A British anthropologist, Leach's criticism is clearly aimed at a mere mirage of Eliade's method and not the real substance of it. Described by two other field colleagues as having a "verve" for anthropological extremism and a "vulgar positivism", Leach is briefly brought to task by Melford E. Spiro and Clifford Geertz (especially the former) : *vide* Michael Banton, ed., *Anthropological Approaches to the Study of Religion* (London : Frederick A. Praeger, 1966), pp. 85ff.

[28] Cf. Jarvie, *The Revolution in Anthropology*, pp. 152ff., 189ff., esp. p. 190 : "One might characterize structural-functionalism roughly as the method of exhibiting the way any social institution under discussion interlocks with and contributes to this structure of structures the social structure".

[29] Cf. Eliade, *The Sacred and the Profane*, p. 232.

[30] Cf. Mircea Eliade and Joseph M. Kitagawa, eds., *The History of Religions : Essays on Methodology* (Chicago : University of Chicago Press, 1959), p. 89. (Hereafter cited as *History of Religions : Methodology*). *Vide infra*, "Structure and Religious Symbolism".

for finding more creative avenues to understanding symbological structures in historical-religious terms. Anthropologists of the Leachean sort, nonetheless, have tended to confuse "re-thinking"[31] within a cherished methodological framework with "rethinking the framework".[32] Thus we are concerned that, insofar as some historians of religions are sometimes tempted to forfeit the possibility of "a historico-religious creative hermeneutics",[33] vis-à-vis even the exaggerated claims of certain scholars in other disciplines, that specifically unfounded criticisms be clarified and corrected.

Our first observation, then, in this direction confronts a methodological misunderstanding which has a rather semantic nature. We refer to the problematic tendency of some scholars to view the very use of the word "structure" in the methodological sense as signifying a type of mono-methodic scholastic formula in religious studies. This, of course, may be due to the influence of the new Lévi-Strauss way of handling myth; that is to say, the methodological disposition to deal with the concerns of myth without due consideration of the ultimate intentionality of myth. Whether in the long run such a tendency will be understood by other anthropologists as just another example of socio-anthropological reductionism remains to be seen. Nevertheless, it is a phenomenon which continues to arouse our own suspicions.

We suggest that the time has come for scholars in all branches of the social sciences to recognize that the mere use of one word (e.g., structure, or structuralist) nead not—indeed, should not— encourage the art of critical oversimplification. Eliade, for instance, hardly, if ever, regards himself as *merely* a structuralist in any self-conscious methodological sense.[34] Is the scholar, perhaps, aware of the tendency

[31] Cf. Edmund Leach, *Rethinking Anthropology* (London : Athlone Press, 1961), p. 1. For Leach's assumptions upon mythic and ritual symbols, *vide* his *Political Systems of Highland Burma* (London : Bell Publishers, 1954), e.g., pp. 10, 13, 14. Cf. Melford E. Spiro, "Religion : Problems of Definition and Explanation", in Banton, *Anthropological Approaches to the Study of History*, p. 122: and a non-Leachean perception of "placing of proximate acts in ultimate contexts ..." in Clifford Geertz, "Religion as a Cultural System", *ibid.*, p. 38.

[32] Cf. Jarvie, *The Revolution in Anthropology*, pp. 172 and 178, n. 1; cf. *ibid.*, pp. 211, 31; and *ibid.*, pp. 188, 171, 217.

[33] Mircea Eliade, "Crisis and Renewal", in *The Quest*, p. 64.

[34] We shall say that there *is* a structuralistic component in Eliade's methodology which, again, is the basis for our brief but explicit attempt to distinguish him, essentially, from the anthropologist, Lévi-Strauss, and his approach towards a common phenomenon-myth. *Vide infra*, pp. 28-34.

which we have described and wishes to discourage the same? Let us recall that he uses the word "orientation" regarding the phenomenon of emphatic differentiations in method within his very own discipline of research. We, ourselves, are inclined to prefer that when one is writing or speaking about a method such as Eliade's, a crucial distinction should be made between the detection of an *emphasis* within what is really a *complex* method and the more responsible description of an *encompassment* of method in more general terms. We understand Eliade's use of the word "orientation", contrary to its apparent misunderstanding by scholars inside and outside of the History of Religions, in the former sense of emphasis rather than encompassment.[35] In other words, we are insisting upon what we might call the case for a specific methodological density : the feasibility of a historico-phenomenological approach to religious studies that has a *structuralist* "density" or centre of gravity in its operation. Our thesis will also reflect this methodological density, though we intend to speak now more distinctly of *structure* as *both* one aspect of a multiple approach and, too, the designation of an overall *themic* unity.

For the purpose of further clarification of other issues with regard to the History of Religions, we focus our attention upon certain methodological oversights by scholars (e.g., of the Leachean disposition) who would recast religion, religious studies, and students of religion within typically reductionist moulds (e.g., social categories, historicism, positivism, etc.).

First, there is the need to recognize that it is the burden and the risk of every discipline that undertakes the art of understanding human culture to make *tentative generalizations*.[36] This is true despite

---

[35] For an encompassment of Eliade's method, we suggest the following considerations : (1) the role of comparison-integration in generalizing upon the religious behaviour of man; (2) the creative adoption of an historico-phenomenological mode of understanding with regard to the symbolized past (i.e., the past as revealed in symbols); (3) the vital notion that "every religious act and every cult object has a meta-empirical purpose", or "aims at a meta-empirical reality". Cf. "Methodological Remarks on the Study of Religious Symbolism", in Eliade and Kitagawa, *History of Religions : Methodology*, pp. 86-107, esp. pp. 89, 90, 91, 95; and/or Mircea Eliade, *Mephistopheles and the Androgyne*, trans. J. N. Cohen (New York : Sheed and Ward, 1965), pp. 189-211, esp. p. 199.

[36] Ironically, Leach (*Political Systems ...*, pp. 14f.) says the following : that "all human beings whatever their culture and ... their degree of mental sophistication tend to construct symbols and make mental association"; but then, acknowledging this as "a very large assumption", made by all anthropologists, he adds : "it is difficult entirely

the fact that civilization may not have reached its final phase of utopia or discontent. As we recall, it is on this basis of the unfinished business of *all* field research that final "histories" cannot now be written. But since we are concerned with both history and religion, there is often both the possibility and the necessity of striving to present a coherent generalization that does justice to the fullness of the historical-religious task.[37] Furthermore, it must also be remembered that every generalization ever made appears to be "final" in its own time. Ours is an appeal for the making and the breaking of generalizations.

Second, there is the need to take adequate account of the phenomenon of *methodological variability* within a single discipline, or even within a department of study within a particular university. This means that individual scholars will tend to manifest varying objective concerns and intellectual talents for breaking new ground for future methodological procedures and hermeneutical criteria. No one scholar, after all, can be expected to solve all of the methodological problems possibly emergent within a particular discipline.

Third, there is the need to develop an *open appreciation* for — not belief in — the kinds of transcendental milieux which have historically so pervaded and encompassed religious mythologies. To be sure, this means that the Sacred is to be approached as sacred (i.e., on its own terms). This assertion need not preclude, however, the awareness of the scholar that there may well be other interpretive options open to himself and other scholars for seeking to understand the religious phenomenon. The important thing is to recognize that "the orientation of the History of Religions field leaves room for an interpretation of transcendence as a specifically *religious* category [italics mine]".[38]

---

to justify this kind of assumption, but without it all the activities af anthropologists become meaningless". Leach's fault consists in failing to see the *extra*-Anthropological significance of that insight.

37 Cf. Eliade, "Methodological Remarks ...," p. 93.

38 Cf. a statement on behalf of the History of Religions field by scholars, in Milton Singer, ed., *South and Southeast Asian Studies* (Chicago : University of Chicago, The Committee on South Asian Studies, 1966), pp. 45f.

Phenomenology and Religious "Anaïveté"[39]

Methodologically speaking, intellectual reductionism [40] tends to become equivalent to purism : the subjection of complex natural and cultural phenomena to simplistic and over-strained methodological principles, however complexly developed. The classical exemplification of this is a certain understanding of the word "phenomenology".[41] So much of our life is phenomenal in the simplest meaning of the word (i.e., that which appears to us); yet the phenomenal for many persons continues, somehow, to connote the extraordinary or the unusual. It is the *logia* aspect of the term which seems to demand an inclusive consideration not only of the ordinary and the extraordinary, but also the objective and the subjective aspects of our natural and cultural experience; that is to say, our experience of the phenomenon of nature and of other "selves" — not excluding our (own-) "selves". In the latter case we refer to the "history" of our own experience.

With regard to the History of Religions it is interesting to notice (in a non-phenomenological, subjective sense) a student's initial discovery of the phenomenological *epoche.*[42] In respect to what appears

---

[39] Cf. *supra*, p. 9, n. 6. Apart from Gluckman's appropriate use of the antonym (naivety) in the context of his own discussion, we find the term used here and there in the literature on phenomenology, Husserl himself, apparently, having used the term vis à vis naturalism, psychologism, etc. *Vide* Marvin Farber, *The Aims of Phenomenology* (Torchbook ed.; New York : Harper and Row, 1966), p. 33; and, *The Foundation of Phenomenology* (New York : Paine-Whitman Publishers, 1962), p. vii. For us, *anaïveté* = our own triangulation of methods. *Vide infra*, pp. 24-25.

[40] Reductionism here, of course, does not refer to the methodological act of "phenomenological reduction", but to the ultimate claims made in its behalf as an epistemological key to understanding.

[41] Cf. Edmund Husserl, *Ideas* : *General Introduction to Pure Phenomenology*, trans. W. R. Boyce Gibson (New York : Macmillan, 1931). Though not the founder, as such, of a general movement, Husserl continues to be regarded as the central figure in discussion upon the history of phenomenological thought. *Vide* both Husserl and "The Essentials of the Phenomenological Method", in Herbert Spiegelberg, *The Phenomenological Movement* : *A Historical Introduction* (2d ed.; The Hague : Martinus Nijhoff, 1965), I, 73-167 and II, 653-701, in turn; and, Edmund Husserl, *Phenomenology and the Crisis of Philosophy*, trans. and introd. Quentin Lauer (Torchbook ed.; New York : Harper and Row, 1965). Cf. H. F. Heinemann, *Existentialism and the Modern Predicament* (Torchbook ed.; New York : Harper and Row, 1958), pp. 47-58.

[42] Cf. Husserl, *Ideas*, pp. 18f., 80ff., 107-111; and, Husserl, *Phenomenology ...*, pp. 168f. and 168, n. 32. The concept is applied by phenomenologist of religion, G. van der Leeuw, *Religion in Essence and Manifestation*, trans. J. E. Turner (Torchbook ed.; New York and Evanston : Harper and Row, 1963), II, 646, n. 1, and 675-677.

to be a goal of "phenomenological revelation" the student undergoes, as it were, certain intellectual "rites of passage"[43] the first stages of which consist in learning *how* to-look-at-what-appears-to-him. A sense of academic elation is apt to be experienced in relation to what seems an all-sufficient passport to a thoroughgoing objectivity. This objective side of the phenomenological process involves the individual's acceptance that the systematic observation and intellectual exposition of natural and cultural phenomena requires the spirit of an artist; that genuine "seeing" and "understanding" must become for him the fruits of a scholarship which constitutes a kind of quest—an Archetype of Discovery.

Beyond the varying conceptions sometimes held concerning Husserl's *epoche* as if it were merely a type of technical mental gymnastic, the concept does have important implications for distinguishing the History of Religions, for example, from explicitly normative disciplines such as Christian or non-Christian theologies. Notwithstanding the probable varieties of methodological "norms" *within* a given religious tradition (e.g., Christian Theology),[44] the individual scholar historian of religions or otherwise, needs to avoid the pendulous reproduction of "cultural fashions".[45] He must develop a receptivity towards transcending the limiting options of his dominant methodological tradition at any given phase of its history in favour of a greater opportunity for objectivity which the phenomenological method or "movement" has certainly encouraged. For objectivity is still the necessary grist of all comparative studies. Max Muller could very well say that "before we comprae, we must know what we compare"; it is also true, however, that before we compare we should know *how* to compare (i.e., in what spirit). To be sure, the phenomenon of methodological overstress or over-straining (*supra*, p. 18) of descriptive principles is not unknown within the community of scholarship.

---

43 Cf. van der Leeuw, *Religion in Essence and Manifestation*, II, 671-689. Cf. Eliade *The Quest*, p. 125.

44 Cf. Albert Knudson, *The Doctrine of God* (New York : Abingdon-Cokesbury Press, 1930), p. 1 and esp. Chap. V. *Vide* also Philip E. Hughes, ed., *Creative Minds in Contemporary Theology* (2d ed. rev.; Grand Rapids, Mich. : Wm. B. Eerdmans Publishing Co., 1969), pp. 1-25. Langdon Gildey, *Naming the Whirlwind : The Renewal of God-Language* (Indianapolis and New York : The Bobbs-Merill Co., 1969), pp. 241-246, shows how a religious tradition in search of contemporary redefinition can be helped *and* hindered by puristic phenomenological notions.

45 Cf. Mircea Eliade, "Cultural Fashions and the History of Religions", in Kitagawa, *History of Religions : Understanding*, pp. 21-38.

Nonetheless, a reasonable intellectual objectivity retains its own importance in all fields of endeavour.

If, as we stated, methodological reductionism amounts to purism, then there is also the question of what we might call *adductionism*. To be sure, Husserl's phenomenology reveals both of these tendencies. On the one hand, his reductionism, though retaining its value for us in the heuristic sense,[46] cannot seem to avoid the practical failure to tell the "truth" about complex historical-cultural phenomena. Indeed, it is the claim of a trancendent act of radical "interiorization"[47] of all the usual notions of subjectivity and objectivity which, ironically, transforms the "pure" phenomenon into a type of *noumenon*.[48] No scholar, irrespective of his level of methodological idealism, can fail to discern the magnitude of Husserl's claim (note : *infra*). On the other hand, Husserl's adductionist tendencies have not gone unnoticed by scholars. In his later writings Husserl is understood as positing a "pre-reflexive, pre-scientific, pre-philosophic consciousness for the philosophic endeavour,"[49] but a consciousness which *pre*supposes a subjective experience of the phenomenal world (in the ordinary sense of the word). Whether this "psychological activity of consciousness" *in addition to* an original phenomenologically reductive "ideal act of consciousness" constitutes in fact a critical modification, if not a reversal in the thought of the (ascribed) "Father of Phenomenology", will probably remain an open question.[50] At any rate, Husserl's larger

---

[46] Bochenski, *The Methods of Contemporary Thought*, p. 17, regards the necessity of the phenomenological method as twofold : (1) "man is so constituted that he has an almost incorrigible disposition to see, in what he look at, extraneous elements which are not contained in the object itself at all. ... (2) No object is simple : every object is infinitely complex, consisting as it does of various components and aspects which are not all equally important. Man cannot grasp all these elements at once ..."

[47] Hussler's own words invite a conclusion which he, certainly, did *not* intend : "We direct the glance of apprehension and theoretical inquiry to *pure consciousness in its own absolute Being*. It is this which remains over as the 'phenomenological residium' we were in quest of : remains over ... although we have 'Suspended' the whole world with all things, living creatures, men, *ourselves* included [italics mine]. We have literally lost nothing, but have won the whole of Absolute Being, which, properly understood, conceals in itself all transcendences, 'constituting' them within itself" (*Ideas*, pp. 154f.). Cf. Lauer in Husserl, *Phenomenology* ..., pp. 67: 73; n. 5; 133 and n. 68.

[48] We are reminded of Pettazzoni's comparatively explicit assertion that "every *phenomenon* is a *genomenon*". *Vide* Eliade, *The Quest*, pp. 29f.

[49] Lauer in Husserl, *Phenomenology* ..., p. 67.

[50] E.g., Lauer (*ibid.*) sees no inherent contradiction or reversal in Husserl's apparent introduction of ideas suggestive of an *Umwelt* or *Lebenswelt*. A change is suggested by

aim has been described as an attempt to "reduce' all being to phenomenality".[51] That task would require such an elusive and abstract intellectual *coincidentia oppositorum* of objective and subjective considerations [52] that it is difficult to avoid the conclusion that we are undergoing a rather noumenal process after all. While the historian of religions bears no uncritical bias against the idea of the noumenal, as such, the irresistible inference is that, in Husserl, we are left with both an ongoing and useful methodological legacy,[53] as well as a methodological overstress of "Idea" which might be legitimately by-passed.

Gerardus van der Leeuw, who declared his intention (in the Preface of the German edition of *Religion in Essence and Manifestation*)[54] to by-pass the then dominant evolutionary, animistic-dynamistic, or monotheistic theories, was seeking to achieve a "phenomenological comprehension of History". Towards this end, in his "Epilogomena" he applies the logic of negation to the role of poetry, psychology, philosophy, theology, and even the *history* of religion as bearing any relevance to a *phenomenology* of religion.[55]

On the face of it, van der Leeuw does a remarkable job of showing how a few of Husserl's basic principles or ideas might be applied to the study of religious phenomena.[56] In fact, even the most learned scholar in or outside of the History of Religions must stand in reverence

---

Long, "Archaism and Hermeneutics", p. 75. The latter scholar adds that Husserl did not seek "to reduce man to a function of his *Umwelt* or *Lebenswelt*", but "to demonstrate the modalities of being in relationship to this dimension of the human consciousness" (*ibid.*, p. 76). *Vide* Husserl's *Phenomenology* ..., pp. 151-155 : here it would appear that even the "introduction" of a relevant corporeality does not mean that the overall Husserlian system is significantly altered. Cf. Farber, *The Foundations of Phenomenology*, pp. viii, 169.

51 Lauer in Husserl, *Phenomenology* ..., p. 47.

52 Cf. Husserl, *Ideas*, pp. 362-363, 366-368. Cf. Quentin Lauer, "The Subjectivity of Objectivity", *Edmund Husserl, 1859-1959* (Phenomenologica; The Hague : Martinus Nijhoff, 1959), p. 167; and, Robert Sokolowski, *The Formation of Husserl's Concept of Constitution* (The Hague : Martinus Nijhoff, 1964), p. 218; also cf. *ibid.*, pp. 222f.

53 Cf. Alfred Schutz, "Husserl's Importance for the Social Sciences", in *Edmund Husserl, 1859-1959*, pp. 97f.

54 G. van der Leeuw, *Phänomenologie der Religion* (1933), trans. Turner, as *Religion in Essence and Manifestation*, Vols. I and II.

55 Cf. *ibid.*, II, 685-689.

56 The degree of his conscious indebtedness to Husserl, compared to others, is not certain. *Vide* Eliade, *The Quest*, pp. 34f.; van der Leeuw, e.g., *Religion in Essence and Manifestation*, II, 646, n. 1.

before the plenitude of this scholar's array of theoretical and ethnographic insights. We are not, of course, concerned at the moment with the author's definitive understanding of the idea of "Power"[57] as essential to and manifested in religious experience. We would merely point out that, like Husserl, van der Leeuw, too, pays the inevitable price of a type of methodological reification of understanding in his endeavour to distinguish, totally, the religious phenomenon from historical-cultural phenomena in general. That is, he goes far enough along the way of "pure" phenomenologists, so that he suffers the ironical disadvantage of over-disengagement, for example, from the socio-cultural sphere in its historical[58] dimension which remains the more pervasive and formal context of the Powerful Sacred. Perhaps what became with Husserl a flagrant advertency was in the case of van der Leeuw a less criticizable inadvertency. What is to be mentioned is that the latter scholar does not entirely ignore form[59] or the structural inner-relatedness of forms; but such forms continue to be subjected to a rather Platonistic conception of form (= Idea).[60]

It is on the basis of his (Idea of) Power, therefore, that van der Leeuw is able to posit the following "double-paradox":

> ... religion is the extension of life to its uttermost limit. The religious man desires richer, deeper, wider life: he desires power for himself. In other terms: in and about his own life man seeks something that is superior, whether he wishes merely to make use of this or to worship it ... Herein consists the essential unity between religion and culture. Ultimately, all culture is religious; and, on the horizontal line, all religion is culture[61].

This highly elusive mutual identification between the verticle and the horizontal (i.e., the ultimate and the intimate), or religion as the search for Power (essence) and culture as the utilization or worship of Power (manifestation), constitutes, ostensibly, a phenomenologico-religious generalization (or "comprehension") of History. At the same time, however, it reveals more precisely van der Leeuw's need to recog-

---

[57] Cf. van der Leeuw, *Religion in Essence and Manifestation*, I, Part I, esp. 23-51.

[58] Cf. Long, "Archaism and Hermeneutics", p. 71. *Vide*, e.g., van der Leeuw's treatment of "The Sacred Community", in *Religion in Essence and Manifestation*, I, 242-274.

[59] E.g., van der Leeuw, *Religion in Essence and Manifestation*, Chaps. IX-X, XV-XVII, XX, LXV-LXVI.

[60] Cf. his Husserlian triumph of Subjectivity, *ibid.*, II, 460-462, 672-673.

[61] *Ibid.*, p. 679, n. 1.

nize the complex historicity of all phenomena. For, though he rightly alludes to the tension ("hostility") between Power and faith,[62] an ordinate historical consciousness would call into question one specific dimension of his paradoxical assertion : which is, that "ultimately", all culture is religious".

It is interesting that the scholar places this weightier side of the paradox in a mere footnote. At any rate, our analysis tells us that, on the one hand, there is a level of comprehension in which the assertion tends to have a certain synchronic validity, i.e., in phenomenological-historical terms. Nevertheless, on the other hand, we are compelled to recognize that the relatedness of diachronic elements to the fuller perception of the "truth" of religious phenomena makes the scholar's assertion itself sound like an affirmation of faith rather than a phenomenological "testimony".[63] In this perspective, then, the "chaotic reality" to which van der Leeuw refers, derives in fact from the *complexity* of historical reality. This complexity requires either a more-than-phenomenological, or a more broadly understood phenomenological viewpoint.[64]

Yet the continuing significance of this scholar's contribution to the phenomenology *and* the history of religions, we feel, really resides in the implications that his methodological reflexions have for all students of *Religionswissenschaft.* In whatever terms the essence or manifestation of religion might be conceived by any one scholar or group of scholars, van der Leeuw's radical meaning for the study of religion

---

[62] Cf. *ibid.*, p. 560.

[63] *Ibid.*, pp. 671, 688. The question of the relation between hermeneutics and *faith* is something that may deserve further reflection by scholars in the Humanities and the Social Sciences. We do not understand this as solely confined to the disciplinary relations between the History of Religions and Theology (Christian or non-Christian); but a faith that may be humanistic and/or "scientific" vis à vis religious studies. Van der Leeuw (*ibid.*, p. 683) insists that, "It is unquestionably quite correct to say that faith and intellectual suspence (the *epoche*) do not exclude each other". Cf. Gunther Spaltmann, "Authenticity and Experience of Time", in J. M. Kitagawa and C. H. Long, eds., *Myths and Symbols : Studies in Honor of Mircea Eliade* (Chicago and London : University of Chicago Press, 1969), pp. 371-372; J. M. Kitagawa, ed., *Understanding and Believing : Essays by Joachim Wach* (Torchbook ed.; New York : Harper and Row, 1968), Part III; *vide* also Gilkey, *Naming the Whirlwind*, pp. 196-203. Cf. Van Austin Harvey, *The Historian and the Believer* (New York : The Macmillan Co., 1966), Chaps. IV and VII. For a detailed but brief analysis of general problems, *vide* Edward Vogt, "Objectivity in Research in the Sociology of Religion", in Joan Brothers, ed., *Readings in the Sociology of Religion* (London : Pergamon Press, Ltd., 1967), pp. 115-125.

[64] *Vide* Joachim Wach, *infra*, p. 24.

consists in how his scholarly work continues to promote the adoption of a phenomenological *attitude* (beyond method as mere *savoir faire*). It is essentially an attitude of phenomenological freedom and humility towards not only the objective data but also the *human* subjects of one's field of inquiry. The individual can thus aspire to apply such an attitude to both his intellectual work and his philosophical life. The fullest, practical implication of van der Leeuw's method of understanding is that it can become a serious existential possibility : a mode of being in the world for the researcher himself.[65]

This being the case, however, it does not undercut but further substantiates the need for a more complex method of approach to the participants *in* religions, because even these human subjects of investigation [66] cannot be adequately "dislocated" or understood apart from their historical-phenomenal milieux : "times" and "histories".

In our overall view, then, a basically phenomenological approach is indispensable to the study of the History of Religions, and, therefore, the method has a type of core role in our present thesis. Generally, however, phenomenology itself is deemed to fall into inadequacy if "overstressed" in terms of a *pure* phenomenology. For, ultimately, the cost of such methodological purism is a not-so-pure (less wholistic) understanding of a project such as ours, for example. Serious account must after all be taken of those "other" relevant phenomena so intertwined with religious expression—what Joachim Wach refers to as "the conditions—geographical, ethnological, political, cultural—which have determined the actual course of events in an ... attempt at a systematization or phenomenological study of socio-religious phenomena".[67]

Our application of the term "anaïveté" bears a three-fold relevance to the foregoing considerations. First, it refers to a methodological position which understands the phenomenological "reduction" as basic to objective intellectual inquiry. Secondly, it also acknowledges the inherent limitations of that "reduction" as an epistemological tool. Our use of the term (anaïveté), therefore, also constitutes a charge

---

[65] Cf. Mircea Eliade, Preface to G. van der Leeuw, *Sacred and Profane Beauty : The Holy in Art*, trans. David E. Green (New York : Holt, Rinehart, and Winston, 1963), pp. v-ix.

[66] Cf. Wilfred Cantwell Smith, "Comparative Religion : Whither—and Why"? in Eliade and Kitagawa, *History of Religions : Methodology*, pp. 31-58.

[67] Wach, *Sociology of Religion*, p. 1c.

against the *naïveté* [68] of a phenomenology whose principle of reduction, when raised beyond a fundamental to a comprehensive status, becomes itself a reductionistic *methodology*. We have already stated that there is nothing inherently wrong with the making of generalizations (*supra*, p. 16). Perhaps what is significant is for scholars to recognize a singular methodological temptation; that is, the fact that every scientific methodology, as it applies itself to the so-called "sciences of the spirit" (*Geisteswissenschaften*), or "the human sphere", tends to test its elasticity to the extent that technical insight becomes unwarranted generalization.

Thirdly, our own methodology is qualified by the use of a "hermeneutical phenomenology".[69] Since all historians "interpret", we wish to emphasize that this additional interpretive dimension [70] comprises the following elements considered in this chapter so far (this section and the previous section, "History and Religious Hermeneutics"), as parts of an overall search for historico-religious meaning: (1) the perception of the religious phenomenon in its historical milieu; (2) the grasping or apprehension of its peculiar form among other forms; and (3) the appreciation of the transhistorical, transformal "reality" which is being symbolized in and through sacred ideas and objects.

Our primary concern in these foregoing, cumulative remarks upon "history", "phenomenology", and *religion* represent an appeal for more scope and depth of methodological concern than the singular search for pure objectivity. For in the Social Sciences and Humanities (perhaps also in sectors of the Natural Sciences) the co-existence of objective and subjective elements is certainly a probability—if not an inevitability. We are convinced that this dual phenomenon, though it is capable of being understood in various ways and degrees of intensity, constitutes both the peril and the prospect of all honest research. But it is a challenge that must be faced with an open mind. It is a task that will continue to demand a response that allows for an "open end".

---

68 Cf. Sokolowski, *The Formation ...*, p. 213 : on Husserl's later thought.

69 Cf. Spiegelberg, *The Phenomenological Movement*, II, 694ff.

70 I.e., concerning "meaning", is theoretically discussed more fully *infra*, "Structure and Religious Symbolism", and is exemplified in the body of this study : Chaps. III, IV, and V.

Structure and Religious Symbolism

Earlier we alluded to the presence of a largely rationalistic modern milieu in which the religious phenomenon tends to be reduced to the categories of one field "logos" or another. It must be recognized, nonetheless, that field approaches other than the History of Religions have their own valid freedom of inquiry beyond questions pertaining to the adequacy or inadequacy of their methods of research.[71] Thus the historian of religions need not be dismayed by this fact of methodological freedom; in fact, he needs and can welcome the findings of other scholars concerning problems and prospects that require highly specialized investigation.[72] Unfortunately, however, the Vogue of Reason (i.e., the Enlightenment legacy) has not always adequately served the purpose of understanding religious phenomena as much as it has the objects of study in the Natural Sciences.

The problem of determining the distinctive meaning of religious ideas and forms has become extremely acute in the minds of scholars in the face of at least three specific developments: (1) the increased awareness of the commonality of much of the date examined and interpreted by several branches of knowledge; (2) the emergence of the History of Religions as a distinctive discipline beyond earlier "Comparative" and "Philological" approaches to the study of religions; and (3) the radical treatment of longtime, vital elements, such as religious myths and symbols, by scholars in the Social Sciences whose methods derive much from the naturo-scientific tradition. It is true, of course, that, due to the influence of both theological and humanistic scholars and writers, our conception of the role of myth in society and culture has not continued to be understood solely in Enlightenment perspectives.[73]

---

[71] Cf. J. M. Kitagawa, "The History of Religions in America", in Eliade and Kitagawa, *The History of Religions: Methodology*, p. 15: "It must be made abundantly clear that the history of religions is not proposed as the only valid method of studying religions".

[72] Cf. Eliade, "Methodological Remarks ...", pp. 90f.: "It is not a question, for the historian of religions, of *substituting himself for the various specialists*, that is to say, of mastering their respective philologies. ... His task is rather to inform himself of the progress made by the specialists in each of these areas.

[73] See Berdyaev on myth, in Wach, *The Comparative Study of Religions*, p. 65. Cf. Amos N. Wilder, *Theology and Modern Literature* (Cambridge: Harvard University Press, 1958), pp. 27-37; "Art and Theological Meaning", in Nathan A. Scott, Jr., *The New Orpheus* (New York: Sheed and Ward, 1964), esp. pp. 415-418; Mircea Eliade, "Myth and Reality", in *Alienation: The Cultural Climate of Modern Man*, ed. Gerald

The relation between religion and culture, generally, and religion and structuralism, specifically (as a method of approach to religion) appears to have reached its controversial apex with the application of the term "structure" to the study of myth in Anthropology.[74]

Vis-à-vis a rationalism which continues to dominate much of Social Science methodologies, it is significant that various scholars (from Rudolf Otto [75] to Mircea Eliade) have insisted upon the *sui generis* character of religion in their work. There is also reflected in their writings an emphasis upon a philosophical-existentialist dimension which is integral to their approach to religious phenomena. More recently, it is doubtless Eliade's *The Sacred and the Profane* [76] and (also what the author still probably considers "the most significant of my books") *The Myth of the Eternal Return*,[77] in which the distinctiveness of the "Holy", the "Sacred", or the "Religious" is elaborated so clearly within a basically structuralist orientation to the study of religion. History and phenomenology are not foresaken by Eliade; but in the light of recent developments it has become all the more important for us to distinguish between Eliade's treatment of mythic symbols and the Lévi-Straussian type of structuralism. For the aphorism "What's in a name"? (or a "term"?) tends to lose its truistic value as we begin to draw out the comparative methodological implications of these two scholars for our present thesis.

Sikes, II (New York: George Braziller, 1964), esp. 751-753; Eliade, *Myths, Dreams, and Mysteries*, pp. 35-38. Cf. James Baird, *Ishmael: A Study of the Symbolic Mode in Primitivism* (Torchbook ed.; New York: Jarper, 1960), p. 8 *et passim*. *Vide* also Nathan A. Scott, Jr., "Theology and the Literary Imagination", in his *Adversity and Grace: Studies in Recent American Literature* ("Essays in Divinity Series", Vol. II; Chicago: University of Chicago Press, 1968), p. 3 *et passim*.

74 Cf. Claude Lévi-Strauss, "The Structural Study of Myth", in Thomas A. Sebeok, ed., *Myth, A Symposium* (Bloomington: Indiana University Press, 1968), pp. 55-66; Claude Lévi-Strauss, *The Savage Mind* (Chicago: University of Chicago Press, 1966), pp. 1-35 *et passim*. Cf. Edmund Leach, "Lévi-Strauss in the Garden of Eden: An Examiation of Some Recent Developments in the Analysis of Myth", *Transactions of the New York Academy of Sciences*, Series II, XXIII (1961), 386-396; Edmund Leach, *The Structural Study of Myth and Totemism* (London: Tavistock Publications, 1967); *vide* also Rob Cooley, "Jung, Lévi-Strauss, and the Interpretation of Myth", *Criterion*, VIII, No. 1 (Autumn-Winter, 1968), 12-16.

75 Cf. Rudolf Otto, *The Idea of the Holy*, trans. John W. Harvey (2d ed.; London: Oxford University Press, 1952).

76 Cf. Eliade, *The Sacred and the Profane*.

77 Cf. Mircea Eliade, *Cosmos and History: The Myth of the Eternal Return*, trans. Willard R. Trask (Torchbook ed.; New York: Harper and Row, Publishers, 1959).

Mythic Language and Sacred Experience

Lévi-Strauss engages in the search for anthropological significance in the patterns that emerge from variant but similar mythic and themic configurations. This structuralist quest for meaning, however, is largely confined to the formal relations of mythical structures without explicit reference to historical, social, or cultural contexts. In short, "myth itself provides its own context",[78] and the scholar's entire endeavour is guided by criteria which have to do with the making of a structural-linguistic science.[79]

> Myth, like the rest of language, is made up of constituent units. These constituent units presuppose the constituent units present in language when analyzed on other levels, namely, phonemes, morphemes, and semantemes, but they, nevertheless, differ from the latter in the same way as they themselves differ from morphemes, and these from phonemes; they belong to a higher order, a more complex one. For this reason, we will call them *gross constituent units* ... However ... it is well known to structural linguists that constituent units on all levels are made up of relations and the true difference between our gross units and the others stays unexplained ... Thus the specific character of mythological time ... remains unaccounted for. Therefrom comes a new hypothesis which constitutes the very core of our argument: the true constituent units of a myth are not the isolated relations but *bundles of such relations* and it is only as bundles that these relations can be put to use and combined to so produce a meaning.[80]

Myth, then, serves a function that by-passes the structural side of language (*langue*), which belongs to "a revertible time"; or the statistical aspect of language (*parole*), which is "non-revertible". Moreover, beyond this "double structure" of myth (i.e., the historical/an-historical) lies a more distinctive level of meaning: "what gives the myth an operative value is that the specific pattern described is *everlasting*; it explains the present and the past as well as the future [italics mine]".[81]

Before going further it should be pointed out that there are at least three specific respects (all in *kind*, the last in *degree*) in which

---

[78] Lévi-Strauss, "The Structural Study of Myth", p. 56.

[79] Cf. Claude Lévi-Strauss, "Structural Analysis in Linguistics and in Anthropology," in Robert A. Manners and David Kaplan, eds., *Theory in Anthropology: A Sourcebook* (Chicago: Aldine Publishing Co., 1968), pp. 531b-532a, 540b.

[80] Lévi-Strauss, "The Structural Study of Myth", p. 53. Cf. Edmund Leach, "Claude Lévi-Strauss—Anthropologist and Philosopher", in Manners and Kaplan, *Theory in Anthropology*, p. 547a.

[81] Lévi-Strauss, "The Structural Study of Myth", p. 52.

both scholars—Lévi-Strauss and Eliade—find common ground. First, both of them are aware of the generality of natural and historical modes of mythical expression;[82] the anthropologist pays more attention to the structural relations of intra-mythic themes as human attempts to transform nature into cultural reality;[83] the historian of religions concentrates more directly upon the structures or modalities of mythic symbols as cultural "creations" that are also sacred.[84] Secondly, they both accept the kinds of existential [85] concerns which are relevant to the shaping of mythic models; the anthropologist is fundamentally committed to the functional-resolutional meaning such models have with regard to the human/natural, human/social "oppositions and correlations":[86] the historian of religions is primarily interested in the distinctiveness and variety of valorizations of mythic symbols as vehicles and "ciphers" for a religious understanding of the world.[87] Thirdly, both scholars recognize—apart from synchronic and diachronic considerations—a durachronic aspect of mythical thinking which qualifies anhistorical events with perpetuity of value; the anthropologist brings this level of meaning almost to the threshold of a radical qualitative distinction; the historian of religions does this much but goes further towards a hermeneutical depth of understanding which introduces a new and crucial (i.e., a fourth) observation.

---

82 I.e., that man tends to interact with his non-human and human "environments" in the making of mythic ideas and forms. For differences in *degree* of "freedom", cf. Lévi-Strauss, *The Savage Mind*, pp. 11-26, esp. pp. 19 and 22; and Eliade, *supra*, p. 11, n. 14.

83 Maurice Merleau-Ponty, "From Mauss to Claude Lévi-Strauss", in *Signs*, trans. R. C. McCleary (Evanston, Ill.: Northwestern University Press, 1964), pp. 114-125, esp. p. 123. Cf. Leach, "Claude Lévi-Strauss ...", pp. 547b-550.

84 Cf. Mircea Eliade, "Approximations: The Structure and Morphology of the Sacred", in *Patterns in Comparative Religion*, pp. 1-33.

85 Conveniently, we note—with Tillich—that "Here the distinction between existential and existentialist should be brought out: 'Existential' points to the universally human involvement in matters of genuine concern; 'existentialist' points to a philosophical movement which fights the predominance of essentialism in modern thought, be it idealistic or naturalistic essentialism". Paul Tillich, "Existentialism, Psychotherapy, and the Nature of Man", in *The Nature of Man: in Theological and Psychological Perspective*, ed. Simon Doniger (New York: Harper and Brothers, Publishers, 1962), p. 43, n. 1.

86 Cf. Lévi-Strauss, "The Structural Study of Myth", pp. 59-64.

87 Cf. Mircea Eliade, "Prolegomenon to Religious Dualism: Dyads and Polarities", in *The Quest*, pp. 127-175, esp. pp. 173-175; *vide* also his "Symbolism and History", in *Images and Symbols*, pp. 151-178, esp. pp. 172-178.

It is a *hermeneutic* which regards the "everlasting" quality of myth as the clue to a *distinction in kind*; and the substantiation of this judgment lies precisely in the latter scholar's understanding of the ultimate intentionality of myth as capable of a decisive disengagement from its own inherent linguistic form.

Here we gain an essential preview of the most serious distinction between Lévi-Strauss and Eliade—their ultimately different understandings of the word "structure", not as a key to social phenomena but to *religious* phenomena—the mythical consciousness.

Doubtless, in the case of Lévi-Strauss, the "unpardonable sin" (reductionism) has been committed. For Lévi-Strauss' sort of neo-functionalism [88] raises the objection that he has unwarrantedly subjected a vital dimension among the "referents"[89] of religious mythology (beyond even its durachronic—"everlasting"—character) to the categories of nature and history. To be sure, his position has been described as reflecting, fundamentally, an anti-existentialist and neo-positivist vogue,[90] since the "everlasting" pattern of myth, though distinct from both its explanatory and expressional character, "remains linguistic by nature".[91]

The duty remains to account for such a procedural abortion of meaning in terms of the Lévi-Straussian methodology. The fault can be directly attributed to the scholar's utterly non-phenomenological approach to what we have already called the "transcendental milieu" (*supra*, p. 17) of myth, or the ultimately *para-linguistic* intention of myth-making. On the one side, Lévi-Strauss seems to equate essence (i.e., meaning) with structure (as formal and infra-formal relation) in a rather one-dimensional manner, so that *langue*,

---

88 Leach ("Lévi-Strauss in the Garden of Eden", p. 387) claims that Lévi-Strauss "has quite explicitly repudiated the functionalist thesis ... in favor of a revised form of 'symbolist' analysis that he calls structural". Lévi-Strauss, in fact, supersedes only the traditional functionalism exemplified by Malinowski and Radcliffe-Brown. The new approach to myth remains basically functionalist in character, insofar as Lévi-Strauss assumes an organic correlation between myth and existence; in the end, however, such a method has only an implicit basis in the forms of social existence; that is, the structural study of mythic *language* tells us something of value about socio-cultural reality. In this regard, we note that many of Eliade's critics overlook the fact that he discerns an important correlation between "the structures of the religious universe" and human social behaviour. Cf. Eliade, *Myths, Dreams, and Mysteries*, pp. 14-17.

89 Lévi-Strauss, "The Structural Study of Myth", pp. 52f.

90 Cf. Eliade, "Cultural Fashions ...", p. 35.

91 Lévi-Strauss, "The Structural Study of Myth", p. 52.

parole, and "everlasting" (-ness) are all identified with a puristic, structural materialism. "In other words, there is no solution of continuity between the polarities and oppositions grasped at the level of matter, life, deep psyche, language, or social organizations and those grasped at the level of mythological and religious creation".[92] In general, then, Lévi-Strauss subjects all the existential concerns and cosmic visions of the myth-makers to the genius and process of their own configurative art. Paul Ricoeur,[93] who remarks upon this interdisciplinary problem, understanding his role as having been that of "arbitrant" between "a hermeneutic of the demystification and a hermeneutic of the recollection of meaning", plays his part well for us here :

> Now the very possibility of divergent and rival hermeneutics ... adheres to a fundamental condition which, to my mind, characterizes *en bloc* the strategic level of hermeneutics. ... It consists in this, that the symbolic is a milieu of expression for an extralinguistic reality ... in hermeneutics there is no cloture of the universe or for an extralinguistic reality ... in hermeneutics there is no cloture of the universe of signs. Whereas the linguistic moves in the enclosure of a self-sufficient universe and never encounters anything but intrasignificant relations of mutual interpretation of signs ... the hermeneutic is under the regime of the open state of the universe of signs. ... It is the *raison d'être* of symbolism to disclose the multiplicity of meaning out of the ambiguity of being.

It is in this sense that the historian of religions understands the mythological-religious structure as having an important architectonic dimension.[94] The viability of that structure includes a conscious and, probably, an unconscious, creative act on the part of the religious being, an act whose symbolic meaning though coincident with, tends to transcend, any given form [95] and points to an ultimate context for all human strivings in the past, present, and future.

Here the phrase "essence of religion"[96] would constitute no mere verbal redundancy or cryptic saying. For though at a certain stage or level of technical (e.g., linguistic) analysis, essence (meaning) and form

---

92 Eliade, *The Quest*, p. 132.

93 Paul Ricoeur, "The Problem of the Double-Sense as Hermeneutic Problem and as Semantic Problem", in Kitagawa and Long, *Myths and Symbols*, pp. 53, 65, 66, 68.

94 "In myth [one] discovers what really happened to constitute his world ... what reality is ... what he must do and be if he is to belong to the level of reality upon which the gods live". Luyster, "The Study of Myth : Two Approaches", p. 236.

95 Charles H. Long, *Alpha, The Myths of Creation* (New York : George Braziller, 1963), pp. 8ff.

96 Cf. *supra*, p. 14.

(manifestation) are indeed contemporal, at another level of phenomenological perception they are finally conceived as having a dialectic-hierophanic relation. The mythic symbol would, therefore, become "a hierophany at the moment of stopping to be a mere profane something, at the moment of acquiring a new 'dimension' of sacredness".[97] This means that vis-à-vis the Lévi-Straussian type of structuralism, there is ultimately a radical discontinuity between the religious meaning-structure and the linguistic meaning-structure as primary goals in the study of myth. Accordingly, the religious meaning-structure of myth is capable of engaging the mind both (a) by accounting for, if not also validating, a concrete world in which the individual may live, move, and have his being; and (b) by pointing to a qualitatively different *order of things*, or reality, in which the individual may participate during sacred "times" (seasons) and within sacred "spaces" (places).

Eliade, then, conceives of the meaning-structure of myth (in phenomenological terms) as also pointing towards a transhuman reality (i.e., Supernatural Beings) whose essence, beyond the mere physics of myth, lies in man's *experience* of the Sacred.[98] It is, therefore, this experience of the Sacred and the Real which is oftentimes manifested in relation to that very realm of "opposition and correlation" mediated through myth as posited by Lévi-Strauss.

Needless to say, it has not been our intention here to discuss *in extensu* the methodologies of these two scholars. Our aim is rather to indicate a decisive methodological thrust in the historian-of-religion's treatment of religious mythology. This involves, again, an attempt to clarify our emphasis upon Eliade's specific contribution to our own "triangulative" method of approach.

There persists, after all, a critical distinction between the two foregoing scholars, which may further have implications for distinguishing certain methodological trends in their respective disciplines. Nonetheless we continue to insist that the most crucial distinction lies in what is conceived to be the ultimate context and purpose of the making of myth. We refer to the vital experiential dimension of myth. For it appears that only Eliade is sufficiently phenomenological to grasp the metastructural ambience of myth as a

---

[97] Eliade, *Patterns in Comparative Religion*, p. 13.

[98] Cf. Mircea Eliade, *Myth and Reality*, trans. Willard R. Trask (New York : Harper and Row, Publishers, 1963), pp. 18f.

sacred literature, a literature which Lévi-Strauss understands as merely "taking off from the linguistic ground on which it keeps rolling".[99] The historian of religious continues to distinguish a living qualitative uniqueness in the structure and function of myth which transcends even its "everlasting" linguistic, social, and cultural value.

> "Living" a myth, then, implies a genuinely "religious" experience, since it differs from the ordinary experience of everyday life. The "religiousness" of this experience is due to the fact that one re-enacts fabulous, exalting, significant events, one again witnesses the creative deeds of the Supernaturals; one ceases to exist in the everyday world and enters a transfigured, auroral world impregnated with the Supernaturals' presence. What is involved is not a commemoration of mythical events but a reiteration of them. The protagonists of the myth are made present, one becomes their contemporary. This also implies that one is no longer living in chronological time, but in the primordial Time, the Time when the event *first took place* ... it is the prodigious, "sacred" time when something *new, strong,* and *significant* was manifested. ... In short, myths reveal that the World, man, and life have a supernatural origin and history, and that this history is significant, precious, and exemplary.[100]

The purpose of the previous comparisons and distinctions has been to show that there is an emphasis in both Lévi-Strauss' and Eliade's approach to the study of myth which is helpful to our study. Through the anthropologist we become acutely aware of a Myth/Socio-World correlation wherein (a) mythic language and natural existence are seen as mutually affecting things in the life of man whose myths themselves are signs of the transformation of natural enigmas into cultural reality and meaning; and (b) mythic language and social relations are understood as mutually analogous, the latter providing the real context of human conflicts, the former being the surrealistic plane upon which the living structural ambiguities are sought to be resolved.

Yet it is the anthropologist's emphasis upon structure as, ultimately, a mytho-social model which will guide much of our thesis. The infra-structuralization of that model is as follows : (1) a systematic character, having a complex of mutually affecting ingredients; (2) an amenability to transformations productive of other homologous sets of sub-structures; (3) an allowance for morphological interaction upon cer-

---

[99] Lévi-Strauss, "The Structural Study of Myth", p. 53. Cf. Edward Sapir, *Language : An Introduction to the Study of Speech* (Harvest Book ed.; New York : Harcourt, Brace, and World, 1949), p. 223 : "The latent content of all languages is the same—the *intuitive science* of experience". Additional italics are the author's.

[100] Eliade, *Myth and Reality*, p. 19.

tain modifications of ingredients; and (4) a provision of a "correspondential framework" for all the mythic, cultic, and symbolic phenomena examined.[101]

Through the historian of religions we are brought face-to-face with a meaning of myth and structure which suggests a distinctive Myth/Religious-Reality correlation wherein (a) there is the factor of the religious participant's conceptual (or theoretical) framework for existence (i.e., socio-historically) as intimately related to his mythic symbolizations; and (b) there is the experience itself of the Sacred that the religious mind has in relation to the conceptualized reality of which myth invites our historical-religious understanding. Here the notion of *eidos* (or the structurological *logos*) represents a phase of method which *complements theoria* (or the phenomenological *epoche*), in that numerous mythic-symbolic "Realities" tend to reveal certain vital characteristics.[102] Thus the "Ultimate Reality" orientation, as it concerns Wach, Eliade, and ourselves,[103] is insisted upon as an "irreducible factor", more particularly reliable, and warranted as a characteristic methodological generalization. Here on the level of generalization the meaning and function of myth tends to "take off", but does not confine itself to the socio-linguistic ground where the researcher first finds it. This new, "transfigured, auroral" *Lebenswelt* becomes, then, the ultimate context of the content of social realities, "proximate acts",[104] and the sacred experience of man.

The Phenomenologic of Symbols

Here we have to do with the structure of mythological symbols as tools of historical research in the specific culture with which we are concerned—India. The methodological rationale that underlies

---

[101] These criteria are adapted from Claude Lévi-Strauss' *Structural Anthropology*, trans. Claire Jacobsen and Brooke G. Schoepf (New York : Basic Books, Inc., Publishers, 1963), p. 279. Cf. Hugo G. Nutini, "Some Considerations on the Nature of Social Structure and Model Building : A Critique of Claude Lévi-Strauss and Edmund Leach", *American Anthropologist*, LXVII (February-August, 1965), 707-731.

[102] Cf. Bleeker ("La Structure de la religion") and these categories, in Wach, *The Comparative Study of Religions*, p. 25. "According to this theory, structure is revealed in four ways : through constant forms, irreducible factors, points of crystallization, and types". Here, to be sure, we are dealing with a more comprehensive idea of phenomenonology. *Vide* Wach, *supra*, pp. 23, 24.

[103] *Supra*, p. 8.

[104] Geertz, "Religion as a Cultural System".

our thinking remains the same : "that the religious symbol provides us with a key for the understanding of that particular response to reality which we call culture".[105] In the main our intended focus is upon the area of Bengal. Our initial emphasis upon the structural aspect of this study as both one aspect of a multiple approach and the designation of an overall themic unity, however, allows us to consider the relevance of other structurally similar ideas and forms within a broader geographical perspective. Structural latitude will nonetheless be held in creative tension with historical and phenomenological longitude because of the *locus classicus* status of the Bengali Pūjā-Festivities. For it is there that so many of the variety of mythic and cultic structures find their co-inherent relation to that "Other" structure of *sacred* experience. Thus it is generally felt that there is a remarkable opportunity to discern a basic continuity and relation of structural conceptualizations between the goddess Durgā-Kālī as found in the Great Traditional elaborations and the numerous religious expressions of the Little Tradition.[106] Yet, because of the formidable variety of religio-symbolic ideas and forms which may be found in any given area of India, however, a few remarks are desirable concerning the "Feminine Cipher".

It will be observed that we have juxtaposed a series of names or goddess-epithets in our discussion of the "Form", "Nature", and "Activity" of the goddess. The comments that follow aim at confirming the enhanceability of our task through the presence of a peculiar (phenomeno-) "logic of symbols"[107] with regard to the Goddess-Symbol. Moreover, in the face of other historical and cultural problems, such remarks will also be supplemented by certain findings brought to our attention by students of Indian Sociology and Anthropology.

The problem of the relation between geographical *locus* and religious *cultus* was stated early by Hornell, who said that "identification and comparison of the deities worshipped in different parts of the country are to be effected at the cost of immense labor, for though the number worshipped in any particular village are few, many are of local origin and are not recognized away from their home country".[108] Although our distinctive approach here is neither that of the culture historian

---

105 Long, *Alpha*, p. 219.

106 On these "Two Traditions", *vide infra* and Chap. II.

107 Cf. Eliade, *Patterns in Comparative Religion*, pp. 453ff.

108 James Hornell, "The Ancient Village Gods of South India", *Antiquity*, XVIII (1944), 81-82.

nor the social anthropologist, Hornell's statement is both borne out and reasonably overcome by more recent studies in village India.

McKim Marriott's study [109] of Indian "Sanskritization" and "Parochialization" processes as they relate to the Great and Little Traditions constitutes in large measure an answer to many of the difficulties implied in Hornell's statement. Marriott's most revealing examination of the geographic distribution of "Sanskritic rationale and nomenclature"[110] is made in connection with the conceptions held of the "mud idol" in the festival of *Nine Durgās* in Kishan Garhi.[111]

For our purposes we would point out two specific factors regarding "distributional" phenomena which are of primary significance to our own study. First there is the discovery of linguistic, symbolic, and functional variations with regard to village deities and festivities. (a) The element of linguistic variation is seen in the festival's own name, i.e., *Naurthā* (*nava rātra*, "nine nights") which Marriott understands as "an old dialectic variant" of the Sanskritic celebration.[112] Naurthā, herself, can be "one of the 'Nine *Durgās*'", or "represent *Durgā, Kālī, et al*".[113] (b) The factor of symbolic alternation is exemplified by *Bhūmiyā*, "Earthy", a mother-goddess of Kishan Garhi; yet *Bhūmiya* or *Bhairon* can also be a local village *godling* of another district, or even a manifestation of Śiva or Viṣṇu. Again, *Cāmaṛ*, conceived as "Mother" in Kishan Garhi, is held to be "masculine in gender" in parts of the Aligarh and Agra Districts; both changing linguistic and symbolic elements characterize the masculine Sanskritic masculine deity, *Kṣetrapāla* ("Field Protector") in the Delhi District; yet this deity can have another identification as "Earthy", the mother-goddess in Kishan Garhi. (c) The matter of variation of function is found with the deity *Patthvārī* (the "Stony One"), who the one hand is associated with sulphurous mountain fires; and, on the other,

---

109 Cf. McKim Marriott, "Little Communities in an Indigenous Civilization", in his edition of *Village India: Studies in the Little Community* (Chicago and London: University of Chicago Press, 1955), pp. 171-222.

110 *Ibid.*, p. 193.

111 The village name is a pseudonym.

112 Marriott observes: "The festival of Nine *Durgās* in Kishan Garhi presents another specimen of parochialization", having "innumerable precedents in Sanskritic literature of the great tradition. The nine days on which it takes place are sanctioned in myth for the worship of *Durgā, Kālī, Parvatī, Śakti* ..." *Ibid.*. pp. 200-201.

113 *Ibid.*, p. 215.

"is said by a different Sanskrit etymology to be the 'Goddess of the Roadways'".[114]

The numerous female deities manifested at the village level in India are encompassed by the category known as "Grāmadevatās". We are informed that "the Grāmadevatā is the 'tutelary deity' or 'protecting mother' of a particular place or locality in India ... Especially in Southern India the cult of these goddesses is very popular, and there is almost no village without the shrine of the Grāmadevatā".[115] As far as these Little Traditional deities are concerned, certain comparative elements should be now noted which suggest a reasonable uniformity in their worship relative to the *cultus* of the Great Tradition, granting the improbability of rigid lines of religio-symbolic separation:[116] (1) the general lack of a Brahmanic priesthood (the exception always exists!); (2) the predominance of "apotheosis" over and beyond "legendary history" concerning the birth of such deities;[117] (3) the almost universal practice of bloody sacrifices; and (4) the commonality of more distinctively *female* deities, in contrast to the general "masculinity" of the gods of the Great Traditional pantheon.[118]

The second factor which bears upon Hornell's problematic of "identification and comparison of deities" has important general significance. It concerns the existence of a fairly widespread (Mother-) Goddess Complex[119] in Indian religion—specifically Hinduism. This has important methodological implications for us in terms of the structural latitude of our study. For this "complex", virtually, bridges

---

114 *Ibid.*, pp. 215-217. "The Stony One", the scholar adds, "has for at least a generation and probably much longer been identified with a famous manifestation of the great goddess *Pārvatī* or *Satī Devī* at Nagarkot in Kangra District, Punjab". *Ibid.*, p. 216.

115 A. P. Karmakar, *The Religions of India* (Lonvala, India: Mira Publishing House, 1950), I, 112.

116 Cf. Edward Harper, *Religion in South Asia* (Seattle: University of Washington Press, 1964), pp. 3-4; Marriott, "Little Communities ...", pp. 207ff.

117 Marriott, "Little Communities ...", pp. 197-201.

118 Cf. Wilber T. Elmore, *Dravidian Gods in Modern Hinduism* (University Studies of the University of Nebraska, Vol. XV, No. 1; Lincoln: University of Nebraska, 1915), pp. 11-17.

119 Cf. Marriott, "Little Communities ...", pp. 201, 215, 216, 217; V. Raghavan, "Variety and Integration in the Pattern of Indian Culture", *The Far Eastern Quarterly*, XV, No. 4 (August, 1956), 501.

the "Two Traditions".[120] Moreover, there is apparently some basis for discerning a stratification of linguistic-cultural and symbolical-religious significance *within* that "complex". On the face of it, it would seem that Marriott's "Mother (*Mātā*) and Goddess complex of Hinduism"[121] would refer, on the one hand, to the Grāmadevatān category of theistic ideas and symbols, and, on the other hand, to the Sanskritic level of thought elaborated in mythic and cultic texts. Both Marriott and Harper, however, have alluded to the highly fluid intermixture of the religious deposits of the "Two Traditions". Thus the symbols of *mātā* and *devī* tend to have largely inseparable "coherence" in both traditions as we find them. The two previous categories suggested, therefore, seem to clarify the stratification as it is. Shah and Shroff show us both of these phenomena—the linguistic-cultural and the symbolical-religious—in their stratification and their mutual relations in a *Mātā* (Goddess) Complex among the Barots of Gujarat.

> The cult has two levels, the Sanskritic and non-Sanskritic. It is known as the Śakti cult at the Sanskritic level, which is elaborated in many Sanskrit works beginning with the sixth and seventh centuries A.D. The mode of worship at the Sanskritic level corresponds more or less to those texts. The two modes of worship are, however, not mutually exclusive. The proportion of the two modes in the worship of *mātās* by a group of devotees varies with the level of Sanskritization archieved by them. ... Bhāṭs and Cāraṇs were called Devīputras because they were *mātā* or Devī worshippers, the former at the Sanskritic and the latter at the non-Sanskritic level. At the Sanskritic level, a *mātā* worshipper looks upon the different *mātās* as different manifestations of Śakti "energy", which is the personification of the female principle in the creation of the universe. The same idea is expressed in different words at the non-Sanskritic level: "The different *mātās* are manifestations of a single *Mātā*, the mother of all creation". The term "Devīputra" is used in this sense, and not in reference to any specific *mātā*.[122]

The specific but complex problem of the *means* of continuity between the Sanskritic and non-Sanskritic traditions continues to be variously understood and discussed by scholars of Indian history,

---

[120] Marriott's essay casts valuable light upon the general question of those "Two Traditions". *Vide* his comments on "circular flow", non-mutual exclusiveness of tradition, and the role of "caste hierarchy" in "Little Communities ...", pp. 202, 207, 209.

[121] *Ibid.*, p. 217.

[122] A. M. Shah and R. G. Shroff, "The Vahīvānca Bārots of Gujarat: A Caste of Genealogists and Mythographers", in Milton Singer, ed., *Traditional India : Structure and Change* (Philadelphia : The American Folklore Society, 1959), p. 43.

sociology, and anthropology.[123] No doubt we shall apply a few of their findings to our treatment of the historical and traditional origins of the goddess Durgā-Kālī. As far as the Mother-Goddess Complex is concerned, nevertheless, three of the main *phenomena* of structural-symbolic continuity are, briefly, the following.

First, there is the conception of the deity as *motherly* : in one sense, that she is transcendentally creative as in the mythological-philosophical constructions of a Sanskritic *literati*; and, in another sense, that she is immanently *protective*, accessible to human need as rituo-pragmatically conceived by the non-elite masses of village worshippers.[124] This latter kind of "accessibility" has oftentimes been taken by scholars as expressing a *do ut des* quality, largely magical in nature.[125] We are reminded in this, however, of the dubious distinction between magic and religion claimed by Frazer and Durkheim.[126] For, though there are certainly specific and, sometimes, weird modes (i.e., ritual

---

[123] Cf. *supra*, Marriott; *vide* also Robert Redfield, "The Social Organization of Tradition", in his *The Little Community and Peasant Society and Culture* (Chicago and London : University of Chicago Press, 1960), pp. 40-59. Cf. Milton Singer, "The Social Organization of Indian Civilization", *Diogenes*, XLV (1964), 84-119; a comprehensive sociological study is Louis Dumont's *Une Sous-Caste de l'Inde du Sud* (Paris and the Hague : Mouton and Co., 1957). *Vide* also significant articles, esp. by scholars Daniel Ingalls, W. Norman Brown, Nirmal K. Bose, Bernars S. Cohn, Surajit Sinha, and Milton Singer, in Singer, *Traditional India*, pp. 3-9, 35-39, 191-206, 217-225; 298-312, 141-182, respectively. A helpful survey is in Barrie M. Morrison, "Sources, Methods, and Concepts in Early Indian History", *Pacific Affairs*, XLI, No. 1 (Spring, 1968), 71-85.

[124] For such *emphases* both in distinction and relation, *vide* David G. Mandelbaum, "Introduction : Process and Structure in South Asian Religion", in Harper, *Religion in South Asia*, pp. 10f. Surajit Sinha's introduction of the relevance of the "Tribals" of India to "the larger universe of Indian Civilization" (he is not conclusive) has significance for our consideration (Chap. II) of the historical and traditional origins of the goddess Durgā-Kālī. *Vide* his article : "Tribal Cultures of Peninsular India as a Dimension of Little Tradition in the Study of Indian Civilization", in Singer, *Traditional India*, pp. 298-312.

[125] Cf. Paul Masson-Oureal, "The Doctrine of Grace in the Religious Thought of India", *The Mysteries*, ed. Joseph Campbell (Papers from the Eranos Yearbooks, No. 2; New York : Pantheon Books, Inc., 1955), p. 9; Norvin Hein, "Hinduism", in Charles J. Adams, ed., *A Reader's Guide to the Great Religions* (New York : The Free Press, 1965), p. 54.

[126] Cf. Lévi-Strauss, *The Savage Mind*, p. 221 : "There is no religion without magic any more than there is magic without at least a trace of religion". Cf. Mischa Titiev, "A Fresh Approach to the Problem of Magic", in W. A. Lessa and E. Z. Vogt, eds., *Reader in Comparative Religion : An Anthropological Approach* (2d ed.; New York : Harper and Row, Publishers, 1965), pp. 316-319.

acts) for "getting-a-goddess-to-do-what-one-wishes", the line of demarcation between this kind of accessibility and response ("ulterior devotion") and the kind of accessibility and response insisted upon in so-called "higher" religions ("disinterested devotion") is not always clear or convincing. Thus even in the case of the transcendental/pragmatic schematization of Mandelbaum one must be careful not to forget that "it is the scale that makes the phenomenon";[127] that is, the historian of religions allows for the possibility that a sacred reality and a sacred experience may underlie the elements of such a schema—the "doings" correlative to the "believings".

Secondly, there is the presence in both traditional, religious "strata" of ambiguity and/or multivalence (which may be nominal, gendric, or dispositional). The possibility of nominal-gendric ambiguity in terms of geographical *loci* has been exemplified in the work of Marriott in Kishan Garhi.[128] Ambivalence of disposition, whether "great god" or godling, is always a probability in India. Although malevolence (vis-à-vis theistic benevolence) comes in varying degrees, it has been observed that the Grāmadevatān type (not excluding male forms) of "lesser deities" tends to be understood as more radically malevolent upon the occasion of ritual defilement or specific displeasure.[129]

The goddess, Durgā-Kālī, of course, reveals all three of the above types of ambiguity. For now, we point out the special exemplificative presence of a "masculinity" within the nature, activity, and (iconographic) form of the goddess. We have to bear in mind that many of the great Epic Motifs of the Vedo-Brahmanic thinkers reflect often martial depictions and resolutions of "Cosmic Questions". Such motifs must have demanded both a theoretical and practical modification of certain mythical symbols in the process of intra-cultural cross-fertilization. It is highly probable, then, that this represents a creative, however tendentious, literary rationalization on the part of Smārta Brahman mythographers both in variation and accommodation with regard to the Little Tradition's tendency towards the dominance of the Feminine Symbol.[130] The process of genealogy and mythography

---

[127] Eliade, *Patterns in Comparative Religion*, p. xiii.

[128] E. g., Bhūmiyā (goddess), Bhūmiya/Bhairon (godling), *supra*, p. 36.

[129] Cf. Mandelbaum, "Introduction: Process and Structure ...", p. 9; Edward Harper, "Ritual Pollution as an Integrator of Caste and Religion", in his *Religion in South Asia*, pp. 183ff., 190f.

[130] Cf. Elmore, *supra*, point 4. "Dominance" more than *presence*, for Vedic religion is not without the presence of feminine deities, which we shall recall later.

seen in Shar and Shroff thus has a much broader application in the history of Indian religion. Hence, in the nature and activity and form of the Martial Goddess in myth, festival, or "cultural performance" (Singer), we are confronted by an epic symbol whose full transparence may be related to ponderous historical and cultural factors in addition to its own religious phenomenology.

Thirdly, the last and most important symbol of structural continuity happens to be the idea of Śakti (power or energy). Śakti remains the underlying conceptual vehicle for mediating and coagulating the religious structures of goddess worship on the two planes of cultic manifestation mentioned earlier. Śakti is the irreducible (*sui generis*) ground for understanding both the non-Sanskritic, popular, and exoteric and the Sanskritic, philosophical, and esoteric participations in eventful symbols varyingly shared by both traditions. Śakti is the dynamic, awesome, and sacred Power which *is* the goddess Durgā-Kālī. She is the *mysterium tremendum et fascinosum* : "the 'great Mother' of Bengal whose worship can appear steeped in an atmosphere of profoundest devotional awe ... a blending of appalling frightfulness and the most exalted holiness".[131] This last and most potent phenomenological symbol—Śakti—permeates and encompasses both the ambivalent structure of the Sacred as religious manifestation and the multivalent structure of the Sacred as religious experience.

The overall significance of the foregoing discussion is that it suggests the following conclusions. (1) The historian of religions is enabled, because of a peculiar "phenomenologic of symbols" in Indian culture, to deal in an effective manner with the problem of regional theistic and cultic variations *as it pertains to the goddess*. The principal *cultural* nexus being (a) distribution of linguistic, symbolic, and functional phenomena, and (b) a stratified but unifying "Mother-Goddess" Complex. The primary *symbols* of structural continuity in religion continue to be (a) the Mother-Motif, (b) the Valence of Symbols, and (c) the idea of Śakti. (2) The variety of elements proposed characterize the fundamental movements of the goddess, Durgā-Kālī, in her historical, phenomenological, and structural expression as a religious object. Understanding, then, what we have referred to as the "phenomenologic of symbols" (Eliade : the "coherence of symbols") has indispensable value for everything that will pertain to the development of our study, especially Chapters III, IV, and V.

---

131 Otto, *The Idea of the Holy*, p. 62.

CHAPTER TWO

HISTORICAL AND TRADITIONAL ORIGINS: FROM ANCIENT TO MEDIEVAL TIMES

The Religio-Morphic Prehistory

The primary sources for a history of the goddess, Durgā-Kālī, take the form of historical, religious, and iconographic studies. In this initial phase these kinds of sources will be supplemented, however, by other types of materials (i.e., archaeological and ethnographic) in our attempt to glance, briefly, at the prehistoric and protohistoric cultural background of that divinity as a religious idea and form. This endeavour involves, to be sure, a reasonably clear perspective of both the possibilities and the limitations of such an approach.

Indeed, in his study of the human community a preeminent historian acknowledges at once that "in the beginning human history is a great darkness". He goes on to say, nonetheless, that archaeological research allows us to "infer ... and to deduce at least some of the characteristics of human life in times otherwise beyond our knowledge".[1] Such as it is to trace the *genera* of the human beings who worship her, Durgā-Kālī presents the historian of religions with both irresistible opportunities and insuperable difficulties in his attempt to discover her *ultimate* origins. Incidentally, British anthropologist L. S. B. Leakey "has already pushed the dawn of the human race back to 1,800,000 years";[2] the Aurignacian artictis heritage takes us back 32,000-35,000 years ago; again, we are told that human beings may have been in India for at least a period of 300,000 years;[3] finally, Indus Valley civilization has been estimated, apart from more romantically remote opinions, to have existed around 2,500 B.C. (with hundreds of years probably separating its demise and the Vedic literary deposit).

---

[1] William H. McNeill, *The Rise of the West* (Chicago: University of Chicago Press, 1963), p. 3.

[2] Cf. Andreas Lommel, *Prehistoric and Primitive Man* (London: Paul Hamlyn, 1966), p. 14.

[3] Cf. K. A. Nilakanta Sastri, *The Culture and History of the Tamils* (Calcutta: Firma K. L. Mukhopadhaya, 1963), pp. 3f. Cf. Joseph Campbell, *The Masks of God*, Vol. II: *Oriental Mythology* (New York: The Viking Press, Inc., 1962), pp. 150ff.

With such gaps in our knowledge, it is no wonder that the question might be asked whether there is any sense in which we might speak of the "history"[4] of this particular divinity any time before the Christian era.

As we indicated earlier, our intention is not to defer to chronologistic enthusiasts who demand specific chronologies in historical-religious studies where they are not always available to us. At the same time we consider it a legitimate enterprise to deduce or infer something valuable about man's long religious heritage, even if such inferences might have a tentative character.[5]

Consistent with our proposed method of approach (Chapter I) history must then be supplemented by phenomenological perception and structural considerations, if it is to be an historico-*religious* study. Thus in terms of "the history of the human spirit"[6] the Hindu divinity that concerns us constitutes an historical-cultural *ideomorphe.* She can be said, therefore, not only to have "descended" from a symbolic prototype in ancient Indian civilization; but she can also be viewed in the most centrifugal historical relation to much more archaic forms of religious expression. In this general sense, we have to combine the historical concerns of archaeological interpretation,[7] the phenomenology of culturo-symbolic creations,[8] and the structural dimensions of religious experience (as "psycho-history").[9]

---

4 Broadly speaking, of course, the term here signifies (a) "the philosophical and general meaning of 'history'" (Eliade, *supra*, p. 12); or that the religious symbol has been a part of human experience, or else the phenomenon of cultural evolution; and (b) part of a specific culture's religious heritage. The general historical sense both allows and requires us to consider, seriously, that as an *ideomorphe* (*infra*) the goddess has archaic religious antecedents — "She" — Durgā-Kālī — has happened to, with, and because of "someone". This approach requires a consciousness of crucial methodological observations (*supra*, pp. 10-11). Again, in a specific sense, Indian history merges with Indian "tradition" ("not, then, the spiritual outpourings of the heart of primitive man at the dawn of history" — Anislee T. Embree, ed., *The Hindu Tradition* [New York : Modern Library, 1966], p. 15); but which happens in this case to be textual and experiential; it, therefore, may include factors : psychological, sociological, etc. In Chapter IV we hope to show that it is in the religious cultus that all these factors find their meaningful integration.

5 McNeill, *The Rise of the West.*

6 Eliade, *Myths, Dreams, and Mysteries*, p. 12.

7 *Vide infra*, Levy *et al.*

8 Eliade, *Images and Symbols*, pp. 151-178.

9 Cf. Erich Neumann, *The Great Mother*, trans. Ralph Manheim (New York : Pantheon Books, Inc., 1955), p. 89.

We grant that there is some basis for skepticism (should one even take as his historical vantage point the matrix of the Indus Valley), when one is confronted by proponents of a sheer Orientalist romanticism. At any rate, that is not the basis of our own prehistoric beginning of the story of the goddess. In our view allowance can be made for such a beginning as long as one does not claim at this point to be doing chronological history but rather using complex and practicable historical-religious criteria. In a fundamental sense the fact remains that

> "primitivity" and "prehistory" have points of contact so that phenomena occurring in archaic or so-called primitive cultures may by way of analogy help us to form an idea of the meaning and purposes of prehistoric finds.[10]

Within this perspective, then, the *ideomorphe* of our study, Durgā-Kālī, rightly belongs to a more expansive sphere of culturo-religious activity which in all probability finds its earliest manifestations in the Upper Paleolithic and Neolithic periods of human evolution. As a "feminine cipher" her origins are thus prehistorical and protohistorical. The beginnings of her cultural lineage and representational genealogy carry us back towards the contemplation of the immemorial figure of the *Terra Mater*. In the widest and longest historical perspective, graphic or agraphic, we cannot thus ignore that very "wide provenance".[11] which was to become known as the realm of the *Great* Mother Goddess.[12] Indeed the religio-morphic historicity of the goddess, Durgā-Kālī, and her relatedness to the primordial *Terra Mater* have already been recognized in the archaeology of religion. Thus E. O. James has said,

---

[10] Jan Gonda, *Change and Continuity in Indian Religion* (The Hague : Mouton and Co., 1965), p. 33, n. 106. Cf. G. Rachel Levy, *Religious Conceptions of the Stone Age* (New York and Evanston : Harper and Row, 1963), p. 28; *vide* pp. 3-122, esp. pp. 56ff., 62f., 78-83, 86f., 119, and Plates 6, 7, 8d; Sybille Cles-Reden, *The Realm of the Great Goddess* (Englewood Cliffs, N.J.: Prentice-Hall, 1962), esp. pp. 9 (and Plate 38), 123-124, 70-74, 102f., 312 *et passim*; Lommel, *Prehistoric and Primitive Man*, pp. 7, 14f., 34 (Plate 14), 66 (Nos. 20-23), 68b; Neumann, *The Great Mother*, pp. 94-120, esp. 94, 106, 120 (Plates 1-3, 6 22); Jack Finegan, *The Archaeology of World Religions* (3 vols.; Princeton : Princeton University Press, 1965), I, 30; E. O. James, *The Cult of the Mother Goddess* (London : Thames and Hudson, 1959), pp. 11, 13-46.

[11] Levy, *Religious Conceptions* ..., p. 103. Cf. Long, *Alpha*, pp. 35-44.

[12] Cf. Neumann, *The Great Mother*, p. 11. Cf. Eliade, *Patterns in Comparative Religion*, pp. 261ff.

In India ... the worship of the active female principle *sakti* as manifest in one or other of the consorts of Shiva (e.g. Uma, Kali, Parvati, Durga) has a long history behind it. ... Shaktism, in fact, is ... an offshoot of the Earth Cultus.[13]

There even appears to be some validity to the idea of an intimate structural connection between the "Feminine Cipher" and the emergent consciousness of man.[14] Moreover, this archetypal intuition of *Terra Mater*—which is shared by so many persons in various and sundry places—reminds us again of the vital relation between symbol and culture.[15] It also signifies the dynamic interchange between man and environment in a more general sense as mentioned earlier.[16] Accordingly, at a certain moment of crucial apprehension in cultural prehistory, human beings began to experience a "primary intuition of the earth as a religious form", an intuition that "is prior to the symbolism of the earth in the form of the Great Mother", and which "is the intuition of the earth as the cosmic repository of all forms, latencies and powers ... the fertile source of being".[17] These amorphous but vital religious valorizations were made in dynamic relation to real "cultural moments" in profane world history.[18] It is, furthermore, noted that this primary intuition was eventually left behind in the shadow of a more anthropomorphically expressed sacred symbol.[19] Yet it is also probable that a semi-conscious, perhaps, also conscious, awareness of "a pervading principle ... a life-substance through which

---

13 James, *The Cult of the Mother Goddess*, pp. 242, 243. Giuseppe Tucci, "Earth in in India and Tibet", *Eranos Jahrbuch*, XXII (1953), 355, has interesting comments on Mother Earth/Mother Goddess. They may symbolize (1) parallel but different ethno-cultural trends and life styles; (2) yet be divergent expressions of an underlying intuition of the same "primordial archetype"; (3) moreover, this image from which female divinities of either Mother Goddess or Earth Mother type (i.e., "stress") emreges has an apparent but indefinite limit; thus (4) we are dealing with a basic phenomenon "capable of infinite modulations" and "recurrent resurrections".

14 Levy, *Religious Conceptions ...*, p. 63: on "anthropomorphic shape" and the "human personality"; Erich Neumann, *The Origins and History of Consciousness*, trans. R. F. C. Hull (New York: Harper and Brothers, 1962), Part II, p. 288.

15 *Supra*, pp. 34-35.

16 *Supra*, p. 11.

17 Long, *Alpha*, p. 38; Eliade, *Myths, Dreams, and Mysteries*, p. 168, n. 1; Eliade, *Patterns in Comparative Religion*, p. 245; Levy, *Religious Conceptions ...*, p. 27.

18 Cf. Mircea Eliade, "Structures and Changes in the History of Religions", *City Invincible*, ed. Carl Kraeling (Chicago: University of Chicago Press, 1960), p. 359.

19 Eliade, *Patterns in Comparative Religion*, p. 245.

that power could act"[20] both previewed and accompanied the later religious-symbolic crystallizations under the form of Woman.

It is this *morphe* of Woman, which, essentially, enables us to posit an *historio*-morphic relatedness — not a necessary chrono-genetic continuity [21] — between Durgā-Kālī and the First Feminine Religious Form wherever it might have occurred. We speak under this morphological and historical aegis with confidence because our discipline concerns itself with both generalization and particularization. These two processes are not, therefore, to be seen as unrelated. But it is in general on the level of "the philosophy of culture"[22] that we now say such things. To be sure, we must acknowledge the existence of what Mircea Eliade calls "limit-situations",[23] stylised cultural differences, as well as the un-interchangeability of individual cultures as historical formations.[24] Yet as culturo-morphic realities that have been lived, valued, and shared, we can also afford to acknowledge that "different" 'histories' can inter-communicate".[25]

> Starting from any stylistically and historically conditioned creation of the spirit one can regain the vision of the archetype : Kore Persephone, as well as Hainuwele, reveals to us the same pathetic, creative destiny of the Young *Woman*.[26]

It is, again, this *morphe* of Woman which became the symbolic "vessel" of two very fundamental religious realities. These realities comprised not only the cultic guarantorship of terrestrial fertility or *cornucopia*. They also gave spiritual direction and a meaningful frame of reference to human beings who had, recurrently, to witness, if not to face, uniquely the phenomenon of death.[27]

---

[20] Levy, *Religious Conceptions ...*, p. 62.

[21] Cf. Neumann, *Origins ...*, Part II, pp. 264ff.

[22] Eliade, *Images and Symbols*, pp. 172f.

[23] *Ibid.*, pp. 174, 176. Cf. *ibid.*, pp. 115ff.

[24] *Ibid.*, p. 173.

[25] *Ibid.*, p. 174.

[26] *Ibid.* (Italics mine.) Eliade, *Myth and Reality*, pp. 103ff.

[27] Cf. Levy, *Religious Conceptions ...*, p. 86. Cf. Eliade, *Patterns in Comparative Religion*, p. 352, and *Myths, Dreams, and Mysteries*, pp. 188f.; J. A. B. van Buitenen, trans., *Tales of Ancient India* (Chicago : University of Chicago Press, 1959), pp. 16-19 (*vide* also *infra*, p. 199); Joseph Campbell, *The Masks of God*, Vol. I : *Primitive Mythology* (New York : Viking Press, 1959), pp. 70, 68; Gerald D. Berreman, *Hindus of the Himalayas* (Berkeley and Los Angeles : University of California Press, 1963), pp. 379-381, 383f., 101; Tara Krishna Basu, *The Bengali Peasant from Time to Time* (Indian Statistical Institute Series, No. 15; Bombay and Calcutta : Asia Publishing House, 1962), pp. 149-151, 153-154; Oscar Lewis, *Village Life in Northern India* (New York : Random House, 1958), p. 238.

Coherent with these two basic concerns both in terms of structure and function were other cultic ingredients which have lingered, though variably, throughout the later Neolithic period and into our own day. They are manifested in the complex phenomenon of the cult of the Mother Goddess in India. These "associative symbols" belong to the provenance of Earth-Mother as a religious form. They do not mean that the goddess, Durgā-Kālī, is merely an earth-goddess; but they are a part of her comprehensive mythic and ritual complex. Such symbols may take a variety of forms though they cannot all be taken into consideration here. Nonetheless

> these symbols — particularly nature symbols from every realm of nature [28] — are in a sense signed with the image of the Great Mother, which, whether they be stone or tree, pool, fruit, or animal, lives in them and is identified with them. Gradually, they become linked with the figure of the Great Mother as attributes [29] and form the wreath of symbols that surrounds the archetypal figure and manifests itself in rite and myth.[30]

Beginning earlier but finding their eventual fruition in the middle and late Neolithic millenia were certain categorical nominals or epithets which, too, became parts of the complex of activities associated with the archaic Earth-Goddess. E. O. James points out that they had to do with her more decidedly anthropomorphic and individualized emergence and capacity as Lady of the Wild Beasts, the Mountain Mother, and the Mistress of Trees.[31]

To be sure, the divinity, Durgā-Kālī, reveals in dramatic fashion her culturo-morphic relatedness to both the Neumannian archetype as well as the functional characterizations indicated by James. For her capacity as Lady of the Wild Beasts, we shall see, is implied in her

---

[28] Cf. W. Crooke, *The Popular Religion and Folklore of Northern India* (2 vols.; rev. ed.; Delhi : Devandra Jain, 1968), I, Chap. I, 26-33, 60-63, 198, 111-117, 119, 42, 55; Chap. III, 125-136, 142f., 151-152, 173f., 236, 283; II, Chap. II, 91, 105f., 108, 180, 184-185, 224, 236f., 271.

[29] Cf. Eliade, *Yoga*, p. 386 : "Like the ancient autochthonous divinities, the ancient religious ceremonies survive, but under different names and sometimes with a changed meaning. The tribes still venerate the sacred places — a tree, a lake, a spring, a cave— haunted by their tutelary divinities. ... Hinduism identified these ... with the many manifestations of Śiva or Kālī (Durgā); as for the ancient sites, they were validated by episodes from Hindu mythology".

[30] Neumann, *The Great Mother*, pp. 9, 12. Eliade, "Methodological Remarks ...," pp. 99f., and *Patterns in Comparative Religion*, pp. 189f., 255, 286, 314, 325.

[31] James, *The Cult of the Mother Goddess*, pp. 128-129.

role as Bana-Durgā ("Durgā of the Forest"), Vanaspatī ("Mistress of the Wood"), or Bana-Devī ("Goddess of the Forest").[32] Her capacity as Mountain Mother finds striking structural continuity in the epithetic Goddess as Haimāvatī Umā ("Daughter of the Himalayas"), or Pārvatī ("Lady of the Hills"), or Vindhyavāsinī ("Dweller of the Vindhyas").[33] Her capacity to be Mistress of the Trees finds its appropriate context in the milieu of the vegetation cult.

P. K. Maity also recognizes the phenomenon of "associative symbols" in his socio-cultural study of Manasā, the snake-goddess of Bengal.[34] In terms of myth and cult, however, many of the various symbolic elements indicated in Neumann and James, though hardly all of them, tend to be encompassed by the categories of (1) aqualithic symbolism, (2) therio-affinal imagery, (3) vegetal cult, and (4) sanguinary rites. Mircea Eliade [35] has taken notice of many of the previous mythic and cultic phenomena in connection with the goddess, Durgā-Kālī, as she is worshipped by members of the aboriginal inhabitants of India.

Aqualithic Symbolism

Among such studies, that of S. C. Mitra [36] is particularly worthy of our attention. For even one reason : it brings together the primeval element — stone and the ever-assimilative element — water. The

[32] Cf. N. M. Chaudhuri, "The Cult of Vana-Durgā, a Tree-Deity", *Journal of the Royal Asiatic Society of Bengal* (Letters), XL, No. 2 (1945), 75-84; Crooke, *The Popular Religion* ..., I, 115.

[33] *Encyclopedia of Religion and Ethics*, 1912, V, 118, and II, 813; Gustav Oppert (*On the Original Inhabitants of Bharatavarṣa or India*, [Westminster : Archibald Constable and Co., 1893]) notes that the goddess lives "in fact on all mountains" : in the Malayas, Vindhya, Kailāsa—in Northern, Central and Southern India (pp. 433, 435-436).

[34] P. K. Maity (*Historical Studies in the Cult of the Goddess Manasa* [Calcutta : Punthi Pustak, 1966], pp. 40ff.) can therefore refer to" ... other beliefs relating to the cult", e.g., "Water spirits", "Ancestor spirits", "... the earth", "tree and serpent", etc. All of this, of course, testifies to the sheer potential of the "Earth", as a religious form to encompass "a wide range of symbolism" (cf. Long, *Alpha*, p. 37 : and to be "the matter from which all forms of life emerge and to which all forms eventually return"). For a classical illustration of the interplay and overlapping of symbols, *vide* H. and H. A. Frankfort, J. A. Wilson, and T. Jacobsen, *Before Philosophy* (Baltimore : Penguin Books, Inc., 1964), Chap. V, esp. pp. 142ff., 149-161, 170-174.

[35] Eliade, *Yoga*, pp. 286-388.

[36] Cf. Sarat Chandra Mitra, "The Cult of the Lake-Goddess of Orissa", *Journal of the Anthropological Society of Bombay*, XII (1920-1924), 190-197.

Orissan lake-goddess is named Kālijai. Her name alone intimates an interesting linguistic affinity with the goddess Kālī. In fact, she is "looked upon as an incarnation of Kālī".[37] Her temple is situated on an island in Chilka Lake.[38] She has, apparently, no anthropomorphic image connected with her worship, except that she is represented by an irregular block of stone (measurements : 4 feet high and 3 $^{1}/_{2}$ feet wide) besmeared with a pasty oil and vermillion. In addition the object is ornamented with cowry shells. Other significant features are the following : (1) Kālijai is worshipped as the "protectress"[39] of "boatmen and fishermen" from storms, which she herself can control for good or ill; (2) Kālijai is the abitress of procreation and death, thereby delivering boons from sickness and disease through the offerings of her devotees; (3) the votive offerings to her range from sheep, goats, fowls (and possibly at one time) human beings.[40]

In addition to its autochthonous aqua-orientation, the aboriginal structure of the Kālijai cult, says Eliade, "is further confirmed by the fact that fowls are sacrificed to her".[41] Its archaic character is also suggested by the presence of cowry shells and blood-coloured substances which are almost universally recognized as having some vital connection with funeral, sacrificial, or apotropaic ends.[42] On the whole, Mitra's

---

37 *Ibid.*, p. 190.

38 Cf. W. W. Hunter, *Orissa* (London : Smith, Elder and Company, 1872), p. 47 : "... the history of Orissa is the narrative of a province at the mercy of a great river, and a short account of the Chilka will make known to European readers the terrible meaning of these words". *Vide* also *ibid.*, pp. 17-80, esp. pp. 81-21, 25, 26, 29, 31, 45f., 63f., 67.

39 In this functional aspect, it appears, Kālijai is historically and structurally related to the Yakṣī-type of divinity. Though of "uncertain" etymology (cf. Ananda Coomaraswamy, *Yakṣas*, Part II [Washington, D.C. : Smithsonian Institution, 1931], p. 1), the term has been assigned multiple meanings both in name, nature, and function in Indian literature. Cf. the same author's "Yakṣas", Part I, in *Smithsonian Miscellaneous Collections*, LXXX, No. 6 (1928-1931), 2ff.; on ambiguity, *ibid.*, pp. 7, 11, 14, 15, 16, and Part II, pp. 1-12. Particularly noticeable are their functions as *guardians* (*ibid.*, pp. 2, 8), *vegetation* spirits, and in relation to *water* (*ibid.*, p. 2, n. 2, and pp. 16f., 19ff.).

40 Mitra, "The Cult of the Lake-Goddess of Orissa", pp. 190, 192, 193.

41 Eliade, *Yoga*, p. 387.

42 Mitra, "The Cult of the Lake-Goddess of Orissa", pp. 192, 193. Here, however, the apotropaic function is assigned by the author to numerous "bangles made of glass or silver", "... used in Indian ritual as spirit-scarers" in the North in the form of a "disease-transference charm"; likewise, clay-made bracelets in the South are used "either as an offering to the disease-spirit or as a charm to drive it away". On "blood" apotropaicism, *vide* Jarl Charpentier, "The Meaning and Etymology of Pūjā", *Indian Antiquary*, LVI (1927), 98f., 133, 134, 136; Elmore, *Dravidian Gods in Modern Hinduism*, p. 125.

study has particular value for us, because it not only relates to the question of magna-minor-traditional processes in India, but it also shows several vestiges of a much more archaic culturo-morphic orientation.[43]

Moreover, Coomaraswamy's studies in Yakṣa iconography, besides showing temple guardianship and vegetal relations, tell us something interesting about their specific association with water symbolism. River goddesses, in part undifferentiated as well as individualized, are recognized in connection with various supportive representations of "mythical aqueous animals, notably the *makara* ..."[44] These *nadī-devatā* found at the Kaṅkālī Ṭīlā site at Mathurā, Deogaṛh, Ajaṇṭā, and other locations, are largely Guptan in chronology (from *ca.* 320 A.D.); the earliest "differentiated goddesses" are probably to be dated around 500 A.D.[45] Pre-Guptan undifferentiated representations are probable with respect to Buddhist naga-affiliated river goddesses. Coomaraswamy, however, offers no approximate dating; but such figures are seen as historico-iconographic links between (a) those of Yakṣas or dryads, on the one hand; and (b) vase attributed, "differentiated" river goddesses in the late Guptan and post-Guptan period.[46] Related, and earlier still, may be the very *motif* of "doorway forms" of distinctively animal nature (*ca.* 130 A.D.), which find some iconographic continuity in *makara*-supported Yakṣas at Candragupta cave.[47] Perhaps what may be the earliest paired-representation of Śiva-Pārvatī of the Dīdargañj Yakṣī type [48] is "embossed on a concave plaque of pure gold, 2 1/2 inches high, found on the site of the Patna fort".[49] On the face of it, Banerjea notes that, in terms of present or missing iconographic features, it could be dated as Mauryan or pre-Mauryan (*ante* or *intra* 322-185 B.C.). Other dates range between the first century B.C. and the first century A.D. Though it is of special

---

[43] Cf. E. O. James, *Prehistoric Religion : A Study in Prehistoric Archaeology* (New York Barnes and Noble, Inc., 1957), pp. 20f., 23ff., esp. 28-30 *et passim.*

[44] Coomaraswamy, *Yakṣas*, Part II, p. 66.

[45] *Ibid.*, p. 68.

[46] *Ibid.*, pp. 70f.

[47] *Ibid.*, p. 67.

[48] Cf. A. L. Basham, *The Wonder That Was India* (3d ed. rev.; New York : Taplinger Publishing Co., 1968), p. 367, Plate 26a.

[49] Jitendra Nath Banerjea, *The Development of Hindu Iconography* (Calcutta : University of Calcutta, 1956), p. 224.

interest to us, the prospect of its age and authenticity has not been without some question.[50]

The significance of the foregoing studies and date (notwithstanding the Dīdargañj Yakṣī question) is the following. They suggest that, probably alongside of the more archaically *un*-anthropomorphic (i.e., lithiconic)[51] representation of Kālijai and the later more anthromorphically cosmic representations of Durgā-Kālī of the Pallava and Gandāra periods of Indian art,[52] might be placed a folkloristic (Kālī-) *Yakṣī*/(Kālī-) Rakṣī type of chthonian representation (aquatic, vegetal, fairy-like, etc.). It is, in fact, regarded a strong probability that

> the goddess Sītalā, Olābībī (goddess of cholera), the Seven Mothers (partly connected with Kubera, "king" of the Yakṣas), the sixty-four Yoginīs and Ḍākinīs, some forms of Devī, almost all the divinities of southern India, and even the great Durgā were originally Yakṣas—that is ... regarded as such in Brāhmanic circles. In any case, the Yakṣas and the Yakṣinīs represent the type-form of aboriginal religious devotion.[53]

Therio-Affinal Imagery

It can be readily seen that the goddess Kālijai, as aqua-symbol, tends to assimilate elements used in a potentially more extensive ritual-structural complex. A similar capacity will be seen to characterize the blood-sacrificial aspect of her cult. It also becomes clearer

---

50 *Ibid.*, p. 224, n. 1 (cf. *ibid.*, pp. 97-99). Cf. N. R. Ray, "Art" (Sculpture), in R. C. Majumdar, gen. ed., *The History and Culture of the Indian People*, II (Bombay : Bharatya Vidya Bhavan, 1968), 517f.

51 Cf. Eliade, *Yoga*, p. 345 : "Altars for the worship of Yakṣas can be raised almost everywhere. The essential element is the stone tablet or altar (Veyaḍḍi, mañco) placed under the sacred tree".

52 Cf., e.g., Heinrich Zimmer, *The Art of Indian Asia : Its Mythology and Transformations*, ed. Joseph Campbell (2 vols.; New York : Pantheon Books, Inc., 1955), esp. I, 93, and Vol. II, Plate 210.

53 Eliade, *Yoga*, p. 345; K. A. Nilakanta Sastri, *Development of Religion in South India* (Bombay : Orient Longmans, 1963), p. 50f. Cf. Crooke, *The Popular Religion ...*, I, 94f., 247, 253, and II, 79ff.; Coomaraswamy, "Yakṣas", Part I, pp. 5, 24ff. Both scholars are aware of the presence of ambivalence of "functional" meaning; "Rakṣa-Kālī", i.e., "the Kālī who protects", appears in Basu, *The Bengal Peasant*, pp. 150, 151. In Chintaharan Chakravarti's "The Cult of Bāro Bhāiyā of Eastern Bengal" (*Journal of the Asiatic Society of Bengal*, XXVI [1930], 380, 388), Raṇa-yakṣinī ("The Yakṣinī of the Battle-Field") appears as a sister alongside of the Twelve Brothers (demons, *daityas*) whose mother (*ibid.*, pp. 382f.) is Vana-Durgā (*dānava mātā*).

how, as a form of ritual behaviour, such worship of the goddess, Durgā-Kālī, happens to be associated with theriomorphic imagery.

Our attention is called at once to many soapstone carvings (20 in number) believed to go back to the Śuṅga Period (around 185-80 B.C.):

> many of them are of a very high order. ... Five of them contain the figures of the nude mother or the fertility goddesses associated with various animals and birds like lions (some of them are winged), elephants, horse, antelope, stag, ram, goose, peacock and parrot. In this strange medley of animals no alligator or iguana is seen, it is true, but the association of lion and other animals and that of birds with the goddesses is very significant.[54]

The reference to the iguana is of special interest to us; for the *godha* (i.e., iguana) as an iconographic element is known to be part of the imagery of the mother-goddess: Pārvatī, Caṇḍī, or Kālaketu (Śiva) in Bengal, as well as in southern India on reliefs of Umā-Mahesvara. In addition an early fifth-century A.D. *godha* is seen with a cave carving of a twelve-armed goddess under the form of Mahiṣamardinī.[55]

Banerjea recognizes these phenomena of therio-kinship as being "of unique importance and interest from the point of view of the developed Śakti cult in India".[56]

The traditional presence of the lion or the tiger as a companion or *vāhana* (i.e., vehicle) of the goddess, Durgā-Kālī, has already been alluded to in its culturo-morphic relatedness to much earlier forms.[57] Interestingly, the structural relation between water *and* animal symbolism is confirmed by the fact that Yakṣas and Yakṣis are said to have symbolic affinities with "supports' [vehicles] representing mythical animals, notably the *makara*,[58] more rarely the fish-tailed horse (*jala-turaga*), elephant (*jalebha*), or lion or the flower of a lotus ... an indication of the ultimate connection of these deities of fertility with life-giving Waters".[59]

---

[54] Banerjea, *The Development of Hindu Iconography*, pp. 172-173; *vide* also the hymn to Tārā (Nilā Tantra), in Arthur and Ellen Avalon, *Hymns to the Goddess*, trans. from the Sanskrit (Madras: Ganesh and Co. Private, Ltd., 1964), p. 54, vs. 7. (Hereafter cited as *H.T.T.G.*).

[55] Banerjea, *The Development of Hindu Iconography*, pp. 172-173.

[56] *Ibid.*, p. 172.

[57] Levy, *Religious Conceptions ...*, p. 119. Cf. *ibid.*, pp. 223f.; Banerjea, *The Development of Hindu Iconography*, pp. 167, 134f., 185ff.; Crooke, *The Popular Religion ...*, II, 210.

[58] Cf. *supra*, p. 50.

[59] Coomaraswamy, *Yakṣas*, Part II, p. 66.

We recall that Durgā-Kālī is not only "mother of demons", but "mistress of the wood" as well. She is "Durgā of the Forest". Her symbolic association with the forest, naturally, implies her sovereign affinality with the living creatures of that realm (i.e., all living things there—including human beings and sundry types of animal spirit-children. She is, therefore, Mistress of all forest life.[60] Among the animals, themselves, the lion and the tiger are well-known "sovereigns" among other creatures. Accordingly, "the fury of Devī, the Supreme Goddess may be projected as a ravenous lion or tiger".[61]

The list of animals of almost fabulous variety [62] mentioned in the Kālikā Purāṇa (*ca.* the tenth century) in connection with sacrifice to the goddess bears witness, no doubt, to human experiences in the ancient forests of India.[63] Whether their nominal selection was ultimately derived from mere propitiatory actions toward them or totemistic ideas may never be known for certain. Nevertheless, phenomena such as these have not gone unnoticed or unentertained by researchers as a basis for such theories.

The totemistic interpretation has been adopted with regard to certain animals which form part of the Mother-Goddess Complex in South India (e.g., the Buffalo Sacrifice).[64] Whitehead's approach involves the assumption that the original rationale of such practices, though conceivably attributable to a gift-theory of sacrifice, or the

---

[60] Cf. Eliade, *Patterns in Comparative Religion*, p. 255.

[61] Heinrich Zimmer, *Myths and Symbols in Indian Art and Civilization*, ed. Joseph Campbell (Torchbook ed.; New York : Harper and Brothers, 1962), pp. 189, 69ff. Cf. Banerjea, *The Development of Hindu Iconography*, p. 166. Cf. Chakravarti, "The Cult of Bāro Bhāiyā of Eastern Bengal", p. 383 : the goddess "who has taken up a tiger's skin as her cloth, who stands on a lion, has the snake as her ornament, and who plays (i.e., moves) like a tiger on the occassion of killing enemies.".

[62] I.e., "Birds, tortoises, alligators, fish, nine species of wild animals, buffaloes, bulls, he-goats, ichneumons [i.e., slender, cat-size, carnivorous mammals], wild bears, rhinoceros, antelopes, iguanas, reindeer, lions, tigers." ... Karmakar, *The Religions of India*, I, 212.

[63] Cf. Crooke, *The Popular Religion ...*, I, 114-115 ("The Jungle Mothers"); Tarak Chandra Das, "Religious Beliefs of the Indian Tribes", *The Cultural Heritage of India*, Vol. IV : *The Religions*, ed. Haridas Bhattacharyya (Calcutta : Ramakrishna Mission Institute of Culture, 1956), p. 431; E. P. Stebbing, *The Forests of India*, I (New York : E. P. Dutton and Co., [*ca.* 1922]), 197f., 200f.; John F. Hurst, *Indika : The Country and the People of India and Ceylon* (New York : Harper and Brothers, 1891), pp. 92ff.

[64] Cf. Henry Whitehead, *The Village Gods of South India* (2d rev. ed.; Calcutta : Association Press, 1921), pp. 56f., 62f., 70, 72f., 93f., 108f., 117ff. *et passim.*

idea of propitiation, is not fully explained by them.[65] All the animal rites connected with South Indian divinities (gods and goddesses) are, therefore, made intelligible by a theory of "communion with the totem spirit".[66]

A contrary viewpoint is advanced by Elmore,[67] who claims that, though useful, the South Indian buffalo is not held in high esteem or is not a probable totemic animal. The author is reluctant, however, to disregard the commonly held opinion of the venerators of the village goddesses; they, apparently, believe that such divinities take "the spiritual part of the food or its essence or spiritual strength".[68] Elmore rejects, nonetheless, the totemistic hypothesis in favour of another quite interesting interpretation; that is, the theory of "the dire punishment and disgrace of a conquered enemy".[69] Claiming that this view is supported by early and later textual tradition (e.g., the Purāṇas), he recognizes, to be sure, that "from such legends ... we may not hope to establish any historical facts about the origin and meaning of the buffalo sacrifice".[70] Psychologically, at any rate, the aim of the sacrifice of the animal(s) is neither totemistic nor "eucharistic" but rather "aversive" in nature.[71]

From a broader perspective it would seem to us, after all, that the natural convergence of impressions of animal-wonder, demonic folklore, and the mystery of death may have formed parts of a complex background of "emotional, religious and ideological"[72] responses. In all probability the affinality of such creatures with the realm of Durgā-Kālī as the Earth-Goddess meant a religious orientation of persons to a divinity who demanded such animals as votive offerings for the welfare of her subjects.

---

65 *Ibid.*, pp. 142-144.

66 *Ibid.*, pp. 147, 148-151.

67 Elmore, *Dravidian Gods in Modern Hinduism*, p. 126.

68 *Ibid.*, p. 139.

69 *Ibid.*, p. 123.

70 *Ibid.*; *vide* also *ibid.*, p. 121.

71 *Ibid.*, p. 123.

72 Cf. John V. Ferreira, *Totemism in India* (Bombay : Oxford University Press, 1965), p. 43. The specific problem of totemism among Indian tribes is breathtakingly complex. Ferreira's critical study is a veritable maze of ethnological data and opinions, but does contain valuable synthetic observations on the problem. *Vide ibid.*, pp. 121ff., and esp. "devaks" and "sakti", pp. 204-206; Chap. X; also pp. 262f., 268f., 280ff. One must recognize the complexity of India's "tribal" world : (1) ethnically, (2) culturally (espeially technologically), and (3) religiously. *Vide ibid.*, pp. 84, 275-279; Surajit Sinha, "Tribal Cultures of Peninsula India ..., pp. 301ff.

Vegetal Cult [73]

The naked goddess—"She who is without her garment of leaves" (*Aparṅa*)[74] is also *Śākambarī* : "She who feeds the herbs",[75] as well as "She who bestows food" (*Annapūrnā*).[76].

Like the goddess Kālijai as aqua-symbol, the goddess Durgā-Kālī, as vegecultural symbol tends to encompass other motifs through the "logic of symbols". If water, as it seems, is the all-encompassing symbolic frame of reference for so many cosmogonic visions, the phenomenon of vegetation would appear to be a center of gravity for a host of floral or vegetal ideas, all of which are assimilable to the goddess in her capacity as Earth-Mother.

The archaic bond between water and vegetation symbolism, however, is the tree as a religious form (*ficus religiosa*).[77] This symbol has been noted not only among the varieties of religious expressions discovered in the Indus Valley but "particularly in association with the worship of the Mother goddess".[78] From at least the Vedic period,[79]

---

73 *Nota Bene* : "... there has never been any real vegetation cult, any religion solely built upon plants and trees. Even the most 'specialized' religions (the fertility cults, for instance), when plant life has been adored and used in the cult, other forces of nature have too. What are generally known as 'vegetation cults' are really seasonal celebrations which cannot be accounted for merely in terms of a plant hierophany, but form part of far more complex dramas taking in the whole life of the universe. Indeed, it is sometimes hard to separate vegetation elements from the religious elements connected with the Earth-Mother ..." Eliade, *Patterns in Comparative Religion*, p. 325.

74 Eliade, *Yoga*, p. 354, n. 178.

75 Devīmāhātmya 91 : 44.

76 Tantrasāra (the Annapūrnāstotra, *H.T.T.G.*, pp. 64-68, 208-214).

77 Cf. Coomaraswamy, "Yakṣas", Part II, pp. 19-26; the water-vegetal bond is thus this (*ibid.*, p. 25) : "from the primeval Waters arose the Plants, from Plants all other beings, in particular the gods, men, and cattle. *Rasa*, as an essence of the Waters, or as sap in trees, is variously identified with *soma*, *amṛta*, semen, milk rain, honey mead (*madhu*) and liquor (*surā*); there is a cycle in which the vital energy passes from heaven through the waters, plants, cattle and other typically virile or productive animals, and man, thence ultimately returning to the waters". Eliade (*Yoga*, p. 350) notes that "Sometimes the symbolism of water resists all mythological and scholastic reinterpretations and ends by forcing its way even into the sacred texts. The *Devyupaniṣad* relates that the gods, having asked the Great Goddess (Devī) who she was and when she came, received the answer, 'The place of my birth is in the water within the sea : he who knows this, obtains the dwelling of Devī'".

78 E. O. James, *The Tree of Life : An Archaeological Study* (Leiden : E. J. Brill, 1966), pp. 20f., 23.

79 A. A. MacDonell (*A History of Sanskrit Literature* [New York : D. D. Appleton and Co., 1900], pp. 146f.) notes the apparent absence in the Ṛg-Veda of the *Ficus*

then, the tree appears to have been a sacred object in two respects: (1) reverence paid to the tree in its natural form, and (2) reverence paid to the tree as a *locus* of some divinity such as "Gods, Gandharvas, Apsarases, Yaksaṣas, Nāgas ... pretas or ghosts".[80] The multiple functions of the sacred tree, in the first case, take the form of efforts to participate in its "magical potency", for physical secutiry, health, wealth, and progeny.[81] In the case of the "anthropomorphic forms" (sometimes independent but still connected with the tree), "they have to be propitiated for granting desires or for averting their displeasure".[82]

The goddess Vana-Durgā, among similar deities [83] variously located in Bengal, is associated with the sheora tree (*Trophis aspera*).[84] Several characteristics of this type of cult are thus pointed out by Chaudhuri.[85] Noting that the Sheora tree is a sacred object worshipped particularly by women, the author infers that such worship

> combines two conceptions, namely, the conception of the fertility-giving powers of trees and the conception of malignant spirits harmful to children residing in the sheora tree who have to be propitiated ... In the cults under notice we have an instance of the fertility conception of the old tree worship being superimposed on an old tradition of demonolatry probably of tribal origin. The former conception appears to have transformed the latter conception with the result that ... a tree

---

indica (i.e., the Nyagrodha, or banyan tree) which he calls "the tree which is most characteristic of India". W. Norman Brown ("The Content of Cultural Continuity in India", *The Journal of Asian Studies*, XX, No. 4 [August, 1961], 433f.) employs by analogy what we might call "the nyagrodha principle" as a key to understanding "the history of Indian civilization".

[80] Cf. N. M. Chaudhuri, "A Pre-Historic Tree Cult", *Indian Historical Quarterly*, XIX (1943), 327; cf. *ibid.*, pp. 319f.

[81] Cf. Chaudhuri, "The Cult of Vana-Durgā, a Tree Deity", pp. 75f. *Nota Bene*, the goddess Jātāpahāriṇī (*et al.*), *ibid.*, pp. 78-79.

[82] *Ibid.* Cf. James, *The Tree of Life*, pp. 24f.

[83] E.g. (Vana-Durgā as) Rupasī, Rupeśwarī (Bengal and Assam), Guṇḍi Thākurāṇī (Goddess of the Tree-Trunk).

[84] Sanskrit: *sakhot* (or *piśāca druma*: ghost tree—"well known in the folklore of Bengal as the favourite haunt of female ghosts or *pretinīs*"). Chaudhuri, "The Cult of Vana-Durgā, a Tree Deity", p. 78.

[85] *Ibid.*, p. 77. The cult of Vana-Durgā was also reported (*ibid.*, pp. 77-78) "in association with the *sal*, *palāśa* and *aśvattha* trees in some of the West Bengal districts and with the *kāmanī* in Comilla in East Bengal. ..." Cf. S. C. Mitra, "On the Cult of the Tree-Goddess in Eastern Bengal", *Man in India*, II (1922), 233ff.; Eliade, *Yoga*, p. 388. Cf. the divinities, Śiva and Pārvatī, *a propos* vegiconography, in J. G. Frazer, *The Golden Bough* (abridged ed.; New York: The Macmillan Co., 1958), p. 372.

> recognized as the abode of malign spirits has been transformed [86] into the abode of the protecting spirit of children called Vana-Durgā, Buḍī, Rupasī, Guṇḍi Thākurā-ṇi ... in different parts in the same fashion as baby-killing demonesses were transformed into protectresses of children ... The process ... has gone further and resulted in affiliating the tree deities to the great Devī under the name of Vana-Durgā.[87]

Phenomenologically, that which Chaudhuri presents within a pattern of evolutionary transformation remains in essence a testimony of both the ambivalent and the multivalent nature of the *ficus religiosa.* Indeed the sacred tree can also serve as an image of the cosmos,[88] a cosmic theophany, a symbol of life, the center of the world and support of the universe, a mysto-anthropomorphic bond, as well as a symbol of vegetal resurrection.[89] Perhaps these are not all; but it is clear that "the presence of the goddess beside a plant symbol confirms one meaning that the tree possesses in archaic iconography and mythology : that of being an *inexhaustible source of cosmic fertility*".[90]

> ... O ye gods, I shall support (i.e. nourish) the whole world with the life-sustaining vegetables, which shall grow out of my own body, during a period of heavy rain. I shall gain fame on earth then as Sakhambhari; and in that very period I shall slay the great *asura* named Durgama.[91]

The Rite of *Navapatrikā* ("nine leaves", or "nine sprouts") involves the use of the branches or twigs of nine trees. The symbolic coalescence of tree and divinity is confirmed in that the taking of a branch brings pain to the divinity symbolized by a particular sacred tree. The severing of a leaf is accompanied by the words' "I take thee away, oh beloved Candika. Dost thou grant one wealth and dominion. Welcome oh Devi Candika".[92] Or, as a personified whole, "Oh, leaf [patrikā],

---

86 Cf. the Rājasūyārambha Parva in the Mahābhārata, trans. P. C. Roy, Vol. I (n.p., n.d.), Sabhā Parvan XIV-XVIII, esp. Secs. XVII-XVIII. Cf. J. N. Banerjea, "Some Folk Goddesses of Ancient and Medieval India", *Indian Historical Quarterly,* XIV (1938), 101f. (note Jarā : "old age", p. 108).

87 Chaudhuri, "The Cult of Vana-Durgā, a Tree Deity", p. 83.

88 Cf. Eliade, *Patterns in Comparative Religion,* pp. 269ff., 273ff.; James, *The Tree of Life,* pp. 148-152.

89 Eliade, *Patterns in Comparative Religion,* p. 267.

90 *Ibid.,* p. 280.

91 Devīmāhātmya 90:43-44. Durgama : a personification of drought. Cf. "Durgama," in Whitehead, *The Village Gods of South India,* pp. 71, 74-76, 86.

92 Cf. P. Ghosha, *Durgā-Pūjā* (Calcutta : Hindu Patriot Press, 1871), pp. 66-68. Cf. Eliade, *Patterns in Comparative Religion,* p. 240 : i.e., the Indian Baiga who "thought it a sin to tear their mother's bosom with a plough".

O nine forms of Durgā! You are the darling of Mahādeva; accept all these offerings and protect me, O queen of heaven. *O, adoration to Durgā dwelling in the nine plants*".[93]

Mitra rightly says that the *Navapatrikā* rite—and, we would add, the other foregoing mythic and symbolic elements—"is ... a survival of the cult of Durgā in her capacity as the vegetation-spirit or the tree-goddess".[94] Moreover, the protection-fertility-vegetation symbological nexus is epitomized in a mantra recited by women in the invocation of the goddess Durgā: "Save sons and give sons, o goddess; make the paddy in the field and the plough for tilling hundredfold; obeisance to thee o goddess of the tree-trunk".[95]

Sanguinary Rites

> The frightening aspect of the Earth-Mother, as the Goddess of Death, is explained by the cosmic necessity of sacrifice, which alone makes possible passage from one mode of being to another and also ensures the uninterrupted circulation of Life.[96]

The relation of the goddess Durgā-Kālī to blood-sacrificial cults in India has, probably, its earliest manifestation among the tribal inhabitants. Here, however, we shall direct our attention only to the phenomenon of human sacrifice. Karmakar shows us that human sacrifice to the goddess Kālī endured well into the nineteenth century.[97] The Meriah sacrifice to the Earth-Goddess among the Khonds of Orissa, Bengal, and Bihar is regarded as typical of ancient Indian human sacrificial activity.[98]

Our earlier statement with reference to the Kālikā Purāṇa—that its sacrificial-animal selections go back undoubtedly to a much earlier milieu of mythic and cultic activity—is further suggested by the religious value placed upon the sacrifice of human beings.

---

[93] Mitra, "On the Cult of the Tree-Goddes in Eastern Bengal," pp. 232-233.

[94] *Ibid.*, p. 233.

[95] Chaudhuri, "The Cult of Vana-Durgā, a Tree Deity", p. 77.

[96] Eliade, *Myths, Dreams, and Mysteries*, p. 189.

[97] Cf. Karmakar, *The Religions of India*, I, 213f.; Crooke, *The Popular Religions ...*, II, 169-174; cf. *ibid.*, pp. 175f.

[98] Cf. a description in Campbell, *The Masks of God*, II, 160-163. For an account with historical and ethnographic allusions, *vide* Arthur Miles, *The Land of the Lingam* (London: Hurst and Blackett, Ltd., 1933), pp. 79-90; *vide* also Eliade, *Patterns in Comparative Religion*, pp. 344-345.

The Kālikā Purāṇa adds: "men, and blood drawn from the offerer's own body, are looked upon as proper oblations to the goddess Caṇḍikā. By a human sacrifice, attended by the forms laid down, Devī is pleased 1,000 years, and by the sacrifice of three men, 100,000 years".[99]

By far one of the most valuable ethnographic studies on the archaic affiliation of the goddess Durgā-Kālī, with *human* sacrifice is E. A. Gait's account [100] of several tribal groups in the area of Assam. The author reports on cultic activities among at least seven groups: the Koches, Kachāris, Chutiyas, Tipperas, Nagas, Manipuris, and Jaintias. The goddesses worshipped bear such names as Kāmākhyā, Kesa Khati, Durgā, and Umā. Gait notices that the attending rites seem to resemble those prescribed by Purāṇas and Tantras, including the "Kalka Tantra" (Kālikā Purāṇa?); for example, "Kāmākhyā is one of the three deities to whom the offering of human sacrifice is enjoined in that Purana".[101]

The sacrificial cultus seems to have had royal patronage, and sacrifices were sporadically demanded of the most loyal and even high-stationed officials, for instance, among the Tipperas.[102] Human offerings (*bhogīs*) were sometimes voluntary, victims were treated with great reverence (as among the Khonds of Bengal), and the occasion tended to coincide with "public calamities, such as war, or for the purpose of obtaining great wealth".[103]

Sacrificial-cult among the Jaintias has special illustrative significance for the association of typically recognized archaic or aboriginal elements with the goddess Durgā-Kālī. The ceremonies in her honour took place at a sacred place said to be one of the 51 *pīṭhas* of the goddess. We would point out the following elements, present at the *Durgā-Pūjā* among the Jaintias, which are important to us: (1) voluntary human sacrifice (as already indicated), (2) the smearing of the victim

---

[99] Karmakar, *The Religions of India*, I, 212-213.

[100] E. A. Gait, "Human Sacrifice in Ancient Assam", *The Journal of the Royal Asiatic Society of Bengal*, LXVII, Part 3 (1898), 56-65. Crooke, *The Popular Religion* ..., II, 170-171, 176. Also in a broad perspective there is R. Mitra's "On Human Sacrifices in Ancient India", *Journal of the Asiatic Society of Bengal*, LXV, No. 1 (1876), 76-118; and H. H. Wilson, *Religion of the Hindus*, II (London: Trubner and Company, 1862), Chap. V, 247-269.

[101] Gait, "Human Sacrifice in Ancient Assam", p. 56. Vide K. B. Kanta, *The Mother Goddess Kāmākyhā: Studies in the Fusion of Aryan and Primitive Beliefs of Assam* (Gauhati, 1967).

[102] Gait, p. 59.

[103] Cf. Gait, pp. 62f.

with red sandalwood and vermillion, (3) the use of garlands of flowers, (4) the victim's partial self-preparation through meditation (*japa*), including sacrificial mantras, (5) the decapitation [104] of the victim and presentation of his head to the goddess on a golden plate, (6) the eating of the victim's cooked lungs by attendant yogis; (7) the royal family's devourment of food (rice) cooked in the victim's blood, and (8) a large communal, vicarious participation.[105]

Heretofore we have sought to exemplify four aspects of the goddess Durgā-Kālī in her chthonian orientation : the aqualithic, therio-affinal, vegetal, and sacrificial. As nominal, functional, and symbolic categories, however, they cannot ultimately be viewed as separate things but rather as interrelated aspects of a larger Goddess-Cultus, which, again, reaches beyond the Earth-Mother or Earth-Goddess orientation. Nevertheless, our primary purpose has been to illustrate the presence of "primitive", aboriginal, and archaic elements that have managed to "survive" into later phases of Indian religious history.[106] Mircea Eliade has said that "Earth religion, even if it is not, as some scholars believe, the oldest of man's religions, is one that dies hard".[107]

---

[104] Cf. Eliade, *Yoga*, pp. 300f., 305f. Karmakar (*The Religions of India*, I, 208) notes the possibility of a "tradition of offering the heads of seven victims" in the Brahmāṇda Purāṇa, i.e. (text) : "It is said that the Goddess Lalitā wore a garland of the seven heads of the Raksaṣas by means of weaving their hair into each other and created a shrilling noise". Cf. a Bhāgavata Purāṇa story of sacrifice to Kālī or Bhadrakālī wherein the victim was spared, *ibid.*, p. 210. Interestingly, Karmakar says, further, that the Ṛg-Vedic "*Puruṣa-sukta* (X.90) happens to be a mystic glorification of the victim who already stands sacrificed ..." *Ibid.*, p. 211; *vide* also *ibid.*, p. 209. Cf. Crooke, *The Popular Religions ...*, II, 167.

[105] Gait, "Human Sacrifice in Ancient Assam", p. 63; Karmakar, *The Religions of India*, I, 213.

[106] Cf. E. O. James, *Origins of Sacrifice* (London : John Murray, 1933), pp. 26-34, 255-257; *supra*, p. 50, n. 43. Tantrasāra (Bhairavīstotra) : "O Mother, how can the ignorant ... know Thy form ravishing with its vermillion" (*H.T.T.G.*, pp. 192, 22). What Ray ("Art", p. 517) says about "Yaksha Primitives" may have the merits of a cultural-religious generalization, i.e., "They are all primitively Indian in form, but they also reflect the currents of the flowing traditions and fashions of contemporary civilized practice". *Vide* also *ibid.*, pp. 526-528, and III, 521f., 539-541.

[107] Eliade, *Patterns in Comparative Religion*, p. 246. Cf. Tucci, "Earth in India and Tibet", p. 346 : the Bengali "Vasumatī". *Vide* also Crooke, *The Popular Religion ...*, II, Chap. VI, 288, 290, 298, 309 *et passim*; Syotirmoyee Sarma, "A Village in West Bengal", in *India's Villages*, ed. M. N. Srinivas (2d ed. rev.; London : Asia Publishing House, 1960), pp. 180-201, esp. pp. 199f.; Verrier Elwin, *Myths of Middle India* (London : Oxford University Press, 1949), esp. p. 40, No. 19; p. 42, No. 21 and cf. with p. 12; p. 42, No. 22; p. 294, No. 92; p. 349, No. 7; p. 428, No. 25 *et passim*.

The creative modifications which this form of religion has undergone in India with regard to the goddess Durgā-Kālī shall become more apparent as we proceed in subsequent chapters.

Devī : The Earth-Mother Par Excellence

For now, we call attention, finally, to Durgā-Kālī in her rôle as Earth-Mother as exemplified in a primary religious text : the Devībhāgavata Purāṇa.[108] This remarkable text contains the mythic rationale for the Earth-Cultus dimension of the larger religious totality over which *the* Devī, Durgā-Kālī, reigns supreme. Book IX, chap. 9, contains an account of the Ending of the Ages, which the goddess effects through the mere closing of her eyes (an interesting gesture-motif);[109] the cyclical appearance and disappearance of the earth in the primal waters, and all the world's attendant natural phenomena and life-forms ("in every world in every universe"),[110] as well as the worship of the Earth by gods and men.[111]

In a key mantra uttered by Bhagavan Viṣṇu, the goddess is called "O Devī Earth!" A meditation hymn of praise includes the petition, "O Devī Earth! Give me the fruits that I desire".

> ... O thou! The Store-house of all grains, enriched with all sorts of corns, Thou bestowest harvests to all; Thou takest away all the grain in this world and again Thou producest all corns of various kinds here. O Earth! Thou art all-in-all to the landlords, the Best source of refuge and happiness. O Bestower of lands! Give me lands ...[112]
>
> Thou art the Earth itself.[113]

It is apparent that the Earth-Cultus scenario of the Devībhāgavata Purāṇa is dominated by elements of Vaiṣṇavite-Śākta imagery

---

[108] This purāṇa, though not usually listed among the so-called 18 Mahā-Purāṇas, has, however, been listed as a Mahā-Purāṇa (e.g., the *Devī*bhāgavata in place of the [Vaiṣṇavite] Bhāgavata Purāṇa). *Vide* A. D. Pusalker, *Studies in the Epics and Purāṇas* (Bombay : Bharatiya Vidya Bhavan, 1963), p. 25 and n. 76. The Devībhāgavata nonetheless lists *itself* as a Mahā-Purāṇa (I.3.1-11, e.g., "the holy [Devī] Bhāgavata") subsequently listing the "Bhāgavata" (Vaiṣṇavite) as an Upa-Purāṇa (I.3.12-17).

[109] Devībhāgavata Purāṇa IX.9.1-4.

[110] *Ibid.*, IX.9.5-23, 38-41.

[111] *Ibid.*, IX.9.24-26, 46-63.

[112] *Ibid.*, IX.9.14-26, 49-63.

[113] *Ibid.*, IX.9.19 (*H.T.T.G.*, p. 148).

(e.g., IX. 9.27-34, 38-41 *et passim*) as part of the multinominal and multimorphic capacities of the goddess. The foregoing observation is interestingly accounted for by two basic characteristics of this purāṇa : (1) the Devībhāgavata Purāṇa reflects an historical situation (*intra* eighth-twelfth centuries) in which there is a more intense Śākta sectarian consciousness;[114] and (2) despite the Vaiṣṇavite *dramatis personae*, Devī remains, tendentiously, "the Supreme Embodiment of Śakti, through which alone even Brahmā, Viṣṇu and Śiva can perform their functions ... She is naturally the Supreme Deity that one must adore".[115] Ultimately, then, the Devas and Viṣṇu himself turn to worship the (body of) Earth as "the incarnate of Devī".

Furthermore, we must consider this purāṇa in a literary-critical perspective. We notice then the severe textual denigration of a variety of chthonian (and, probably, Tantric) cultic elements.[116] These elements represent a medley of cultic acts and objects either originally unassociated with classical Brāhmanic practices or later de-valuated by a Brāhmanic *literati*,[117] who were more receptive to the idea of elevating the *form* of the "Goddess" (*Devī*) than many of her (and, probably, Śiva's) chthonian-tantric parphernalia.[118] This is not all. These tend-

---

114 Cf. Dasharatha Sharma, "Verbal Similarities between the Durgā-Sapta-śatī and the Devī-Bhāgavata-Purāṇa and Other Considerations Bearing on Their Date", *Purāṇa*, V, No. 1 (January, 1963), 110.

115 *Ibid.*, pp. 90f. : apparently, the Purāṇa does not have the non-sectarian quality of the Durgā-Sapta-śatī (*vide ibid.*. pp. 96f., 100, 109).

116 I.e., Devībhāgavata Purāṇa IX.IX.5.38-41 : "... pearl, small shells, Śālagrāma (a black stone, usually round, found in the river Gaṇḍaki, and worshipped as a type of Viṣṇu), the phallus or emblem of Śiva, the images of the goddesses, conch-shells, lamps (lights), the Yantras, gems, diamonds, the sacred upanayana threads, flowers, books, the Tulasī leaves, the bead (Japa mālā), the garland of flowers, gold, camphor, Gorochanā (bright yellow pigment) prepared from the urine or bile of a cow), Sandal, and the water after washing the Śālagrāma stone. I will not be able to bear. I will be very much pained in case I were to bear these on Me". We note that damnation (*ibid.*, IX. IX.5.42f.) comes upon those would dare.

117 *Supra*, p. 40; G. V. Devasthali, "Literature", in Majumdar, *The History and Culture of the Indian People*, III, 297ff.; H. C. Hazra, *Studies in the Purāṇic Record on Hindu Rites and Customs* (Dacca : The University of Dacca, 1940), pp. 218ff., 238ff., 241f.; Gonda, *Change and Continuity in Indian Religion*, pp. 224ff., 226f.

118 Cf. Hazra, *Studies in the Purāṇic Record*, p. 226. Apart from Hazra's note (Devībhāgavata Purāṇa VII.39.31) that no sin is incurred by Brahmins who abide by Vedic passages, another thing is noticeable vis-à-vis the "damnation-passage" (*ibid.*, IX.IX.9.42f.); that is, the *acceptance* of typically "unacceptable" elements (*ibid.*, VII.39.38ff.) is accompanied by a stratification of cultic homage to the goddess (cf. *ibid.*,

entious re-creators of myth, cult, and symbols were also in tension themselves with other adherents of an even more rigid Vedo-Brāhmanic orthodoxy. The latter, in turn, were more receptive to that which had been heard (*śruti*) than that which had been remembered (*smṛti*).[119] This accounts in large measure for the fact that, among the sacred objects and acts repudiated by Devī, the (Earth-) Goddess (Devībhāgavata Purāna IX.9), there are also mentioned other *Brāhmanically* associated phenomena : for example, the Śālagrāma Stone [120] and the *upanayana* threads. It is thus apparent that one can hardly attempt to offer an oversimplification of this historico-religious situation or literary-historical process, if, indeed, that were possible (hence *infra*, "The Centripetalization of the Goddess Durgā-Kālī"). For it is hard to speak of these things at all with any legitimacy without showing some indication that one is aware of their comoplexity.[121]

Smārta Brāhmans, then, could exist among Vaiṣṇavites and Śaivites, as well as Śāktas.[122] In general, therefore, a renascent Brāhmanic-Hinduism appears to manifest literary-religious creativity and variety of response (i.e., sectarian Smārtas) in the face of heterodox (non-brāhmanic) but theistic religious groups.[123] These more "popular" religious ideas and expressions, however, were *also* creative and diverse but more oriented toward an earthier life-experience and more pregnant religious symbols; specifically, a broad "leftist" (but multisectarian) neo-Brāhmanic religious force would "have its cake and eat it too" :

I.18-19; Hazra, *Studies in the Purāṇic Record*, pp. 229f.); for comments on theologico-symbolic stratification, *vide* Eliade, *Patterns in Comparative Religion*, pp. 28, 7, and *supra*, pp. 37f.

119 It is not our intention to exaggerate the distinctiveness of the content of much of these traditions, revealed or remembered, as much as it is to emphasize the variabilities of literary-religious temperament and practical experience. *Vide* Gonda, *Change and Continuity in Indian Religion*, pp. 334f. On the other hand, *vide infra*, p. 93, n. 256.

120 For this object, *vide* Oppert, *On the Original Inhabitants ...*, pp. 337-359.

121 Devasthali ("Literature", p. 298) mentions "Smārta-Śaivas" and "Smārta-Vaiṣṇavas", but not, apparently, Smārta-Śāktas. The last term is used by Hazra, *Studies in the Purāṇic Record*, p. 225 *et passim.*

122 Cf., e.g., Gonda, *Change and Continuity in Indian Religion*, pp. 400f.

123 Majumdar, *The History and Culture of the Indian People*, III, 370ff. Hazra (*Studies in the Purāṇic Record*, pp. 225f.) shows us some of the nominal diversity. To these Hazra adds Buddhism, Jainism, and foreign influences (*ibid.*, pp. 216ff., 228-231). The view : an anti-Buddhist, anti-Jainist rationale behind the Purāṇas is challenged by K. M. Panikkar (*A Survey of Indian History* [Bombay : Asia Publishing House, 1954], pp. 55f.) who, however, merely attributes more significance to the "foreign and erotic elements" (*ibid.*, p. 56, esp. pp. 148ff.) that were invading India.

making remarkable use of the *adhikārabheda* principle and having, still, a tacit "open-door" policy toward old and new, but nonetheless strange mythic and cultic ideas; while a far less broad "rightist" force of Vedo-Brāhmaṇic persuasion would find a path of revealed traditional continuity amidst vast cultural changes; it survives (though still modified) in the modern Ārya and Brāhmo Samāj type of renascent Vedism.[124]

In another sense, the primary Earth-worship intentionality of the text (Devībhāgavata Purāṇa IX.9) requires a critical observation regarding mythical cosmology and the cultic milieu which underlies the Purāṇas and Tantras in general.

The mythic "time" is the cosmic period of the Kali-Yuga; so that, here, through Earth-Worship (i.e., Devī) "people become certainly freed of their sins, if they read this stotra ... Religious merits, equivalent to one hundred horse sacrifices accrue from reading this stotra".[125] The cultic milieu is one in which it happens that "the turning of the Earth-Mother into the Great Goddess of agriculture is the turning of simple existence into living drama".[126] Finally, it must be borne in mind that the primary Earth-Worship intentionality involves, in all probability, the phenomenon of change-and-continuity so characteristic of Indian religion.[127] For, apart from the rejection of chthonian-associated ingredients in the Earth-Devī Cultus, the text reveals additional elements and ends alongside of "the day when tilling the ground commences".[128]

We close this portion with comments which illustrate, further, the culturo-morphic recurrence of structural motifs and religious valorizations in the history of Durgā-Kālī under the form of the glorious Devī. That is, it is remarkable to see that the *hieros gamos*

---

[124] Cf. Gonda, *Change and Continuity in Indian Religion*, pp. 10f., 16.

[125] Devībhāgavata Purāṇa IX.9.52.63.

[126] Eliade, *Yoga*, p. 261.

[127] *Vide*, e.g., Eliade's comments on the medieval Śābarotsava in honour of the goddess Durgā-Kālī in Bengal, *ibid.*, pp. 342f.

[128] Devībhāgavata Purāṇa IX.9.35-37. Cf. *ibid.*, "Ambuvachi" (Ambubachi). According to R. C. Muirhead-Thomson (*Assam Valley : Beliefs and Customs of the Assamese Hindus* [London : Luzac and Co., Ltd., 1948], p. 37) the Ambubachi refers to the "menses of the earth. This is known throughout Assam as Haht, when the earth is supposed to have its annual menstrual period [mid-summer : June and July]. In the Assam villages this festival may last for five to seven days, after which time, all articles in the house must be purified. It is also said that Brahmin widows must not walk on the earth during this period when it is considered unclean".

theme [129] has been conveniently interweaved with the overall Earth-Cultus in the Devībhāgavata Purāṇa. In connection with an astrological motif of "the auspicious birth of Maṅgalā (Mars)",[130] we are told something interesting that occurs after Varāha Deva has re-creatively performed the classical Indra-Vṛtra (or Devāsura) cosmic event, and Brahmā has in turn effected "the wonderful creation on the surface of the earth ..."

> Bhagavān Hari, in his boar form [131] and brilliant like ten million suns saw the beautiful and lovely appearance of the presiding deity of the earth, possessed of amorous sentiments. He then assumed a very beautiful form, fit for amorous embraces. They then held their sexual intercourse and it lasted day and night for one Deva year. ... Now the Earth became pregnant ...[132]

We share the view of Dikshitar that, as it is the case with other agrarian (and pre-agrarian) ideas and forms already presented, the Devībhāgavatan Earth-Cultus aetiology may be "primitive" as well as "belong to pre-Vedic days when man was still in a low level of culture";[133] we modify this, of course, with the point that the pre-Vedic period itself may have been characterized by parallel yet differing cultural-religious strata. Dikshitar is more critical, however, when he says that

> the conception [134] may be older than the Vedic times and a pre-Vedic one. But one cannot subscribe to the view that it is un-Vedic or non-Vedic. It may be that the Vedic Indian absorbed the existing belief or developed an independent cultus.[135]

With regard to the emergence of the Earth-Mother toward the status of the Great Mother Goddess of Time and Eternity, it has

---

[129] Cf. Frazer, *supra*, p. 56, n. 85. The Śālagrāma Stone (See Oppert, *On the Original Inhabitants ...*, pp. 337-359) "is sacred even now, because it is taken as a symbol of the Goddess Lakṣmī. ... in fact the religious coupling of stone and plant was a primitive symbol of the 'holy place', of the primitive altar, and was so over the whole Indo-Mediterranean area" : Eliade, *Patterns in Comparative Religion*, p. 226. Cf. the Khasis (*ibid.*, p. 219) and the Oraons (ibid., p. 356); Eliade, *Myths, Dreams, and Mysteries*, p. 186. James, *The Cult of the Mother Goddess*, pp. 121-124.

[130] Devībhāgavata Purāṇa IX.9.23.

[131] Cf. Zimmer, *Myths and Symbols ...*, pp. 17f., 77-79, 36f., 51; Vasudeva J. Agrawala, *Solar Symbolism of the Boar* (Varnasi, India: Devkumar, Prithivi Prakashan, 1963), pp. 1f.

[132] Devībhāgavata Purāṇa IX.9.27f., 42ff.

[133] V. R. Ramachandra Dikshitar, *The Lalitā Cult* (Bulletin of the Department of Indian History and Archaeology, No. 8; Madras: University of Madras, 1942), p. 42.

[134] I.e., the Earth-Cultus: Earth as guardian deity.

[135] *Ibid.*, pp. 45f.

been recognized that a creative valorizational "arrest" probably took place along the way, i.e., "by her hierogamy with the sky and by the appearance of divinities of agriculture".[136] It is important, again, to observe that in the process of continuity and change, discernible residues of earlier religious ideas, acts, and forms are retained amongst human beings (i.e., tribal and peasant), who, themselves, are now in a period of cultural-religious transition and transformation in India. Presently, we shall be witnessing the further glorification of the Earth-Goddess, Durgā-Kālī, on a cosmic scale calculated to stagger anyone except the individual with a veteran religious imagination. Further on—in retrospect—however, it will be incumbent upon us to remember that

> ... the Earth-Mother never entirely lost her primitive prerogatives of being "mistress of the place", source of all living forms, keeper of children, and womb where the dead were laid to rest, where they were reborn to return eventually to life, thanks to the holiness of Mother Earth.[137]

The Indusian "Mother Goddess"

The Earth-Mother finds her culturo-morphic recurrence in a specific sub-continental matrix that has much to do with our ongoing study. Here in the Indus Valley of northwestern India, however, the rudiments of the earlier history of the goddess Durgā-Kālī present themselves in stirring fashion.

It should be remembered right away that the term "Indusian" bears an archaeological significance before we can approach the subject of (proto-) history. "Indusian" calls to mind at once the work of several pioneers over the past four decades, especially Sir John Marshall,[138] at the more familiar archaeological sites: Harappā,

---

[136] Eliade, *Patterns in Comparative Religion*, p. 262.

[137] *Ibid.*

[138] Cf. Sir John Marshall, ed., *Mohenjo-Daro and the Indus Civilization* (3 vols.; London: Arthur Probsthain, 1931), I, 48-78. Marshall's oft-quoted statement (*ibid.*, p. vii) is that" ... as a whole, their religion is so characteristically Indian as hardly to be distinguishable from still living Hinduism or at least from that aspect of it which is bound up with animism and the cults of Śiva and the Mother Goddess still the two most potent forces of popular worship". Cf. Ernest J. H. Mackay, *Chandu-Daro Excavations, 1935-36* (American Oriental Society Series, Vol. XX; New Haven, Conn.: American Oriental Society, 1943); M. Wheeler, *The Indus Civilization* (3d ed.; Cambridge: The University Press, 1968); V. Gordon Childe, *New Light on the Most Ancient East* (London:

Mohenjo-Daro, and Chandu-Daro. It was Marshall's optimistic statement about the symbolic "finds" in the Indusian area which gave impetus to new thought on the nature of ancient Indian history and religion.[139] From this, however, there has grown up a fairly inveterate "tradition" of opinion about the relation between pre-Vedic religion and Hinduism. That "tradition" of opinion still tends to regard the original archaeologico-religious conclusions of Marshall, Mackay, Pigott, and others—despite the obscurity of the Indus script — as solving much of the problem of historical and religious continuity in Indian culture.

In the broadest culturo-morphic sense, the problem bears some relation to the concerns of comparative ethnography and culture-history when focused upon the so-called "Āryan-Dravidian" question.[140] The fact of religio-symbolic resemblances between, apparently, the oldest Indian civilization and those of the Middle or Late Neolithic Mediterranean area or Central and Western Asia has led scholars, both Western and Hindu, to adopt conclusions ranging from theories of extra-Indian diffusion eastward to pan-indigenous religious development (but heading westward).

Laksmanshastri Joshi,[141] for instance, is one scholar who is overwhelmed by the religious and symbolic resemblances :

Routledge and Kegan Paul Ltd., 1964), Chap. IX. *Vide* also Finegan, *The Archaeology of World Religions,* I, 123-128; A. D. Pusalker, "The Indus Valley Civilization", in Majumdar, *The History and Culture of the Indian People,* I, 169-198.

139 H. D. Lewis and R. L. Slater, *The Study of Religions* (Pelican Books; Baltimore : Penguin Books, Inc., 1969), p. 36.

140 The arguments are many. They range from an insistence upon pro-Indian (= uniquely indigenous), extra-Indian (= Western-Central Asian, cultural diffusion), to multi-Indic (= convergent multi-ethnic, or cross-cultural, creations). Cf. a brief resumé of a variety of earlier views : Karmakar (*The Religions of India,* I, 316ff., esp. 318f.) where the author supports an Indusian diffusion westward to other high civilizations; very early historical relations (West-East) are still supported by various scholars : Mortimer Wheeler, *Early India and Pakistan to Ashoka* (rev. ed.; New York and Washington : Frederick A. Praeger, Inc., 1968), pp. 100-107. Cf. Elizabeth Bacon, "A Preliminary Attempt to Determine the Culture Areas of Asia", *Southwestern Journal of Anthropology,* II, No. 2 (Summer, 1946), 122, 131; McNeill, *The Rise of the West,* pp. 84f.; William H. McNeill, *A World History* (New York : Oxford University Press, 1967), pp. 31f.; D. P. Singhal, *India and World Civilization,* I (East Lansing, Mich .: Michigan State University Press, 1969), xiif., 2, 3, 5ff. *et passim* (and cf. *ibid.*, p. xvii); a recent distinctive contribution : Geoffrey Bibby, *Looking for Dilmun* (New York : Alfred A. Knopf, 1969); cf. Wheeler, *The Indus Civilization,* p. 81.

141 Laksmanshastri Joshi, *A Critique of Hinduism,* trans. G. D. Parikh (Bombay : Modern Age Publications, 1948), pp. 102, 103.

> In the earlier civilization of Egypt, Crete, and Mesopotamia are ... found the Gods of Shiva, Vishnu, the Goddess Kali and the worship of the Naga (Cobra), Linga (genital organs), the moon, the Graha (the planets), and the ancestors. ... Hinduism thus inherits a number of things peculiar to the civilization which arose along the banks of the Nile, the Tigris and the Euphrates and the Indus.

On the other hand we are cautioned by Sir Mortimer Wheeler with regard to the urge to make bland connections between the archaeo-religio-cultural contributions of the Harappān civilization and the existence of definite sectarian forms of Śaktism. That is to say, "a large number of the terra-cottas represent females ... and there has been perhaps an exaggerated tendency to regard these as a manifestation of the Great Mother Goddess familiar in the religions of western Asia and parts of Europe".[142]

An apparently moderate, still cautious, view is adopted by S. G. F. Brandon, [143] who claims that (1) it cannot be demonstrated that there is a culturo-genetic relation between the goddesses depicted on Indus Valley figurines and Minoan-Mycenaen amulets; (2) later Hinduism's divinities, Śiva and Śakti (i.e., Umā, Pārvatī, Durgā, Kālī) reflect man's religious experience in response to the cycle of natural creation and destruction, and (3) the matter remains speculative until more evidence is placed at our disposal. Nonetheless

> of what we can be certain is that these Indus Valley peoples believed that the dead required proper burial and some funerary equipment and that they worshipped, undoubtedly among other deities a goddess which appears to approximate to the type of Mother Goddess known throughout the ancient world of the Near East.[144]

We have already suggested a level of understanding upon which all these religio-artifacts are humanly and morphologically related. But we shall say more of this presently.

When we pass beyond questions of Western, Mid-Eastern, and Eastern historical-religious continuity, there still remains the problem of the Indus Valley and its relation to later Hinduism, particularly the Śaktite goddess par excellence — Durgā-Kālī. The traditionality of opinion to which we referred earlier, nevertheless, continues. The pan-indigenous religious view itself, however, has been supported by scholars who vary in their special *emphases*. One approach, for instance, would have us believe that the only prestratum to be recognized as

---

142 Wheeler, *The Indus Civilization*, p. 91.

143 S. G. F. Brandon, *Man and His Destiny in the Great Religions* (London : Manchester University Press, 1962), p. 304.

144 *Ibid.*

the basis of later Hinduism is a Ṛg-Vedic one.[145] Another substratum approach allows for some foreign instrusions or elements, including the "Dravidians", but regards the overall religious and cultural reservoir of the Indus Valley as an essentially *Indian* creation.[146] A third variant approach looks at the development of the two key religious figures at Mohenjo-Daro — the "proto-Shiva" and "proto-'Mother-Goddess'" artifacts — as non-Āryan in origin, but specifically, the result of a "mixed Aryo-aboriginal" process.[147]

The specific question of the cultural-historical origins of the ("Indusian") Indian Mother-Goddess, therefore, has not been unshrouded by scholarly controversy. Indeed, it must be admitted that the opinion that one adopts, finally, concerning even the *intra*-cultural ideas and objects of the Indusian religious heritage can affect both one's perspective of the history of Indian religion and the philosophy of human culture.

The most serious challenge in recent times to the traditional interpretations of religious artifacts found in the Indus Valley has been launched by the Indologist Jan Gonda.[148] Gonda deserves special attention with regard to the specific issue of an Indusian "mother-goddess" and her possible relation to the Hindu goddess Durgā-Kālī. His work is of particular interest to us because it is a critique of general Indian religious "substratum theories" and, therefore, warrants a new appraisal of the possibility of discerning the origins of Durgā-Kālī even within an indigenous historical frame of reference.

Gonda confronts the reader with a rather imposing and highly skeptical evaluation of the traditionally accepted "finds" and interpretation of them by earlier and later scholars. He thus attacks the general tendency "to undervalue the complicateness of the problems ... and to simplify intricate historical processes which moreover are never more than incompletely recognizable".[149]

---

[145] Swami Sankarananda, *The Rig Vedic Culture of the Prehistoric Indus*, Vol. I (2d ed.; Calcutta : Abhedananda Academy of Culture, 1946).

[146] R. K. Mookerji, *Hindu Civilization* (London : Longmans, Green and Co., 1936); S. K. Chatterji, "Race Movements and Pre-historic Culture", in Majumdar, *The History and Culture of the Indian People*, I, 158. Cf. Pusalker, "The Indus Valley Civilization", p. 186.

[147] D. C. Sircar, "The Indian Father-God and Mother-Goddess", in *Parliament of Religions (1963-64*, in honour of Swami Vivekananda (Calcutta : Swami Sambhuddhananda, Publisher, 1964), pp. 321-326.

[148] Cf. Gonda, *Change and Continuity in Indian Religion*, Chap. I, "Some Critical Remarks Apropos of Substratum Theories", pp. 7-37.

[149] *Ibid.*, p. 15; *vide* also *ibid.*, p. 24.

The scholar's specific remarks on much previous scholarship having to do with historical-religious generalizations upon the Indusian religious deposit may be summarized as follows. The author, first of all, calls our attention to (what has been noted before him as) the notorious lack of the proper sense of history by many Hindu scholars.[150] They, it appears, are indeed apt to concern themselves with practical "patterns of life, religion and culture", but only in relation to "the corpora of the Veda" as the "basis which, being eternal and 'revealed' in 'the beginning' of history, is infallible and absolutely true and reliable".[151]

Again, he refers to other Hindu Orientalists or Western Indologists (some with whom he is in partial agreement) who have accepted some kind of Harappān-Hinduist continuity but on far less hasty or romantic grounds.[152] Nonetheless, in the case of the "Mother-Goddess", most conveniently, the traditionally accepted religio-artifacts derived from the Harappān sites are challenged by Gonda, when they are considered to be without doubt the historical prototypes of the Hindu Mother Goddess in terms of religious significance.[153] And, finally, the author turns the emphasis upon the phenomenon of cultural-religious change or fluidity of concepts in Indian culture.

---

150 *Ibid.*, pp. 7-11, 14 and n. 24.

151 Ibid., p. 9. The question of Indian scholars' and their understanding of the nature of "history" has been frequently noted, criticized, and defended. *Vide*, e.g., the early remarks of A. Banerji-Sastri, "Ancient Indian Historical Tradition", *Journal of the Bihar and Orissa Research Society*, XIII, Part 1 (1927), 62-79, and also *The Cambridge History of India*, I, ed. E. J. Rapson (Cambridge : University Press, 1922), 56ff., 274ff., 299f., 306ff.; F. E. Pargiter (*Ancient Indian Historical Tradition* [London : Oxford University Press, 1922]) pleads the case for Purāṇic "histories". Cf. R. N. Dandekar, *Progress in Indic Studies* (Poona : n.p., 1942), pp. 39-151, esp. p. 139; Pusalker, *Studies in the Epics and Purāṇas*, pp. 22, 41-42, 105-109. An overview is presented by U. N. Ghoshal, *Studies in Indian History and Culture* (Calcutta : Orient Longmans, 1965), esp. Chaps. I and III. For an excellent discussion on "Itihāsa" as a term, its historical relation to "Purāṇa" and modern historiography, *vide* R. C. Majumdar, "Ideas of History in Sanskrit Literature", in *Historians of India, Pakistan, and Ceylon*, ed. C. H. Philips (London : Oxford University Press, 1961), pp. 13-28. Cf., among other scholars, especially V. S. Pathak, "Ancient Historical Biographies and Reconstruction of History", in *Problems of Historical Writing in India*, Proceedings of the Seminar held at the India International Centre, New Delhi, January 21-25, 1963, pp. 11-21. Cf. R. Thapar, *ibid.*, pp. 90-96.

152 Gonda, *Change and Continuity in Indian Religion*, p. 14, n. 25; pp. 34f., n. 16; pp. 25ff.

153 *Ibid.*, pp. 32-34, 20f.

That is, he insists upon the unequivocal acknowledgment by scholars of the equivocal archaeological evidence.

> The serious drawback of all purely archaeological argumentations, the very incapacity of the "symbols" to reveal their true content and to explain the beliefs of those who created and used them, comes to light when discussion is opened on such questions as the religious functions of the material objects.[154]

The sum of Gonda's critical scholarship about "substratum" historical-religious theories is that too many scholars have indulged in the repetition of a traditionality of opinion established by "archaeologists and students of the history of Indian religion".[155] Such persons have thus tended to confuse mere "traces" of cultural-religious orientation with "historical reality".[156] The more critical scholar, then, by inference, can only be far more certain of the origins of theoretical historical connections made by romantic researchers than the origins of the cultural-religious forms and ideas now clearly seen in the "Hinduist" religious tradition.

Our initial response to Gonda's argumentation about theoretical substratumism with regard to Indian religion is rather positive; that is, the establishment of the traditionality of an interpretative vogue is something with which we are familiar.[157] Furthermore, in light of the mere frustration experienced by scholars facing the Indus Valley, it becomes understandable how one might choose to drift with the winds of interpretive optimism rather than pessimism.

A more thoughtful consideration of the specific implications of Gonda's presentation for the historian of religions, however, leads us to make a few critical observations about his remarks and certain conclusions that he has drawn.

We shall maintain that the more appropriate and eclectically considered "Earth-Goddess" or "Mother-Goddess" evidence tends to override (not his general, but) a few of Gonda's specific claims. It should be understood that the grounds of our interpretation of the evidence are not the same as those of Indian or Western "orientalist" romantics; that our grounds are partially those of Gonda himself (for Gonda is not a proponent of absolute historical-religious discontinuity when it comes to the Indus culture and later Hinduism);[158] and then,

---

[154] *Ibid.*, p. 31; cf. *ibid.*, p. 20, n. 42 (Boas); pp. 21, 27-30.

[155] *Ibid.*, pp. 32, 24.

[156] *Ibid.*, p. 21.

[157] *Supra*, pp. 18-19.

[158] Cf. Gonda, *Change and Continuity in Indian Religion*, pp. 13, 22.

that there are other *Indian* factors which the scholar has apparently not taken into account.

To begin with, let us say right away that his assertion about Przyluski's introduction of a possible Austroasiatic cultic element (i.e., the liṅga) into the Indusian problem appears inefficacious regardless of the validity or invalidity of Przyluski's overall conclusions. For Przyluski's idea, after all, does not require the assumption that the Austroasiatics "produced the Indus culture".[159] It means, of course, that the Austroasiatic religious language may have contributed to the Indusian repertoire,[160] as they were probably an ethno-historical component in the broad cultural complex of the Indus in diachronic terms.[161]

Somewhat in this same connection Gonda underestimates the nature of symbols, especially religious symbols, and tends to exaggerate their historical relativity.[162] He, therefore, shows no objective interest in the larger context of world religious history (not instead of, but) beyond mono-cultural historical change and continuity.[163] We recognize that his book is concerned primarily with India. The historian of religions, nonetheless, is interested in the particularity of Indus Valley artifacts, but insists also that they cannot ultimately be divorced from man's general knowledge of the history of religious symbolic forms. Religious visions in various cultures can "inter-communicate".[164] We apply this principle in the two following ways.

First, we should make it clear that we are only in partial disagreement with Gonda's overall analysis;[165] but that portion with

---

159 *Ibid.*, p. 31. It is to be noted in the following pages that we, too, agree (cf. *ibid.*, p. 33) that not all the Indusian female figurines may have been necessarily understood by them as deities. We are more wary of Gonda's subtle religious-symbolic distinctions among *types* of goddesses (*ibid.*). *Vide infra*, p. 73.

160 Cf. Eliade, *Yoga*, pp. 352f., 429, 349, and 351, on the nature of *specific* religious symbols and culture.

161 Cf. Karmakar, *The Religions of India*, I, 31-34. On the causes of the collapse of the Indus civilization, *vide* H. T. Lambrick, *Sind : A General Introduction* (History of Sind Series, Vol. I; Hyderabad [Sind], Pakistan : Sindhi Adabi Board, 1964), Chap. VI, esp. pp. 84ff.; Wheeler, *Early India and Pakistan to Ashoka*, pp. 111-114.

162 Cf. *supra*, p. 73f., n. 154.

163 The scholar is not unaware of this point, however. *Vide* Gonda, *Change and Continuity in Indian Religion*, p. 344.

164 *Supra*, p. 46.

165 With Gonda, for example, we are cautions not to extend morphogenetic continuity and historical relevance to the "seven female figurines" of the Indus and "'the

which we cannot agree remains radical in nature, because of the difference in our disciplinary perspectives. We contend, therefore, that his actual admission, yet hypercritical presentation, of a diversity of interpretive possibilities about specific religious meanings, for example, the Indusian sacred figurines,[166] overlooks a very important thing about the nature of *religious* symbols. That is to say, if there is anything that they teach us in general, and especially in India, it is their potential capacity for logical distinctiveness and generality through the phenomenon of modality and multivalence (i.e., conscious or unconscious coalescence of religious meaning);[167] the scholar's undue concern, therefore, about "the strict sense of the term" (i.e., mother-goddess) not only presumes that it has in fact a universal mono-valent meaning, but disregards the fact that (femino-morphic) artifactual "representatives of the creative and nourishing powers of the earth", "mothers of the gods", "mothers of life", and "parochial goddesses presiding over wind or water, fire or forest", may all constitute symbolic aspects of a perceptual field of human experience and a matrix of religious and symbolic expression; that is, a religious experience, expression, and understanding of the world which suggests a vivid and varied chthonian depth as an essential valuation of life.

The most important thing to recognize, secondly, is that, when the historical "evidential complicateness" of the religious artifacts is taken into account under the added perspective of the phenomenology and the structural study of symbols, something *different* happens. It is discovered that certain of the Indusian sealings or pictographs suggest a particular kind of religious orientation as the logical context of their original viability. It is our opinion, then, that these (ideogramatic) *scenarios* also suggest a legitimate type of Indusian-Hinduist continuity. It remains for us to demonstrate this fact in more specific terms and to generalize upon the type of continuity that we mean.

In the meantime let us not forget that, here, we are dealing primarily with no question of *Kulturkreislehren* but with the fact that we are now on *Indian soil.* With regard to the Indus Valley, then, we insist that due to geographic homogeneity (notwithstanding the ethno-linguistic diversity) of India, we do not have to argue from one extra-

---

primitive Indian cult regarded as indigenous' of the smallpox goddess Sītalā and her six sisters"; on other such observations, *vide infra*, pp. 75, n. 177; p. 76 n. 180; p. 78f.

166 Cf. Gonda, *Change and Continuity in Indian Religion*, p. 33.

167 Cf. Eliade, "Methodological Remarks ...", pp. 98f., 105ff., and *Patterns in Comparative Religion*, pp. 453ff.

Indian civilization to another (i.e., India itself) in technical terms; but that India as a culture area is conducive to the change and continuity of ideas as well as the presence of what we would call a perennial, undercurrent, religious naturalism as part of its "principle of consciousness".[168] It is this religious naturalism which has pervaded (and continues to pervade) Indian civilization throughout so much time;[169] and, as we have seen (*supra*, pp. 44, 48-60) it has not permitted us to leave (as Gonda has done) "the prehistoric 'parallels' on one side".[170] For the ancient religious naturalism to which we refer has to do with the presence of a deeply ingrained "terranean awareness" on the part of India's inhabitants. It is reflected in their mythology, their theistic sects, as well as their artistic creactions. This terranean awareness has persisted despite the possibility of the early co-existence or emergence of similar or more daring *cosmic* visions of man's place in the world.[171] The continuing relevance of the Earth-Mother/Earth-Goddess presentation above, however, is that it goes to the heart of that ancient Indian "awareness"; and the Indus Valley shows irresistible signs of having nourished that same consciousness. Moreover, evidence in the *later* Hinduist tradition in other times and parts of-India substantiate its capacity to effect "successive periodic reincarnation"[172] of aspects of that terranean religious syndrome.

In the main the particular kind of religious orientation that is evident to us in the Indus Valley (withstanding other beliefs and symbols not evident) has to do with symbols with a collectively impressive *terranean orientatio*. They are, too, (a) lithiconic,[173] (b) therio-affinal or theriomorphic, (c) vegetal, and (d) sacrificial. These symbolic manifestations,[174] however, tend to be iconographically interrelated,

---

168 Cf. Brown, "The Content of Cultural Continuity in India", p. 434.

169 Cf. James, *The Cult of the Mother Goddess*, p. 113 : "—the sanctity of the Earth has remained a fundamental belief throughout India for all time, and around it the Goddess cult has found its several modes of expression".

170 Gonda, *Change and Continuity in Indian Religion*, p. 33.

171 *Vide infra*, Chap. III.

172 Brown, "The Content of Cultural Continuity in India", p. 429. We have already noted that the (*post*-Indusian) Devī-Māhātmya and the later Devībhāgavata and Kālikā Purāṇas "reincarnate" elements of agricultural religious symbolism into their imagery alongside of a more cosmically developed mythology.

173 As also elsewhere : i.e., a stone that is an icon (as compared to an icon of any shape which might be made of stone).

174 *Supra*, pp. 48ff.

if not intermingled,[175] so that a given seal, disc, or stone may combine all of the previous orientative elements in highly suggestive fashion and, in fact, evoke a highly plausible religious interpretation. They are, therefore, of special interest to us, for, all together, they point up the unwarranted degree of skepticism which Gonda expresses about them (as a category). The truth is that, though we do not possess comprehensive[176] knowledge of the Indus Valley religious *Weltanschauung*, there is nothing wrong with making thoughtful inferences about *complex scenarios*. The latter are not to be assigned the same interpretive value as, for example, the comparatively simple proto-historical seals of C. L. Fabri.[177] There, detailed figures appear but, as Gonda rightly remarks, no contextual meaning can be inferred.

The ideogramatic scenarios, however, in their implicit cultic[178]

---

[175] Cf. Banerjea, *The Development of Hindu Iconography*, p. 489 : "The nude female figurines very often shown in ... ornamented 'ringstones' and 'discs' are almost invariably associated with plants and vegetation (sometimes with men and animals) ..."

[176] D. H. Gordon, *The Prehistoric Background of Indian Culture* (Bombay : M. D. Desai, 1958), cited in Gonda, *Change and Continuity in Indian Religion*, p. 19, n. 40; pp. 21f., uses the term "precise knowledge" while noting its slightness with regard to the nature of Harappān religion; we agree with the dignity that he assigns to "inference from the testimony of scenes depicted on the seals"; but we prefer to say that we lack "comprehensive" knowledge — the combined dramatic quality of the scenarios allows only a key interpretation of an aspect of the Harappān religious *Weltanschauung*, but, for all that it is, it is a plausibly inferred one.

[177] Cf. Gonda, *Change and Continuity in Indian Religion*, pp. 26f. Gonda is impressed, on the whole, with the scholar's "earlier" and "later" correspondences. His prospective opinion of our few specific correspondences and a certain milieu (*vide infra*, pp. 77f.) is another thing. Nonetheless we maintain that, juxtaposed with other data from later India, certain artifacts point to a type of religious orientation which becomes more implicitly an "historical reality".

[178] Eliade (*Patterns in Comparative Religion*, p. 324) remarks that there is a "difference between a(n) ... *ideogram* and a ritual. The formulae for carrying out a rite are not those for stating an ideogram, myth or legend. But all of them express the same idea. ..." (The remark's context is "terranean"). Gonda's remark on "an 'amulet' showing ... one tree that has been torn asunder", for instance (*Change and Continuity in Indian Religion*, pp. 31-32), is an over-simplification of the seal (*infra*, p. 77, Point 2), if, in fact, the author has the same in mind. The peculiar impression is that the scholar seems to apply non-religious criteria to data which he has already acknowledged as fundamentally religious; moreover, his insistence upon scholars' need to "occupy themselves with elements of the material culture, means of subsistence, food and dress" (Gonda, *Change and Continuity in Indian Religion*, pp. 19f.) in contrast to a host of other "substratum" particulars which he accurately describes as exaggerated (*ibid.*, p. 20)... if the claim is made — remains something quite different from the religious implications that we discern about a distinctive aspect of the total world-view (whatever it might have been).

complexity are far more convincing. They are re-represented to us by Campbell [179] under these rubrics : (1) The Sacrifice, (2) The Goddess of the Tree, (3) The Lord of Beasts, and (4) The Serpent Power.[180] This scholar (via Marshall) has done little disservice to the *religious* significance of these seals. For the cultuc "acts" implicit upon them are are reasonably decipherable, particularly against the general background of the history of religions symbolization. Briefly, let us take a closer look at not only these symbolic phenomena but also, in conjunction, "other Indian factors" (*supra*, p. 72) which simply cannot be ignored.[181]

---

[179] Cf. Campbell, *The Masks of God*, II, 166-170. We are, of course, not primarily concerned with this "proto-Śiva" at this time. Cf. Finegan, *The Archaeology of World Religions*, I, 127, Fif. 49. Finegan's succinct and effective (Indus-Hinduist) correspondential description warrants the phrase "plausible deduction" not "plausible guess"; much of the difficulty arises merely from the use of the *name* "Śiva" at all. H. P. Sullivan ("A Re-examination of the Origin of the Indus Civilization", *History of Religions*, IV, No. 1 [Summer, 1964], 115-125) says that "if there was any distinct male deity it is impossible to say just what his nature and his role were". This is overstatement, especially about his "nature" (*vide* O'Flaherty, *infra*). We find it difficult to see how he transforms *that* seal into a "goddess", though other more plausible ("goddess") seals are so indicated by the same author (and Mackay)., Wendy D. O'Flaherty ("Asceticism and Sexuality in the Mythology of Śiva, Part I", *History of Religions*, VIII, No. 4 [May, 1969], 300-337) finds "good reason to support the identification of this figure with Śiva ..." (*ibid.*, p. 308 and n. 34). Her more significant adduction, however, is that it "is evidence of a very early correlation between asceticism and sexuality", controversy not-withstanding; for she illustrates that it is possible to insist upon non-nominal but real-life categories (i.e., asceticism, sexuality) as validly represented by the "seal"; we, likewise, make no claims of an Indusian Śakti cult or Indusian "Kālī", but rather a correlation between Indusian "goddess-motifs" amidst complex epigramatic terranean symbolism and later forms of Indian religion—but *particularly* the religio-symbolic totality of the goddess Durgā-Kālī (*infra*, p. 77f.). We have taken no position on the Indus "stones" (i.e., "Phallic and Baetylic Stones" : Marshall, *Mohenjo-Daro and the Indus Civilization*, I, 58-63; *vide* Gonda, *Change and Continuity in Indian Religion*, p. 31); although we agree as to the inevitable difficulties of ascertaining the religious intentionality of such evidence, the stones do present tempting prima facie *religious* significance (e.g., Plate XIII : 1 and 7; XIV : 2 and 4). This, *plus* Marshall's own persuasive argument against their alternative possible uses or purposes, makes the controversy still potentially a live one.

[180] Here, with the use of the "leading" phrase "The Serpent Power" (Tantrism ?), Campbell may well have invited a criticism of his understanding of the relation between "Scholarship and Romance" (*The Masks of God*, I, 8).

[181] *Vide* notes to Table 1. Notice Gonda, *Change and Continuity in Indian Religion*, p. 27 : "i.e. two thousand years earlier ..." The author makes no distinction between the ephemerality and the perenniality of "symbolic value".

TABLE 1

Archaeological, Iconographic, and Literary Correspondences

Indus Valley . 2500-1500 B.C.)	*Extended India* (in time and space)	*Texts* Goddess Durgā-Kālī with Body-Vegetation [c]
al : Upside-Down Nude Female with Womb-Plant, etc.[a]	Terracotta Relief: Upside-Down Nude Female with Neck-Plant (*ca.* 320-650 A.D.)[b]	Śākambarī/Navapatrikā (Devī-Māhātmya 90.43-44; *ca.* third-fifth centuries A.D.; Mahābhārata VI.23.9; *ca.* 400 B.C.-400 A.D.; Rāmāyana V.22.39f.; *ca.* 400 B.C.-200 A.D.)
. Seal : Nude Female standing between "Pronged" Pipal Tree[d] with apparent Sacrificial Motif (*ca.* 2000 B.C.)	"Meriah" of the Khonds: Neck (or Chest) between Cleft tree [e] Victim (boy *or* girl) = Goddess incarnate (ancient: *ca.* ?)	(Durgā-Kālī as Tree Goddess): Bana-Durgā (who dwells in trees (ancient motif) Victim in Kālikā Purāṇa (i.e., Rudhirādhyāya): Worshipped as divinity: (Śiva-) Kālī (*ca.* tenth century)[f]

---

[a] Joseph Campbell, *The Masks of God*, Vol. II: *Oriental Mythology* (New York: The Viking Press, Inc., 1962), p. 166, Fig. 16; S. Chattopadhyaya (*The Evolution of Theistic Sects in India* [Calcutta: Progressive Publishers, 1962], p. 54) calls our attention to another goddess/plant type: a Bhadragoshan coin (*ca.* first century B.C.); on the reverse side of his coins are found "a female deity *standing* on a lotus" (italics mine). She is apparently either Lakṣmī or Durgā. Cf. Jitendra N. Banerjea, *The Development of Hindu Iconography* (Calcutta: University of Calcutta, 1956), p. 168, n. 2. Chattopadhyaya points out that Bhadra is the name of Durgā in the Purāṇas. Here, again, however, we note that the point should be "scenic" and not "nominal". Incidentally, it is pure romance and not scholarship for the author to say(*The Evolution of Theistic Sects in India*, p. 50) that the Indusian seal "undoubtedly represents the Mother Goddess, *bhū* or *Pṛthivī*", or the Ṛg-Vedan Aditi.

[b] Cf. Banerjea, *The Development of Hindu Iconography*, p. 168; Campbell, *The Masks of God*, II, 166f.

[c] *Supra*, p. 58. In the Rāmāyana, Sītā is called *Dhanyāmalaī*, "the Corn-crowned One". Cf. Chattopadhyaya, *The Evolution of Theistic Sects in India*, p. 57; Mircea Eliade, *Patterns in Comparative Religion*, trans. Rosemary Sheed (Cleveland: The World Publishing Co., 1963), p. 260.

[d] Campbell, *The Masks of God*, II, 167, Fig. 17; Banerjea, *The Development of Hindu Iconography*, pp. 168, 173f.

[e] *Supra*, p. 58 and n. 98 on that page. In the origin-legend of the Khonds (cf. Arthur Miles, *The Land of the Lingam* [London: Hurst and Blackett, Ltd., 1933], pp. 89f.) a female is sacrificed, or a male; the sacrificial motif attends the "Upside-Down Goddess" (*supra*, Point I of this table); Durgā-Kālī is a tree -goddess (*bana-durgā* : *supra*, pp. 56f. and notes). The goddess Bhagavatī of the Oraons is worshipped under a tree (Mircea Eliade, *Yoga: Immortality and Freedom*, trans. Willard R. Trask [New York: Pantheon Books, Inc., 1958], p. 386); masked dancing worshippers of the goddess Kālī pay homage to her under a banyan tree (*ibid.*, p. 388). We do not adopt the Marshall-Campbell (*The Masks of God*, II, 167) identification of the Indusian "tree" (*ibid.*, Fif. 17) as the "*bodhi*, or *bo*-tree", however, "under which the Buddha gained enlightenment.

[f] Cf. Sir Charles Eliot, *Hinduism and Buddhism: An Historical Sketch*, II (New York: Barnes and Noble, Inc., 1968), 289. (Reprint).

TABLE I — *Continued*

III. Seal : Nude Female in presence of Animals or Theriomorphes (*supra* : Seals I and II), e.g., Pair of Tigers [g]	Stone disc : Nude Female Figure with Animals : including *godha* (*ca.* fifth century or earlier A.D.)[h]	Goddess Durgā-Kālī with Vāhana/Makara symbolism : (Devī-Māhātmya in Mārkaṇḍeya Purāṇa LXXXII : with lion); Goddess Caṇḍī (in Mangal-Kāvyas, fifteenth century) :[i] with *godha* symbolism

This eclectic array of phenomena, we believe, constitutes potent evidence at least that the matter of Indusian-Hinduist religious continuity, though capable of being grossly exaggerated in favour of one fond artifact or another, is not to be taken lightly. Here it means, again, that the subject of Indusian-Hinduist religious continuity becomes intelligible concerning the "mother-goddess" in particular, according to the level upon which one conceives that it is possible to understand such continuity.

Gonda's general skepticism regarding the figurine-scenarios is the source of our contention that (1) there can be in fact "recurrent continuity" of religious ideas and forms, even where there are apparently no adequate grounds for "absolute continuity"; (2) the probability is, in the case of a specific Hindu divinity (especially Durgā-Kālī as "Earth-Mother"), that the Indusian religio-artifacts suggest, strongly, a general kind of milieu (i.e., a "terranean awareness", or "intuition"[182]) out of which a divinity of the "earth-mother" type (e.g., Durgā-Kālī) might well have emerged.

With Gonda, to be sure, we agree that these types of Indusian "goddesses" are not to be blandly *identified as Durgā-Kālī* in every specific sense; for example, her (sometimes) tiger accompaniment would not automatically establish that the Indusian divinity-with-

---

[g] Campbell, The Masks of God, II, 166-167; Banerjea, *The Development of Hindu Iconography,* pp. 167, 168. B. Yu. Volchok, "Figures on Objects With Proto-Indian Inscriptions", Field and Laird, (*infra,* p. 81n.).

[h] *Supra,* pp. 52-53; cf. Moti Chandra, "Studies in the Cult of the Mother Goddess in Ancient India", *Bulletin of the Prince of Wales Museum of Western India* (No. 12, 1973), pp. 1-47, esp. pp. 28-36.

[i] Cf. R. C. Agrawala, "Some Sculptures of Durgā-Mahiṣāramardiṇī from Rājasthāna", *Adyar Library Bulletin,* XIX, Part 2 (1955), 37-46; Chattopadhyaya, *The Evolution of Theistic Sects in India,* p. 54; Edward C. Dimock, Jr., *The Thief of Love* (Chicago: University of Chicago Press, 1963), p. 243; *supra,* pp. 74-78.

[182] *Supra,* p. 45.

tigers *is* indeed our goddess. But on another level of historico-phenomenological comprehension the *collective* import of the kinds of symbols above (Table 1 and notes) do support the view that both (3) in a certain general sense that pervasive, undercurrent, chthonian orientation may have had a genuine perpetuity of its own throughout Indian religious history; and (4) the development (not necessarily the "creation") of a specific kind of divinity, such as Durgā-Kālī, was indeed enchanced by that kind of "environment" indicated. We now turn to that environment, which was essentially a *human* environment, in order to make explicit that what was always an ever-present undercurrent religious reality also had (and still has) its concurrent *historical* reality in the early and later Vedo-Brahmanic period.

The "Dravidian" Strain

Earlier [183] we said that the Indus Valley discoveries had an important effect upon the one-sidedly held belief that the Āryans were the sole culture-bringers into the Indian sub-continent. It was, further, the contemplation that a people, long designated as the Dravidians, had been the source of its own culture and religion which changed the "colour" of Indian history. The insistence upon the term Dravidian, however, does not automatically clarify the nature of the sources of the religion or civilization of ancient India. The issues continue to be discussed. For questions then arose as to whether (a) the Dravidians were in fact the original cultural inhabitants of the Indus, (b) the Dravidian content of Indian religion could be ascertained apart from the Vedic religious institutions; even (c) the recognition of the complex make-up of the total Indian population necessitated a distinction between the Dravidians and the Tribal Cultures, and (d) (whether) it is possible that an Āryo-Dravido-Aboriginal synthesis of races and cultures has indeed characterized the history of India's religious development.

Most respectable scholars today would state quite frankly that no one probably knows for certain who the Ādi-Indusians were.[184]

---

183 *Supra*, pp. 66ff.

184 Contrary to Sankarananda, *The Rig Vedic Culture ...*, Chap. II, esp. pp. 78 and 155, and others. Cf. Gonda, *Change and Continuity in Indian Religion*, p. 22 and n. 49; Surajit Sinha ("Tribal Cultures of Peninsula India ...", p. 302, last paragraph) entertains an interesting "probability", but still refers its content to the realm of "historical speculations"; G. E. Sen (*Cultural Unity of India* [rev. ed.; Delhi: Publications Division,

Furthermore, the eventual development of a consensus that the term "Dravidian" should not simply refer to a *race* of presons [185] showed the need for a modification of the assumption either that they are to be radically distinguished from all Indian tribals,[186] or that they were necessarily the source of all the deepest moral and philosophical ideas which are now so interwoven in the Hindu religious totality.[187] It can be readily seen, of course, that this subject tends to be a logical extension of the issue maintained before concerning the discovery of the Indus Valley artifacts and their bearing upon comparative ethnography and culture-history. At any rate, our more limited concern involves no attempt to solve all such problems; although we are apt to make use of a variety of insights about the issue, which may happen to help us to clarify our own position. Thus it is to be understood, from our own perspective, that the term "Dravidian" may be adequately comprehended as a *convergent culturo-nominal*. This means that it encompasses, broadly, linguistic, ethnographic, socio-political, and mythological realities in Indian history. None of these factors, however, can be thoroughly divorced from the others, and the phenomenon of *religion* is what brings them all into meaningful relevance with regard to our study.

The relevance of the "Dravidians" to our account of the emergence of the goddess Durgā-Kalī begins with the acknowledgment that a certain amount of linguistic borrowing or intermixture has occurred over a long period of time in India.[188] This phenomenon involved, mainly, the "three major families, Indo-Aryan (a sub-family of the

---

Ministry of Information and Broadcasting, Government of India, 1965], p. 13) seems inclined to say "proto-Dravidian", but ultimately "still wrapped in mystery". Cf., briefly, von Fürer Haimendorf *et al.* in Ferreira, *Totemism in India*, p. 263, n. 3. The sources are many; the opinions are basically few.

[185] Cf. Ferreira, *Totemism in India*, p. 84. The term "Language-Culture(s)" is used by Suniti Kumar Chatterji in *The Indian Synthesis and Racial and Cultural Inter-Mixture in India* (Poona: Bhandakar Oriental Research Institute, 1953), pp. 9, 12 *et passim*, and in "Race Movements and Pre-historic Culture", p. 145. Cf. W. H. Moreland and A. C. Chatterjee, *A Short History of India* (4th ed.; New York: David McKay Co., Inc., 1957), pp. 4ff.

[186] Cf. M. B. Emeneau, "Linguistic Prehistory of India", *Proceedings of the American Philosophical Society*, XCVIII (1954), 282-292, esp. 285b.

[187] As in Campbell, *The Masks of God*, II, 183f. *Vide* Gonda, *Change and Continuity in Indian Religion*, p. 15.

[188] Gonda *Change and Continuity in Indian Religion*, p. 13.

Indo-European), Dravidian, and Munda.[189] Philological studies [190] have contributed to our understanding of this process. But we are reminded by Emeneau [191] that the long-range occurrence of this phenomenon in India's history will require further study for a detailed comprehension;[192] moreover, theories of "general displacement" through the expansion of population are still rather simplistic and should be deferred to the greater likelihood of "absorption" [193] as the main cultural medium. This medium, itself, however, is complex, involving political, economic, and religious considerations.[194] Though general philological investigations remain fluid, there are, of course, specific linguistic whose investigation has contributed much to our understanding of Indian religion.[195]

One of these studies has been made by Jean Przyluski, much of whose contributions have had to do with the non-Aryan (e.g., Austro-Asiatics) linguistic content of the Indian cultural matrix. Przyluski helps us particularly with regard to the probable historico-religious background of the name *Kālī*.[196] To be sure, we are not at the moment

189 M. B. Emeneau, "India As A Linguistic Area", *Language*, XXXII (1956), 5, 6. Cf. Chatterji, *The Indian Synthesis* ..., pp. 11-18.

190 C. S. Lévi, J. Przyluski, and J. Bloch, *Pre-Aryan and Pre-Dravidian in India*, trans. P. C. Bagchi (Calcutta: University of Calcutta, 1929); B. M. Barua, "Indus Script and Tantric Code", *Indo-Iranica*, I (1946), 15-21; G. V. Alekseev, Yu. V. Knorozov, A. M. Kondratov, and B. Yu Volchok, *Soviet Studies on Harappan Script*, ed., Henry Field and Edith M. Laird (trans., H. C. Pande), Florida : Field Research Projects, 1969; A. Parpola, S. Koskenniemi, S. Parpola, and P. Aalto, *Decipherment of the Proto-Dravidian Inscriptions of the Indus Valley*, Copenhagen : The Scandanavian Institute of Asian Studies, 1969. Larger cross-cultural possibilities are suggested in Hans Jensen, *Sign, Symbol, and Script*, trans., George Unwin (3rd ed. rev. and enl.; New York : G. P. Putnam's Sons, 1969), pp. 353-361.

191 Emeneau, "India As A Linguistic Area", p. 6 and n. 4.

192 Cf. Luigi Pareti, *History of Mankind*, Vol. II : *The Ancient World*, trans. G. E. F. Chilver and S. Chilver (New York : Harper and Row, Publishers, 1965), pp. 60f.; Emeneau, "Linguistic Pre-history of India", pp. 291f.

193 While the term "absorption" seems to supersede "general displacement" in a critical sense, S. K. Chatterjee's use of "intermixture" also has its own critical appeal. Perhaps both scholars intend to indicate similar processes, i.e., including but going beyond linguistic considerations.

194 Cf., in the case of Bengal, Barrie M. Morisson, "Social and Cultural History of Bengal : Approach and Methodology", in *Nalini Kanta Bhattasali Commemorative Volume*, ed. A. B. Habibullah (Dacca : n.p., 1966), pp. 323-338, esp. pp. 323-327.

195 E.g., *supra*, p. 72, n. 160.

196 Cf. Jean Przyluski, "From the Great Goddess to Kāla", *The Indian Historical Quarterly*, XIV (1938), 267-274. For the mythonominal "Durgā", *vide infra*, p. 114 and n. 387 of that page.

concerned with the author's insistence upon discussing that name within the broad framework of cross-cultural religious developments.[197] It is significant enough that, apart from the scholar's cultural-religious generalizations, his essay offers a plausible exemplification of how language and religion have affected one another in the development of the Indian ethno-cultural synthesis. Przyluski first inquired "whether Kāla [198] means the Black god only and Kālī the Black goddess, or if those names allude to Time also, destroyer of everything. ... are kāla 'black' and 'kāla' 'time, fate' two different senses for the same word?"[199]

Otto Schraeder [200] acknowledges that the Sanskrit *kāla* (time) and a non-Āryan word *kāḷa* (black) are juxtaposed in the Pāli. But the scholar makes the following two critical observations: (1) that neither of these terms (non-Aryan *kāla*, Sanskrit *kāla*) has "a common origin with Sanskrit *kāla* 'time'"; the reason is that this last term denoted only "the sense of a definite and recurrent time" (i.e., seasonal);[201] (2) the term's association with *kāla* (black) was an even later development which followed upon *kāla's* (time's) abstract usage and nomination as "the great Destroyer".[202]

Przyluski points out, however, that "time" (*Kāla*) finds its philosophical-religious place already in the Atharva-Veda Saṃhitā.[203] He further calls our attention to a linguistic variation of meaning found in the Buddhist Dīgha Nikāya,[204] which suggests to us the capacity of a certain root (*kāl*) for aesthetic, moral, theological, and

---

197 Cf. Jean Przyluski, "The Great Goddess of India and Iran", *The Indian Historical Quarterly*, X (1934), 405-430, and *La Grande Déesse* (Paris : Payot, 1950).

198 Kāla is thus distinguished in the Sanskrit dictionary as (1) kāla, dark, blue, black; (2) kāla, time, fate, death, god of death. Przyluski, "From the Great Goddess to Kāla", p. 267.

199 *Ibid.*

200 F. Otto Schraeder, "The Name Kalki(n)", *Adyar Library Bulletin*, I, Part 2 (1927), 21, n. 1.

201 Ṛg-Veda X.42.9 (and in the early Brāhmaṇas).

202 Schraeder, "The Name Kalki(n)", p. 21, n. 1.

203 Atharva-Veda XIX.53.5 and 54 in fine : "Praise of Time (Kāla)", trans. William Dwight Whitney (Harvard Oriental Series, Vol. VIII; Cambridge : Harvard University Press, 1904).

204 I.e., "and just as a clear cloth from which all *stain* [italics mine] has been washed away will readily take the dye, just even so did Pokkarasādi, the Brāhmaṇa, obtain, even while sitting there, the pure and spotless Eye for the Truth". *Dialogues of the Buddha*, trans. T. W. Rhys Davids, I, 135, quoted by Przyluski, "From the Great Goddess to Kāla", p. 268.

philosophical nuances of meaning — but also with an altogether symbolic capacity for logical coherence in a religious sense. In the main, Przyluski's linguistic contribution to our understanding of cultural-religious processes *within* Indian is summarized in these words:

> a non-Aryan root attested in Dravidian has been borrowed by Indo-Aryan under different forms: *kāl-*, *kal-*, *khal-*, *kāḷ-*, and this diversity in sounds added to the converging of the senses is explained by the non-Aryan origin of this root. Between *kāla* "black" and *kāla* "time, destiny", then, a series of intermediates can be exposed, which form an uninterrupted chain: *kālaka, kalka, kaluṣa, kali, kalki*, so that one passes gradually from a concrete "dark blue, black" to abstract and general notions "time, fate, death".[205]

The extended relevance of this observation will become more evident when we comment upon the literary-historical aspects of the emergence of Durgā-Kālī within the Hindu pantheon. For now, it suffices to say that the philologist would further emphasize these additional factors. First, he ventures to say that alongside of the specific meaning of the word *kāla* (time) in the religious texts one must allow for its wider application "in the spoken language";[206] secondly, the possible, affective nuance of *kāl-* as "all that is black and terrible" might well have had connotative application in the case of the other terms mentioned above, insofar as the effects "of such a principle in the religious domain are wider than is believed generally".[207]

---

205 *Ibid.*, p. 272. M. B. Emeneau (*Brahui and Dravidian Comparative Grammar* [Berkeley and Los Angeles: University of California Press, 1962], p. 18: DED 1772 and n. 26) remarks that "a wide range of meanings" is possible for *kaḷ* and its nominal verbal variations. Cf. T. Burrow, "Dravidian Studies VII: Further Dravidian Words in Sanskrit", *Bulletin of the School of Oriental and African Studies*, (= BSOAS hereafter) XII (1948), 371; *vide* also *ibid.*, XI (1943-1946), 132-133.

206 What Przyluski affirms was asked earlier but not then answered by Jules Bloch, "Some Problems of Indo-Aryan Phonology", (= BSOAS, V, 1930), 744: "... shall we suppose that words which appear in later texts were already in use among the real vernaculars before having been accepted by the written language?"

207 Przyluski, "From the Great Goddess to Kāla," pp. 267, 268, 270. Cf. Maurice Bloomfield, *American Journal of Philology*, XVI (1895), 409-434: "Every word, insofar as it is semantically expressive, may establish by haphazard favoritism, a union between its meaning and any of its sounds, and send forth this sound (or sounds) upon predatory expedition into domains where the sound is at first a stranger and a parasite". Quoted by M. B. Emeneau, "Onomatopoetics in the Indian Linguistic Area", *Language*, XLV, Part 1, No. 2 (June, 1969), 286, n. 12. *Vide*, for example, Dūgī, as a Prakritic survival of the deity Durgā, but also used in Bangeli folk-form as an appellation of "contempt"— S. K. Chatterji, "Purāṇa Legends and the Prakrit Tradition in New Indo-Aryan", BSOAS, VIII (1936), 466. Following Bloomfield's idea we note also the Tamilian *kara*

Burrow reminds us that "etymologies ... are as a rule of two sorts : either they are self-evident, or they are a matter of probability and to a certain extent of faith".[208] Like him, we should like to believe that our *religio*-linguistic correlations at least "are of the second kind".[209] However, we must not fail to mention at this point the historical likelihood that even if there may be some probable validity in such correlations, certain critical reservations should be acknowledged. Initially, then, there is also the strong probability that the varieties of meanings or nuances that seem to be relevant to the goddess Durgā-Kālī may not have all co-existed either in time or space; again, there may have been an element of "chance"integral but somehow related to what Burrow calls the "affective value"[210] of certain words; and finally, it is hardly necessary to posit the idea that the goddess Durgā-Kālī was the cause of all the variations and distinctions of meaning derived from the basis root *kāl-*, or the like; for, historically, it has most likely been both a matter of (1) a gradual coherence of symbolic experience in the secular commonplace, and (2) a religious response to a particular manifestation of divinity, be it Durgā-Kālī or another kind of sacred object.[211] At most, therefore, we can say that at a crucial but, at present, indeterminable historical-religious period in Indian culture, the goddess Durgā-Kālī became the absorbing focus

---

and *kaḷ* to steal; also *kal* = art (Burrow, "Dravidian Studies VII", p. 371, No. 52); (Telegu) *kar-* = to learn (T. Burrow, "Some Problems of Indo-Aryan Phonology, BSOAS, V [1930], 740f.). Cf. the goddess as "Kalavati" in the Mahānirvāṇa Tantra (H.T.T.G., p. 40, n. 8). Cf. "*Kharapaṭa*" (Sanskrit *Karṇīsuta*, Tamil *Karavaṭaṉ*), an author, and *karaviṭam*, a treatise on the "art" of *stealing* (*karavaṭam* = act or practice of stealing, in T. Burrow, "Some Dravidian Words in Sanskrit", *Transactions of the Philological Society* [1945], pp. 97-98). Although "other meanings ... seem unconnected" (Emeneau, *Brahui ...*, p. 18, n. 26) it interests us that a rough synthesis of a variety of meanings (cf. Burrow, "Dravidian Studies VII", pp. 132-133) tends to have some relevance to the sundry "attitudes" and "doings" of the goddess Durgā-Kālī in myth, cult, and symbols. Consider, for example (in Tamil, Malto, and Cannada) thd word *kal* = stone (*ibid.*, p. 132) vis-à-vis the lithiconic goddess Kalijai; *kalaha* = fight vis-à-vis Durgā-Mahiṣāsuramardinī (in Tulu) *kala* = (bed of) "flowers" vis-à-vis Durgā-Pūjā. Others are possible; however, no final conclusions may be drawn at this time. Cf. Jules Bloch, "Sanskrit and Dravidian", in Bagchi, *Pre-Aryan and Pre-Dravidian in India*, pp. 35-59, esp. p. 46.

208 Burrow, "Some Problems of Indo-Aryan Phonology", p. 743.

209 *Ibid.*

210 *Ibid.*, pp. 741, 743.

211 We shall be returning to the goddess as "Time" throughout Chapters III, IV, and V, but especially during Chapter V, when we shall embark upon the subject of "eschatology" and the goddess.

of human sensitivities that were largely sombre and turbid; but that the element of paradoxical valuation was never lost. It made her the source of both a tremendous *and* fascinating mystery.

Beyond the linguistic aspect of the "Dravidian" strain there lies the relevance of an ethnographic factor of great significance. This element has to do, again, with our former recognition of the complexity of the term "Dravidian". First of all, we note, as before, that, culturo-linguistically, "Dravidian" may include an ethnic *component* but hardly a mono-ethnic one; that it is more of a linguistic designation. The ethnic (i.e., in the sense of "racial") connotation, by itself, implies an oversimplification in the context of Indian history and culture. For "there is only a very rough correlation between ethnic stock and language".[212] Nevertheless—granting no necessary mono-ethnic substratum theory, the Indusian population may very well have included peoples of proto-Dravidian or Dravido-Mundic stock.[213] Furthermore, it is extremely interesting that, linguistically, "Dravidian" does not refer only to much of the southern area of the sub-continent; it happens also that most of the peoples of these stocks are now either "represented only by a handful of languages in the backwoods of Central India",

---

212 Cf. O. H. K. Spate and A. T. A. Learmonth, *India and Pakistan* (3d rev. ed.; Bungay, Suffolk: Richer Clay [The Chaucer Press], Ltd., 1967), p. 153; Sen, *Cultural Unity of India*, p. 13. Cf. Chatterji ("Race Movements and Pre-historic Culture", p. 145), who reminds us that "even in some cases the economic milieu transcends the diversity of language and language-culture and tones down very largely, within a given economic area, the more aggressively prominent or more easily noticeable special cultural traits that go with language—religion, social usage, customs, etc. Thus in the Chota Nagpur, in spite of diversity of language the Dravidian-speaking Oraons and the Austric (Kol)-speaking Mundas are within the fold of a common culture". *Vide* also John J. Gumpery, "Some Remarks on Regional and Social Language Differences in India", in *Introduction to the Civilization of India* (Chicago: The College Syllabus Division, University of Chicago, September, 1957), pp. 31-38, esp. p. 33.

213 Emeneau ("Linguistic Prehistory of India", pp. 287f.) intimates that the presence of Ṛg-Vedic (Dravidian) loan-words suggests an hypothesis of it as either the "nature of the Harappa language or of *one* of the Harappa languages [italics mine]"; although Emeneau says that "attempts at interpretation have not been convincing" (*ibid.*, p. 283b), he adds that the presence of such Dravidian loan words in "the earliest Sanskrit recorded" (*ibid.*, p. 286b) "fills this regrettable vacuum satisfactorily"; he praises Manfred Mayerhofer's earlier (apparently later abandoned) position that "Dravidian speakers were among the early peoples met by the invading Indo-European speakers" (*ibid.*, p. 287b, n. 23 continued). Cf. Yu V. Knorozov, "Characteristics of the Language of the Proto-Indian Inscriptions", Field and Laird, eds. *op. cit.*, pp. 17-22; note (p. 21) the probable connection between symbols No. 15 and 183 (in combination, similar to Dravidian) and the mytho-nominal "Mahādevī".

or "spoken by backwoods 'primitives' ..."[214] To be sure, in the most technical philological sense, we should not over-complicate the meaning of "Dravidian" to the extent of undermining the diversity of tongues in India. But neither has it been overlooked that by and large, linguistically, "the most important distinction is that between the Dravidian tongues of the south and the Indo-Aryan of the north and centre".[215]

Gonda[216] casts a favourable glance at the probability that the ancestors of the "'aborigines' ... may have played a certain role in the formation of Hinduism". Following an earlier study,[217] the scholar itemizes these kinds of *differentia* with regard to the aboriginals: generally, they have no caste distinctions ('Hindus'[218] are caste-divided); (2) they do not forbid widows to remarry ('Hindus' often do so); (3) they make no distinctions about the edibility of animal foods ('Hindus', "a large majority", prohibit beef-eating, especially the sacred cow); (4) they drink fermented liquors freely, especially during ceremonial occasions[219] ('Hindus' "often abstain"); (5) they are markedly contrary in their acceptance of "the spilling of blood" (to the 'Hindus'); (6) they have no restrictions regarding commensality (upper-class 'Hindus' do); (7) they have their own (non-Brāhmanic) priests (contrary to the 'Hindu' veneration of Brāhmins); (8) they bury their dead ('Hindus' burn their dead); (9) they have patriarchal institutions ('Hindus' as a rule have municipal civil

---

214 Emeneau, "Linguistic Prehistory of India", pp. 284a, 285b; Campbell, *The Masks of God*, II, 157f.; Sylvan Lévi, "Pre-Aryan and Pre-Dravidian in India", in Bagchi, *Pre-Aryan and Pre-Dravidian in India*, p. 95.

215 Spate and Learmonth, *India and Pakistan*, p. 154.

216 Gonda, *Change and Continuity in Indian Religion*, p. 25.

217 *Ibid.*, n. 49.

218 Gonda's "inverted commas" suggest his awareness—which we share—that Briggs was probably thinking in more restricted terms of the meaning of 'Hindu', though Briggs' analysis, apparently, continues to have some general value as a beginning for an even more critical (diachronic) historical-religious analysis. In this direction, *vide* L. S. S. O'Malley, ed., *Modern India and the West* (London: Oxford University Press, 1941), Chap. XII (Hutton), pp. 417-444, and Chap. XVI (O'Malley), esp. pp. 725-739; Nirad C. Chaudhuri, *The Continent of Circe* (New York: Oxford University Press, 1966), pp. 66-85; Nirmal K. Bose, "The Hindu Method of Tribal Absorption", in *Introduction to the Civilization of India*, pp. 349-363; Nirmal K. Bose, *A Common Perspective for North-East India*, National Seminar on Hill People of North Eastern India (Calcutta: n.p., 1966).

219 *Infra*, p. 122.

institutions); (10) they have tribal or family heads as lifetime arbiters of justice ('Hindus' have courts with judgment by one's peers).

The consideration of "two strands in Indian traditional religion, philosophy and ritual—the Vedic, and the non-Vedic" is included in the analysis of S. K. Chatterji concerning the general Indian "cultural synthesis". He posits that Nigamic (Vedic) and Āgamic (non-Vedic) traditions [220] in the course of time have undergone a process of unification or "intermixture". The former tradition is "'that which has come inside', evidently as a later cultural imposition"; and the latter is "'that which has come down' from the time immemorial".[221] This tradition, the author acknowledges, includes in all probability elements derived from "largely Dravidian" but also Austric and Sino-Tibetan sources.[222] Accordingly, among the early "Aryan-non-Aryan" elements which comprised the eventual Indian synthesis, the following are emphasized: the Vedic Fire Ritual (*Homa*) and the non-Vedic Flower Ritual (*Pūjā*):

> The ideas of *homa* and *pūjā*,[223] as it is apparent, had their birth in different milieus.[224] The mixed Hindu people, and the Brahmanical faith of mixed origin, inherited both. The *homa* was exclusively Aryan, to which non-Aryans had no right as it was the special privilege of the Aryan. But everybody was welcome to the *pūjā* ritual. *Homa* was a rite in which ordinarily animal sacrifice was a necessary part: it was known also as a *paśu-karma*. In *pūjā*, flowers are essential: it was, so to say, a *puṣpa-karma*.[225]

It seems to us that the two foregoing considerations of religiomorphic *differentia* by a late nineteenth-century observer and a scholar of our century tend to reflect, respectively, a synchronic and a diachronic mode of analysis. We also realize that, apart from the attempt to clarify essential elements—Vedic or non-Vedic—the process was, and probably has been, far more complicated than any one individual could ever hope fully to explain. Perhaps this accounts in large

---

220 Cf. Chatterji, "Race Movements and Pre-historic Culture", p. 160; *supra*, p. 2.

221 Chatterji, *The Indian Synthesis* ..., p. 51.

222 *Ibid.*

223 On the question of the term's origin and meaning, *vide infra*, Chap. IV.

224 Cf. Chatterji, "Race Movements and Pre-historic Culture", p. 161; Eliade, *Yoga*, p. 348.

225 Chatterji, *The Indian Synthesis* ..., p. 53. The author (*ibid.*, p. 54) refers to a verse in the Bhagavad-Gītā (IX.26) which appears to be "the great charter for the *pūjā* ritual within the milieu of Vedic Brāhmanism", i.e., "If anyone offers me with devotion a leaf, a flower, a fruit, and water, I receive that, offered by the person whose soul is disciplined". *Vide* Chatterji, "Race Movements and Pre-historic Culture", p. 161.

measure for the greater emphasis in recent times upon the apparent inextricability of what might have been religio-morphic ingredients peculiar to either "strand" (or "strain") of cultural orientation.[226] It is also evident, however, that it is possible to overstate the legitimate acknowledgment of synchronically inextricable religious elements, as if diachrony had no place in the study of Indian ideas, forms, and events. The elusive relationship (though certainly valid use) of these terms (i.e., synchronic/diachronic) is suggested and clarified by Merleau-Ponty, who says (in another connection) that "diachrony envelops synchrony" : "we must recognize that the present diffuses into the past to the extent that the past has been present. History is the history of successive synchronies".[227]

Chatterji, then, presents a diachronic religious portrait of Vedic-Hinduist mythic, cultic, and symbolic traits.[228] He also says that the Nigamic (or Vedic) religion and ritual have had quite an effect upon the Nigamic mode, but that the latter constitutes another world. Having pointed this out, however, the scholar does not appear to be fully aware that an adequate diachronic approach merits even further synchronic but critical observations.

To begin with, the scholar does not acknowledge that the rudiments of a Cosmic Force are already anticipated in the (Ṛg-) Vedic tradition, for example, in the concept of *ṛta*;[229] or, in the case of the Tantras, that it may well be a matter of comparative emphasis rather than exclusive Tantric belief that "the whole universe is filled with a Cosmic Force or Divine Spirit".[230] Moreover, he does not mention that the *do ut des* description [231] (though controversial as far as we are concerned) has also been applied even more emphatically to the *pūjīc* devotional forms. Again, his description of the Vedic *haomic* devotional forms as "simple and very primitive",[232] is rendered without regard to the due necessity of making a similar observation

---

[226] Cf. *supra*, p. 37 and n. 116.

[227] Merleau-Ponty, *Signs*, pp. 86, 87.

[228] *Vide* Chatterji, "Race Movements and Pre-historic Culture", pp. 160f.

[229] Cf. Maurice Bloomfield, *The Religion of the Veda* (New York : AMS Press, Inc., 1969), pp. 126-128; Campbell, *The Masks of God*, II, 178-179.

[230] Chatterji, *The Indian Synthesis* ..., p. 52. His point is valid, however, that in the case of the pūjīc vogue, "the worshipper wants to have a personal communion or touch with it" (*ibid.*).

[231] *Ibid.* Cf. *supra*, p. 39.

[232] Chatterji, *The Indian Synthesis* ..., p. 52.

concerning certain (but not all)[233] aspects of the *pūjic* rites.[234] And, finally, his most glaring oversight is that there also exists among the non-Āryan populations more or less "humanized forms of natural forces", but which, admittedly, include by and large (natural) "disease", "plague", and "calamity" deities.[235] Here, again, to be sure, there is no *absolute* conceptual correlation but only a relative one (in fact, the Ṛg-Vedans are generally *aniconic*); however, the basic religious humanization of natural forces is present among the Grāmadevatān worshippers though they can include iconic representations as well.[236] Furthermore, the oft-noted henotheistic nature of Ṛg-Vedic religion is partially realized in myth and cult among the popular strata.[237]

We notice, therefore, that, in the passage of time and during the course of Indological research, the case becomes more accurately described as one of Vedic-Hinduist difference *and* continuity, or continuity and difference.[238] The difficulty with Chatterji's analytical *differentia*, then, is that, ultimately, in a more critical perspective, they tend to attest to matters of "degree" concerning Vedic-Hinduist relations rather than matters of absolute distinction. As we said, the scholar shows his awareness of the fact of no absolute distinction (*supra*, p. 88) but, seemingly, in passing.[239] This is one reason that Gonda's work is so valuable. Gonda, too, nevertheless, says that "continuity is no identity";[240] yet our point is that continuity would be more appropriately recognized in terms of *comparative emphasis* instead of identity. The basis of this assertion happens to be the phenomenon of a more intense consciousness amongst the "Dravidian" populations of that terranean reality—to which we referred earlier

---

233 Cf. Chatterji, "Race Movements and Pre-historic Culture", p. 160 : e.g., "yoga as a special form of mystico-religious ideology and practice".

234 Cf. *ibid.*, pp. 160f.; Chatterji, *The Indian Synthesis ...*, pp. 52f.

235 Cf. James, *The Cult of the Mother Goddess*, p. 116; Crooke, *The Popular Religion ...*, Vol. I, Chap. III.

236 *Vide* Oppert, *On the Original Inhabitants ...*, pp. 452, 455.

237 I.e., the Pañcāyatana Pūjā : the symbols "are arranged in five different methods according to the preference given any one of the five deities at the time of worship'.' *Vide* M. Monier Williams, *Brahmanism and Hinduism* (4th ed. enl. and improved; New York : Macmillan and Co., 1891), p. 412.

238 Cf. Gonda, *Change and Continuity in Indian Religion*, pp. 16-17.

239 Cf. Chatterji, *The Indian Synthesis ...*, p. 51, par. 2, where the author's description of the Nigamic/Agamic pantheonic combination is characterized by language almost equally applicable to either milieu.

240 Gonda, *Change and Continuity in Indian Religion*, p. 17.

in connection with the Earth (Mother) Goddess and/or the goddess Durgā-Kālī.

Thus Briggs and Chatterji, together, serve to make us recall that, though the Vedic world-view involves "some individual gods and goddesses who are humanized forms of natural forces",[241] the "Dravidian" depth of religious experience tends to find its more marked focus in the human entrancement with the sacredness-in-the-profane, the temporalization of the Eternal. Both the aboriginal funeral interments and the "Dravidian" megalithic [242] valuations of the meaning of existence testify, probably, to an ancient, more rustic, lithiconic,[243] and sensual orientation towards the mystery of life and death. In the later, more developed aspects of Tantric myth and ritual, is there not a literal and decisive mergence of the idea and the form of Sacred Power (nāma = rūpa; Puruṣa = Prakṛti)? Fundamentally, it is against this particularly inveterate background of "spiritual terraneality" that we are inclined to agree that the Grāmadevatān religious beliefs and expressions may be indeed the "rural, larval, 'popular' forms" of the earlier Indusian religious matrix.[244]

The third important element in this discussion of the "Dravidian" strain is socio-political in nature. It is at this level of historical-religious investigation that "the more complex picture" or "more complicated" early Indian situation to which both Sastri and Heine-Geldren refer [245] is considered with remarkable discernment by Panikkar. This scholar points out the following things during the course of his survey of Indian history: (1) the literary portrayal of the "Battle of the Ten Kings"[246] suggests, already, that there was no simple ethno-political

---

[241] Chatterji, *The Indian Synthesis* ..., p. 52.

[242] Cf. Eliade, *Patterns in Comparative Religion*, pp. 217-218, 219, 220; Nilakanta Sastri, *Development of Religion in South India*, pp. 1-2. Cf. N. R. Banerjee, *The Iron Age in India* (Delhi : Munshiram Manoharlal, 1965), pp. 51-67.

[243] Cf. a discussion of this particular sub-strain in J. N. Farquhar, "Temple-and-Image Worship in Hinduism", *Journal of the Royal Asiatic Society of Great Britain and Ireland*, 1928, pp. 15-23.

[244] Eliade, *Yoga*, p. 358. It should be clear by now that we would not reduce the total Indusian religious milieu to Earth (Mother) Goddess worship; however, we do insist that Gonda's rebuttive analysis concerning over-optimistic conclusions about the Indusian culture and religion, though generally meritorious, does not necessarily invalidate the "dynamic" comparative-historical interpretation of the Harappan aftermath rendered, for instance, by Eliade.

[245] Nilakanta Sastri, *Development of Religion in South India*. p. 3; Heine-Geldern, in Ferreira, *Totemism in India*, p. 263.

[246] I.e., *Dāśa-rājña* (Rig-Veda VII.33.2, 5; 83.8).

or mono-religious dichotomy characteristic of the Āryan long-range advancement into the Indo-Gangetic plain;[247] the "Battle", for instance, "was not ... solely of Āryan peoples. Non-Āryans under their own kings were ranged on both sides";[248] (2) although, in general, the Āryans were probably contemptuous of their "dark-skinned" neighbours, "before the caste system took shape such intermixture of blood has already taken place";[249] and (3) the later criteria of authentic "Āryanhood" were less ethnic and caste-centered, being more distinctively religious as far as "status and culture" were concerned.[250]

In terms of historico-religious development, then, the following phases of intra-cultural relations probably occurred. First, at the earliest, though still a not precisely determined period in Indian history,[251] a situation prevailed in which the Indo-Gangetic community was characterized by a more simply polarized ethno-political situation. This was the natural outgrowth of the initial wave (or waves)[252] of Āryan invaders who confronted the indigenous populations whose appearance, speech, and customs were more conspicuously "different".[253] A subsequent phase of development saw the emergence of

---

247 Note that even if the "Battle" is considered purely mythological, it still suggests a complex intermixture of "cultural" elements *inside* the epic story itself.

248 Panikkar, *A Survey of Indian History*, p. 7.

249 Panikkar, *A Survey of Indian History*, p. 10; Mookerji, *Hindu Civilization*, pp. 68f.

250 Panikkar, *A Survey of Indian History*, p. 10; Mookerji, *Hindu Civilization*, p. 70, n. 1, can, therefore, point out that "some of these [derogative] epithets are also applied to Āryans". It is for us to note that in this context there could be (ethnically) non-Āryan (religious) "Āryans" as well as (religiously) "non-Āryan" Āryans; unorthodox Āryans *and* non-Āryans thus incurred derogative epithets. R. P. Chandra (*ibid.*) understands the historical situation in dynamic terms (i.e., cultural synthesis); but it is not clear that he values adequately the religious factor to be creative (then and thereafter) of *both* a distinctive harmony *and* radical cleavage. Cf. Buddha Prakash, *Political and Social Movements in Ancient Panjab* (Delhi : Motilal Banarsidass, 1964), p. 32.

251 The Ṛg-Vedic "Age" is most often estimated, despite plausible variations, to begin around 1500 or 1200 B.C. Cf. Prakash, *Political and Social Movements in Ancient Panjab*, p. 23. *Vide* also this author's socio-cultural account of the ancient Panjab, *ibid.*, Chap. VI.

252 *Ibid.*, pp. 32f. Besides noting religious elements the author includes for our consideration the notion of a plurality of Aryan settlements or incursions. *Vide ibid.*, pp. 17-23.

253 E.g., "Dasyus", "Vṛtras", "Vrātyas", "Asuras", etc. : Ṛg-Veda I.35.10; 130.8; 174.7-8; 175.3; IV.16.9-12; V.29.10 (cf. I.2-8). Cf. a host of passages in H. Daniel Smith, *Selections from the Vedic Hymns* (Berkeley, Calif. : McCutchen Publishing Corp., 1968), pp. 37-42; Mookerji, *Hindu Civilization*, p. 30, and esp. p. 70; Karmakar, *The Religions*

more practical socio-political interrelations under the influence of the normal exigencies of cultural life. During this phase, on the whole, a considerably fluid historical situation developed in which there was more cosmopolitanism, syncretism, and parallelism both in terms of religious ideas as well as institutions; yet this was notably accompanied by the search for, and the claim of, *distinctiveness* in the spiritual path. A still later, more crucial period saw, finally (if not the emergence, at least) the intensification of a trend for making derogative value judgments. 'But they were now made against a broader target, yet specifically with reference to persons (e.g., the Vrātyas)[254] of *various* ethnic, social, and political backgrounds,[255] including *Āryans* themselves—who failed or refused to adopt or follow with fidelity certain

---

of India, I, 9ff.; S. Chattopadhyaya, *The Evolution of Theistic Sects in India* (Calcutta: Progressive Publishers, 1962), p. 6. *Vide* also Prakash, *Political and Social Movements in Ancient Panjab*, pp. 33-42, 27.

[254] Though mentioned above, the term has special historical-religious significance in light of the long-run emphasis upon "ritual performance" as a major criterion of socio-political status. Both Gonda and Karmakar indicate that the term "vrātyas" tells us something about the nature of ancient Indian religion and society. Thus, it appears, (1) the Vrātyas were known for their association with certain paraphernalia; (2) they were said to speak the language of the consecrated; (3) the Vrātyas' ritual institution was probably borrowed by the Vedic-Brāhmans (cf. Gonda, *Change and Continuity in Indian Religion*, pp. 326, 289; Karmakar, *The Religions of India*, I, 23, 25). These scholars disagree upon the ethnic identification of the Vrātyas. Gonda (*Change and Continuity in Indian Religion*, p. 289) says that they are "authentic Vedic Āryans" (cf. Keith and others in Karmakar, *The Religions of India*, I, 18, n. 3, and p. 26); Karmakar (*ibid.*, pp. 18, 24, 28 *et passim*) sees them as "non-Āryans" whose cult was associated with the "Dravidian" peoples (*ibid.*, p. 26). He alone appears to consider them adequately in a diachronic perspective; that is, the dignity and status of the Vrātyas *change* with the passage of time (*ibid.*, pp. 26ff.; cf. Basham, *The Wonder That Was India*, pp. 245f.). On the historical-religious significance of the Vrātyas, *vide* also Eliade, *Yoga*, pp. 103-104. This scholar calls our attention (*ibid.*, p. 105) to the possibility of an additional, though hardly extricable, "aboriginal, pre-Āryan" component and contribution to a particular type of religious discipline and experience—a significant observation in that the earliest orientations, whether "parallel" or complicated, suggest the *pre-conditions* for an eventual culturo-religious synthesis.

[255] On the whole it would seem that Gonda's "authentic Vedic Āryans" were probably not such at least in an ethnic sense, but adjudged so (i.e., authentically Āryan) in a rituological sense. It was most likely the cultural heterogeneity and heterodoxy which eventually came to characterize the Vrātyas which brought about their reclassification by the orthodoxists as "non-Vedic"; non-Vedic, however, need not have meant non-Āryan ethnically (as we indicated—*supra*, p. 91, n. 250); nonetheless, with the broadening of the Vrātyas' cultural base, it (i.e., *vrātya*) came in turn to mean non-Āryan both religiously and ethnically.

distinctive *religious* rites or sacred status-valuations. Such things were, by then, taking shape in the hands of a Brahmanic aristocracy which was itself, probably, not "purely Āryan".[256]

Our historical and religious judgment is, therefore, that what may have begun (at the earliest Vedic period) as an ethno-political *confrontation* and, later, as well, a socio-political *encounter*, became in the final analysis a creative religious *transvaluation*. It was the nature of this transvaluation that it conjoined and undergirded all the pervious forces within a decisive framework or *religious* understanding of man in the world. Thus, while the linguistic, ethnographic, and socio-political elements never entirely disappeared, the eventually dominant *Weltanschauung* was to be a cosmo-anthropomorphism,[257] or as J. M. Kitagawa prefers, a "socio-religious order ... including morals, economics, politicals, and all aspects of culture and society".[258]

The last important element in this phase of our discussion is a mythological one. However, its nature and significance are not unrelated to the historical factors just indicated. Certainly the relations between Hindu mythology and Indian history allow for no easy solution.[259] For example, no less than half a dozen interpretations

---

256 Cf. Przyluski, in Prakash, *Political and Social Movements in Ancient Panjab*, p. 63; *vide* also *ibid.*, pp. 241ff. Religious rites were thus the norm more than "belief content" : *orthopraxis* beyond professed orthodoxy; hence this criterion would tend to affect (Ādi-) Āryans as well. *Vide* Harper, "Ritual Pollution as an Integrator of Caste and Religion", p. 151 (*supra*, Chap. I); J. A. B. van Buitenen, "On the Archaism of the Bhāgavata Purāṇa", *Krishna : Myths, Rites, and Attitudes*, ed. Milton Singer (Honolulu : East-West Center Press, 1966), p. 30.

257 Cf. "The Primeval Sacrifice", in Wm. Theodore de Bary, gen. ed., *Sources of Indian Tradition* (Paperback ed.; New York and London : Columbia University Press, 1958), I, 13-15; also *ibid.*, pp. 214ff., 219ff.

258 Joseph M. Kitagawa, *Religions of the East* (Philadelphia : The Westminster Press, 1960), p. 125. For an excellent discussion of the *varieties* of forces at work in the Indusian matrix, *vide* S. C. Malik, *Indian Civilization : The Formative Period* (Simla : Indian Institute of Advanced Study, 1968), pp. 73-146; esp. pp. 99-105; 121ff., 127ff., 137-146.

259 For example, a fairly early attempt was made by A. Banerji-Sastri in a series of articles (*Journal of the Bihar and Orissa Research Society*, XII [1926], 110-139, 243-285, 334-360, 503-539) to promote a myth-and-history approach to the Vedas and Itihasa-Purāṇas; although the author preferred the term "traditional history" ("Ancient Indian Historical Tradition", pp. 62-79), his view appears very much like a "myth-*as*-history" endeavour. Cf. V. S. Agrawala, *Vedic Studies* (Banaras : Banaras Hindu University, School of Vedic Studies, 1953), p. 111. Agrawala rightly suggests the matter's complexity; however, he does not mention that the Śatapatha-Brāhmaṇic textual allusion (XI.1.6.10), probably, represents a post-Ṛg-Vedic mystical valorization. It, therefore, need not be regarded as an "historical" contradiction : sacred or profane.

have been advanced or supported by various scholars concerning the precise *rationale* which underlies the Vedo-Brāhmaṇic religious literature.[260] Nonetheless, all such solutions or keys, ranging from the naturistic to the metaphysical, tend to have or simply imply an *historical* dimension in the light of our earlier proposed methodological understanding of the term "history" (Chap. I, and p. 43, n. 4). Accordingly, whether one ventures to say that the Vedo-Brāhmaṇic *rationale* is "an attempt to conceptualize and establish relations with the conspicuous forces of nature" (Müller); or a "reflection of a tripartite Indo-European class structure" (Dumézil)[261] : or, indeed, "symbolic expressions of monistic teaching",[262]— the context of such religious strivings still remains history as encultured nature and history as religious being (i.e., existence).[263]

The mythological analogue to the process of Indian history discussed heretofore around the word "Dravidian" as a convergent culturo-nominal finds a highly appropriate focus in the term *asura*. Although we have subsumed this term under the topic "Dravidic", *asura* itself tends to have the character of a *convergent mytho-nominal*. As such, there is a sense in which it integrates in part several zones of Indian history and religion into a symbolical whole.[264] This is especially the case when *asura* is considered in relation to the term *deva* (e.g., the Devāsurasangrāma or Devāsuram). As part of this perennial Hindu theme, *asura* is the polaric symbol par excellence and has continuing relevance to the myth, cult, and symbols of the goddess Durgā Kālī. For it is she who confronts in the most dramatic and epic fashion *the asura* of all *asuras*—the Mahiṣāsura.

By far the most sophisticated and thought-provoking but complex analysis of the problem is a monograph by K. P. Chattopadhyay, *Ancient Indian Culture Contacts and Migrations* (Calcutta Sanskrit College Research Studies, Vol. XLIII, No. 25; Calcutta : Sanskrit College, 1965).

260 Cf. Hein, "Hinduism", p. 50.

261 Cf. C. Scott Littleton, *The New Comparative Mythology* (Berkeley and Los Angeles : University of California Press, 1966).

262 Hein, "Hinduism", p. 50.

263 Cf. *supra*, pp. 29-30, 33, 34.

264 I.e., *asura* has the symbolic potential vis-à-vis Brahmanic Hinduism to point to all the negative valuations of Indian myth *and* history. Thus Asura, Dasyu, Vṛtras, Vrātyas (cf. Verrier Elwin, *The Religion of an Indian Tribe* [London : Oxford University Press, 1955], pp. 11-13; Lévi, "Pre-Aryan and Pre-Dravidian in India", pp. 88, 89, 90; *supra*, pp. 90-93); or any other competitive forces or unorthodoxies (e.g., Jainists, Buddhists); for this last, *vide* Pargiter, *Ancient Indian Historical Tradition*: pp. 291, 292.

The term *asura* encompasses both positive and negative valuations in Indian history; so that it is not unrelated to previously considered historical and religious realities. 'It shows its own linguistic relevance, first of all, insofar as the term seems to have had its own "history"[265] prior to its utilization by the Ṛg-Vedic poets. In a second case, the Vedic hymns reveal indications of a tendency to regard certain segments of the ancient Indian population, as we said, as worthy of derogation. The *asuras* are included among them;[266] for we recognize that the term was indeed applied on the historical level even if it be granted that the Devāsuram theme may not correspond solely, if at all, to *mere historical events.*

At any rate, the term *asura* under literary criticism presents us with significant insights concerning both the relation between language and culture, as well as phenomenon of paradoxical nominal valuation. Studies by Bergaigne [267] do much to establish the fact that there was an *earlier asura* "dignity" in ancient Indian literature; that, specifically, there are evidences in the Ṛg-Veda, to be sure, of the positive valuation of the term *asura.*[268] Furthermore, it is important to see that the very attempt to establish or confirm an *asura* "dignity" in the earliest Veda led Bergaigne to discern a virtually "superior" dignity in which the *asuras* were held. The scholar affirms that "supe-

---

[265] Cf. Finegan, *The Archaeology of World Religions*, I, 69, 89, 131; B. K. Ghosh, "Indo-Iranian Relations", in Majumdar, *The History and Culture of the Indian People*, I, 218-224; Prakash, *Political and Social Movements in Ancient Panjab*, pp. 38ff.; Chattopadhyay, *Ancient Indian Culture Contacts ...*, pp. 15f. *Vide* also H. D. Griswold, *The Religion of the Rig Veda* (London: Oxford University Press, 1823), Chap. I, esp. pp. 20ff.

[266] *Supra*, p. 91, n. 253.

[267] Abel Bergaigne, *La Religion védique*, Vol. III (Paris: F. Vieweg, Librairie-Editeur, 1883).

[268] Ṛg-Veda I.35.7, 10; 151.4; II.27.10; 28.7. Writing of Avestan and Vedic parallels, A. A. MacDonell (*Vedic Mythology* [Varanasi, India: Indological Publishing House, 1963], p. 7) says that "in both religions the term *asura* = *ahura* is applied to the highest gods ... as mighty kinds ... almost entirely free from guile and immoral traits". Max Muller (*Contributions to the Science of Mythology*, I [London: Longmans, Green and Co., 1897], 126) refers to "Asura Varuna" as "the most powerful and sometimes supreme deity"; he is noted for his "universal monarchy" (*sāmrājya*) and especially his "occult power" (*māyā*). Others, "Indra ... Agni ... Savitṛ ... also share the dignity of being Asura-like" (A. Banerji-Sastri, "The Asuras in Indo-Iranian Literature", *Journal of the Bihar and Orissa Research Society*, XII [1926], 123-124). Cf. Karmakar, *The Religions of India*, I, 10. *Vide* especially Bergaigne, *La Religion védique*, pp. 70-71.

riority" in a statement which combines both the intimations of etymology and mythology regarding the name *asura*.

> It is itself derived from *asu* "breath, life"[269] (met with in the R.V. two times accompanying the epithet *jiva*, "the living one"—I.140.8; 113.16) and must mean "he who is in possession of the breath of life ... [i.e., more than just "living" but] rather he who is "master of the sources of life, himself drawing from them at will". It appears synonymous with a compound ... *asutrip* "he who delights in the breath of life, who enjoys it fully", or as it were, "he who drinks at the sources of life".[270]

Yet this priority of the *asuras* looms before us still more dramatically in the Ṛg-Veda when we read that "the gods maintained faith in the mighty asuras";[271] but, then, *another* attitude toward them is present which seems to signify the *de-dignification* of these "Masters of the sources of life": "... Who, Indra, dares withstand thy bolt of thunder? Weaponless are the Asuras, the godless! scatter them with thy wheel, Impetuous Hero".[272] As a potential problem of Ṛg-Vedic literary criticism it is interesting to notice the textual position of these positive and negative valuations.[273] More intriguing,

---

[269] Cf. John Dowson, *A Classical Dictionary of Hindu Mythology* (3d ed.; London: Kegan Paul, Trench, Trubner, and Co., Ltd., 1891), p. 27; J. G. R. Forlong, *Encyclopedia of Religions*, I (New York: University Books, 1964), 158; W. Norman Brown ("Mythology in India", in S. N. Kramer, ed., *Mythologies of the Ancient World* [New York: Doubleday and Co., Inc., 1961], p. 21) refers to *asura* as "a name which means something like 'living power'". C. W. J. van der Linden ("The Concept of Deva in the Vedic Age, I" [Dissertation, University of Utrecht, 1954], p. 32) wonders whether the term *asuratva* might not be rendered as "creative power". Cf. Gonda, *infra*, p. 133; Bergaigne, *La Religion védique*, pp. 70-71.

[270] Bergaigne, *La Religion védique*, p. 73 and n. 2. Prakash, *Political and Social Movements in Ancient Panjab*, p. 37; van der Linden ("The Concept of Deva in the Vedic Age, I", pp. 31, 32, 33) points out that "Asura as epithet to *deva* occurs unfrequently, e.g. 3.55.1 (*devānām asuratvan*). This certainly points out that the Vedic Indian considered the *asura*-ship as an addition or something superior to *deva*. Here, too, there is a hyperbolic use as this is a litany with the repeated recurrence of *devānām asuratvam*"; "7.65,2 shows to us Mitra-Varuna as both *asura* and the lords of the *devas*. *Asura* seems to be superior to *deva*. 8.25,4 expresses that Mitra-Varuṇa are devas *and* asuras. ... There is an essential difference between deva and asura and it proves itself in 7.66,2: where Mitra-Varuṇa are said to have destined the *devas* to the dignity of *asura*. *Asuratva* is superior to *deva*". "The Maruts do not have the *Asura*-title. But Sūrya, Mitra-Varuṇa and Aditi share this title, and the other *devas* are clearly separated from them".

[271] Ṛg-Veda X.151.3.

[272] Ṛg-Veda VIII.85.9.

[273] Cf. Bergaigne, *La Religion védique*, pp. 68, 69.

however, is the discovery of certain textual indications of the "polarization-process" of certain principal Vedic divinities.[274]

At any rate, the period of the Brāhmaṇas witnesses the beginnings of a steadier, more intense, and more thoroughgoing symbolic polarization : between *asura* and *deva*. Here in the Brāhmaṇas terms such as *deva* and *asura* become employed as collective representations of mighty hosts in a tradition of mutual hostility, with the latter group as the express enemies of the former.[275] In the Atharva-Veda and other Puranic sources *asura* means "demon" only, or "a demoniacal being",[276] and goes on to be applied

> to the expressions like Rākṣasas, Daityas, Dānavas ... The epics and the Purāṇas prominently describe the names of the following *Asuras* : Rāvaṇa, Bali, Kaṁsa, Jarāsandha, Naraka, *Mahiṣāsura*, Hiraṇyakaśipu, and others.[277]

The Brāhmaṇas apart, Eliade calls our attention to the fact that although the Indra-Vṛtra battle plays a considerable role in the Ṛg-Veda, "numerous myths bring out the consubstantiality or brotherhood of the Devas and Asuras".[278] Moreover, we note with interest two other observations by Eliade which delineate the paradoxical relations of such divinities. First, there is a non-Providential dimension in the character of these divinities which "is thought proper for the Gods" ; and, second, "the Gods *are, or once were, or are capable of becoming* Asuras or non-gods".[279] So much for a linguistic-theological

---

[274] Cf. W. Norman Brown, "Proselyting the Asuras", *Journal of the American Oriental Society*, XXXIX (1919), 100-103. Cf. Prakash, *Political and Social Movements in Ancient Panjab*, p. 59.

[275] MacDonell, *Vedic Mythology*, p. 156. Because of an apparent original equality of Devas and Asuras, as offspring of Prajāpati, MacDonell adduces (*ibid.*) that "it is perhaps for this reason that malignant spirits are sometimes included by the term *deva* (T.S. 3, 5. 4; A.V. 3, 15)". Some interesting nominal dichotomies are "Deva"-"A-Deva" (Bergaigne, *La Religion védique*, p. 68); "Sura" (a purported Upanishadic usage)-"A-Sura", "not (a) god" (but *vide ibid.*, p. 68, n. 1); in the case of other Asuras, e.g., the Ādityas, there is "A-diti"-"Diti" (Brown, "Mythology in India", p. 282; Sankarananda, *The Rig Vedic Culture ...*, p. 138). On a similar symbolical ambiguity (i.e., with "Yakṣa") in Jainism, *vide* Coomaraswamy, "Yakṣas", Part I, pp. 37, 11 and n. 4.

[276] MacDonell, *Vedic Mythology*, p. 156.

[277] Karmakar, *The Religions of India*, I, 10 (italics mine). For Mahiṣāsura, *vide infra*, Chap. III.

[278] Cf. Eliade, *Mephistopheles and the Androgyne*, pp. 88-89. Cf. Chāndogya Upaniṣad I.2.1; Bṛhad Āraṇyaka Upaniṣad I.3.1; 5.2.1ff.

[279] Eliade, *Mephistopheles and the Androgyne*, pp. 89, 90. Cf. A. Coomaraswamy, "Angel and Titan : An Essay in Vedic Ontology", *Journal of the American Oriental Society*, LV (1935), 373-419.

paradox which has significance for any consideration of the fundamental nature and categorization of divinities in the Hindu pantheon.[280]

A final point about the term *asura* yet remains. It concerns the question of the historical reality of the *asura*, that is, beyond the realm of a mere mytho-nominal or epithetic application of the term to various non-desirable groups. The modern *Asur* of India represent a tempting focal point in the perennial problem of the relation between myth and history. The solution of continuity here, however, does not seem to have been established. And it does not edify our overall discussion to attempt to discuss the matter at any length. For it might better become the subject of a study by another student of religion who, like ourselves, finds that there are things about those "ironsmelters" which continue to make the mind wonder.[281]

The Centripetalization of the Goddess Durgā-Kālī

The natural wonderment and uncertainty that the scholar might experience regarding the question of historical continuity concerning the mythical *asuras* and the modern *Asur* do not apply to the goddess Durgā-Kālī, as she is understood to have become a part of the Hindu pantheon and the Smārta-Brahman tradition. For, here, we are primarily interested in the way in which the attempt was made to incorporate and to assimilate an ineradicable religious experience which subsisted parallel to mainstream Vedo-Brāhmaṇic thought. To be sure, that endeavour also involved the search to maintain and perpetuate a fundamental religious vision of time and eternity.[282]

Our use of the word "centripetalization" bears at once some significance, of course, for the way in which we have suggested the historical

280 Cf. Eliade, *Patterns in Comparative Religion*, p. 419 : "In India, every divinity has a "gentle form' and equally a 'terrible form' (*krodha-mūrti*).

281 Cf. "Asurs", *Encyclopedia of Religion and Ethics*, 1910, pp. 157b-159a. Cf. Banerji-Sastri, *supra*, p. 93, n. 259; and also on the Asurs, S. C. Roy in *Journal of the Bihar and Orissa Research Society*, I (1915), 229-253; *ibid.*, VI (1920), 393-423; *ibid.*, XII (1926), 147-152. The question of mythological-historical continuity and correlation is critically discussed by Verrier Elwin, *The Agaria* (Calcutta : Oxford University Press, 1942), Chap. II, which includes the conclusions, however uncertain, of Walter Reuben's *Eisenschmiede und Dämonen in Indien* (Leiden, 1939). Cf. .K K. Leuva, *The Asur : A Study of Primitive-Ironsmelters* (New Delhi : n.p., 1963); *vide* also Banerjee, *The Iron Age in India*, pp. 182-186, 220-222.

282 *Vide infra*, Chap. III.

relatedness of Durgā-Kālī to the immemorial *Terra Mater*. That is, we have presented the "story" of the goddess, heretofore, in terms which are more concentro-historical than chrono-genetic, while insisting that history, phenomenology, and structure are at present inseparable for our immediate task. In more specific terms, nonetheless, "centripetalization" refers here to two Sanskritizational processes : mythological magnification and devotional glorification.

It, therefore, seems to us that such phenomena were not born "ex nihilo", but had their "creation" and viability vouchsafed in large measure by two very important factors in ancient Indian religion and society. First, there was the presence of sufficient theoretical and experiential variation within the Vedo-Brāhmaṇic community itself to allow for the emergence of the former "processes"; and, secondly, there was the reality of what we have chosen to call "parallel and transitional ciphers" in the Vedic mythological tradition itself which in all probability facilitated the emergence and fulfillment of those "processes". This does not mean that such processes have come to an end. For the previous discussion [283] of ideas and events highly germane to the sectarian structuralization of the myth, cult, and symbols associated with the goddess as a religious object tastify to an ongoing interaction between various intra-cultural forces in ancient and modern India. What is important to notice is that the parallelism just mentioned was the natural accompaniment or corollary, perhaps even the mutually effective product, of the co-existence of "two worlds" which may broadly "stand as symbolic poles representing the interplay of ... contrary mythologies",[284] as well as general orientations toward the world.

It does not seem clear to us, of course, that Campbell is aware of factors other than that there is contrariety in the broadly "Vedic" and "Dravidian" mythic and existential symbolizations. For example, it should be recognized that the parallel symbols which we shall point out are considered such just because they are fairly similar morphological expressions (but varying apprehensions) of the sacred-in-the-profane. Moreover, other symbols (or, perhaps, a few of the same) tend to have a plausible "transitional" value and efficacy; these, we believe, were the logical symbolic precedents to be employed

---

283 *Supra*, Chap. I, section entitled "The Phenomenologic of Symbols", pp. 34-41.

284 Campbell, *The Masks of God*, II, 198. Cf. *ibid.*, p. 172 : "a two-ply cult of the goddess", i.e., *ibid.*, p. 171 (top).

by persons who themselves (or the forbears) had apprehended nature and Ultimate Reality (or Ultimate Reality *through* nature), but now with renascent novelty and creativity.

It must be said at once that scholars tend to concur in their denial of the Vedic origins of any definite form of Mother-Goddess *cult.*[285] Few, if any, however, have felt the need to deny that the Vedic mythological deposit was the natural seed-bed[286] for the potential development of such a cult. Louis Renou, for instance, with reference to the belief in Śakti as the basis of the cult of Durgā-Kālī, tells us that "this belief", Śakti, "is an ancient one, the first *traces* of it being discoverable in the Veda ... it made its way into various forms of worship that are not specifically of the *Śākta* persuasion [italics mine]".[287] Even more plausible an opinion is expressed by Alain Daniélou,[288] who epitomizes, adequately, the general and particular nature of a critical outlook :

> The conception of supreme divinity as a woman, a mother, a womb, does not seem to have had at first any place in the Aryan scriptures. But the prehistoric cult of the mother goddess can be found there, too, as in all other religions, *latent*, ready *to spring forth.* (Italics mine).

One must grant the foregoing observations concerning the absence of a distinctive Vedic-Śaktic cult. There are, nonetheless, other considerations in our account of the goddess' emergence which, in fact, do bear significant relation to the feasibility of the Great Traditional recognition and acceptance of such a cult. Those considerations take the form of *Vedic* feminine deities which constitute legitimate and important "traces" (Renou) to be taken into account as part of the historical-traditional growth of the Śākta faith.

---

[285] Cf. R. G. Bhandakar, *Vaiṣṇavism, Śaivism, and Minor Religious Systems* (Strasburg : Karl J. Trubner, 1913), p. 142; Karmakar, *The Religions of India*, I, 96; Chattopadhyaya, *The Evolution of Theistic Sects in India*, p. 49.

[286] For the "Goddesses Mentioned in the Vedic Hymns", *vide* Sec. 20 of the same title in *Original Sanskrit Texts*, coll., trans., and illus. John Muir (3d ed.; 5 vols.; Amsterdam : Oriental Press, 1967), V, 337-349. For subsequent use of Muir's volumes, "Texts" will be referred to in the following manner : name of text, place (*O.S.T.*, Vol., and page); "commentary" by Muir *et al.* : Muir, Vol., and page. J. Muir's "Contributions to a Knowledge of the Vedic Theogony and Mythology" (including reference to Vedic goddesses) may also be found in the *Journal of the Royal Asiatic Society of Great Britain and Ireland*, New Series, I (1865), 51-140; *ibid.*, II (1866), 1-25, 26-43.

[287] Louis Renou, *The Nature of Hinduism*, trans. Patrick Evans (New York : Walker and Company, 1962), pp. 114-115.

[288] Alain Daniélou, *Hindu Polytheism* (New York : Random House, Inc., 1964), p. 256.

Parallel-and-Transitional Ciphers

Pṛthivī

Pṛthivī is the "Earth" (*pṛthivī*), or "the Extended One".[289] As a terranean Vedic deity, she is often seen in co-relation with her male counterpart, the celestial god Dyaus,[290] "in the compound Dyāvāpṛthivī, the Universal Parents, who are celebrated in six hymns".[291] Though neither of these divinities tends to have any well-defined anthropomorphic nature,[292] Pṛthivī in her symbolic capacity of the divinization of the earth (*tellus mater*) tends also to have "a status of her own".[293] For instance, it is noted that "often Heaven and Earth are called the 'two mothers', even when Dyaus is one of them. Thus, the Earth is besought to be 'kindly, full of dwellings and painless', and to give protection.[294] The dead are exhorted to 'go into kindly mother earth who will be wool-soft like a maiden'".[295]

It is in the Atharvavedan hymnic presentation of the goddess Pṛthivī that the "Earth" as a religious symbol receives its "broadest" and most inclusive manifestation.[296] The Atharva-Veda has long been recognized as having a more conspicuous popular character among the four classical Vedas. It also seems to provide a probable historical-religious link between the earliest Vedic period and the later emergence of other popular-oriented epics (or "purāṇas") such as the Mahābhārata

289 Taittirīya Samhita VII.1.5.1ff.; Taittirīya Brāhmaṇa I.1.3.5ff. (*O.S.T.*, I, 52, 53).

290 Cf. Eliade, *Patterns in Comparative Religion*, pp. 66f., 77f. Cf. *ibid.*, pp. 82-84.

291 V. M. Apte, "Religion and Philosophy", in Majumdar, *The History and Culture of the Indian People*, I, 364-365. *Vide* Ṛg-Veda I.159, 160, 185; IV.56, VI.70, VII.53. *Vide* Muir, V, 21-24. Cf. Eliade, *The Sacred and the Profane*, pp. 145ff.

292 Cf. Tucci, "Earth in Indian and Tibet, p. 329, i.e., "how difficult it is to disentangle the various elements which flow together in this archetype of Earth-Mother". *Vide ibid.*, pp. 325ff., 333, for earth image nominals in Sanskrit.

293 James, *The Cult of the Mother Goddess*, p. 101. Cf. *ibid.*, p. 243. *Vide* Ṛg-Veda VI.84 and cf. Bloomfield, *The Religion of the Veda*, p. 110.

294 James, *The Cult of the Mother Goddess*, p. 113. Cf. Crooke, *The Popular Religion ...*, I, 26ff., and II, 288, for the goddess Pṛthivī's connection with agrarian rites. For other mythic expressions, *vide* Viṣṇu Purāṇa I.4.1ff. (cf. *supra*, p. 101, n. 289); Liṇga Purāṇa I.4.59ff. (*O.S.T.*, IV, 36-39); Zimmer, *Myths and Symbols ...*, pp. 77ff. Cf. *supra*, pp. 61.

295 James, *The Cult of the Mother Goddess*, p. 133 (Ṛg-Veda I.22; I.5; X.18.10); Eliade, *Patterns in Comparative Religion*, p. 252 and nn. 2-6.

296 Atharva-Veda XII.

and the Rāmāyaṇa.[297] Pṛthivī is described in the Atharva-Veda [298] in terms which suggest not only her all-inclusive "motherhood" in the face of the vicissitudes of life on "earth"; but in the hymnic laudation there is also the suggestion of a cosmopolitan *Sitz im Leben* in which subsides

> on the earth, brown, black, ruddy and every-coloured, on the firm earth that Indra guards from danger.[299]

It is the "Earth as Motherland".[300] C. K. Raja says in this regard that the text shows that the poet sings of people "who live together without any over-crowding and mutual enmity. There is the picture of the happy humanity living on the earth on account of her Grace as a loving Mother".[301]

Sarasvatī

This goddess is usually consorted by or associated with the god Brahmā.[302] She has been called "the goddess of music, wisdom and knowledge, the mother of the Vedas".[303] But Sarasvatī has also been recognized as having linguistic and symbolic affinities with terranean realities.[304] For instance, her name "contains an allusion to a river" :[305] She is "the watery one" ;[306] and she can be iconographically depicted as a beautiful four-armed being whose personification of the virtues ini-

---

297 Cf. Bloomfield, *The Religion of the Veda*, pp. 40-43; Embree, *The Hindu Tradition*, pp. 36-41; Tucci, "Earth in India and Tibet", pp. 330-332. The Atharva-Veda is, nonetheless, not without its own deep and sophisticated passages : Embree, *The Hindu Tradition*, pp. 33, 23-24; *supra*, p. 82 and n. 203 of the same page.

298 Atharva-Veda XII.1ff., or Embree, *The Hindu Tradition*, p. 46.

299 Embree, *The Hindu Tradition*, p. 46.

300 Cf. *ibid.*, p. 45.

301 C. K. Raja, *Survey of Sanskrit Literature* (Bombay: Bharatiya Vidya Bhavan, 1962), p. 25.

302 *Vide* her consortive relation to "a river god, called Saraswat" in Ṛg-Veda VII.96.4-6 (Muir, V, 430). Cf. "Brahmā and Sarasvatī", including iconography, in *New Larousse Encyclopedia of Mythology*, Introduction by Robert Graves, trans. R. Aldington and D. Ames (rev. from French ed.; London : Paul Hamlyn, 1959), pp. 344-345.

303 Mahābhārata, Śānti-parvan 12920 (cf. Muir, III, 14, 10, 12).

304 This divinity can, however, have her *celestial* manifestations : "Ṛg-Veda V.43.11 (*O.S.T.*, V, 340), and in Ṛg-Veda VI.49.7 the epithet "daughter of the lightning" is applied to her. Cf. Ṛg-Veda VI.61.11f.

305 *New Larousse Encyclopedia of Mythology*, p. 344b.

306 James, *The Cult of the Mother Goddess*, p. 109.

tially mentioned correspond to a little drum and/or the *vina*, as well as a book of palm leaves.

Significant, however, is the thought that Sarasvatī might originally have been a river-godddss, or perhaps a goddess of the waters".[307] It is not unusual, therefore, to see her seated upon a lotus. E. O. James connects her with Vedo-Brāhmaṇic river-located rites,[308] and alludes to her historical-mythological transpositions in the sectarian tradition, especially among the Vaiṣṇavas of Bengal.[309]

Araṇyānī

Having various meanings attributed to her: "Goddess of Forest Solitude,,'[310] "Mother of Beasts",[311] or "Lady of the Forest",[312] this Vedic goddess arouses in us a peculiar fascination. Ragozin calls her hymn "a pretty thing".[313] She appears to enter our vision not as an object of mere Vedic research but almost surreptitiously, tending to invite contemplation instead of critical comment. Perhaps we should sympathize with A. L. Basham, who refers to her as "the elusive spirit of the forest".[314]

> Araṇyānī is lauded by the worshipper as the mother of wild, the unctuous-scented, the fragrant, who fields abundance of food though has no hinds to till her.[315]

---

307 *New Larousse Encyclopedia of Mythology*, p. 344b. *Vide* also Ṛg-Veda X.30.10-12; V.46.7, and Zimmer, *Myths and Symbols ...*, pp. 109ff.

308 James, *The Cult of the Mother Goddess*, p. 110; also Ṛg-Veda X.17.7-10, VIII.96. V, 339-341.

309 James, *The Cult of the Mother Goddess*, p. 110; Zimmer, *Myths and Symbols ...*, p. 88.

310 Muir, V, 346; cf. "the personified Forest": Zénaïde A. Ragozin, *The Story of Vedic India* (New York: G. P. Putman's Sons, 1895), p. 272.

311 James, *The Cult of the Mother Goddess*, p. 120. T. H. Griffith (cf. H. D. Smith, *Selections from the Videc Hymns*, p. 33) translates "Araṇyānī" as "Goddess of wild and forest ..."

312 Basham, *The Wonder That Was India*, p. 404. Cf. Crooke, *The Popular Religion ...*, I, 114f.; *supra*, p. 53.

313 Ragozin, *The Story of Vedic India*, p. 272; Ṛg-Veda X.146.

314 Basham, *The Wonder That Was India*, p. 404.

315 Ṛg-Veda X.146.6. We employ Muir's translation because of its "flavour"; he also renders a free metrical version of verses 1, 5, and 6 (Muir, V, 423). The use of "no hinds" suggests Araṇyānī's sovereignty over and independence of animals in the spirit of a true "Mother of the Beasts" or "the mother of all things wild". Basham (*The Wonder That Was India*, p. 404) notes the problem of variant translation. Cf., for example, this scholar's first verse: "Lady of the Forest/ ... who seems to vanish from sight in the distance/ why do you never come to the village ? /Surely you are not afraid of men"—with Ragozin's

Although this goddess appears to be just another vivid expression of Vedic man's religious apprehension of Nature, the hymn may well have been born out of the same contemplative milieu which eventually produced the kind of literary expressions known as the Āraṇyakas. These type of contemplative works tend to have a "transitional" status in Vedo-Brāhmanic history similar to that which the Atharva-Vrda has in relation to the three other Vedas : the Rig, Sāma, and Yajur Vedas. It is stimulating enough that they are called "Firest Books".[316] Moreover, they are said to have appeared "toward the end of the Brāhmana period, that is, c. 600 B.C. ..."[317]

> The exact implication of this term is uncertain, but it seems probable that these works were recited by hermits living in the forests ...[318] The Āranyakas contain transitional material between the mythology and ritual of the Samhitās and Brāhmanas on the one hand and the philosophical speculations of the Upanishads on the other. The ritual is given a symbolic meaning, and knowledge of this becomes more important than the actual performance of the ritual itself. This principle then becomes the starting point of Upanishadic speculation.[319]

No historically organic but rather a phenomenologically dynamic relation between the goddess Araṇyānī and the Āraṇyakas is posited here. This does not mean, however, that in an historico-phenomenological sense the two religious manifestations are unrelated to a certain milieu of *religious experience.* For it was more than likely the kind of creative interaction between man and Nature and man and his *religious* posterity which was the occasion for both the "discovery" of Araṇyānī and the graphic productions of the Aranyaka (or "Forest Priests").[320] Furthermore, although the goddess reveals some degree of ambivalence in her activities.[321] the philosophical-religious contem-

---

(and similarly Muir's, V, 423) : "Araṇyānī ... thou seemest to have lost thyself there; why doest thou not ask the way to the village ?/ Does terror not seize thee ?" Ragozin, *The Story of Vedic India*, pp. 272-273.

[316] I.e., Forest Texts. For Arani (*infra*, p. 121)/Aranya/Aranyaka, *vide* Raja, *Survey of Sanskrit Literature*, p. 35, aǹd also Sir Charles Eliot, *Hinduism and Buddhism : An Historical Sketch*, I (New York : Barnes and Noble, Inc., 1968), 87f. Cf. Campbell, *The Masks of God*, II, 197-203.

[317] De Bary, *Sources of Indian Tradition*, I, 24.

[318] For these and other types of ascetics, *vide* Basham, *The Wonder That Was India*, pp. 245-249, and also pp. 159f., 252.

[319] De Bary, *Sources of Indian Tradition*, I, 24; Swami Prabhavananda, *The Spiritual Heritage of India* (Garden City, New York : Doubleday and Co., Inc., 1963), p. 37.

[320] Cf. Eliot, *Hinduism and Buddhism*, III, 53; cf. *ibid.*, p. 54.

[321] Ṛg-Veda X.146.5 : "The Goddess never slays, unless some murderous enemy approach ..." (Griffith). On the whole, nonetheless, the mood of the hymn is "sensitive" (Basham), vivid, and gay.

plations by teachers at whose feet were to sit novices in spiritual sessions, would give birth to the interiorization of the wiles of the forest through a decisive integration of opposites (*coincidentia oppositorum*).[322]

Uṣas (Rātri/Diti)

The Goddess "Dawn" (Uṣas) is celebrated in several hymns of the Ṛg-Veda.[323] Her divinity in most naturally praised with numerous allusions to her various associations with "light";[324] and her lustrous though diverse manifestations or descriptions range from "Mother of the gods" (Ṛg-Veda I.113.19), "Daughter of the Sky", to "wife of the sun" (Ṛg-Veda VII.75.4). She rouses "into motion every living thing...," and "everything that moves bows down before her glance" (Ṛg-Veda I.92.9 and I.48.8).[325]

Uṣas' connection with a chariot drawn by steads (Ṛg-Veda I.113.14) becomes the focal point of her tense relations with the impetuous divinity Indra. The god destroys her celestial car which is presumed to be owned by an evil woman, and the indictment is that the "daughter of the sky ... was exalting herself" (Ṛg-Veda IV.30.9).

> The bright Uṣas was afraid of the destructive thunderbolt of Indra; she departed and abandoned her chariot. (Ṛg-Veda X.138.5.).

Dawn's chariot is not the chariot of war, like Indra's; but a chariot of resplendence whose occupant, the "young Dawn", does a part that constitutes her own quiet epic. She dispels the Darkness through the unstentorian spreading of light upon and before and ahead of the paths of men. The goddess Dawn's hymn is said to reflect "a vivid, colorful delight in the bounty of life's onward flow ..."[326]

The counterpart of Uṣas' resplendence is Rātrī, the Goddess of the Night (Ṛg-Veda X.127). As "the personified night"[327] she is the natural symbolic polarity of "her sister Dawn"; yet Rātrī expells the "Dawn" with a radiance of her own; so that "now darkness also dis-

---

322 Cf. Eliade, *Mephistopheles and the Androgyne*, pp. 82, 88ff., 92ff.; *Images and Symbols*, pp. 73ff.; *Patterns in Comparative Religion*, p. 420.

323 I.e., Ṛg-Veda I.48, 49, 92, 113, 123, 124; III.61; IV.51, 52; V.79, 80; VI.64, 65; VII.75-81; X.172.

324 E.g., Ṛg-Veda I.48.15; I.89; 92.1-5 ("Dawns"); 124.4; 62.2; 113.1, 2, 14.

325 Cf. *New Larousse Encyclopedia of Mythology*, p. 332b.

326 Campbell, *The Masks of God*, II, 180.

327 Basham, *The Wonder That Was India*, p. 404.

appears".[328] For though the goddess Rātrī is the "Night", she is essentially the "starry night", and daughter of Dyaus.[329] Thus, while the goddess Rātrī is the personification of the Night, she is a divinity who gives protection to persons during that period of time. Her hymn is often noted as one of beauty.

> The immortal goddess now has filled
> wide space, its depths and heights
> Her radiance drives out the dark.
> . . . .
> And so you have drawn near to us,
> who at your coming have come home,
> as birds to their nest upon the tree.[330]

Nirṛti

The faint mutual ambiguity [331] of Uṣas and Rātrī which does not endure because paradox prevails—the Night also casts out the Darkness—becomes with the goddess Nirṛti a stronger symbolic negation. Nirṛti is "the goddess of Evil",[332] or, as another scholar has put it, "the goddess of all evil".[333] She is also alluded to as the wife of one Adharma and the mother of Rākṣasas, her offspring, as well as three "terrible" sons : Bhaya, Mahābhaya, and Mṛtyu. This last is Death, the "ender of beings" who thus has no family of his own.[334]

It is observed that though Nirṛti is a divine representation of evil and "destruction", she is "an only halfway visualized and personified figure".[335] This means that the later, more visualized and personified Mahābhāratan symbolization of her may reflect the more vivid creation of the popular mind.[336] We are reminded (in another context)

---

328 *Ibid.*

329 Dikshitar, *The Lalitā Cult*, p. 46.

330 Cf. Basham, *The Wonder That Was India*, p. 404; Ṛg-Veda X.127.2, 4.

331 Cf. Ṛg-Veda I.124.8; 11.2, 3.

332 Dikshitar, *The Lalitā Cult*, p. 56.

333 Weber, in Chattopadhyaya, *The Evolution of Theistic Sects in India*, p. 51.

334 Mahābhārata, Ādi parvan 2617 (*O.S.T.*, I, 124.)

335 George Widengren, "The Principle of Evil in the Eastern Religions", in *Evil : Essays ...*, ed. The Curatorium of C. G. Jung Institute, Zurich (Evanston : Northwestern University Press, 1967), p. 27.

336 Cf. Sukumari Bhattacharji, *The Indian Theogony : A Comparative Study of Indian Mythology from the Vedas to the Purāṇas* (Cambridge : At the University Press, 1970), p. 85 : "Although Nirṛti virtually disappears in the epic-Purāṇic age, her functions are discharged by other deities and her evocative associations are distributed among goddesses like Kālī, Karalī, Cāmuṇḍā, Chinnamastā, Manasā and such other minor, sectarian and regional goddesses".

of the "faineant" character of certain divinities in primitive culture. Such beings have formed part of the recurrent controversy of "Primitive Monotheism" (or the search for "Supreme Beings").[337] With Nirṛti, nonetheless, even a pre-Mahābhāratan, Vedic verse renders a most apprehensive protrayal of her as a divinity to be feared. Hence the suppliant entreats the gods Soma and Rudra to

> Chase Nirṛti far away from us
> May we have excellent renown [338]

Vāc/Vāgdevī

In the symbol Vāc (the Goddess of Speech) we encounter the potentiality of a Vedic "female" divinity for having a role which merits the modification of the oft-held opinion that there are no goddesses of considerable status in the Vedas.[339] For Vāc appears not only to have a type of divine ambiguity [340] but also to be present in numerous texts of the Vedo-Brāhmaṇic tradition. Her merely apparent but relative omnipresence in various *texts*, however, is not the thing to which we would call special attention.

As a goddess of "Speech", of course, the great mythological potentiality noted seems to be ultimately related to the serious emphasis placed upon the "Word" or the "utterance" of words in Vedic sacrifices.[341] The cosmic structure of the sacrifices makes it symbological that Vāc is conceived as having been present at the beginning, pervading all things.[342] Generated by the gods and envisioned as a Holy Cow yet "queen of the gods", she is first heard to "speak" of "unintelligible things"; but men praise her because she nourishes and sustains them.[343] It is she who not only enabled the men of old to obtain the *soma*, but can, too, be petitioned by (and *as*) the Holy Word (Vāc Sarasvatī)

---

337 Eliade, *Patterns in Comparative Religion*, p. 43; Paul Radin, *Primitive Religion* (New York : Dover Publications, Inc., 1957), p. 266.

338 Ṛg-Veda VI.74.2; cf. Ṛg-Veda VII.37.7; *vide* Gonda, *Change and Continuity in Indian Religion*, p. 151. For a ritual exemplification of the quest to turn Nirṛti away through homage, *vide* Bhattacharji, *The Indian Theogony*, p. 81.

339 Ṛg-Veda X.125.

340 Śatapatha Brāhmaṇa VI.1.1.9.

341 *Vide infra*, p. 108, n. 344; Gonda, *Change and Continuity in Indian Religion*, p. 364.

342 Śatapatha Brāhmaṇa VI.1.1.9.

343 Ṛg-Veda VIII.89.10-11; also Bṛhad Āranyaka Upaniṣad V.8.1. On Vāc's "unintelligible things, *vide* Muir, II, 213.

for the sake of gaining "Faith" (*śraddhā*) through *soma*.[344] In fact, Vāc, whose ultimate source and the ground of whose activities is Brahman is both formed of the Vedas as well as mother of the Vedas.[345] She is, therefore, the goddess who "inspired" the ancient Ṛṣis and gave men a sacred promise.[346]

The goddess Vāc's most primordial and cosmic status is more than suggested by the fact that she was present at the beginning (*supra*). This goddess is, again, associated with Prajāpati as both a consort as well as a power through whom the cosmogony is effected.[347] Hence

> Prajāpati was the universe
> Vāch was a second to him
> He associated sexually with her;
> she became pregnant;
> she departed from him;
> she produced these creatures;
> she again entered into Prajāpati.[348]

Elsewhere Prajāpati says

> "Let me send forth this Vāch
> She will traverse and pervade all this"
> He sent her forth ... she extended
> aloft, diffused like a stream of water.[349]

Finally, this Goddess of Speech has an exalted status implied in her discovery by the Ṛṣis. For when they "followed the path" (or "came upon the track of speech") through sacrificial rites, they "found her entered into the rishis" (Ṛg-Veda X.71.3). The commentator (Muir) notes that this means "that Vāch already existed when she was discovered". The thrust of the specific cosmological interpretation, however, rests upon the consideration of a continual paradoxical relationship between "history" and "religion" is one's approach to Vedic thought; that is, the (religious) assumption of the

---

[344] Aitareya Brāhmaṇa I.27; Śataphata Brāhmaṇa III.2.4.1ff.; Atharva-Veda V.7.1, 5. Cf. Bloomfield, *The Religion of the Veda*, pp. 186-191.

[345] Taittirīya Brāhmaṇa II.8.8.5; cf. Śatapatha Brāhmaṇa 14.4.3.12; Mahābhārata, Śānti parvan 8533 (*O.S.T.*, III, 9, 10, 16).

[346] Ṛg-Veda X.71.3; cf. I.37.4; X.125.5.

[347] *Vide* Weber, *Indische Studien*, IX, 477f., cited in Muir, V, 391f.

[348] Kāṭhaka XII.5; cf. Śatapatha Brāhmaṇa X.6.5.4 (*O.S.T.*, V, 392).

[349] Pañchavimsa Brāhmaṇa XX.14.2. *Vide* mythic variations and commentary on "Prajāpati's status", Muir, V, 392; *ibid.*, pp. 390-393.

eternity of the Vedas [350] alongside the observer's knowledge of the (historical) priority of the participants or practitioners of the Vedic "words" as Speech (Vāc).[351]

Vāc is understood in the highest sense, when it is observed that in the Bṛhad Āranyaka Upaniṣad that this goddess is co-identified with the traditional Ultimate Reality of Hindu religion and philosophy : "By speech alone, Your Majesty, Brahman is known, speech, indeed, O King, is the Highest Brahman".[352]

Aditi

The Ṛg-Vedic divinity, among the thirty and three divinities [353] who appears to us as the most exalted "female" symbolization of the sacred is the goddess Aditi. The question of the exact derivation and significance of her name is probably capable of various plausible answers. A textual aetiology, for example, accounts for the name through an association with the idea of food;[354] the notion, however, is doubtless culto-linguistic in intention and context, having only indirect bearing upon her precise origins. The opinions of scholars are many, though it is noticeable that such opinions tend to be variations on a specific orientation : towards "the Unbounded".

Consistent with an "astral" mythological hermeneutics, Max Müller regarded Aditi as "the earliest name invented to express the Infinite";[355] moreover, the goddess was not the product of ratiocination but an immediate apprehension of the "visible Infinite" beyond earth, clouds and sky".[356] Other explanations (e.g., Böhtlingh and Roth) account for the name in terms similar to Müller; but they suggest another sense of the word in connection with the general notion of boundlessness, i.e., "inviolability", "imperishableness"—yet boundlessness and infiniteness are understood in contrast to "the

---

350 *Supra*, pp. 69f.

351 The commentary is interesting in its implications for Vāc, especially the Vedāntic interpretations. *Vide* Muir, III, 98-108, Chap. I, "Opinions Regarding the Origin, Division, Inspiration and Authority of the Vedas. ..."

352 Bṛhad Āraṇyaka Upaniṣad IV.1.2, in *The Upaniṣads* (Sacred Books of the East, Vol. I, Part II; Oxford: The Clarendon Press, 1897), p. 153; cf. Brhad Āraṇyaka Upaniṣad I.3.20-21.

353 Ṛg-Veda I.34.11.

354 Bṛhad Āraṇyaka Upaniṣad I.2.5b.

355 Quoted in Muir, V, 37.

356 *Ibid.*

finiteness of the earth, and its spaces".[357] Oldenberg and others emphasize the designation of Aditi as "liberty, absence of bonds", or even "free from bonds".[358] We employ the word "Unbounded", because this goddess' status in the Ṛg-Veda is highly fluid, despite her potentiality for symbolic magnification. She then can thus express the Unbounded *both* in terranean and celestial terms. For Aditi is also associated with the Earth (*pṛthivī*) which, in a sense, might be conceived as the "unbounded" earth or expanse or wide.[359]

As the "goddess", the "divine", or the "irresistible goddess",[360] Aditi, again, has her familial associations. She is the daughter of Dakṣa (and she is the "mother" of Dakṣa !). This paradox is an extremely interesting one in Ṛg-Vedic mythology and has invited commentary.[361] Aditi's sons are the Ādityas, seven, eight, or twelve in number;[362] and, in later mythology, the god Viṣṇu appears to be a divinity born of her as the last or youngest son.[363] The intensity of the paradox is increased by the familial status of Dakṣa himself as the father of the gods,[364] just as Aditi is the mother of the gods.

Although posited as the Infinite by Müller and others, Aditi is also encountered as a goddess who *acts*.[365] She is not only Mother of the gods, the mother of excellent sons, kings, and heroes, but men appeal to her and her celestial family for protection in their verbal petitions.[366]

The divine supremacy, it seems, of the goddess Aditi is based upon two notable factors—which, interestingly, tend to apply to other Ṛg-Vedic divinities : (1) her associability or mutual identification with other deities of potentially "unbounded" status; and (2) her own peculiarities with regard to theological qualities which, probably, relate to her very name itself. In the first case, if we recall,

---

357 *Ibid.*

358 Cf. B. S. Upadhyaya, *Women in Rigveda* (Benares : Nand Kishore and Brothers' 1941), pp. 3-8; *New Larousse Encyclopedia of Mythology*, p. 333b.

359 Cf. Muir, V, 35; cf. Ṛg-Veda V.46.6 : "widely expanded" (Muir, V, 46).

360 Muir, V, 46.

361 Ṛg-Veda X.72.45; cf. X.90.5. *Vide* Yāska's commentary in Muir, IV, 13.

362 Ṛg-Veda IX.114,3; X.72.8, 9; Śatapatha Brāhmaṇa IX.6.3.8.

363 Mahābhārata I.2522, 2600; Rāmāyaṇa I.32.14, 19 (*O.S.T.*, IV, 118, 134); *ibid.*, V, 53 (Vājasaneya Samhitā 29.60; Taittirīya Samhitā VII.5.14.1). Aditi is represented as the spouse of Viṣṇu.

364 Ṛg-Veda VI.50.2; 66.2. Cf. Dakṣa as Creator : Śatapatha Brāhmaṇa II.4.4.2.

365 Ṛg-Veda VII.35.9; Atharva-Veda XIX.10.9.

366 Ṛg-Veda VIII.101.15; I.153.3; Atharva-Veda VI.4.1.

the goddess Vāc tended to have her "cosmogonic" status increased (but not decisively) through her association with both Prajāpati and the supreme Brahman. Aditi, likewise, has been identified symbologically with Vāc (i.e., Voice, Speech)![367] The semblance of deistic ambiguity arises in connection with the mytho-nominal doublet: Aditi/Diti, who seem to constitute intentional symbolic antitheses,[368] much like those "*naktośasā* (a dual feminine word)"[369] which we find elsewhere in Indian mythological thought.

The cosmic range of Aditi's religious symbolization is most fully apprehended by the thought that she might be a personification of the all-embracing realm of Nature. That is to say (Ṛg-Veda I.89.10):

> Aditi is the heaven;
> Aditi is the atmosphere;
> Aditi is mother, and is father,
> she is son;
> Aditi is all the gods (*viśvadeva*)
> and is five sorts of beings;
> Aditi is that which is born,
> Aditi is that which is to be born.

It is the height, breadt and depth of this hymnic imagery and praise of Aditi which so exhilarated Jean Przyluski, leading that scholar to postulate that this goddess is probably "akin to the Great Goddess of Asia Minor ..."[370] Przyluski's claim was that "in the Vedic mythology, the gods have a limited power and they have ascendancy over the goddesses. Aditi, however, is an exception to this rule: her sovereignty is unlimited and she is superior to the gods".[371]

At any rate, the same scholar further acknowledges that, though, here, we may be "close upon monotheism", "a monotheistic conception is not yet realized".[372]

Granting their lofty roles, functions, and attributes, it would still seem that Aditi (and other divinities such as Vāc and Rātrī) represent a peculiar phenomenon in Vedic mythology. Max Müller

---

367 Muir, V, 35.

368 Ṛg-Veda V. 62.8; *supra*, pp. 97, n. 275.

369 Cf. Eliade, *Patterns in Comparative Religion*, p. 145.

370 Przyluski, "The Great Goddess of India and Iran", p. 413.

371 *Ibid.*, pp. 412f.

372 *Ibid.*, p. 418. Cf. Griswold, *The Religion of the Rig Veda*, pp. 108-110, 347, 348. Cf. Roth, *Journal of the German Oriental Society*, VI, 68f., quoted in Muir, V, 37.

used to refer to it as *henotheism* or *kathenotheism* :[373] the presence of a tendency in the inchoate orchestra of divinities of the Ṛg-Veda to play "solo" parts (i.e., roles, function, attributes) which, occasionally, impress us as unique; but which never completely drown out similar capacities and powers of other divine players in the background... "ready to spring forth" (Danielou).

Before proceeding to discuss aspects of the mythic and *sectarian* magnification of the goddess Durgā-Kālī, further observations need to be made concerning the foregoing Vedic divinities : Pṛthivī, Sarasvatī, Araṇyānī, Uṣas, Rātrī, Nirṛti, Vāc, and Aditi.

We hardly need to reiterate that the Vedic repertoire of "female" divinities is far more extensive than these that are treated here. Their appropriateness as choices, nonetheless, resides not only in the fact that they, too, tend to illustrate the phenomenon of henotheism; such divinities are also in all probability the kinds of mythological religious symbols which, as we earlier indicated, served as "parallel and transitional ciphers" that facilitated the mythic and cultic, and symbolic characterization of the goddess Durgā-Kālī in role, function, and attributes in the later Purāṇic and Tantric literary formations.

The literary-historical plausibility of this vital Vedic-Hinduist continuity has been enhanced by B. L. Mukherji [374] with regard to several basic ideas and practices : gods and goddesses, symbols and gestures, rites and purposes. For now, we are primarily concerned with the mytho-nominal symbolizations, that is, "female" divinities. Mukherji finds a Sarasvatī/Kālī/Durgā correspondence suggested in the Vedic portrait of Sarasvatī in the Nighantu and other ideas in the Sāma-Vidhāna Brāhmaṇa (III.8).[375] Her expression of "nudeness" and "that age of a woman when womanhood has not expressed itself"[376] (analogous to "Kumārī" ?) are cases in point. He refers, again, to deonominations that are found in Bṛhaddevatā (II.79), where the god-

[373] Cf. Renou (*Religions of Ancient India*, p. 12) who notes that, though Müller's use of the term "was later ridiculed ... it expressed his meaning, and represents a permanent feature of Indian thought, which is especially noticeable in Śaktism. It is the tendency of a worshipper to ascribe the attributes of other gods to the particular deity whom he is honouring". *Vide* also Bloomfield, *The Religion of the Veda*, pp. 164, 199; E. W. Hopkins, *Ethics of India* (New Haven : Yale University Press, 1924), pp. 35-38.

[374] In John G. Woodroffe, *Śakti and Śākta* (5th ed.; Madras : Ganesh and Co. Private, Ltd., 1959), pp. 103-113.

[375] *Ibid.*, p. 110.

[376] *Ibid.*, p. 111. It is also noticed that Sarasvatī receives animal sacrifices (*ibid.*).

desses Aditi, Vāc, Sarasvatī, and Durgā are mentioned as being the same divinity; and Vāc's metamorphosis into a lion appears to the scholar as an item which explains "how Durgā has a lion to carry her".[377] Vāc's alliance with the Devas, with her stipulation that offerings be made to her prior to the god Agni,[378] has interesting significance for Mukherji. For, somehow (though it cannot seem unusual in Indian mythology) Vāc (or Vāgdevī) and Rātrī are sometimes worshipped interchangeably,[379] the goddess Rātrī being "substantially' the same with, but in form different from", the Goddes of Speech.[380]

Rātrī, it appears, is described most appropriately in her *sūkta* as having a black colour;[381] and the Pariśiṣṭa portion of the Ṛg-Veda [382] (vss. 5 and 13) allows us to draw an even more intimate symbolic connection between Rātrī Devī and Durgā. Of the most interesting significance is Mukherji's observation of the symbological association of Durgā with the "Tongues of Agni". In the Ṛg-Vedic Pariśiṣṭa, then, Rātrī Devī (or now, symbologically, Durgā-Rātrī) is referred to as the "carrier of oblations" and thus associable with the sacrificial fire.[383] The scholar, therefore, understands Durga (-Agni) to possess the Vedic god's traditional tongues (of fire) which are these: Kālī (black), Karālī (terrific), Manojava (swift as thought), Sulohitā (very red), Sudhūmravarṇā (purple), Sphulingini (sparkling), and Śucismitā (or probably, Viśvarūpā: "having all forms").[384]

Accordingly, another scholar [385] postulates the following:

> The first two of these names were at a later period personified, and came to represent Durgā (the consort of Śiva, who has developed out of Agni), who (Durgā) ... became the object of bloody sacrificial-worship under the names Kālī (the dark, black), Karālā, Karālevadanā, Karālānanā, Karālamukhi. It is evident that a considerable

---

377 *Ibid.*, p. 112.

378 *Ibid.*, p. 109.

379 *Ibid.*, p. 110.

380 *Ibid.*

381 Ṛg-Veda X.127.7.

382 I.e., "the *Rātrī-Pariśistha* between the fourteenth and fifteenth divisions of the seventh section of the eight Ashṭaka of the R.V. (i.e. between Maṇḍala X.127 and 128". *Vide* Muir, IV, 427; also Appendix note i, 497-500.

383 *Ibid.* ("bearer"). Cf. Ṛg-Veda X.6.4; Taittirīya Brāhmaṇa II.4.1.6 (*O.S.T.*, IV, 499) and II.4.1.7 (O.S.T., IV, 427).

384 Mukherji, in Woodroffe, *Śakti and Śākta*, p. 110. *Vide* also Muṇḍaka Upaniṣad I.2.4 (Sacred Books of the East, Vol. I) for these "tongues" (Muir, IV, 429, for text and commentarv).

385 Weber, *Indische Studien*, I, 286f., quoted in Muir, IV, 429-430.

> time was required for the sense of the word to become developed from that of the "dark, terrific, tongue of fire" to that of a goddess Kālī, Karālā, worshipped with bloody sacrifices : and since we find the latter in the drama of "Mālati-Mādhava", by Bhavabhūti who is assigned by Wilson to the eighth century,[386] the Muṇḍaka Upanishad must be considerably older; unless ... the ancient signification of these names maintained itself at a later period alongside of the popular one.

The coalescence of the appellations Durgā [387] and Kāli is partially seen by Weber as related to at least two specific factors. First, the Ṛg-Veda alludes to the god Agni as one disposed to aid the worshipper to overcome "all 'durga' and 'durita' (difficulties and evils").[388] Weber understands Durgā here, however, as having originally had a positive role and function; so that even her association with Agni's "violent flame",[389] similar to fire per se, was *religiously* conceived as something which "delivers, atones, and frees from" evils and difficulties; Durgā was, then, essentially "a protecting fortress against them" much like the character of Ambikā, Śiva, and Umā.[390] Secondly, Durgā's eventual connection with Evil (e.g., the personification, Durgati) is related to her connection with Śiva (as Rudra) and, again, with Agni (via the "tongue", Karālī). In this latter *negative* symbolization (i.e., with Evil), Weber considers that Durgā's malevolence might "have arisen out of Nirṛiti ... at a later period", when "the original signification had been lost".[391] This association of the goddess Durgā with Vedic Nirṛti was also made by Mukherji in his attempt to establish the mythic and cultic continuity between the Vedas and the Tantras :[392]

> Nirṛti is black and is a terrible Devī and punishes those who do not offer Soma to her. She is the Devī of misfortunes and removes all misfortunes. She is the genetrix and she is fond of the cremation ground (S.B. VII. 2.1; A.B. IV.2.4).[393]

---

[386] Cf. Louis Renou, *Hinduism* (New York : George Braziller, 1962), pp. 187f.; 246, n. 35.

[387] I.e., "... she who is 'difficult (*dur*) to go against (*ga*)'; that is to say, 'the unassailable, unconquerable one'". Zimmer, *The Art of Indian Asia*, I, 90-91. Other variations are these : "the Inaccessible" (Renou and Dowson); "the Goddess-Beyond-Reach" (Danielou); "difficult of approach" (Campbell). Cf. Durgā (Mahābhārata VI, Virāta Parvan), the goddess who "savest ('rescues') men from difficulty"; who (*ibid.*, Bhīṣma Parvan—Sec. XXIII) dwells in "inaccessible regions" (*H.T.T.G.*, pp. 144, 156).

[388] Ṛg-Veda I.99 (Muir, IV, 427f.)

[389] Cf. Ṛg-Veda V.2.4, 6; VI.10.4; VII.8.2; VIII.23.19; and also I.143.5; V.41.10; VI.60.10.

[390] Muir, IV, 428.

[391] *Ibid.*

[392] In Woodroffe, *Śakti and Śākta*, p. 113.

[393] *Ibid.*, p. 112.

It is immediately apparent that Weber's notion of the symbolic odyssey of Durgā has a chronological (evolutionary) character: benevolent Durgā to malevolent Durgā, with a divine ambiguity implied only insofar as the "fire" of Durgā is a "violent flame". Mukherji, nonetheless, attributes both a malevolence and a benevolence to Nirṛti herself. This should make us recall the almost omnipresent ambiguity of character in Hindu divinities and, therefore, realize that even Rudra (-Śiva) and Durgā (-Karālī) reflect the same phenomenon.

A brief but critical review of the foregoing remarks warrants at once that we recognize the inevitable partiality or incompleteness of all attempts to tell the "story" of Durgā-Kālī within a framework of *mere* Vedic-Tantric continuity. Such a procedure, though componential, has only a relative degree of validity and thus tends to betray a rather reductionist character. The problem is far more complex and allows no easy solution.

We come closer to a reasonable solution of the process of mythological magnification with regard to Durgā-Kālī, when we consider other factors in addition to those already discussed. Those factors, though literary, cannot be dealt with outside of the context of religion (especially religious *experience*) and culture (i.e., a specific orientation). Culturally it has already been shown that the term *kālī* in all probability was not of Vedic origin; that it belongs properly to what has been considered the "Dravidian Strain", or, at least, a non-Vedic milieu.[394] A partial synthesis of the previous remarks begins with the fact that the *name* Kālī does not appear in the Ṛg-Vedic literary deposit.[395] When it does occur, however, it is in materials which appear to be in peripheral or in transitional relation to the four classical Vedas. Incidentally, the "popular" aspect of the Atharva-Veda need not indicate a chronological advancement but, perhaps, a coming of the popular element to the fore.

The stimulating question of how the names Kālī, Karālī did in fact enter into these "Vedic" literary extensions—Brāhmaṇas, Āraṇyakas, or Upaniṣads, etc.—we feel, has much to do with the factor of religious experience notwithstanding the existence of other "profane" forces. This is only one reason that we cannot agree with A. L. Basham's comment that "Araṇyānī, the Lady of the Forest", is

---

394 *Supra*, p. 82f.

395 Cf. H. H. Wilson on the Ṛg-Veda in Muir, II, 201.

"a nature goddess of little importance who is praised in one very *late* hymn", playing no "significant part in the cult [italics mine]".[396] Indeed, it is precisely the probability that the goddess Araṇyānī represents a *late* but still a type of *mytho-nominal paradigm* in the context of Indian religion and culture that concerns us. For this divinity is a product of "forest" contemplation. She suggests the beginnings of a new trend and period of spiritual apprehension in Indian religion which challenges our historical-religious imagination. Such a period has the character of a "twilight zone" between the classical Vedic-Brāhmaṇic sacramentarian tradition and the ascetic-Yogic-Upaniṣadic subjectivization of much of the objective ritual intentions of the former.[397]

The important thing to realize is that the process of Sanskritization that even underlies the literary magnification of the goddess Durgā-Kālī was derived *in part* from non-Vedic, ascetic, yogic, and mystical experience *as well as* Vedo-Brāhmaṇic ascetic-yogic and mystical experience. The mere fact that an eventual *literati* will commence to dominate the orthopraxis does not signify either that the new, radical, subjectivist "interiorization"[398] of earlier sacramentarian intentionalities was contemplated or experienced by heterodoxists alone; or that the traditional objectivist redintegration of cosmic realities (e.g., Puruṣa/Prajāpati)[399] has no part in the making of "Forest Philosophy".[400]

To be sure, what we merely sense in the Araṇyānī/Āraṇyaka symbolic-literary correlation becomes more strongly manifest in the Kena Upaniṣad.[401] Here a "popular" mountain goddess, Umā, appears to have undergone a decisive mythic-magnification process, rendering

---

396 Basham, *The Wonder That Was India*, p. 235.

397 Eliade discusses this important phenomenon, "Yoga and Brāhmanism", in *Yoga*, Chap. III, pp. 101-142.

398 *Ibid.*, pp. 111ff. The author (*ibid.*. pp. 102f.) notes, briefly, that the Yogic vogue, as a striking "phenomenon of Hinduization", incorporates "two traditions : (1) that of the ascetics and ecstatics, documented from the time of the Ṛg-Veda, and (2) the symbolism of the Brāhmaṇas, especially the speculations justifying the "interiorization of sacrifices".

399 Cf. *supra*, p. 93, n. 257. Cf. Renou, *Hinduism*, pp. 64f., 66f., 82f.

400 *Supra*, pp. 103-105.

401 Cf. Paul Deussen, *The Philosophy of the Upanishads*, trans. A. S. Geden (Edinburgh: T and T Clark, 1919), pp. 2-7, esp. p. 3 : "Even ... if in the schools of the Sāmaveda the name Āraṇyaka is not employed [see listed Sāmaveda—Kena (Talavakāra) Upanishad—p. 7], yet there also the introductions to the Upanishads (note 1) bear throughout the character of Āraṇyakas".

her the status of mystagogue of the gods. The gods (Agni, Vāyu, Indra) having failed to perceive who the "spectre" (*yakṣa*)[402]was—to the last divinity, Indra, she reveals *the* Yakṣa to be "Brahman" : "the life-force of the Universe that secretly dwells within all things".[403] Heinrich Zimmer calls our attention to the idea that

> In this episode of the Kena Upanishad,[404] where the mother goddess appears for the first time in the orthodox religious and philosophical tradition of India, she—womanhood incarnate—becomes the guru of the male gods. She is represented as their mystagogue, their initiator into the most profound and elementary secret of the universe ... her own essence.[405]

What concerns us most is that one observe that a text, estimated to date around the seventh century B.C., shows us already the mythological magnification of a "parochial" divinity, Umā Haimāvatī ("Daughter of the Snowy Mountain").[406] For we maintain that a similar phenomenon has occurred with regard to the names "Kālī", "Karālī", for example, in the Muṇḍaka Upaniṣad.[407] There is basically a mutual soteriological intention in these texts, a difference probably existing with regard to their functional contexts. The mythological context of the "victory" of the gods in the Kena Upaniṣad is doubtless the Devāsurasangrāma : the conflict between the Devas and Asuras, and the conquest of the latter by the former.[408] The "rituological" context of the Muṇḍaka Upaniṣad's reference to the "tongues of Agni" is a mantrayānic though *not* a sacrificial one. That is to say, soteriologically, the latter (as well as the Kena Upaniṣad) has as a didactic intention the pre-eminence of attaining "the highest knowledge, the knowledge of Brahman, which cannot be obtained either by sacrifices or by worship (upāsana) but by such teaching only as is imparted in the Upanishad".[409] Yet here, again, it is not beyond the realm of

---

402 Cf. *supra*, p. 51.

403 Cf. Campbell, *The Masks of God*, II, 204, 205.

404 I.e., Kena Upaniṣad III.11, 12 and IV.1-2. For commentary and interpretive variation, *vide* Muir, IV, 420-425; also T. M. P. Mahadevan, trans., *The Kena Upaniṣad* (Madras : Ganesh and Co. Private, Ltd., 1958).

405 Campbell, *The Masks of God*, II, 205.

406 *Supra*, p. 48.

407 Muṇḍaka Upaniṣad I.2.4.

408 Kena Upaniṣad III.1, 2; Campbell, *The Masks of God*, II, 204. Zimmer : "Ours, indeed, is this victory! Ours the glory!' Brahman, therefore, understood their pride and appeared before them; but they did not know what Brahman was".

409 Max Muller, "Introduction", to *The Upanishads* (Sacred Books of the East, Vol. I, Part II), p. xxvi; *vide*, however, "lightning" in the Kena Upaniṣad IV.4f. Cf.

probability that the adoption of the non-Āryan term *kālī* ("black") or karālī ("terrific") may indeed reflect the discreet assimilation and adaptation of a *goddess*: Kālī (i.e., the Black One). Similarly, in a mythological sense, the designation Viśvarūpī ("having all forms") might analogically present itself so easily as symbologically associable with the deity Viśvakarman. It would mean the continuity between "act" and "form",[410] just as Kālī, Black/Kālī, the Black One would mean, potentially, the homologative correspondance between "tongue" and "body".

Yet this amounts to no invitation to adopt a simplistic *nomina numina* formula for Kālī, Black in relation to Kālī, the Black Goddess. For we submit that the ("Dravidian") goddess Kālī was *already a divinity* as well as a personification of "forest phenomena" and "forest contemplation" *before* her actual association with the god Agni. There is, then, no overwhelming reason to believe that the process need to have involved a passage from the more abstract (neuter or adjectival) to the personificatory as Weber claims.[411] In the most general terms it means that the ascetic, yogic, or mytstical tendencies that availed were then capable of varying responsive representations of religious self-abnegation, self-control, or self-transcendence. In rather specific terms it would signify that we might plausibly *reverse* (i.e., "explode") Weber's procedure and entertain another religious phenomenologic: that a "multiplicity of hierophanies"[412] presented themselves to the diversity of *homines religiosi* who existed during the Vedic period (usually 1500-800 B.C.) but particularly beyond that period (*ca.* 800-200 B.C.);[413] and that whether or not the "ancient signification"[414] of Kālī, Karālī, etc., is fairly old or coexisted with other popular notions (i.e., personifications) at a later time—no requirement of "considerable time"[415] for *nomen* to *numen* is a necessary hypothesis. What did in fact require considerable time was the

---

Muller, *The Upanishads*, p. 152, n. 1. Cf. Eliade, *Images and Symbols*, p. 75. *Vide* Umā as "Brahmanvidyā" (*infra*).

410 Cf. Ṛg-Veda V.63, where Agni, for example, combines both the characteristics of *viśvakarman* and *viśvarūpa*; he is said to have "stretched out the whole universe, and, though one, to exist in manifold shapes" (*O.S.T.*, IV, 501).

411 *Supra*, pp. 113f.

412 Cf. Eliade, *Patterns in Comparative Religion*, pp. 10ff.

413 Brandon, *Man and His Destiny in the Great Religions*, p. 307 and n. 1.

414 Weber, *supra*, pp. 114.

415 See *ibid.* I.e., a development from descriptive function (black tongue of fire) to theistic nomination (black goddess of sacrificial worship).

process of "orthodoxizing" (i.e., bringing the goddess Kālī [-Durgā] and other like phenomena) within the realm of the Great Tradition on acceptable terms.

Epic and Purāṇic Transitions

The historical and traditional interstices which remain in the account of the goddess Durgā-Kālī's emergence to *sectarian* prominence take the more crucial form not of Tantras but that body of literature known as the Purāṇas and/or the Itihāsas. The graphic relevance of this statement becomes evident as soon as we consider, for example, the quite interesting text, the Mārkaṇḍeya Purāṇa, which might well stand between the Muṇḍaka Upaniṣad and the Mālatī-Mādhava of Bhavabhūti.

Pargiter and Agrawala estimate that the Mārkaṇḍeya Purāṇa is "a product of the Gupta Age and that its redaction had been finalized by the time of Chandragupta Vikramaditya at the end of the 4th century A.D."[416] Even granting the variability of this date (i.e., the Devī-Māhātmya is regarded as the latest portion and extends not beyond the ninth century), the portion of interest to us at present (chap. 99) is still considered part of the original Purāṇa (chaps. 45-81, 93-136, respectively) which was "very probably in existence in the third century, and perhaps even earlier ..."[417]

In the textual section mentioned (specifically, 99.52-58) reference is made to the "tongues of fire" of the god Agni. Of Kālī and Karālī (vss. 52-53) it is said" "By the tongue Kālī, the final destroyer (of the world), preserve us from sins and from great present alarm. By thy tongue Karālī, the cause of the great mundane dissolution, preserve us ..."[418] It is indeed a hymn to Agni; but it is also clear that, there, we are not dealing with Kālī as a hyperbolic or somatic-symbolic description of the god Agni. Kālī, Karālī, etc., are here beginning to assume cosmic soteriological "functions" though still in traditional relation to the Vedic deity. Yet the implications of the foregoing

---

416 Cf. V. S. Agrawala, *The Glorification of the Great Goddess* (Ramnagar, Varanasi: All-India Kashiraj Trust, 1963), p. iv. For literary-historical data on the Mārkaṇḍeya Purāṇa (including the Devī-Māhātmya) *vide ibid.*, the Preface, pp. i-xiv; F. E. Pargiter, trans., *The Mārkaṇḍeya Purāna* (Calcutta : The Asiatic Society of Bengal, 1904), pp. iv-xii; Hazra, *Studies in the Purāṇic Record*, Chap. II, pp. 8-13.

417 Pargiter, *The Mārkaṇḍeṇa Purāna*, p. xx.

418 Cf. Muir, IV, 500.

considerations for Weber's remarks are that in the case of Kālī, we are met with more than a word (i.e., "dark", terrific, or "tongue of fire") but as much and more, a *divinity*, a *goddess*, whose representation as a tongue of Agni *both* in the Muṇḍaka Upaniṣad and the Mārkaṇḍeya Purāṇa marks a literary-historical process which cannot be ultimately separated from the phenomenon of religious experience. On the one hand, that experience came into paradigmatic focus in the milieu of the *vānaprastha* (with this contemplative "forest" orientation) which, so naturally, took the form of an esoteric [419] philosophicalization of a mythic reality (i.e., Umā as *Brahmavidyā*).[420] On the other hand, that experience found another exemplary center of gravity in the milieu of the Śākta or the Bhakta (with his devotional "iconic" orientation) which so appropriately took the form of an exoteric, mythic symbolization : Kāli (-Agni)-Karālī, as the "final destroyer ... the cause of the mundane dissolution [of sin and suffering]".

When we come to the great Indian epic, the Mahābhārata,[421] and a supplement of it, the Harivamśa,[422] the account fo the goddess introduces elements which, apart from the item of literary chronology, render a more complex picture of Durgā-Kālī. Amidst that complex characterization, nevertheless, there are references to role, function, and attributes that have great significance for our previous discussion.

The goddess (as Durgā and/or Kālī) is referred to in two specific hymns of the Mahābhārata,[423] as well as two portions of the Harivamśa.[424] The manifold imagery of praise for the goddess reveals at least the following significant things : (1) there are mythonominal symbols of continuity in the form of "female" divinities drawn from the Vedas;

---

[419] Cf. Deussen, *The Philosophy of the Upanishads*, p. 2 : "... until quite late times ... no strict line of demarcation was drawn in most instances between *vānaprastha* and *sannyāsin*". Cf. Āraṇyaka Upaniṣad, *ibid.*, and pp. 10f.

[420] Cf. Weber, in Muir, IV, 422ff., who reviews the commentary in Śaṇkara and Sāyana on the goddess Umā. The scholar shares Śaṇkara's view that Umā is "Vidyā" (Knowledge) or (Weber) "Brahmavidyā" (Divine Knowledge); Oppert, *On the Original Inhabitants* ..., pp. 418-419. The identification, soma : *sa- uma* (Taittirya Araṇyaka X.1. 150) appears to remain too textually tendentious for us to begin to speculate. We note that it is mentioned by Weber in Muir, IV, 422ff.; Oppert, *On the Original Inhabitants* ..., pp. 418-418; and also by Lévi, "Pre-Aryan and Pre-Dravidic in India", p. 98.

[421] *Ca.* 400 B.C.-400 A.D.

[422] *Ca.* fourth-fifth century A.D. References which follow for both of these texts are in the main from *H.T.T.G.*, pp. 142-157.

[423] Mahābhārata VI (Virāta Parvan) and XXIII (Bhīṣma Parvan).

[424] Harivamśa LVIII (for other text, *vide O.S.T.*, IV, 435).

(2) there are manifest several items of a cultic nature which indicate a certain kind of Vedic but *typically non*-Vedic ritual practice in connection with the worship of the goddess; and (3) there are also sundry natural phenomena symboligically associated with the goddess as a chthonian religious reality.

In the first case, our divinity is, to be sure, called "Devī", alongside of Durgā, Kālī, Mahākālī, or Mahādevī, among other nominals.[425] The Vedic mytho-nominal background is generally evident, for example, in the ideas (a) that she is "praised and worshipped by the Devas for the protection of the three worlds"; (b) that she conquers the Dānavas (i.e., the sons of Danu, the enemies of the Devas) in battle; and (c) that for incarnate beings she is "the knowledge of Brahman".[426] More notably, the goddess is referred to as "Aditi of Devas" (i.e., the children of Aditi), Sāvritī, Indrāṇī, Sarasvatī, and Svāhā, the wife of Agni. Indeed she is Mother of the Vedas and the Vedanta.[427]

In the second case, several elements of a cultic nature are also present among the many lines of adoration contained in the foregoing texts. Described as a dark, virgin being, the goddess has the character of a *brahmacarya*; she observes not only the traditional rites for gaining spirituality,[428] but is herself gracious to the Brahmans who handle the sacrificial fires. In truth it is she who is the *Āranī* which make for the Agnihotra of the Brahmans. The goddess is the gift which the priests are offered for their sacrificial work.[429] Alongside of these descriptions, however, which have a rather Vedic or Vedo-Brāhmaṇic character, there are other cultic elements which suggest a markedly different background. Our attention is called, for example, to two such elements: (a) the goddess is said to be

---

[425] E.g., Mahābhārata XXIII: Kumārī, Bhadrakālī, Caṇḍī, Karālī, Umā, Bhagavatī, Jātaveda, i.e., Jātavedasī (the former a name of Agni); Harivamśa LVIII: Raudrī, Lakṣmī; Eldest Sister of Yama, Pārvatī; Younger Sister of (Kṛṣṇa), etc.

[426] *H.T.T.G.*, p. 143 and n. 6 (cf. Muir, V, 39 and n. 73); H.T.T.G., pp. 156, 155, 151 (*supra*, pp. 94, 97, 120, and n. 420 of p. 120).

[427] *H.T.T.G.*, pp. 148, 149, 150, 151, 156.

[428] Cf. also the story of Umā and her ascetic quest for Śiva's nuptial devotion: Rāmāyaṇa I.36.13ff.; Harivamśa CMXL (*O.S.T.*, IV, 430-432). *Vide H.T.T.G.*, (esp. the Viśvasāra Tantra and Harivamśa), p. 82 and n. 1: "ascetic one"; *ibid.*, p. 146: "She who undergoes great austerities"; *ibid.*, p. 150: "Devi of ascetics"; *ibid.*, p. 153 and n. 3 (Mahābhārata XXIII [Bhīṣma Parvan]): "leader of Yogīs"; *supra*, p. 116 and n. 398 on that page.

[429] *H.T.T.G.*, pp. 142 and n. 8; 146, 149, 150, 155: Mahābhārata (Virāta and Bhīṣma Parvans) and Harivamśa.

fond of "wine, meat, and animal flesh", and (b) she is reported to delight in the blood of buffaloes.[430]

In the third case, the sundry natural phenomena associated with the goddess are marked by their particularly terranean or chthonian nature. The goddess is pictured as having a body like a serpent; in fact, she is called the mother a serpentine divinities, as well as the "foremost Yakshi of the Yakshas".[431] Dwelling in inaccessible places such as the forests or the wildernesses and oceans, the goddess is then portrayed as the protector of persons who travel there; or who may be in danger in such regions; indeed she resides in "rivers ... caves, forests, and groves".[432] In her loftier dwelling places (i.e., the mountains) she is depicted as accompanied or surrounded by various creatures such as fowls, goats, sheep, lions, and tigers.[433] Most interesting of all, the goddess is noted to be an object of special worship by such traditionally derogated groups as the Śabaras, Barbaras, and Pulindas—who are tribesmen.[434]

If we move from literary text to historical-religious context it is thought that the celebration of Durgā-Kālī in the Mahabharata by Arjuna (Bhiṣma Parvan) and Yudhiṣṭhira (Virāta Parvan) raises the question of the relation of the goddess to other sectarian movements before and after the Christian era. The following factors suggest such relations: (1) an allusion to Durgā-Kālī as the sister of Kṛṣṇa or Vasudeva;[435] (2) her description as having Kṛṣṇa's hue—a dark, blue colour and wearing a crest of peacock feathers;[436] and especially

430 *H.T.T.G.*, p. 144: Mahābhārata (Virāta Parvan); *ibid.*, p. 154: Mahābhārata (Bhīṣma Parvan); *ibid.*, p. 148: Harivamśa; Oppert, *On the Original Inhabitants ...*, p. 433; *supra*, p. 86 (Gonda's Point 4); Bhattacharji, *The Indian Theogony*, p. 168 and n. 1a.

431 *H.T.T.G.*, pp. 143, 149.

432 *Ibid.*, pp. 153, 144, 151, 147.

433 *Ibid.*, p. 147; *supra*, pp. 49, 52.

434 Oppert, *On the Original Inhabitants ...*, p. 431; Harivamśa LVIII.7, 8 (*H.T.T.G.*, p. 147); Muir, IV, 434; *supra*, p. 92, n. 255 and p. 94, n. 264. The nominal fluidity and meaning of such names is mentioned by Elwin, *The Religion of an Indian Tribe*, pp. 1, 497. "Śabara", alone (e.g., "Savara, Saora") may have as many as *thirty* variant spellings (*ibid.*, p. xx).

435 Mahābhārata VI (Virāta Parvan): *vide* Roy, *Mahābhārata*, III, 10; sister of Indra and Viṣṇu (Harivamśa: *O.S.T.*, IV, 435).

436 Mahābhārata VI (Virāta Purāṇa) (*H.T.T.G.*, pp. 142, 143): "Dark art Thou like the blue-black cloud"; Roy, *Mahābhārata*, III, 11: "Sable as the black clouds, thy face is beautiful ..."; the goddess is *Kṛṣṇachavisamakṛṣṇā*, i.e., "dark as dark can be": Bhattacharji, *The Indian Theogony*, p. 173.

(3) an invitation by Viṣṇu to the goddess (as Nidra-Kāla-rūpinī) to help him to effect a simultaneous and strategic rebirth of them into the world for the sake of thwarting his enemies' designs, promising her a celestial reward, sisterhood, epic conquest, and worship;[437] finally, (4) the goddess is addressed as Umā, the wife of Kāpāla (Rudra, Śiva).[438]

By far the most plausible theory of the inter-sectarian relations that avail at this time in Indian history is that Vaiṣṇavite and Śaivite sects,[439] themselves evolving, are attempting to absorb the parallel emergence of worshippers of the goddess Durgā-Kālī. On the one side, it is noted that the goddess is the object of worship by Vindhyan tribal groups (*supra*); and an attempt appears to have been made [440] to connect the goddess with the myths and legends of Kṛṣṇa. On the other side, the goddess continues to be related to the mythic and legendary "history" of Kṛṣṇa—but now she becomes more specifically the spouse of Śiva (i.e., addressed as Umā).[441] While the goddess (as Ambikā) might be regarded as the sister of Rudra,[442] symbologically she can just as well become the spouse of Rudra.[443] The foregoing views on implicit sectarian relations are supported by Farquhar [444] and others; although in the case of the "sexuality" of the god Śiva much more needs to be said.[445] With regard to the Mahābhāratan reference to the goddess as "Kumārī", that motif (i.e., "the girl, representing womanhood in the making")[446] is thought by Chattopadhyaya to have some possible connection with Cape "Comorin" as well as Gauri's (Durgā's) association with the mountains of southern India. It is more than of passing interest to notice that, though we accept the dynamic relation between the Great and Little Traditions as being more accurately described as one of "circular flow",[447] the

---

437 Cf. Chattopadhyana, *The Evolution of Theistic Sects in India*, pp. 103f.

438 Mahābhārata XXIII (Bhīṣma Parvan) (*H.T.T.G.*, p. 153, n. 7).

439 *Infra*, pp. 137ff.

440 *Supra*, p. 122f.

441 J. N. Farquhar, *An Outline of the Religious Literature of India* (London : Oxford University Press, 1920), pp. 150f.

442 Vājasaneyi Samhita 3.57 (*O.S.T.*, IV, 321).

443 Cf. Chattopadhyaya. *The Evolution of Theistic Sects in India*, pp. 52-53; Muir, IV, 422.

444 Farquhar, *An Outline of the Religious Literature of India*, pp. 150f.; Chattopadhyaya, *The Evolution of Theistic Sects in India*, pp. 101f.; Muir, IV, 433-434.

445 *Vide infra*, Chap. IV.

446 Cf. Tucci, "Earth in India and Tibet", p. 360.

447 *Supra*, p. 38, n. 120.

case for occasionally distinctive directional currents is still recognized. B. C. Mazumdar,[448] for instance, calls our attention to "a hitherto unnoticed Kumārī worship prevalent among the non-Aryan Śūdra castes in the Oriya-speaking hill tracts in the district of Sambalpur, lying on the south-western border of Bengal ..." :

> As the Brahmins and other high-caste Hindus of Sambalpur do not take any part in the Kumārī-Osā of the Śūdras, and as the Durgā-Pūjā in Bengal style is wholly unknown to the people of Sambalpur, no one will venture to say that the power-caste Śūdras in those inaccessible hilly tracts imitated the Durgā-Pūjā of Bengal.[449]

The goddess Durgā-Kālī reaches a "higher rank"[450] in the Devī-Māhātmya portion of the Mārkaṇḍeya Purāṇa. As we have indicated, the literary-historical criticism of this work as a whole is chronologically irregular. That is, the Devī-Māhātmya (or Caṇḍī-māhātmya) is regarded as a unit in itself,[451] whereas the work *in toto* falls within the first 1000 years of the Christian era. Farquhar estimates that "all the Purāṇas, except the *Bhāgavata*, seem to have been in existence by the end of this period [i.e., 500-900 A.D.], and probably earlier".[452] The Mārkaṇḍeya Purāṇa shows some signs of being moderately non-sectarian as a literary totality.[453]

At any rate, in the Devī-Māhātmya portion the goddess has a status which marks a definite critical transition in her historical-religious development. The probable yet nebulous nominal affiliation with forerunning Vedic divinities and symbols now becomes a more pronounced acclamation of a "Female" Dinivity with tremendous and fascinating cosmic powers. Yet, as we shall see in our next chapter on cosmology, the goddess—even in the Devī-Māhātmya—is not yet elevated *radically* beyond "male" divinities who have lingered, some old, some originally latent (e.g., Viṣṇu) well on into the time of the Epics and Purāṇas. For the goddess in the Devī-Māhātmya is still "the perfect form of the powers of countless Devas". Nonetheless, the goddess is portrayed in paradoxical relation to such "Powers" so that in another sense,

> ... O Devī ! those great deeds of Thine
> Done in battle midst hosts of Devas, Asuras, and others ...

---

[448] Cf. B. C. Mazumdar, "Durgā : Her Origin and History", *Journal of the Royal Asiatic Society of Britain and Ireland*, 1906, pp. 355-362.

[449] *Ibid.*, pp. 358ff.

[450] Muir, IV, 435ff.

[451] Mārkaṇḍeya Purāṇa LXXXI-XCII; Pargiter, *The Mārkaṇḍeya Purāṇa*, p. vii.

[452] Farquhar, *An Outline of the Religious Literature of India*, p. 179.

[453] Pargiter, *The Mārkaṇḍeya Purāṇa*, p. xv.

> Incomprehensible art Thou even to Hari, Hara, and other Devas,
> Thou art the refuge of all.
> The whole world is but a part of Thee,
> Unmanifested, primeval, supreme Prakriti.[454]

It is in this dimension of the theogonic paradox that the goddess will surely "come into her own" in the immortial Saundaryalaharī [455] which we shall presently introduce. For it is here that the lingering, ever-present tension between the polytheism and dualistic monism of so many texts becomes a radical mystical monism—which is *the* Devi.

For now, we point out that the goddess as a religious symbol had probably achieved theogonic differentiation well before the rise of the literature known as the Tantras. However, it was only with the emergence of the *cultural vogue* which was so fundamental to those Tantric works that the sect formally associated with goddess-worship (i.e., the Śāktas) gained its ultimate momentum.

The Vogue and the Vehicle

The work of centripetalizing the goddess Durgā-Kālī, we have said, involved processes which had to do with two important Sanskritizational factors: mythological magnification and devotional glorification. These phenomena, however, did not occur in an historical vacuum. Neither had they, each, the character of a distinct and an independent set of responses on the part of myth-makers or ritual performers, whether they might be designated as Vrātyas, Smārta Brahmans, or "Dravidian" religionists. As religious products and valuations those processes were more than likely cultural realities which had their mutually influential source in an also complex milieu of personal motivation and social feeling; but it was a milieu in which the factor of religious experience was vital alongside of considerations of both a political and social nature. The element of "devotional glorification", though it is to receive treatment in Chapter IV, is extremely relevant. All this means that cultural process and religious experience were complementary and co-extensive phenomena in the gradual development of the goddess as an object of worship in Indian history prior to and after the beginning of the Christian era.

---

454 *H.T.T.G.*, pp. 111, 112.

455 Cf. W. Norman Brown, ed. and trans., *The Saundaryalaharī* (Harvard Oriental Series, Vol. XLIII; Cambridge: Harvard University Press, 1958), esp. the "Introduction", pp. 1-24.

Especially in the aftermath [456] of Christian beginnings the Vogue happens to be *Tantrism* and the "Vehicle", specifically, is known as *Śaktism* (i.e., Śaktivada, Śāktayāna).

It is no easy matter to define Tantrism. Such is the opinion of Mircea Eliade [457] who notices, moreover, that, though we may not be able to ascertain the reasons and historical conditions of its emergence, Tantrism has become at least as early as the fourth century A.D. "a great philosophical and religious movement"—indeed (by the sixth century) "a pan-Indian vogue" :[458]

> Quite suddenly, tantrism becomes immensely popular, and not only among philosophers and theologians, but also among the active practitioners of the religious life (ascetics, Yogins, etc.) and its prestige also reaches the "popular" strata. In a comparatively short time, Indian philosophy, mysticism, ritual, ethics, iconography, and even literature are influenced by tantrism.

Nonetheless, Bhattacharyya likens the search for definitions of *tantra* as "not unlike the description of an elephant by a number of blind men".[459] The root of the term (i.e., *tan*) has been understood with varying nuances of meaning. To be sure, another root (i.e., *tattri* or *tantri*) has also been suggested; the former root signifying "to spread", the latter "to explain".[460] The relation between these two senses, it appears, is established by the idea that a narrowing down of the process of "spreading" implies the objective of "explaining".[461] At any rate, the root (*tan*), as it related to the word *Tantra*, bears the meaning of "loom, web", along with other specific connotative literary and sectarian significations.[462] In the *soteriological* sense the meanings proposed by both Eliade and Chakravarti tend to apply. On the one hand, the *tantra* is "what extends knowledge"; on the other

---

456 Renou, *The Nature of Hinduism*, p. 88.

457 Eliade, *Yoga*, p. 200.

458 *Ibid.* Cf. "Tantra", "Āgama", and "Yāmala", in Benotosh Bhattacharyya, *An Introduction to Buddhist Esoterism* (London : Oxford University Press, 1932), pp. 51-52.

459 *Ibid.*, p. 51.

460 Eliade, *Yoga*, p. 200 : "extend, continue, multiply"; the author prefers "succession, unfolding, continuous process". Chintaharan Chakravarti (*The Tantras : Studies in Their Religion and Literature* [Calcutta : Sankar Bhattacharya, 1963], p. 12) also considers "that which gives account".

461 Chakravarti, *The Tantras*, p. 12.

462 Lal Mani Joshi, *Studies in the Buddhistic Culture of India* (Delhi : Motilal Banarsidass, 1967), p. 302, n. 3; p. 322; Campbell, *The Masks of God*, II, 359; Karmakar, *The Religions of India*, I, 118.

it is "that which spreads and saves".[463] Speaking of tantrism in its character as a soteriological *discipline*, Louis Renou understands it to be "an autonomous development of Yoga, taking as its point of departure some of the fundamental yogic formulations in physiology and cosmology".[464]

Still the relation between tantrism and Śaktism does not readily appear in the light of day. For there is a sense in which one might view the question—as we have sought to do heretofore in this chapter—as an historical, phenomenological, and structural phenomenon. By way of one quite general definition which would seem to integrate these three aspects of *tantra* or tantrism, N. N. Vasu [465] says the following :

> The word Tantra is very loosely used.[466] Ordinary people understand by it any system other than the Vedas. But it really means the worship of Śakti, or female energy. The female energy is worshipped in conjunction with male energy. The union of male and female is the essence of Tantra.

Although there is little to be learned from the abstractness of the statement itself, it does point up the need to think of the term *tantra* as a religio-cultural force. Having already suggested some of its linguistic nuances of meaning, let us briefly turn to some historico-phenomenological considerations.

The situation at Mohenjo-Daro and Harappa, it was held for some time, provided "no direct evidence"[467] of a distinctive Śakta *cult*, anymore than the Vedas reflect a cult of the Mother-Goddess. And there are scholars who might say that in both cases the evidence "is merely suggestive".[468] Yet one should say now, in the light of recent announcements (*supra*, pp. 81, 85), that the evidence is indeed not "merely" but "highly" or "seriously" suggestive of a cultic *milieu*. Marshall, at any rate, does imply that the Śaktism

---

463 Eliade, *Yoga*, p. 200; Chakravarti, *The Tantras*, p. 12. Cf. Bharati, *The Tantric Tradition*, p. 285.

464 Renou, *The Nature of Hinduism*, p. 70. Cf. Nilmani Mukhopadhyaya, ed., *The Kūrma Purāṇa : System of Hindu Mythology and Tradition* (Calcutta : The Girisavidyaratna Press [Asiatic Society], 1890), pp. xi-xv.

465 In Bhattacharyya, *An Introduction to Buddhist Esoterism*, p. 53; *vide* also *ibid.*, p. 54.

466 On other usages of Tantra, *vide* S. B. Das Gupta, *An Introduction to Tantric Buddhism* (Calcutta : University of Calcutta, 1958), p. 2.

467 Marshall, *Mohenjo-Daro and the Indus Civilization*, I, 57.

468 *Ibid.*

of later India might well have developed out of the antiquitous cult of the Mother-Goddess; that is, such a 'primitive' goddess might have been "transformed into a personification of female energy (*śakti*)"; that, moreover, what followed was a conception of "the eternal productive principle (*prakṛti*) united with the eternal male principle (*puruṣa*"; and that these became "the creator and Mother of the Universe (*Jaganmātā* or *Jagadambā*) including the gods themselves". Finally, the scholar regards the consummation of such a development to be the supreme form of Mahādevī but as the consort of Śiva, so that Śaivism and Śaktism are seen as "inextricably bound up" together.[469] Following other Indianists and presenting no conspicuous historical chronology, Marshall's "cult-development" does capture, nevertheless, much of the structural dimensions of what the vision of Śakti was later to become.

The specific geography of Tantrism's emergence would seem to elicit no noticeable consensus of scholarly opinion. Favourable locations of historical development and concentration are multiple and go in many directions. Eliade notices the peripheral nature of at least two particular loci: (1) the Afghan frontier (Nortwest India) and (2) Western Bengal, especially Assam.[470] In fact, Assam (Kāmarūpa) is referred to as the "tantric country" par excellence".[471] This relatively "borderland" character of Tantric loci makes it understandable that Tantrism has been thought to be of extra-Indian origins [472] (contrary to other opinions concerning indigenous areas). The precise historical geography of its origins, however (as we earlier indicated), are not known. But many of the areas suggested as de-

---

[469] *Ibid.* Cf. Karmakar (*The Religions of India*, I, 119f.) for a theological and structural summary of the content of the Purāṇas; *vide* also Mukhopadhyaya, *The Kūrma Purāṇa*, pp. xi-xv.

[470] Eliade, *Yoga*, p. 201. Cf. Bhattacharyya, *An Introduction to Buddhist Esoterism*, pp. 42-46. Karmakar (*The Religions of India*, I, 119) notes a geographic-literary division. On Tantric Buddhism's origins, *vide* Lal Mani Joshi, *Studies in the Buddhistic Culture of India*, pp. 324-329. Tucci ("Earth in India and Tibet", p. 355) introduces the possibility that the search for a pre-eminent place of origin may not be fruitful "whether north or south India, Central or Eastern India"; accordingly, different places may have focused upon (a) the mother aspect, (b) the sensuous, or (c) the terrific. Cf. Chattopadhyaya (*The Evolution of Theistic Sects in India*, pp. 56f.) for another threefold schema.

[471] Eliade, *Yoga*, p. 202. *Vide* "Bengal" in the *Encyclopedia of Religion and Ethics*, 1924, II, 479b: "In the time of the *Mahābhārata*, North and East Bengal, with Assam, formed the kingdom of Prāgjyotisha, or, as it was called later, Kāmarūpa".

[472] Cf. Chakravarti, *The Tantras*, pp. 46-49; Lal Mani Joshi, *Studies in the Buddhistic Culture of India*, pp. 304ff.

velopmental strongholds have their historical value insofar as they are oftentimes held to be "sacred spaces"[473] (*pīṭhas*) where parts of the body of the goddess were "discovered" and venerated.[474] On the whole, the historical probability of certain early Tantric centers is not so controversial as the indulgence in a kind of romantic antiquarianism by certain scholars. While Bhattacharyya rightly claims, for example, that Tantrism (eventually more fully developed) ran counter to original Buddhism,[475] the scholar yet ventures, dubiously, to say that Buddha himself taught Tantric instructions and practices.[476]

Perhaps the same scholar is more accurate in his presentation of the phenomenological background of what was to become the Tantric Vogue. Tantrism's emergence is here seen within a general milieu of "primitive magic", and, of course, "Buddhist magic".[477] Aside from the author's questionable emphasis upon the term magic, if we acknowledge with Eliade [478] that "tantrism developed in provinces ... where the spiritual counteroffensive of the aboriginal inhabitants was in full force", then the former scholar's account of the protohistoric Indian *Sitz im Leben* further attests to our earlier perception of the basic cultural fluidity and religious dynamism of the ancient "Āryan" hegemony.[479]

It is in Bhattacharyya's third chapter, "Growth of Buddhist Magic", that certain important elements in the consideration of Tantrism's emergence prove to be remarkably salient factors. First, there is the element of custom or folkways [480] which probably existed prior to, and accompanied, the *Sangha* of Buddha; specifically, the thing to be grasped is the ever-present humanness beyond the religiosity of religious adherents. For we know that not only was there a multiplicity of approaches to Reality germinating before and during Buddha's time;[481] but, most likely, "the members of the Sangha must

---

473 *Supra*, p. 31f.

474 *Vide infra*, Chap. IV.

475 Bhattacharyya, *An Introduction to Buddhist Esoterism*, pp. 22ff., esp. pp. 24,32.

476 *Ibid.*, pp. 48f. Cf. Eliade, *Yoga*, pp. 201, 401. *Vide* the discussion of Lal Mani Joshi, *Studies in the Buddhistic Culture of India*, pp. 307-311.

477 Cf. Bhattacharyya, *An Introduction to Buddhist Esoterism*, pp. 1-9 and Chaps. II and III.

478 Eliade, *Yoga*, p. 201.

479 Cf. *supra*, pp. 90-93.

480 Bhattacharyya, *An Introduction to Buddhist Esoterism*, p. 23.

481 Cf. Surendranath Das Gupta, *A History of Indian Philosophy* (Cambridge : At the University Press, 1951), I, 80.

have revolted from time against the unnatural rules of discipline, and party quarrels ... were already in evidence in the second great council" *within* Buddhism itself.[482] Secondly, there is the factor of temperament, or what one anthropologist calls "individual variability".[483] Here, among the followers of Buddha "all were not of the same mentality".[484] Granting the emergence of the traditional dichotomy between the Great Vehicle (Mahāyāna) and the Little Vehicle (Hināyāna), the rise of the Buddhist Vajrayāna [485] (and others : Mantrayāna, Kālacakrayāna, Sahajayāna) represents more clearly the factor of a perennial capacity in the human spirit for varieties of religious experience. This historico-religious phenomenon is fundamentally confirmed even in the tendency of religionists in many places to bifurcate themselves into exoteric and esoteric orders or levels [486] of spiritual comprehension and depth notwithstanding their claims of experiential authenticity.

Though traditionally regarded as a "non-founded" religion (or a religion-without-a-founder), Hinduism was largely characterized by a similar kind of historico-religious instability—or better still —dynamism. Before mentioning, however, several important cultural phenomena which were relevant to the Hindu "renaissance",[487] one in-

---

482 Bhattacharyya, *An Introduction to Buddhist Esoterism*, p. 23. Cf. N. Dutt, *Early History of the Spread of Buddhism and the Buddhist Schools* (London : Luzac and Co., 1925), pp. 198f., 200-216.

483 Robert H. Lowie, *Primitive Religion* (Paperback ed.; New York : Grosset and Dunlap, 1952), pp. 221ff. For the "temperamental" factor as a problem of theory and practice in Mahāyāna Buddhism, *vide* W. C. Beane, "Buddhist Causality and Compassion", *Religious Studies* (Dec., 1974), Vol. 10, pp. 441-456.

484 Bhattacharyya, *An Introduction to Buddhist Esoterism*, p. 23.

485 Shashi B. Das Gupta, *An Introduction to Tantric Buddhism*, pp. 5-33, 52-76.

486 Cf. *supra*, pp. 37f.

487 D. S. Sarma (*The Renaissance of Hinduism* [Benares : Benares Hindu University, 1944], pp. 1-70), though mainly interested in the modern period, appears to suggest an outlook of "recurrent renaissance". Renou (*Hinduism*, p. 49) sees some relation between royal patronage and the thrust of the "renaissance", but regards the notion as exaggerated in the case of Hinduism; for "there is nothing to indicate that in the prior period [e.g., before the Guptas] Hinduism has been deeply encroached upon by Buddhism or that it had undergone any internal degeneration". Cf. Sarma, *The Renaissance of Hinduism*, pp. 30f. Perhaps the usage (Hindu) "renaissance" may be attributed to those who rejoiced to see "the restoration of Vedic ceremonies" (Renou, *Hinduism*, p. 49); or, in part, to Westerners who adopted notions of "orthodoxy" held mainly by Āryo-Brahmans. Or, again, as Sarma's work suggests, it might apply to the manner in which Hinduism as a remarkably versatile religious phenomenon has been characterized by both continuity and change.

dispensable point must be made. It is that the peculiar turn of events which now occasioned the rise of the Tantric Vogue as it appears in several Indian sectarian or heterodox expressions was essentially *religio-experiential* in nature. Preferring to refer to the Tantric philosophy as "psycho-experimental speculation", Bharati [488] calls us to the heart of the matter—whether Hindu or Buddhist:

> Tantric literature is not of the philosophical gendre; the stress is on *sādhanā* ... the doctrinary discrepancies between the various schools of speculative thought are *really* resolved in Tantric *sādhanā* : all scholastic teachers in India declare that there is *samanvaya*, but the tantric actually experiences it ...

Despite the radical importance of this point, there has been some question concerning the historical priority of either *Hindu* Tantrism or *Buddhist* Tantrism. Scholarly views tend to run in two specific directions of original Tantric influence: (a) either that Hinduism borrowed Tantric beliefs and symbolism from Buddhism;[489] or (b) that the latter faith adopted methods of "Hinduist magic".[490] Bharati's statement on the experimental (-experiential) focus of Tantric *sādhanā*, of course, has already suggested a kind of "key" to understanding Tantrism. At any rate, we are inclined to doubt that either of the two initial opinions has any absolute validity. We grant, however, that the idea of a movement of "circular flow" implied in one view is highly probable. But, perhaps, through tendentiousness (Bhattacharyya) or antiquarianism (Eliot) the temptation could arise to insist upon an "either/or" approach to the problem. Nonetheless, we prefer at this time a position which, too, appears rather antiquarian, yet far more plausible in light of the multiplicity of factors already presented; that is, the problem requires no necessary assumption of Buddhist influence (e.g., via Mahāyāna circles) upon the popular Hindu religionists, or vice versa; but, rather, that a

---

488 Bharati, *The Tantric Tradition*, p. 18. For similarities and differences in the theological and experiential structures of Tantric Hinduism and Tantric Buddhism, *vide* Shashi B. Das Gupta, *An Introduction to Tantric Buddhism*, pp. 3f., 99ff. *et passim*. Cf. Bharati, *The Tantric Tradition*, Chap. I.

489 Bhattacharyya, *An Introduction to Buddhist Esoterism*, p. 147: "Though in the earlier period both Buddhism and Jainism exploited Hindu gods, the Buddhist pantheon was commonly ransacked by Hinduism and Jainism in the later and more promiscuous Tantric age". Cf. "Kālī", *ibid.*, pp. 156f.

490 Cf. *supra*, p. 129; Eliot, *Hinduism and Buddhism*, I, xl; II, 126: "If Hinduism could summon gods and goddesses by magical methods, they [Buddhists] could summon Bodhisattvas, male and female, in the same way ..."

peculiar "strain" of autochthonous religion "unrelated to either Buddhist or Brahmanical higher conceptions"[491] (re-)emerged as permeative regarding sectors of both which signaled "a new victory for the pre-Āryan popular strata".[492]

It is nonetheless (not because, but) *in the light of* the following factors that Hindu Tantrism is to be viewed in terms of its development: (1) the very emergence of Buddhism and Jainism as religious "offshoots" in tension with Vedo-Brāhmaṇic tradition; (2) the existence of a growing popular current of *bhakti* around (and possibly earlier than) the beginning of the Christian era, which permeated especially the Vaiṣṇavite cult-legends, not exlcuding the Pāśupata cult, or the followers of Śiva;[493] (3) the appearance of epic-Purāṇic literature which, though offering no consistent trustworthiness of historical detail, does comprise a storehouse of myth, cult, and symbols, bearing upon and reflecting the former two divinities as well as, in our case, the goddess Durgā-Kālī; and (4) a factor of crucial importance was that of "royal patronage".[494]

To determine exactly, however, "when the sects came into being ... to trace their origins ..."[495] remains a difficult task. We have to remember that the central theological symbol of a cult or sect (i.e., a god or goddess), as well as other cultically unifiable ingredients, are sometimes present before an actual, definitive self-conscious body of believers with a crystallized and coherent tradition has come into being. The religious phenomenon known as Śaktism (i.e., the Śāktas) is no exception.

Whereas Tantrism was the vogue or the crucible through which various and sundry protohistoric (possibly "Indusian") religious currents permeated the foundations of Hindu orthodoxy and orthopraxis,

---

491 Maity, *Historical Studies in the Cult of the Goddess Manasā*, p. 74. Cf. Shashi Bhushan Das Gupta, *Obscure Religious Cults as a Background to Bengali Literature* (Calcutta : University of Calcutta, 1946), 1946), p. xxxiv.

492 Eliade, *Yoga*, p. 202.

493 Cf. Nilakanta Sastri, *The Development of Religion in South India*, pp. 50, 51, 54; Renou, *Hinduism*, Chap. V, esp. pp. 48f.

494 Cf. R. R. Diwakar, *Bihar Through the Ages* (Bombay : Orient Longmans, 1959), pp. 254, 273 (royal "names" of the Guptas), 280, 282, 333; Eliot, *Hinduism and Buddhism*, I, xxxvii; II, 280, 288f.; III: 115ff.; 119; Muirhead-Thomson, *Assam Valley*, pp. 47, 48, 49; Basu, *The Bengali Peasant*, pp. 22-23, 137, 145; *supra*, p. 59. Cf. Rokeya Rahman Kabeer, "Sultans of Bengal : Charges of Religious Intolerance", in Habibullah, *Nalini Kanta Bhattasali Commemorative Volume*, pp. 339-345, esp. p. 341.

495 Renou, *Hinduism*, p. 47.

Śaktism was the specific vehicle [496] through which (we might say) the "densification" process reached its apex. For the Śāktas, as a sect [497] of Hinduism have become the *focus classicus* of a religious apprehension which amounts to the feminization of Ultimate Reality as "Creative Power".[498] The proper relation of Śaktism to Tantrism, then, is not grasped if one insists upon any rigid dichotomy between the two phenomena.[499] To suggest that Tantrism can be independent of, or even that it "accompanies" Śaktism, is to indulge in a type of historico-religious reification; to take no account of the possibility of the *sui generis* character of the meaning of such terms as *religious realities*—realities that shook the foundations of the "orthodox"[500] proprieties of Hinduism, Buddhism and, to some extent, Jainism. Eliot's distinction *in extensu* between Śaktism and Tantrism is the following:

> The former means the worship of a goddess or goddesses especially those who are regarded as forms of Śiva's consort .... Tantrism is a system of magical or sacramental ritual, which professes to attain the highest aims of religion by such methods as spells, diagrams, gestures, and other physical exercises. One of its bases is the assumption that man and the universe correspond as microcosm and macrocosm and that both are subject to the mysterious power of words and letters.[501]

So far, the following discernments have presented themselves as phenomenological aspects of the Tantrism/Śaktism relation: (1) Tantrism has its practical roots in a milieu of "primitive" magic;[502] (2) Tantrism is a fixation upon the essential unity of male and female but this means, fundamentally, the adoration of Śakti; (3) Tantrism is an independent offshoot of the Yoga (*darśana*);[503] (4) Tantrism is sacramental ritual which is underlined by the homologation of man and cosmos. All these perspectives (doubtless there are variations) only suggest the extreme difficulty of trying to distinguish two cultural forces which are largely inseparable. In fact they were better

---

496 *Supra*, p. 41.

497 Cf. Louis Dumont, "World Renunciation in Indian Religions", *Contributions to Indian Sociology*, No. 4 (1960), pp. 55, 59ff.

498 Cf. Gonda, *Change and Continuity in Indian Religion*, pp. 195, 196.

499 Cf. Eliot, *Hinduism and Buddhism*, I, xxxvi, n. 1.

500 I.e., that which was *non*-Tantric.

501 Eliot, *Hinduism and Buddhism*, II, 274. Cf. Dumont, "World Renunciation in Indian Religions", p. 53: "I take Tantrism ... as being essentially the literature of the *śākta*, and secondarily the related texts of other movements".

502 Cf. also Eliot, *Hinduism and Buddhism*, II, 121 and Chap. XXIV.

503 *Vide infra*, Chap. III.

understood as having the nature of an historico-phenomenological continuum. Ideologically, Tantrism and Śaktism might be be seen as a *conical continuum* : with the former visualized as the *vortex*—a dynamic mass of irresistible chthonian and homologative symbols projecting outward as the well-spring of sectarian systems;[504] while Śaktism could be understood as the *vertex* of such systems : the saturation point of tantric symbols that were originally diffusive and relentless,[505] now phenomenologically dominant,[506] but always potentially expulsive [507] in the aggregate of religious thought, feelings and expressions.

An outlook of degree, emphasis, and intensification is employed by the author of a primary source on the Śākta aspect of Indian Hinduism.[508] Payne, therefore, lists the following three underlying characteristics of the Śākta Vehicle : (1) the idea of Deity as Destroyer, (2) the conception of God as Mother, and (3) the attention to ceremonial.[509] He acknowledges at once, of course, that such "marks" are shared by "other forms of Hinduism", but, also, insists that "nowhere are they so combined and emphasized as in this sect".[510] Perhaps the qualification, their being *in combination,* may bear out the remarks of the author.[511] Yet one would have to place the above criteria against the background of the larger, broader, and deeper Tantric Vogue either in the manner previously suggested (i.e., a

---

[504] I.e., that which was *Tantric.*

[505] Tucci, "Earth in India and Tibet", p. 357.

[506] Dumont, "World Renunciation in Indian Religions", pp. 55f. : "... the *female principle* is at the heart of Shaktism ... the couple ... regarded as essential ... *the woman* ... becomes *dominant* in the cult [italics mine]".

[507] E.g., the ultimately independent status of the goddess in the Saundaryalaharī. This is an important consideration in the light of varying descriptions of the Śākta sect which reflect the traditional "alliance" between "Kālī" and "Śiva". Cf. Renou, *Hinduism,* p. 45 : "Śāktas ... the third branch, can be treated as a subdivision of the Shaivites"; G. W. Briggs, *Gorakhnāth and the Kānphaṭā Yogīs* (Calcutta : YMCA Publishing House, 1938), p. 164 : "Today Śaktism is essentially a branch of Śaivism"; he adds, however, that the latter branch "of Hinduism looks to the consort of Śiva for its exemplification". The phenomenological dimension of our study, nonetheless, allows for a Tantric biunity but, ultimately, also an (anthropo-) monism wherein the goddess reigns supreme—even beyond Trimūrti (e.g., *supra,* p. 125 and n. 455 on that page; the *iśtadevatā* concept).

[508] Payne, *The Śāktas* (*supra,* p. 10, n. 11). The author's value judgments upon the moral rectitude of certain phases of Tantric-Śaktic development and expression should not be allowed to override the general usefulness of the work as an historical source.

[509] Payne, *The Śāktas,* p. 3.

[510] *Ibid.*

[511] On these three characteristics, *vide ibid.,* esp. pp. 114, 128-131.

conical continuum) or (as we did Durgā-Kālī in Chapter I)[512] in "concentric" relation to Tantrism : Śaktism as the "inner circle" of the process of Tantricization of Hinduism. If there is any source of difficulty in Payne's book, apart from his historico-religious moralism,[513] it resides in his reductionist understanding of the relation between history and religion. In the work, to be sure, Śaktism is portrayed as an historically evanescent phenomenon. It is easily explained away as an "impermanent" page in the history of Indian religion, as well as universal religious history. The phenomenon of Śaktism, then, is largely attributed to factors that are climatological, existential, and (in the case of some mystical adherents) interactionary.[514] On the whole, nonetheless, Payne's introduction of an "existential" dimension into the complex of human religious responses does have its relevance. It would not, however, account for the emergence, continuity, and recurrence of a religious sect whose "inexhaustible character and meaning"[515] have by-passed even its oft-made comparison with the Mystery Religions of the ancient Near East. For the Śāktas continue to be a vital religious expression of "being in the world" for millions of Hindus of every station.[516]

It is, after all, most important to consider the crucial position of Bengal as the *locus classicus* of the festive celebration of the goddess ("Śakti"). For the idea of religious celebration, particularly in the face of the occurrence and recurrence of natural calamity and socio-political conflict should turn our minds away from the oft-expected conclusion that, at bottom, we are studying Indian religious response as chronic pessimism. Payne thus pays insufficient attention to religious festivity *as a creative answer* to calamitous natural environment or tragic historical event.

---

512 I.e., from goddess worship in general (prehistory) to goddess worship in particular (India).

513 For an historian's indictment of decadence, *vide* Panikkar, *A Survey of Indian History*, pp. 110ff. For an impartial but critical view, *vide* Edward C. Dimock, Jr., *The Place of the Hidden Moon* (Chicago and London : University of Chicago Press, 1966), pp. 112ff., esp. pp. 103-110.

514 Payne, *The Śāktas*, pp. 82ff. A similar perspective is detected in the work by E. J. Thompson and A. M. Spencer, trans., *Bengali Religious Lyrics* : *Śākta* (Calcutta : Association Press, 1923), pp. 13-15; Morisson, "Sources, Methods, and Concepts in Early Indian History", pp. 71-85; Eliot, *Hinduism and Buddhism*, II, 287.

515 *Supra*, p. 11.

516 Briggs (*Gorakhnāth and the Kānphaṭā Yogīs*, p. 351) sees more perpetuity for the Śāktas.

At any rate, the historico-structural aspect of centripetalization of the goddess Durgā-Kālī finds a paradigmatic location in Bengal, because it is here that a few crucial religious ideas and mutually enhancing sectarian relations are so demonstratively present.

First of all, let us remember the fact (via Renou) that we may not after all be able to determine the earliest historio-genetic details of the Hindu sects. Moreover, our allusion to the critical distinction between historically pre-existent yet non-crystallized and cultically coherent ingredients should be borne in mind. Accordingly, neither the presence of a variety of "Devīs" in the Vedas (including the name': "Durgā", or "Kālī" in "Vedic" literary extensions, i.e., beyond the Four Vedas) or other "epic" traditions, the reference to epithets and exploits performed by the goddess, iconographic representations of her, nor hymns to the goddess by early poets,[517] per se, corroborate by necessity the existence of a Śākta *sect*. These factors in their *collectivity* might nevertheless establish both a cult and sect "in the making".

Following Renou's theory that in the main the *context* of the Ṛg-Vedic texts is a religious *cultus*,[518] however, we might postulate that as early as the fourth century onwards there are more or less explicit grounds for maintaining the existence of an independent goddess-oriented cult. For the Devī-Māhātmya or Caṇḍī-māhātmya narrative, it is noted, "forms the chief background of Bāṇa's *Chaṇḍī-śataka* [and] ... the *Chaṇḍī-māhātmya* [519] celebrates the mighty deeds of the goddess and refers to her daily worship and autumnal festival, while the three hymns contained in it and the hymns from the Harivamśa contain the theology of the cult".[520]

In a general sense, we can allow that, probably, all three of Hinduism's pre-eminent sects—the Vaiṣṇavas, Śaivas, and Śāktas—had their constitutive beginnings before the Christian era, in that many of their cultic "constituents" may have existed *in nuce* in the Vedic

[517] E.g., Kālidāsa (fifth century) : his "Kumārasambhava"; Bāṇa (seventh century). *Vide* Payne, *The Śāktas*, pp. 39ff. For Bāṇa, *vide* G. P. Quackenbos, "Bāṇa's Caṇḍīśataka", *The Sanskrit Poems of Mayura* (Columbia University Indo-Iranian Series, Vol. IX; New York : Columbia University, 1917), pp. 245-357.

[518] Renou, *Religions of Ancient India*, p. 11. Renou, however, makes no claim to have found a (single) key to the interpretation of the Veda (*ibid.*, p. 18).

[519] Cf. Dinesh Chandra Sen, *History of Bengali Language and Literature* (Calcutta : University of Calcutta, 1911), pp. 225-235, 294ff.

[520] Farquhar, *An Outline of the Religious Literature of India*, pp. 150f.

period, if not earlier, i.e., in the pre-Vedic Indusian period. It is only during the first six or seven centuries A.D., however, that a *sectarian crystallization prosess* was under way. During the latter part and, certainly, after the Gupta Period (*ca.* 300-*ca.* 600) the group known as the Śāktas came in as a crest on the wave of a Tantric high-tide.[521] The literary evidence already presented attests to the worship of the goddess Durgā-Kālī,[522] if not sporadically by some, more seasonally by others. To be sure, during the period following the fifth century "we find in the literature of Vaiṣṇavism, Buddhism and Jainism, as well as in works connected with Śiva, traces of Śākta ideas".[523]

Moreover, the episode of Yuan Chwang (seventh century A.D.), the Buddhist missionary scholar, who was reportedly almost sacrificed to the goddess Durgā by devout brigands,[524] suggests the cultic notoriety as well as the accessibility of the "Inaccessible One" during those times. Payne points out the following four religious trends': (1) there was an increase in the use of magic spells, (2) a new type of hypnotic meditation, (3) a growing belief in the occult, and (4) the thought of the time was permeated by conceptions of power personified as a goddess.[525]

The centuries that follow in Bengal (up to at least *ca.* the eleventh century) witness a period of flourishing theogonic activity, which is characterized by the birth of "innumerable divinities of local origin", which included, or were akin to, the Grāmadevatān type.[526] It is this syncretistic milieu[527] in which thrived a phenomenon mentioned earlier: the Buddhist and Hinduist unilateral absorption of chthonian and psycho-mental religious elements, as well as the mutual fertilization of Buddhism and Hinduism. This phase of

---

521 Renou, *Hinduism*, p. 49. Cf. Finegan, *The Archaeology of World Religions*, I, 158ff.

522 Cf. Panikkar, *A Survey of Indian History*, pp. 58f.; Chattopadhyaya, *The Evolution of Theistic Sects in India*, pp. 160ff.

523 Payne, *The Śāktas*, p. 42.

524 Cf. J. Estlin Carpenter, *Theism in Medieval India* (London: Williams and Norgate, 1921), pp. 4f.

525 Payne, *The Śāktas*, p. 42; Maity, *Historical Studies in the Cult of the Goddess Manasā*, p. 73.

526 Maity, *Historical Studies in the Cult of the Goddess Manasa*, p. 73. Cf. *ibid.*, pp. 72, 73.

527 As early as the Emperor Harṣa (*ca.* 606-648 A.D.) we see signs of such a trend: *vide* Finegan, *The Archaeology of World Religions*, I, 165- Eliot, *Hinduism and Buddhism*, II, 98f.

theogonic fluidity tends to correspond on the phenomenologico-historical plane to the aforementioned Ur-Vedic situation when the peoples of successive Āryan incursions into the Indus were beginning to settle down and to adapt to the naturalness of a growing multi-cultural life. Analogically, the result of that earlier religious inter-mixture, as much as this later fusion of thought-currents in Eastern India,[528] was no mono-genetic product; for, though religious, it was in both cases a cultural "creation" whose rich source of imagery and reality was related to its own relentless, fascinating, and complex nature.

A development of primary significance, then, occurred in the Pāla-Sena period (*ca.* fifth-eleventh centuries A.D.) when Bengal was fast becoming a Brāhmanical stronghold : the locus of a Neo-Brahmanization of a multiplicity of religious ideas and practices which had proved to be both awesome and mysterious to contemplate.[529] Certainly the process of Neo-Brāhmanization had begun as early as the period of the Guptas. Now, however, a deliberate effort was made to synthesize and harmonize various and sundry "gods" and "god-desses" with certain divinities who had by then gained pre-eminence (e.g., Viṣṇu, Śiva) over the more classical (Vedic) deities (e.g., Indra, Varuṇa, etc.).[530] The cultural media through which this was accom-plished were the (Vedo-) Purāṇic customs and traditions, although the Tantras accompanied them and represent a highly intensified stage of Śākta self-consciousness as a sect. Nonetheless, Purāṇic literature, many of whose images and symbols go back, perhaps, to pre-Purāṇic times,[531] become the literary vogue of "New Brāhmins", who continued to reflect in their loyalty a type of orthodox-heterodox ambiguity.[532] Their influence, of course, was not confined to religion but also extended to the fabric of social life. According to Maity,[533] this "Purāṇic Renais-sance" meant the new birth of Sanskritic ideals, the toleration of

---

528 Cf. D. C. Sen, *History of Bengali Language and Literature*, pp. 406f.

529 Cf. Diwakar, *Bihar Through the Ages*, pp. 340-344.

530 Cf. *The Cultural Heritage of India*, II, 238.

531 E.g., on the "age" of such legends, *vide* Edward C. Dimock, Jr., *The Thief of Love* (Chicago : University of Chicago Press, 1963), pp. 197f.

532 *Supra*, pp. 61-64. Cf. Van Buitenen, "On the Archaism of the Bhāgavata Purāṇa", pp. 24f. *Vide infra*, p. 247, n. 120.

533 Maity, *Historical Studies in the Cult of the Goddess Manasa*, p. 75. Hence : "the Sanskrit Purāṇa tradition", in Chatterji, "Purāṇa Legends and the Prakrit Tradition in New Indo-Aryan", p. 466.

popular creeds, and the appropriation of stories [534] which the Hindu priests now represented in alluring and novel dress.

For the Śākta sect this later phase of "Brāhmanization" signified three decisive developments.[535] First, it meant the dignification and elevation of the cult to a level which Brāhmins could consider "a highly refined and spiritual faith"; secondly, it meant the more conspicuous "Sanskritization" of the vocabulary of literary art and popular communication; and, in the third place, it signaled the transformation of the Śākta modes of worship into orthodox moulds.[536]

The specific significance of the foregoing trends and developments for the "character" of the goddess Durgā-Kālī is mainly theological and inter-sectarian in nature. Durgā-Kālī, of course, had been among the emergent divinities who were recognized and called upon by name in the Itihāsic-Purāṇic traditions. Also, we have already shown that this process of theogonic readjustment and assimilation must have begun fairly early in the post-Vedic mythological period. Needless to say, the phenomenon at hand is partially pretypified in the Vedic period proper, especially the Ṛg-Veda.[537] This process in Bengali religious history, however, is most dramatically manifested in the case of Durgā-Kālī. For, in her gradual ascendancy to theistic supremacy (particularly beyond and over the numberless local divinities or little *mātās* or *ammās*), scholars have seen a phenomenon which they have not hesitated to describe, historio-metaphorically, in terms of devourment and imperialism.[538]

> Durgā or Umā ... was an insignificant goddess in the beginning, but she steadily grew in stature until finally she absorbed all her rivals in her personality and became

---

534 Chatterji, "Purāṇa Legends and the Prakrit Tradition in New Indo-Aryan", pp. 400, 457f., 459; Maity, *Historical Studies in the Cult of the Goddess Manasā*, p. 56; *vide* also a highly useful comment on the relation between the Epics and the Maṅgal poems, in Dimock, *The Thief of Love*, p. 198.

535 Cf. D. C. Sen, *History of Bengali Language and Literature*, p. 251.

536 There are basically two structural branches: the devotees of the right-handed path (the Dakṣiṇāmārga), who find more acceptance with orthodox Brāhmans; and the left-handed path (the Vāmamārga), the more notorious and controversial, perhaps misunderstood, branch, especially by some Westerners as well as Indian intellectuals.

537 *Nota bene*, that in Ṛg-Vedic henotheism there is more distinctively an absorption of "functions" and "attributes" than the assimilation of gods themselves. Cf. Griswold, *The Religion of the Rig Veda*, pp. 352-353.

538 Cf. Marriott, "Little Communities ...", pp. 201, 202; Eliade, *Patterns in Comparative Religion*, pp. 452-462.

> the supreme mother-goddess[539] ... One by one she absorbed the main traits of regional mother-goddesses, household deities who were worshipped for different things by different tribes. Some were fierce and awe-inspiring, others were mild, benign and motherly, yet others were embodiments of lofty ideas—all these were fused into one composite supreme goddess—Durgā. Each of the component deities brought with her a special ritual, specific cultic practices and a different mythological and religious significance to the devotee. A supreme goddess who commanded the whole-hearted allegiance of various types of people, had to combine in her per-personality all the different traits that would satisfy these manifold demands.[340]

Although we are inclined to agree with Farquhar that "a Devī-worshipping *sect*"[541] was formed by the time of the Devī-Māhātmya and Harivamśa, the actual *momentum* of the sectarian cult is, furthermore, intimately related to the co-emergence of other sects such as the Vaiṣṇavas[542] and Śaivas, but particularly the latter. It was indeed both in theistic conflict and creative tension with the devotees of Śiva that the Śāktas gained much of their decisive thrust as a religious movement in Bengal.[543]

Thus another significant phenomenon which throws light upon the historical and traditional growth of the Śākta sect is its peculiar relation to the Śaivas. In this regard, we point out, first of all, that there is a natural tendency for persons to take for granted a perennial harmony between the three major Hindu sects. This outlook, to be sure, has been influenced by typical references to Hindu pantheism, trimūrtism, pañcāyatanism, and the like, as well as the attribution of all Indian philosophy to the Upaniṣadic-Vedāntic tradition.[544] In a more historically dynamic perspective, nevertheless, we see that among the sects the later blending occurred only after "a hard

---

539 *Supra*, p. 124f.

540 Bhattacharji, *The Indian Theogony*, pp. 172, 174.

541 Farquhar, *An Outline of the Religious Literature of India*, pp. 150f.

542 If, at one time, the Vaiṣṇavas sought to conciliate or absorb the Śākta legends and cult (*supra*, p. 123 and n. 437 of that page), at other times the Vaiṣṇavas (even after the "Vaiṣṇava Renaissance" : cf. D. C. Sen, *History of Bengali Language and Literature*, pp. 398-405, 408f. *et passim*) were heatedly opposed to the increasing distinction of the Śāktas within the Bengali stronghold : *vide* Payne, *The Śāktas*, pp. 86, 87, 88. This situation seems to have availed even while under Islamic hegemony.

543 The probable effects of medieval Muslim theology and its strict monotheism upon Hindu theism have been noted : cf. Panikkar, *A Survey of Indian History*, pp. 148ff. The author shows that the issue need not be understood in mere causational terms, however. *Ibid.*, pp. 150f. Cf. Aziz Ahmad, *Studies in Islamic Culture in the Indian Environment* (Oxford : The Clarendon Press, 1964), pp. 140-152 and also pp. 85f. (Guru Gobind Singh), 153f., 163f. *et passim.*

544 E.g., Panikkar, *A Survey of Indian History*, pp. 150f.

contested fight on either side".[545] Such was the case as touching the Śaivas and their Śākta counterparts. This struggle is believed to be exemplified in that form of Bengali literature known as *maṅgalkāvya*.

> The term mangal means something like "eulogy", and the maṅgal poems eulogize one or another of the gods and goddesses—Śītalā, "the cool one", goddess of small-pox; Caṇḍī, slayer of demons; and Manasā, the goddess of snakes, among others.[546]

It is the cycle of Manasā myths, intermingled as they are, with epic and purāṇic content, which has suggested to scholars their historico-religious paradigmatic value. For the cult of the goddess Manasā is type of "competitive" religious expression which the Śaivas are said to have resisted [547] during their sectarian evolution. Obscurities and inconsistencies apart, there are basically two views upon the character of the religious situation (which may be quite pre-Medieval) as suggested by this interesting poetry (the Maṅgal-kāvyas):

> Some scholars have felt that there is in the *maṅgal* poems an indication that early and indigenous mythology and belief have been overlaid with Brahmanism. Others have felt that the legend represents a decaying Śaivism being replaced by the encroaching cult of the female divinity, here represented by the serpent goddess.[548]

We have already accepted the former part of this observation—an overlaying Brahmanism—as constituting a rather general process which involved other coeval (e.g., sociological) factors. The Śaivism/female divinity side of the observation has a more specifically religious character, and such religious forces are probably representative of crucial mutations among the indigenous religious forms themselves; so that what must have occurred were theological and sectarian tensions between the Great and Little Traditions as well as *within* each of these traditions, especially the latter with its greater variety.

At any rate, it is noted that this sectarian struggle constitutes the beginnings of Bengali literature.[549] Certainly, it may not be regarded as the cause of the Bengali religious *experience*; but at the outset the

---

545 D. C. Sen, *History of Bengali Language and Literature*, p. 252. For an example of creative Vaiṣṇava *adaptation* to the Goddess of the Śāktas, *vide* L. P. Vidyarthi, ed., *Aspects of Religion in Indian Society* (Meerut: Kedar Nath Ram Nath, 1961), p. 51.

546 Dimock, *The Thief of Love*, p. 198.

547 D. C. Sen (*History of Bengali Language and Literature*, p. 253) claims Śaivite resistance to the Manasā cult even before its recognition "as a form of Sakti worship".

548 Dimock, *The Thief of Love*, pp. 199-200.

549 D. C. Sen, *History of Bengali Language and Literature*, p. 251.

question of the actual opposition or the potential "interplay of the gods" was a prominent factor. And the *dramatis personae* of the Manasā Episode (specifically, Cāndo and Behulā) would seem to represent differing attitudes toward the goddess Manasā as (paradoxically) a "compelling *iṣṭadevatā*" for all humanity. According to Dimock,[550]

> The basic theme of the tale is that of killing and revival, repeated and varied from episode to episode. All the chief protagonists except Lakhindar have the power to do both : Śiva, Dhanvantari, Cāndo, Manasā; and Behulā is instrumental in both the death and the revival of Lakhindar. All Manasā's antagonists are killed and revived at least once; every act of the tale contains this motif. Power is power for life as well as death.

In what appears to be another of its themes—blessed devotion through suffering[551]—the story resembles the biblical account of the personage Job.[552] However, other attendant themes are implicit to the basic one mentioned above, such as the desire to choose with reward or to resist with retribution;[553] lovers who suffer unfulfilled love; the inescapableness of death as divinely ordained fate; the eventual triumph and vindication of the *bhakta* whose devotion persists; and the subjection of even a *divinity*—Manasā—to a Higher (i.e., Ultimate) Court of Justice, which challenges totally outrageous fortune in the life of man.[554]

More significant than this, nonetheless, is the fact that whether or not there was a Śiva/Goddess sectarian competition, no decisive and permanent unaffiliation of these two groups was inevitable. Perhaps the totality of reasons for this may never be known. Still there are at least a couple of indications as to why these two sects have become traditionally related.

---

550 Edward C. Dimock, Jr., "The Goddess of Snakes in Medieval Bengali Literature II", *History of Religions*, III, No. 2 (Winter, 1964), 317.

551 Dimock, *The Thief of Love*, p. 294.

552 *Ibid.*, p. 199. Notice that, unlike Cāndo, Job believed himself at first to be in a state of devotion to the "proper" god. *Vide* the *blind* Śākta poet, Bhavani Prased Kar, in D. C. Sen, *History of Bengali Language and Literature*, pp. 229f.

553 For the divine-human confrontative pattern of the Manasā-devī, *vide* T. W. Clark, "Evolution of Hinduism in Medieval Bengali Literature", *Bulletin of the School of Oriental and African Studies*, XVII (1955), 507. Cf. the opposition-struggle-surrender pattern of the Dionysian cult in W. K. C. Guthrie, *The Greeks and Their Gods* (Paperback ed.; Boston : Beacon Press, 1966), pp. 165-173, esp. pp. 172-173. The beauty of the author's language itself is intoxicating. On the historical geography of the Manasā cult, *vide* Clark, "Evolution of Hinduism in Medieval Bengali Literature", p. 509.

554 Cf. Dimock, *The Thief of Love*, esp. pp. 209-212, 239-241, 246-248, 253-255, 259, 264ff., 271, 274-278.

One reason has to do with the fundamental serpentine phenomenology of the goddess Manasā. Interestingly enough, as a chthonian religious symbol this divinity, Sen notes,[555] is (a) conceived as intrinsically related to snakes as natural phenomena; (b) capable of being propitiated as the Goddess of Snakes;[556] and (c) representative of the divine power manifested in snakes.[557] The long-time traditional association of the god Śiva with snakes or serpents is fully attested to in Indian literature.[558] To be sure, the account of Manasā as the *daughter* of Śiva lends weight to one possible Śiva-and-goddess affiliation whether or not her eulogies are a productive response to a thriving or a decaying Śaivite cult. Moreover, there is the final reckoning of Manasā's behaviour before a Divine Council which included a few of what we might call the "Old Gods".[559] This would not prove but might suggest an underlying Brahmanic intentionality in the Manasā Episode.

Another reason has to do with what Chattopadhyaya poses as the concurrent but variant emergence of an Ardhanārīśvara motif or cult associable with the Śāktas. Here we seem to be confronted by a religious symbol which turns our minds in another direction—that of *inter*-sectarian theology. The historico-religious meaning of such an intriguing phenomenon has been variously understood : (1) the symbol reflects an attempt by Śaivite devotees to absorb the goddess into the Being of Śiva; (2) it represents an *hieros gamos* rite born out of the practical concerns of an agrarian community; (3) it reveals an attempt to raise the rank of the mother-goddess to equality with her consort.[560] Chattopadhyaya acknowledges these possibilities, but the author prefers, it seems, to emphasize the Upaniṣadic and (to some extent) the Ṛg-Vedic precedents for such a phenomenon. He, therefore, does not disown the fundamental objective of intersectarian relation. Indeed, those relations are seen to represent congenial efforts on the part of Śāktas, Śaivas, and Vaiṣṇavas (e.g., Śiva-and-Umā; Hari-

---

555 D. C. Sen, *History of Bengali Language and Literature*, pp. 252, 253. Cf. *supra*, p. 122.

556 Cf. Crooke, *The Popular Religion* ..., I, 151-152.

557 Cf. Edward C. Dimock, Jr., "The Goddess of Snakes in Medieval Bengali Literature I", *History of Religions*, I, No. 2 (Winter, 1961), 313.

558 Cf. Bhattacharji, *The Indian Theogony*, pp. 148, 151, 152; cf. *ibid.*, pp. 111, 176f.

559 Dimock, *The Thief of Love*, p. 271 : e.g., "Varuṇa", "Yama", etc.

560 Chattopadhyaya, *The Evolution of Theistic Sects in India*, p. 78. The author uses the term "sub-sect" (?); *vide ibid.*, pp. 77ff.

Hara; Kṛṣṇa-and-Radha) to bring about a creative and tolerant interplay of the gods.[561]

Among the local feminine deities with whom Śiva, as a typical rustic "Zeus" affiliates himself, the goddess Caṇḍi is notable as one divinity who does not become Śiva's daughter but his *consort.*

> Śiva and Caṇḍī are husband and wife, in which relationship is to be found an anthropomorphic figure of their unity within the person of the primal being. Caṇḍī is Śakti. Further evidence lies in the indiscriminate use for her of the names of other incarnations of Śakti in the varied stories of the puraṇās: Pārvatī, Ūmā, Bhavānī, Abhayā, etc. She is also frequently referred to as Caṇḍikā, the name of the goddess of "Mārkaṇḍeya Purāṇa". When she appears in her glory to Kālhetu, she does so under the guise of *mahiṣamardinī,* one of the best known figures of Dūrgā; and she is attended by the eight traditional aspects of Śakti, the *aṣṭa nāyikā.* She is also, Mukundarām's *kāvya,* referred to as *ādya-śakti,* the "primal Śakti", in which epithet the metaphysical identification is complete.[562]

It is the recognition that there is a stratification of theistic imagery [563] in the characterization of the god Śiva which helps to clarify both (1) the apparent "epithetic polygamy"[564] of this divinity in legend and art, and (2) the facilitation by which the sectarian interplay of the gods was accomplished on the plane of metaphysical religious thought. Far from being mere divine polygamy, however, we shall see (Chapter V) that this is more a matter of religious experience than preferential morals.[565] At any rate, studies in Śiva's focal relation with the germinal Pāśupata cult suggest, again, that a process of cultic bifurcation and valorization was later probably under way, which may have been connected with similar processes of Brahmanization that we mentioned earlier.[566]

The "heterodox" Pasupatas remain significant, nevertheless, because they can be viewed as a type of chthonian ("left-handed') Śaivism;[567]

---

[561] *Ibid.,* pp. 78, 79-81. Cf. D. C. Sen, *History of Bengali* Language and Literature, pp. 231, 234; and a similar view: "the union of various cults", in R. C. Agrawala, "Some Sculptures of Durgā-Mahiṣāsuramardiṇī from Rājasthāna", *Adyar Library Bulletin,* XIX, Part 2 (1955), 40.

[562] Clark, "Evolution of Hinduism in Medieval Bengali Literature", p. 517.

[563] Cf. Dimock, *The Thief of Love,* p. 198; Clark, "Evolution of Hinduism in Medieval Bengali Literature", p. 504.

[564] E.g., what were probably legendary cycles: Śiva-Kālī, Śiva-Umā, Śiva-Caṇḍī, etc.

[565] Cf. Guthrie, *The Greeks and Their Gods,* p. 55.

[566] Cf. Chattopadhyaya, *The Evolution of Theistic Sects in India,* pp. 67-77, esp. pp. 70ff. For more on the Pāśupatas, *vide* Briggs, *Gorakhnāth and the Kānphaṭā Yogīs,* pp. 218ff.

[567] Briggs, *Gorakhnāth and the Kānphaṭā Yogīs,* p. 171.

they could the more easily develop mythic, cultic, and symbolic "liaisons" with the Śākta sect. Most important, after all, is the fact that "it is in Śaivism that the ideas centering round Śakti have found a soil most favourable for their expression ..."[568]

Once a Śaivite-Śākta interrelation was established among popular circles, despite "primitive" elements,[569] the magnification by the Brahmanic *literati* of these two deities (Śiva and Śakti) became a quest for mythological continuity, relatedness, and originality. In the cultic domain these goals were also pursued but were concurrently under attack within the sects by ideas of either Tantric or Bhakti sectarian democracy.[570] Although, soteriologically, this democracy, too, had its initiatic prerequisites, the Tantric mode of salvation was "revealed" for the sake of an adharmic age. Within those circles where the worship of the god and the goddess was regarded as the epitome of a new cosmology, anthropology, even a theology, Śiva and Kālī were conceived and experienced as "the highest destinies"[571]—(Mahā-) Kāla and (Mahā-) Kālī.

In the next phase of our discussion (Chapter III) the goddess will remain bound to her consort, yet (reminiscent of Aditi), also, Unbounded, a Flood of Cosmogonic Bliss.

A Brief Historical-Religious Overview

In the present chapter we have sought to develop the "story" of the Indian mother-goddess Durgā-Kālī historically, phenomenologically, and structurally in keeping with already discussed methodological criteria (Chapter I). The task began with an attempt to place this divinity, however briefly, within a broader perspective of the history of religion, though in largely historio-morphological terms. Granting the inherent limitations of such an endeavour, it was yet considered that the goddess Durgā-Kālī was indeed an ideomorphic epiphany of the Primordial Earth Mother (*Terra Mater*). Consequently, this venture pursued by way of a developmental movement from concentric generality to concentric specificity, or from the centrifugal to the centripetal; or again, from the prehistoric to the protohis-

568 *The Cultural Heritage of India*, IV, 73. The sectarian impulse, however, is seldom completely abandoned : *vide* Banerjea, *The Development of Hindu Iconography*, pp. 552f.

569 E.g., Śiva as *Śmaśāna-Vasin* ("dweller in burial places"); Kālī as *Chinnamastā*.

570 I.e., *Avarṇāśramadharma*. *Vide* Hazra, *Studies in the Purāṇic Record*, pp. 224f.

571 Przyluski, "The Great Goddess in India and Iran", p. 429.

toric (the Indus Valley) and, finally, the historic (Vedo-Brahmanism, and thereon) as that religious symbol became manifest in a specific area and period of religious concentration and development—Bengal in Eastern India.

Further on, our efforts were directed toward the development of various aspects of the Indian mother-goddess as a religious form. It was important, however, to point out the vital forces of mythic, cultic, and symbolic modification, intrusion, and fusion in the light of other cultural and intra-cultural phenomena, such as historical, political, social, and artistic elements. Within the Indusian matrix, which, we have held, was or became eventually a complex ethnic, cultural, and religious milieu, there was an Harappān-Āryo-Aboriginal confluence of humanity. It was with remarkable discernment that Hinduism was once described as "an anthropological process". For it was essentially this confluence of humanity which gave birth to an influence of religion whose richness has become perennial in its effects upon Hindu life and culture. Another thing to remark is that the medley of religious evidence gathered by Marshall and others in the Indus Valley lends itself to both (1) the presence of proto-Hinduist embodiments indicative of an Earth-Cultus Orientation as at least part of the not now completely known Indusian *Weltanschauung, and* (2) the absence of a quality of data or artifacts which could prove incontestably the case for any *absolute* Harappān-Hinduist continuity of myth, cult, and symbols. It remains our contention, however, that the "substratum" analysis of Jan Gonda underestimates the composite value of the intimated ritual character of certain seals in the Indusian deposit and overemphasizes the range of symbolic diversity amongst admittedly religious artifacts to the detriment of the application of specifically historico-religious criteria. On the whole, nonetheless, the work of this Indologist still provides scholars with a helpful and critical corrective vis-à-vis the continual temptation among researches to indulge in romantic scholarship.

When we come to the Vedic period of Indian history, it becomes apparent that the compositeness of the earliest Indusian matrix has undergone a gradual process of hierocratization which finds its decisive focus in an emergent socio-religious stratification; but this development was yet accompanied, if not pervaded, by the coexistence of two rather *broad* life-orientations. One of these orientations continued to be pastoral, semi-nomadic, martial—however overarched by a celestial vogue of religious belief and symbolism. The other, which we have designated as "the Dravidian strain", was decidedly chthonian or terranean as a life-orientation, as well as more prone to explore and to express a primary intuition of the Earth as a source of Power-and-Being. Yet though other factors were integral to the total *Sitz im Leben*, it is not solely in linguistic, ethnic, or socio-political terms that the goddess Durgā-Kālī is to be religiously understood. For, in actuality, it was the latter of the two broad life-orientations—"the Dravidian strain"—which provided the *sacred* milieu which was so appropriate for the emergence of our particular divinity, Durgā-Kālī, as a chthonian deity. Hence we are reminded of her troublesome unlikeness to the "female" divinities among the Vedic Aryans. With regard to that particular life-orientation, however, including its religious symbols, it were better in a more general sense referred to (paraphrasing Tucci)[572] as a "phenomenon of *stress*", but always potentially pervasive even as an undercurrent among "the conflicting trends of Indian culture". When it concerns the goddess Durgā-Kālī, as the specific divinity upon whom we focus our attention, it is important also to recognize that, granting her general "unlikeness" to the Vedic divinities, the latter as religious symbols were not totally disparate symbolic phenomena in the matter of many specific elements regarding role, function, and attributes. Thus looms the partial validity for maintaining the "priority" of the Vedas in relation to later Hinduism.[573]

Notwithstanding these observations it must be emphasized that the goddess Durgā-Kālī should not be conceived merely as the product of Vedo-Brāhmaṇic myth-making or image-creation (e.g., Kāli a tongue of Agni, per se); she is not, again, a convenient integration of *all* the Vedic "female" divine symbolizations at a later stage of religious contemplation; nor still is she the fruit of an "aboriginalization" of a Sarasvatī, a Rātri, or an Aditi. To be sure, these may very well be relevant historical-religious phenomena in her comprehensive divine biography. In a word, Durgā-Kālī remains pre-eminently a religious creation of the "Dravidian" strain, but this, too, only at a relatively indeterminable stage of Indian religious history.

What, then, Vedicist and Dravidianist antiquarians tend to overlook is the fact that within a diachronic historico-religious perspective

572 Tucci, "Earth in India and Tibet", p. 355.

573 Griswold, *The Religion of the Rig Veda*, p. 328; M. Winternitz, *A History of Indian Literature*, trans. S. Kethar (3d ed. rev.; Calcutta: University of Calcutta, 1962), I, Part 1, 45.

the crux of the matter of the origin and character, for example, of a divinity such as Durgā-Kālī does not lie in *traditionalizing* her station in either of the foregoing orientations; but, instead, it lies in the realization that at a certain "moment" of crucial religio-*cultural* synthesis in Indian history a Pārvatī, Umā, Koṛṛavai, Kumārī, or Kāmākhyā becomes, paradoxically, the "discovery" and the "creation" of a religious history which is essentially *Indian* and not merely Vedic or Dravidian in nature. Furthermore, Tantric Buddhism as a relative but not necessarily an outgrowth of Tantric Hinduism also bears some relevance to the former point. For it is clear that having indeed found a plausible religious "beginning" (i.e., the Earth Cultus) for the Indian goddess Durgā-Kālī, the researcher is ironically denied within a perspective of cultural change a divinity that ultimately belongs to any single historical moment or religious source of creativity. It is true, of course, that the relation of the goddess to the god Śiva is enough to make us wonder whether we not are witnessing another crucial "arrest" of the type mentioned by Eliade—here : the historical-religious reactualization of an *hieros gamos* sacred apprehension in myth, cult, symbol. But, ultimately, again, this religious reality which is *the* goddess was not satisfied with having merely selective associations with "male" divinities, or with certain relative zones of the Sacred. This goddess seems really to return to her originally "unbounded" capacity (like Mother Earth), but now claims more than an earthly expanse, world, or wide. She symbolizes a cosmic expanse which has earned her the name of Ādyakālī.

It is thus that the Mātās of the north and the Ammās of the south of India can both [574] become engulfed in the Mahādevī—the "Great Goddess". But, then, this could only become so within a circular movement of mutual cultural enrichment within the sub-continent itself. It is this remarkable phenomenon in Indian history which continues to testify to the humanness beyond the religiosity of religions; that is, it seems that an earlier religious apprehension of the Infinite Sacred (in Vedo-Brāhmanism) lingering between henotheism and a threshold of monotheism could be transformed into a personal theistic (perhaps monotheistic) experience of the Holy (i.e., Śaktism). In another sense it is a tribute to sacred experience *beyond* mythic language [575] that the Brāhmaṇic priests could ignore the lower-

---

574 James, *The Cult of the Mother Goddess*, p. 116.

575 *Supra*, pp. 28-34.

caste rites to Durgā-Kālī but not so easily the *experience* of the Sacred and the Real which this religious symbol could evoke in the human spirit. Held suspect by some, worshipped by many, this Indian divinity assumes (as we shall see) a position so grand among her devotees that, for all practical purposes, she has become a kind of "unofficial" theological and experiential replacement for Brahmā of the traditional *Trimūrti*. India has a new creator—a *Creatrix*.

CHAPTER THREE

THE COSMOLOGICAL STRUCTURE OF MYTHICAL TIME : KĀLĪ-ŚAKTI*

Cosmogenesis

The form of the Goddess : Mahādevī

The goddess Durgā-Kālī thus appears within an historical-phenomenological perspective to be the structural and functional successor to the Creator (Brahmā) of the traditional Hindu Trimūrti. Yet we shall see that there is another sense in which this new *Creatrix* would seem to explode even that Trimūrtian structure. For in her most elevated cosmic phenomenology this divinity supersedes in resplendence and authority all the "forms" of the gods (*devas*) as well as the great gods (*Iśvaras*), especially Viṣṇu and Śiva. Nonetheless, as we stated much earlier, the paradox is that, in non-phenomenological terms, the history of the goddess and her manifestations remains inseparable from the historicity of the human beings who worship her. Accordingly, when we speak of the "Form" of the goddess (i.e., particularly as "Abstraction"), we are bound to acknowledge a perennial historical and religious truth; that is, man's irrespressible sensitivity to form,[1] even when he insists upon speaking of the Ultimate Reality as itself the Formless.

> The Devī, as Para-Brahman, is beyond all form and guṇa. The forms of the Mother of the Universe are three-fold. There is first the Supreme (*para*) form, of which, as

*This chapter was previously published, with minor modifications, in *History of Religions* 13 (Aug. 1973) by the University of Chicago, Chicago, Illinois, U.S.A.

[1] Cf. Ernst Cassirer, *The Philosophy of Symbolic Forms*, Vol. II : *Mythical Thought*, trans, Ralph Manheim (New Haven : Yale University Press, 1959), pp. 83, 90 : "Perception does not know the concept of infinity; from the very outset it is confined within certain spatial limits imposed by our faculty of perception .... Even the mythical world view starts from the most restricted sphere of sensuous-spatial existence. ... The objective world becomes intelligible to the mythical consciousness and divided into determined spheres of existence only when it is thus analogically 'copied' in terms of the human body". As the matter concerns the phenomenology of religious experience, of course, Cassirer's assertion does not apply to the perceptual possibilities of the "initiated consciousness". *Vide infra*, Chap. V. The author's statement does call attention, however, to a troublesome paradox in all theological and philosophical-religious epistemology.

the Viṣṇu-yāmala says, "none know". There is next her subtle (*Sūkṣma*) form, form, which consists of mantra. But as *the mind cannot easily settle itself upon that which is formless*, She appears as the subject of contemplation in Her third, or gross (*Sthūla*), or physical form, with hands and feet and the like as celebrated in the Devī-stotra of the Purāṇas and Tantras. (Italics mne.)[2]

Indeed, with Durgā-Kālī, as also other Hindu divinities, the Vedāntic-Upaniṣadic type of perception of the goddess as (either the wife of, or) the Para-Brahman is seldom found, if ever, to divorce itself radically from the morphic vision of her as the Macro-anthropic Feminine (i.e., Feminanthropos).[3] The devotees of the goddess, therefore, tend to confirm their irrespressible sensitivity to form per se,[4] in that the goddess is often textually portrayed as having at least, fundamentally, an Ultimate Form (= Formlessness, i.e., to the un-initiated)[5] and an Intimate Form which is accessible to men of faith through iconic or aniconic contemplation. In this regard it is interesting to notice that the gods (*devas*) themselves cannot know even the "Wonderful Cosmic Form" of the goddess without the personal extension of her Grace (*Anugraha*), to the comparative depreciation of practically all other modes of pleasing her except loving devotion (*bhakti*).[6]

The "Absolutely Ultimate"[7] Form (= Formlessness) of the goddess, then, transcends the basic dual stratification previously mentioned (i.e., subtle and gross) in terms of initiatic and experiential

---

[2] Sir John Woodroffe, *Introduction to Tantra Śāstra* (5th ed.; Madras: Ganesh and Co. Private, Ltd., 1969), p. 14. Devībhāgavata Purāṇa III.7.1-10, 16.

[3] Or, "Makranthropos", as used by Tucci, "Earth in India and Tibet", p. 358; also *supra*, p. 45, n. 14.

[4] For signs of the same in the Vedic period, *vide* Banerjea, *The Development of Hindu Iconography*, Chap. II, esp. pp. 42ff., 49, 57.

[5] Cf. Arthur Avalon (John Woodroffe), trans., *Karpūrādi-Stotra* (Hymn to Kālī) (Madras: Ganesh and Co. Private, Ltd., 1965), p. 36: Śiva to Kālī, in the Kubjikā-Tantra, "O Lady of Maheśa. One should meditate on the Formless ... along with the form. It is by constant practice, Oh Devī, that one realizes the formless". *Vide* Bharatan Kumarappa, *The Hindu Concept of Deity* (London: Luzac and Co., 1934), pp. 92-94; cf. *supra*, p. 62, n. 118.

[6] Devībhāgavata Purāṇa VII.34.1f. Cf. Brahmavaivartapurāṇa II.1.41.-50 ("Prakriti-Khanda"), especially the words: "She is Supreme, eternal and primordial. ... But she is imperceptible to the philosophers, gods and saints". For these purāṇas *vide* The Sacred Books of the Hindus, Vols. XXIV and XXVI; cf. Avalon, *Karpūrādi-Stotra*, "Introduction", esp. pp. 36-38; *vide* also Devībhāgavata Purāṇa VII.33. 20-53 and Bhagavad-Gītā XI.

[7] Cf. King, *Introduction to Religion*, p. 282.

significance. It would seem that this Para-formal Being of the goddess which "none know(s)", this Incomprehensible Reality, means the last endeavour of her devotees to extol her theologico-metaphysical greatness and grandeur beyond all contemplatable divine forms (devas, Īśvaras). Paradox, nonetheless, prevails because, on the one hand, man's visualizations of the omni-Sacred still tend to be correlative with "sensuous-spatial existence", the contingency of form; and, on the other hand, the "mythical-religious intuition" allows for the multi-valuation of profone existence[8]—here, for the *sādhaka* vis-à-vis the goddess, the whole of Reality will be seen to be characteristic of a cosmic anthropomorphism. For, as the Para-Śakti, the goddess is the Power beyond "powers"; she thus constitutes the Abyss of Power as Transcendental Form. Yet this remains a meaningless, abstract idea to those who have not entered into her secret Self, or allowed her to enter into their deluded self-understanding. The goddess, therefore, remains a mystery to all those who have not sought to grasp (or be grasped by) the truth of what it is to have the Power of Being (= sacred existence) in the world.

The Abstraction of Time : *Ādyakālī*

As that "Form" (-lessness) which it is not possible for the profane mind to imagine, grasp, or reach, the goddess is Non-Creative Power. She is pre-dynamically the Unmanifest, the Primeval, and the Supreme Prakṛti. She is the ultimate trans-theistic symbol of Timelessness—the Not-Time.[9] whose unmanifested and primordial supranature merit her the name of Ādyakālī. In her most transcendental status as the Primordial Goddess, our divinity possesses a fundamental *aseity*,[10] i.e., she is (a) without beginning, (b) without attributes, and (c) without contingency.

With a sense of inquiry which calls to mind the question of revelational continuity once asked by a forerunner's disciples, "Art thou he that should come ...",[11] another seeker after the vision of Ultimate Truth asks, then, the goddess, "Art thou the Brahman, the one and

---

[8] Cassirer, *The Philosophy of Symbolic Forms,* II, 118.

[9] Cf. Maitrāyaṇī-Brāhmaṇa-Upaniṣad VI.15a; Chāndogya Upaniṣad VI.2.1-2.

[10] Cf. William James, *The Varieties of Religious Experience* (enl. ed.; New York: University Books, Inc., 1963), pp. 439-442. *Vide* the commentary and n. 7 on the goddess as *Asite* (i.e., Unlimited, the Unlimited One), in Avalon, *Karpūrādiā-Stotra,* pp. 72-73.

[11] Matthew 11:2-3.

the secondless ... mentioned in the Vedas? ... Kindly solve this doubt of mine ... Whether Thou art male or female ... So that, knowing the Highest Śakti, I be freed from this ocean of Saṃsāra".[12]

The cosmological answer is given at once : that, though distinctions may emerge in the Being of the goddess at the time of Creation, *before* Creation there is no duality in this goddess of Eternal Being, Consciousness, and Bliss (*Saccidānanda*). To be sure, the testimony of a Ṛṣi to a king is that the goddess "is beginningless" and "therefore ... that Highest Devī is Eternal and ... always the Cause of all Causes".[13] Being absolutely beyond the opposites of phenomenal existence the goddess proclaims that "when everything melts away, i.e., there comes the Pralaya or general dissolution, then I am not female, I am not male, nor (am I) hermaphrodite".[14]

The dramatic primeviality of the goddess is again affirmed as a prelude to her epic confrontation with Demonic Powers. She, as Chandikā, is declared to "exist eternally". Her eternal existence is lauded in that she is not only the foundation of the universe, but once it is established she also maintains and protects the world. In fact, in words that suggest a pan-en-theistic imagery the traditional creator-god, Brahmā, extols her as "thou who containest the world". The goddess is, therefore, the "Queen of the Universe", and is the eternal World-Soul which resides in everything.[15]

That absolute ultimacy whose divinity as Supreme Form remains "Formlessness" to those who would dream of truth rather than live with it is affirmed by the goddess herself in words [16] that also reveal the limitations of language for men *and* divinities :

> I resemble in form Brahman ... from me emanates the world which has the Spirit of Prakriti and Purusha
> I am empty and not empty,
> I am delight and non-delight,
> I am knowledge and ignorance,[17]

---

[12] Devībhāgavata Purāṇa III.6.38ff.

[13] *Ibid.*, V.33.55ff.

[14] *Ibid.*, III.6.

[15] Mārkaṇḍeya Purāṇa LXXXI.47, 56, 63; cf. vss. 49-73 (text by Pargiter).

[16] Devī-Upaniṣad 1-3, quoted in Oppert, *On the Original Inhabitants ...*, p. 425. For another version *vide* Alain Danielou, "The Devī-Upanishad, A Śākta Upanishad", *The Adyar Library Bulletin*, XIX, Parts 1-2 (1955), 77-84, esp. 77-78.

[17] Cf. Mārkaṇḍeya Purāṇa LXXXI.1-44, esp. vss. 42-44 and 58; Devībhāgavata Purāṇa V.33.45-53.

I am Brahman and not Brahman,
I am the five perishable and imperishable elements
I am the whole world
I am the Vedas and not the Vedas ...
I am not born and am born [18]
I am below, above, and horizontal ...

Besides her eternity ("beginninglessness" : *Devī Sanātanī*) another dimension of her fundamental *aseity* is attested to by the affirmation that the goddess is beyond the "Forms" (attributes) of the great gods, singly or together, even beyond Trimūrti. Perhaps the paramount (though not the only) textual testimony of this distinctive "Aloneness"[19] of the goddess, is found in a delightful text of the Tantric-Śaktic tradition, the Saundaryalaharī (or "Flood of Beauty").[20] This artistic textual adoration of the goddess, which W. Norman Brown calls "a great work of religious literature",[21] is cherished by followers of both the Dakṣiṇācāra and Vāmācāra in the Hindu Tantric tradition.

It is hardly a wonder. The goddess in the text is portrayed as the One Supreme Being of obsessing beauty. She is there the ultimate *mysterium fascinans.* It was stated before that this is the text in which the goddess truly "comes into her own". Whereas other texts which regard her highly—not excluding the Devībhāgavata Purāṇa—tend to include multiple theologico-metaphysical structures, in the Saundaryalaharī it appears that the cosmogonic and the cosmo-redemptive are brought together in uniquely striking fashion amidst an outpouring of poetic adulation. Here the cosmogonic and cosmo-redemptive are merged in personalistic-pantheistic imagery in behalf of a divinity who is ultimately perceived as an Eternal Ground of Supra-conscious Being. In the Saundaryalaharī we seem to move beyond the rampant

---

[18] *Infra*, pp. 169.

[19] Cf. Devī : of the Bahvṛcopanishad, in Oppert, *On the Original Inhabitants ...*, p. 424; Karpūrādi-Stotra 12. Cf. the "Aim" of the "Invocation", Avalon, *Karpūrādi-Stotra*, p. 17; Devībhāgavata Purāṇa VII.32.1ff.

[20] *Vide* Brown, *supra*, p. 125, n. 455; also S. S. Sastri and T. R. Srinivasa Ayyangar, *The Saundaryalaharī* (Madras : The Theological Publishing House, 1965). The complete text has three parts : (1) Ānandalaharī (or "Wave of Bliss"), vss. 1-41; this single portion translated by Arthur Avalon (John Woodroffe), *Ānandalaharī* (Wave of Bliss) (multp. eds.; Madras : Ganesh and Co. Private, Ltd., 1961); (2) Saundaryalaharī (proper), or "Wave ('Flood') of Beauty", vss. 42-99, and (3) a "final stanza", vs. 100. For origins and analysis of content, *vide* Brown, *The Saundaryalaharī*, p. 1; also Sastri and Ayyangar, *The Saundaryalaharī*, pp. v-xv.

[21] Brown, *The Saundaryalaharī*, "Introduction", p. 30.

dualistic-monistic tension of the Devī-Māhātmya,[22] as well as the erotic, paradigmatic duality-in-unity of the Kālikā Purāṇa,[23] toward the radical structure of a theologico-mystical monism.

> The knowers of the scripture (āgama) speak of Druhina's
> wife (Sarasvatī), the goddess of speach, [as you,][24]
> Padmā (Lakṣmī), the wife of Hari, [as you,] the mountain's
> daughter (Pārvatī), Hara's mate, [as you],
> *you are an ineffable fourth* [beyond these three], hard
> to reach
> with power unbounded [by space, time, cause and effect,
> substance],
> O great power of creation (mahāmāyā), O wife of the supreme
> brahman (Sadāśiva), you put the universe through its revolution of appearances.[25]

In keeping with our former remarks, however, upon the irrepressible human sensitivity to "form", it must be recognized that the monism which belongs to the goddess in the Saundaryalaharī is, finally, a cosmic anthropo-monism or an anthropocosmic vision of Ultimate Reality.[26] Through his spiritual perception, then, the Śākta *sādhaka* realizes that the periodic Great Dissolution (*Mahāpralaya*) may occur through the mere closing of Devī's eyes,[27] at which time even the Trimurtī is obliterated. The mystery of Form and Non-Form is complete : whatever the goddess as the Eternal Form does not "see" (i.e., acknowledge as acceptable to her) does not *exist.* To be sure, her mere glance heals, renews,[28] which confirms that she has the Power of *Sat* and *Asat*—Being and Non-Being.

The goddess "without continguity" is paradoxically presented to us, insofar as "She is the three great goddesses—Sarasvatī, Lakṣmi, and Pārvatī",[29] while remaining the Surpassing Ground of their

22 *Supra*, p. 124f.

23 *Vide infra*, pp. 173.

24 All square brackets are those of the translator (Brown).

25 Saundaryalaharī 98; Sastri and Ayyangar, *The Saundaryalaharī*, pp. 247-248. (Italics mine).

26 Cf. Brown, *The Saundaryalaharī*, "Introduction", pp. 13-15, for the infra-kuṇḍalinīc development of the universe (vss. 36-41) *within* and *as* the goddess. *Vide* the ritual *reversal* of this process as soteriological act, *infra*, Chap. V.

27 Saundaryalaharī 56, 53; cf. Devībhāgatavata Purāṇa IX.9.1. For this "Eye Motif", *vide* W. Norman Brown, "The Name of the Goddess Minakśi 'Fish-Eye'", *Journal of the American Oriental Society*, LXVII (1947), 209-214, esp. 212-214.

28 Saundaryalaharī 13.

29 Brown, *The Saundaryalaharī*, p. 5. Cf. T. A. Gopinath Rao, *Elements of Hindu Iconography*, I, Part 2 (Madras : Law Printing House, 1914), 336-337.

divine particularity. For when she is referred to as the "ineffable fourth", such a symbol does not simply point to her as "another" goddess, superior in beauty and power, or even the totality of the other great "Lords"[30] but, rather, the revelation of a unique dimension of Being as Boundless Plenitude. In this vein such a vision is shared by other textual glorifications of her. The members of the Trimurti, too, therefore, are eschatologically swallowed up [31] and their traditional functions as Creator (Brahmā), Preserver (Viṣṇu), and Destroyer (Śiva) of the world are ultimately understood to be merely *instrumental* to the eternal Play (*Līlā*) of the goddess whom they, too, worship.[32] For she is both "Mother of Time" (*Kālamāta*) and the "Destroyer of Time" (*Kalāharshinī*).[33] Thus, if she should choose,[34] she may demonstrate her absolute Incontingency by aborting the existence of even that Consort whom mythological and theological tradition have persistently given her.[35]

> At the Dissolution of things, it is Kāla Who will devour all, and by reason of this He is called Mahākāla and since Thou devourest Mahākāla Himself it is Thou who are the Supreme Kālikā. Because Thou devourest Kāla, Thou art Kālī, because Thou art the Origin and devourest all things Thou art called Ādyā Kālī ... dark and formless, ineffable and inconceivable Thou alone remainest as the One.[36]

The Shape of Time : *Mahākālī*

> ... the mythical world achieves its true and specific articulation only when its dimension of depth ... opens up with the form of time.[37]

That which is One, Unmanifest and Primordial before the time of "Creation"[38] is also the dynamic Prakṛti—the key to the unfolding

---

[30] Cf. A. S. Gupta, "The Problem of Interpretation of the Puraṇās", *Purāṇa* VI,, No. 1 (January, 1964), 57f.

[31] Saundaryalaharī 26,29.

[32] Devībhāgavata Purāṇa V.33.60ff.; VII.29.1-19; III.5.28-37; *vide* also "Jagadambikā", in *H.T.T.G.*, p. 128, vs. 1; pp. 129f., vs. 5, and Kālikā Purāṇa 60:64-66 (tr. K. R. Van Kooij, *vide* bibliography).

[33] I.e., as "Ādyākālī" (*H.T.T.G.*, p. 40, vs. 1; p. 41, vs. 9).

[34] *Vide infra*, p. 169.

[35] Saundaryalaharī 26, 29. For a striking account of Śiva's humility before the omnipotence of Durgā (-Kālī), *vide* "an ode to the great goddess", or "the princely ode of Durgā", in Brahmanavaivartapurāṇa LXXXVIII.1-49 ("Krisna Janma Khanda").

[36] Mahānirvāṇa Tantra IV.30-33; IV.25-28; Devībhāgavata Purāṇa III.7.15. Cf. Brahmavaivartapurāṇa LVII.12ff. ("Prakriti Khanda").

[37] Cassirer, *The Philosophy of Symbolic Forms*, II, 105.

[38] *Vide infra*, pp. 157, 169, n. 111.

of the universe as the Great Time and the appearance of the multitudinous array of life-forms and natural phenomena; as one text puts it, her "wondrously variegated universe".[39] The goddess Durgā-Kālī is, then, cosmologically, soteriologically, and eschatologically related to the phenomenon of time as manifest being : (a) she, as Prakṛti, is the source of being as time (Kālī); (b) she, as Mahāmāyā, is the redemptrix of time as power (Śakti); and (c) she as Mahākālī is the destroyer of time as Śiva (Kāla).[40]

All three of these dimensions of her cosmogonic status and activity, however, are co-inherent, so that at any given "moment" in the drama of Creation via emanation or manifestation, we are dealing with the Inaccessible One who has chosen to become the Many.[41] Thus that which began as the most gloriously incontestable Fact (the goddess as *Asite*) now becomes actualized : a variegated Expression of her Being through an imaginative and playful contingency as Self-Manifestation.[42] We cite at length the following Śākta schematization by Radhakrishnan [43] of the emanation of the universe, because it epitomizes both the main stages of a highly complex process as well as refers to conceptual relations concerning the Śākta and other relevant philosophic orientations.

> Prakṛti or māyā is looked upon as of the substance of Devī. Within the womb of Śakti is māyā or prakṛti, the matrix of the universe, potential in pralaya and active in creation. The Sāṁkhya account of evolution from prakriti is followed.[44] Under

[39] Devībhāgavata Purāṇa III.6.38f. Cf. John Woodroffe and P. N. Mukhyopadhyaya, *Mahāmāyā, The World as Power : Power as Consciousness* (Madras : Ganesh and Co. Private, Ltd., 1964), p. 171.

[40] *Supra*, pp. 81-84. *Vide infra*, Chap. V.

[41] Cf. Chāndogya Upaniṣad VI.2.3ff.

[42] Cf. Herbert V. Guenther, "Tantra and Revelation", *History of Religions*, VII, No. 4 (May, 1968), 287ff.

[43] S. Radhakrishnan, *Indian Philosophy*, II (London : George Allen and Unwin, Ltd., 1962), 776. Cf. Woodroffe, *Śakti and Śākta*, pp. 362-390. This latter account appears earlier as a singular essay (pamphlet) entitled, "Creation As Explained in the Tantra", delivered by John Woodroffe at Calcutta, Bengal (1915); or *vide* "Extracts" of the same in B. D. Basu, ed., *Śrī Mad Devī-Bhāgavatam* (Sacred Books of the Hindus), Vol. XXVI; (Allahabad : The Panini Office Bahadurganj, 1921-1923), pp. 800-803.

[44] E.g., Devī-Māhātmya 4.6, 4.9 : *vide* these verses (text) and "Annotations", by V. S. Agrawala, *The Glorification ...*, pp. 198, 199. Cf. John Woodroffe, *The World As Power* (3d ed.; Madras : Ganesh and Co. Private, Ltd., 1966), pp. 283-285; Brown, *The Saundaryalaharī*, pp. 7f. On the Sānkhya *darśana*, *vide* Radhakrishnan, *Indian Philosophy*, II, 248-335, esp. 256-277; Surendranath Das Gupta, *A History of Indian Philosophy*, I, 245-259; S. Prabhavananda, *The Spiritual Heritage of India* (London : George Allen and Unwin, 1962), pp. 208-225.

Śakti's direction, māyā evolves into the several material elements [45] and physical portions of all sentient beings. In all living beings, caitanya or consciousness is present, though it appears as broken up into a multiplicity of beings on account of the varying physical adjuncts. Instead of the twenty-five [46] tattvas of the Sāṁkhya, we have thirty-six,[47] which are classified into: (1) Śivatattva, the supreme; (2) Vidyātattva, or the subtle manifestations of Śakti; (3) Ātmatattva, or the material universe from way down to earth.[48] These three answer to prakāśa (Śiva), vimarśa and the not-self. The supreme spirit of the Śākta scheme has inner differences,[49] though frequently we meet with ideas of salvation and oneness of the world, which remind us of Śaṁkara's more rigorous non-dualism.[50] We have, first of all, the absolute Brahman; next, we have the determinate subject endowed with Śakti. Nāda issues immediately and from nāda bindu appears, and then the Śuddhamāyā. These five answer to Śiva, Śakti, Sadākhya, Īśvara and the Śuddhamāyā of the Śaivas. The rest of the evolution is not different from the Śaiva scheme.[51]

In consideration of the foregoing schematization we would call attention to two pertinent theologico-metaphysical concepts as

---

[45] Ānandalaharī 35; cf. *ibid.*, 37-41; Devībhāgavata Purāṇa III. 6; III.7.11-52. Cf. Woodroffe, *The World As Power*, pp. 176-186.

[46] Twenty-four (minus "Puruṣa"); *vide* Radhakrishnan, *Indian Philosophy*, II, 273.

[47] Cf. Woodroffe, *The World As Power*, p. 157: *vide* Woodroffe, *Śakti and Śākta*, pp. 273-276 and diagram on p. 272; John Woodroffe, trans., *Varnamālā*; [Garland of Letters] (Madras : Ganesh and Co. Private, Ltd., 1963), pp. 83-92; Sastri and Ayyangar, *The Saundaryalaharī*, pp. 50-60.

[48] Woodroffe's account of Prakṛtic evolution (*supra*, p. 157, n. 43) appears to include no details of what M. Hiriyanna (*Outlines of Indian Philosophy* [London : George Allen and Unwin Ltd., 1967], p. 276) calls "secondary evolution"; *vide* Radhakrishnan, *Indian Philosophy*, II, 271-274; Eliade, *Yoga*, p. 21. Woodroffe (*Śakti and Śākta*, pp. 366f., 387, and "Creation as Explained in the Tantras", pp. 4, 21) does, however, point out the main categories for such a subsidiary development. His general objective is (a) an "exposition of the nature of Shaktitattva"; (b) an "account of its manifestation in the universe" (*Śakti and Śākta*, p. 387; "Creation as Explained in the Tantras", p. 14). Notwithstanding his remark that "the Sakta Tantra is not a formal system of philosophy (*Darśana*)", the author betrays an intense interest in attempting to distinguish the Śaktivāda approach to Ultimate vis-à-vis other Indian systems : *vide Śakti and Śākta*, pp. 362-408, 705-717, and also *The World As Power*, pp. 19-22.

[49] Cf. Shashi B. Das Gupta, *Obscure Religious Cults*, pp. 379-389; Prabhat Chandra Chakravarti, *Doctrine of Śakti in Indian Literature* (Calcutta : General Printers Limited, 1940), pp. 71-86, 88-122; also Surendranath Das Gupta, *A History of Indian Philosophy*, III, 496-511.

[50] *Supra*, pp. 152-154; Devī-Upaniṣad 26; Mahānirvāṇa Tantra IV.25-28, 34; cf. *ibid.*, II.33-44. On Vedānta, *vide* Radhakrishnan, *Indian Philosophy*, II, Chaps. VII and VIII, 445-461, 520, 533-541, 565-574; Surendranath Das Gupta, *A History of Indian Philosophy*, I, 429-452, 485-489; Prabhavananda, *The Spiritual Heritage of India*, Chaps. XV and XVI.

[51] Cf. Arabinda Basu, "Kashmir Śaivism", in *The Cultural Heritage of India*, IV, 79-91; J. Sinha, *Shakta Monism*, pp. 1-9, 19-22.

being singularly and coherently important to the cosmological structure of the Śāktas. They are these : (1) the idea of Kālī-Śakti as a symbol of monadic multivalence, and (2) the idea of Kālī-Śakti as a symbol of diadic univalence.

The idea of Kālī-Śakti as a symbol of monadic multivalence was earlier intimated in the portrayal of the goddess as the Flood of Beauty and Bliss, which envelops the Trimūrti, their Śaktis, and all other beings. Moreover, in her distinctive dimension as the "Fourth" Reality, not "next in" but envoloping and "beyond"[52] Time, the contemplation of her divine creativity raises at once the question concerning the Absoluteness and the Relativity of the goddess as Fact (Essence) and Expression (Manifestation). Her divine *aseity* cannot, therefore, be separated from her cosmogonic activity; for "insepara-bility is the key word in Tantrism : inseparability of the absolute and the relative, of the divine and the human, and, by implication, of fact and expression".[53] The goddess, then, is "the Absolute Spiritual Whole (*Pūrna*)", as much as she is also "the relative psychophysical whole (*māyā*)".[54] She is the One

> who is pure Being-Consciousness-Bliss, as Power, who exists in the form of Time and Space and all that is therein, and who is the radiant Illumination in all beings.[55]

Being both the Abstraction (Incomprehensibility) and the Shape (Personification) of Time, the goddess holds within herself the Power (Śakti) which is also *Maya*, so that she is known as Mahā-Śakti, Mahāmāyā, and Mahākālī; the dynamic aspect of the Supreme Time (*Parākāla*) or the Great Time (*Mahākāla*) corresponds to her Timeless *aseity* and Relative time corresponds to her cosmic creativity. Yet her Self-exfoliation is a creative continuum, along which Time comes into being only with the appearance of the heavenly bodies after the underlying constituents of the universe (*tattvas*) have evolved.[56] Furthermore, her creativity as cosmic continuum presupposes the supersession of all the ordinary conceptions of the relation between cause and effect. The goddess as the Translogical Whole (Devī) "does

---

52 Cf. Woodroffe and Mukhyopadhyaya, *Mahāmāyā*, pp. 6ff.

53 Guenther, "Tantra and Revelation", p. 289.

54 Woodroffe, *Śakti and Śakta*, p. 402.

55 Yoginīhṛdaya Tantra, quoted *ibid.*, p. 26.

56 *Ibid.*, p. 407.

not cease to be the cosmic cause because it evolves as the universe its effect".[57]

A glance at certain synthetic but varying views regarding Time in monistic (Advaita) cosmology reveals the following possibilities which aid in clarifying the glory of the goddess as Chronic Multi-form: (1) "time is an effect (*Kārya*) of *avidyā* or *Māyā* like space ... (2) time is not an effect of *avidyā* but is the relation between it and spirit or Brahman ... (3) time [is identifiable] with *avidyā* ... (and, 4) time [is] an aspect (*rupā-bheda*) of Brahman itself".[58] To begin with, let us note that the goddess as the Personification of Time through *māyā-Śakti* remains unchanged in her comprehensive quintessence (*saccidānanda*), and Time as the exfoliation of that quintessence does not constitute a quantitative or qualitative reduction of her Being as emanation.[59] Thus *māyā*, whose nature as "measure" has lured many to understand it as solely "illusion", becomes more decisively in the Śākta Cosmogonic world-view the source of natural phenomenality and/or human *delusion*,[60] as well as the redemptive milieu through which the goddess "as Liberatrix" delivers man "from the ignorance of the forms which are of Her making ...".[61] In her capacity, then, as Mahāmāyā (i.e., The Great Measurer), the goddess Durgā-Kālī can be not only

> the Veiler even of the Creator, Sustainer and Destroyer of the World. But, fundadamentally, She is ... the Whole Reality-Power both in Its veiling and revealing, binding and liberating aspect ... As the Supreme Veiler [62] She is ... Mahā-mohā, and as the Supreme Revealer She is Mahā-vidyā. [Yet] in her aspect of Māyā, She is, generally, described as the veiler, creating and drawing the veil over all particular existences. ...[63]

The significant thing to be grasped is that both of these cosmogonic *desiderata* ("veiling" and "revealing") are integral to the creativity of the goddess, i.e. (*Mahā-*) *vidyā* and (*Mahā-*) *māyā* are *real* [64] aspects

---

[57] *Ibid.*. p. 408; Woodroffe, *The World As Power*, pp. 339-365, esp. pp. 360-365; cf. *ibid.*, p. 47. Notice (*ibid.*) the use of the term "Śākta Darśana" (*supra*, p. 158, n. 48).

[58] M. Hiriyanna, "Advaitic Conception of Time", *Poona Orientalist*, IV, Nos. 1-11 (April-July, 1939), 47-48.

[59] The transcendence-immanence problematic is also noted by Kumarappa, *The Hindu Conception of Deity*, pp. 102-105.

[60] Devībhāgavata Purāṇa VI.31.22-51; Gonda, *Change and Continuity in Indian Religion*, pp. 164-176, 186-187.

[61] Woodroffe and Mukhyopadhyaya, *Mahāmāyā*, p. 260.

[62] Cf. *ibid.*, pp. 46-72.

[63] *Ibid.*, p. 260; *supra*, p. 153, n. 17.

[64] Woodroffe and Mukhyopadhyaya, *Mahāmāyā*, pp. 11-13.

of Ultimate Reality (= the goddess). In this perspective, therefore, (1) Time is not an effect but (like "Space" : *Dik*)[65] a *medium* of *avidyā*; (2) Time is not the "relation" between *avidyā* and Brahman (= the goddess) but the empirical energy of Brahman as *avidyā* (= *māyā*); (3) Time *is* thus a *practical* aspect of *avidyā* (i.e., "Time as (a) śakti (*kriyā-śakti*)",[66] of the goddess; but, again, (4) Time is also an aspect of Brahman (= the goddess) as a "created" (emanated, devolved) *Eternal Continuum*.[67]

Through and within her creative "chronicization" (the goddess as Time and "times" = yugas)[68] there then emerges the variegation of her Cosmic Consciousness (*cit*) as Multiform.[69] Devolved forms of being, ranging from the dimensionalization of the heavens with their sundry beings; devolved forms of life, ranging from man to various microscopic and sub-microscopic organisms, are manifestations of (and pervaded by) the goddess as *Saccidānanda-mayī*).[70]

> The world [as manifested in Time] is not something which has reality independent of Consciousness. It is the transforming and transformed Power of Śakti .... the Divine Mother of the Universe. The Mother as Material Cause ... is not thus, as the Sāṁkhyas affirm, something unconscious. The Mother-Energy is the Source of all mind, life, and matter and their energies which are all modes of Her as Substance-Energy. The Power which evolves the world is both Consciousness (*Cit-Śakti*) and *Māyā* or the finitising power (*Māyā-Śakti*) which manifests as mind and matter. ... Śakti is the Principle of Change and assumes the changing forms which constitute the universe.[71]

---

65 Woodroffe, *The World As Power*, p. 309; also Hiriyanna, "Advaitic Conception of Time", p. 48. Cf. Yoginīhṛdaya-Tantra (Woodroffe, *The World As Power*, p. 229): "I salute Her the *Samvid Kalā* who shines in the form of Space and Time, words and meanings, and in the form of all things which are in the Universe".

66 Hiriyanna, "Advaitic Conception of Time", p. 48.

67 *Ibid.* Cf. Woodroffe, *The World As Power*, pp. 263-268, 392-398; *vide* also Stanislaw Schayer, *Contributions to the Problem of Time in Indian Philosophy* (Cracow: Nakadem Polskiej akademii umiejtęności, 1938), pp. 6-12.

68 *Vide infra*, Chap. V.

69 *Vide* "Mahādevī" and "Ambikā", in *H.T.T.G.*, pp. 100ff., vss. 2, 3, 5, 7, 22, 31a; pp. 119-127, esp. vss. 2v, 6, 12, 15, 28; also Sita Upanishad 1-37, esp. vss. 3-4, 10, 12, 13, 14, translated by Alain Danielou in *Adyar Library Bulletin*, Vol. XIX, Parts 3-4 (1955). Cf. Woodroffe and Mukhyopadhyaya, *Mahāmāyā*, pp. 35f. (cf. pp. 32f.); *ibid.*, pp. 84-96, 127-132.

70 Cf. Woodroffe and Mukhyopadhyaya, *Mahāmāyā*, p. 258; also *ibid.*, pp. 214-217, 153-165, 226-229 *et passim*; Woodroffe, *The World As Power*, pp. 99, 176f., 217-234, esp. pp. 219-221, 230-233, 299, 332f., 243, 260-266, 278-285 (cf. pp. 54-58); and, *Introduction to Tantra Śāstra*, pp. 25f.

71 Woodroffe, *The World As Power*, pp. 356-357.

The conception of Kali-Śakti as a symbol of diadic univalence is particularly relevant to both the phenomenon of anthropogenesis as well as the structural phenomenology of Ritual Time (presented in Chapter IV). To be sure, the relation between these two theological symbols ("Śiva" and "Śakti") has often been considered a subject of religio-symbolic and metaphysic curiosity. Our present purpose, however, is to emphasize the importance of them in at least two specific respects. First, there is the way in which they illustrate, further, not only some of the basic features of the cosmogony rendered above; but they also represent the Śākta solution to the problem of the ontological homogeneity and creative differentiation of the cosmos.[72] Secondly, there is the way in which such symbols (Śiva-Śakti) suggest (a) the prototypical basis for the structural homologation of man and cosmos, as well as (b) a new phenomenological possibility: that such symbols represent a distinctive *raison d'être* or *raison de créer* with regard to both cosmogenesis and anthropogenesis.

A tantric literary production which is frequently alluded to even by other texts and contains a description of Śiva-Śakti in cosmogonic mutuality is known as the Kāma-Kalā-Vilāsa, i.e., "the spreading or emanation or evolution of the Kāmakalā that is the Supreme Triangle of the Bindu and Visarga, or Prakāśa and Vimarsā, of Śiva and Śakta, of the 'I' (*Ahaṁ*) and 'This" (*Idaṁ*) or Universe ... the Śiva-Svarūpa and the Śakti-Svarūpa".[73] Attributed by Woodroffe to a tantric scholar, Punyanandanatha, and said to be a text of some (unascertained) antiquity,[74] the Kāma-Kalā-Vilāsa is a literary-religious portrayal of the Divine Diad (Śiva-Śakti) through which is effected the "phenomenalization" of the Ultimate Reality as the Universe (*Prapañca*). The diadic motif, moreover, is correlated with the yantra par excellence, the Śri-yantra,[75] which in turn is accompanied by both mysto-alphabetic and mantrayanic symbols, in order to schematize the basic features of the cosmogony which occurs through changeless Consciousness (Cit, Samvit) and changing Power (Cit-Śakti, Māyā-Śakti).

---

72 *Supra*, p. 158f.

73 Arthur Avalon (John Woodroffe), trans., *Kāma-Kalā-Vilāsa* (Madras: Ganesh and Co. Private, Ltd., 1961), pp. ix, xf., and vss. 25, 39.

74 *Ibid.*, pp. v, ix.

75 Cf. John Woodroffe, *Tantrarāja Tantra: A Short Analysis* (Madras: Ganesh and Co. Private, Ltd., 1964), the Frontispiece and pp. 1-14, esp. pp. 5-10; and *Śakti and Śākta*, pp. 408-410.

The Śiva-Śakti symbolism illustrates, further, the process of cosmogenesis by, first of all, bringing to a focus the paradoxical problem of of Absolutivity and Relativity mentioned earlier. They are, then, cosmic personifications of the macroscopic Impersonal (= Nirguna Brahman) and, as such, symbolize the creative process as Being and Becoming, Cause and Effect, Power-Holding and Power-Holder.[76] In their Sagunic Duo-Form they are also cosmo-chronic personifications i.e., Mahākāla-Mahākālī) which encompass the transcendent being of Time as disinterestedness, satiation, and immortality, as well as the transcendent power of Time which brings partiality, hunger, and death.[77]

Phenomenologically, there is an implicit or intentional *monadic ambivalence* in this Diad which derives, ultimately, from their very nature as Univalent Being (Śiva = Śakti). Accordingly, Śiva and Kālī-Śakti can be conceived as *dynamically* interrelated, so that whether in āgamic-nyamic pedagogical relation, maithunic activity, or legendary tension,[78] their ultimate (actual) unity remains structurally inseparable from their intimate (potential) disunity as a reflection of sensuous-spatial human experience (Cassirer). Moreover, this monadic ambivalence, though subsumed under the term, diadic univalence, includes a further devolvement which intrigues us and to which we tend to refer as "the ambivalization of the ambivalent"; that is, as distinct (sectarian) divinities both Śiva and Kālī are, *each*, ambivalent : benevolent *and* malevolent in character. Thus, whereas the term diadic univalence refers properly to their metaphysical "mutual identity", it is infrastructurally continuous with their singular sovereignty (as *iṣṭadevatās*) *within Time* for good *and* ill.[79] Finally, in a very specific sense, the former two broad dimensions—the ultimate and the intimate—are structurally mergent, insofar as the Śiva-Śakti symbolism is a cosmogonic *metasexual* prototype of the process of mundane procreation, i.e., in their act of

---

[76] Woodroffe, *The World As Power*, pp. 46f., 143f., 377, 385; Woodroffe and Mukhyo-Caphyaya, *Mahāmāyā*, pp. 4f., 24f., 80-83; Kāma-Kalā-Vilāsa 28.

[77] Danielou, *Hindu Polytheism*, pp. 270f. Schayer, *Contributions ...*, pp. 6f.; Woodroffe and Mukhyopadhyaya, *Mahāmāyā*, p. 171. *Vide* also H. Zimmer, "Some Aspects of Time in Indian Art", *Journal of the Indian Society of Oriental Art*, I, no. 1 (June, 1933), 30-51, esp. 49-51.

[78] Cf. A. Coomaraswamy and Sister Nivedita, *Myths of the Hindus and Buddhists* (New York : Dover Publications, Inc., 1967), pp. 295-301.

[79] *Supra*, pp. 40, 143; Briggs, *Gorakhnāth and the Kanphaṭā Yogīs*, pp. 152, 164.

now expanding and now contracting ... now entering and now separating from one another. ... These two Bindus [Śiva-Śakti] which enter one another and separate ... are the united white and red Bindus (*Sita-śoṇa-bindu-yugalam*) which are known as Kāma-Kāmeśvari, the divine Husband and Wife ...[80] the pair, one namely *Vimarśa* is the Red Bindu, and the other, *Prakāśa*, the White Bindu, and the union of the two is the mixed (*Miśrarūpa*) and all powerful (*Sarvatejomaya*), the *Svarūpa* of which is the Paramātmā (*Paramātmā-svarūpa*).[81]

At this point a critical observation should be made regarding the foregoing diadic dynamism at the level of the cosmogony. For, if we allow that the Śiva-Śakti diad represents the cosmological "tantricization" of earlier darshanic categories (especially the Sānkhya's "Puruṣa-Prakṛti"),[82] then the Śaktivada theory of *Adṛṣṭa-Sṛṣṭi*[83] raises a question similar to that concerning the consistency of Sānkhya cosmology.[84] Whether or not the literary opinion that the Śākta ontology was designed "to establish unity amongst worshippers" has any historical validity,[85] the Śākta approach to the metaphysic of an "Unmoved Mover" has its merits. Their solution to the problem involves again a theology of diadic univalence; that is, *a theory of mutual reality*: the interchangeability of identity, power, and activity of the (two Sānkhyan) Primary Ultimates: Puruṣa (= Śiva) and Prakṛti (= Śakti). Posing, therefore, no original ontological independence of these primordial realities, the "mutual reality" of Śiva and Śakti required no additional rational exposition of the eventual "perturbability" of the Imperturbable (Puruṣa); for the mutually *affective* reality[86] of Śiva (= Puruṣa) and Śakti (= Prakṛti) was not

---

[80] I.e., *Divya-daṁpati-māyā*; hence, *Śiva-Śakti-mithunapiṇḍa.*

[81] Kāma-Kalā-Vilāsa 6, 7, and commentary, p. 16.

[82] Woodroffe, *The World As Power*, p. 46.

[83] Woodroffe, *Śakti and Śākta*, pp. 365, 378-380, 389-390; and "Creation as Explained in the Tantras", pp. 3, 14f., 22-24.

[84] Cf. Radhakrishnan, *Indian Philosophy*, II, 303ff.; *vide* "Pralaya and ... Prakṛti", and the teleological assumption, in Surendranath Das Gupta, *A History of Indian Philosophy*, I, 247f., 258f. (cf. Hiriyanna, *Outlines ...*, pp. 273, 279f.); Surendranath das Gupta, *A History of Indian Philosophy*, I, 440-441; Eliade, *Yoga*, pp. 17f. *Vide*, esp. Karl H. Potter, *Presuppositions of India's Philosophies* (Englewood Cliffs, N.J.: Prentice-Hall, Inc., 1963), pp. 150-153. Cf. "a classical problem of metaphysies", in Heinrich Zimmer, *Philosophies of India*, ed. Joseph Campbell (Meridian Books: Cleveland and New York: The World Publishing Co., 1964), pp. 527ff.

[85] The Śaktisaṅgama-Tantra: according to Woodroffe, *The World As Power*, p. 77.

[86] *Vide* in this connection the remarkably interesting "Mirror-Motif", Kāma-Kalā-Vilāsa 2, 4 and commentary, pp. 7f., 11f. Devībhāgavata Purāṇa III.6: "There is oneness always ... there is no difference whatsoever at any time between me and the

now preconceived without explanation of an implicitly necessary relation [87] but took the form of a distinctive (though yet another) a priori, in that its very paradoxical quality might render it intelligible to the imagination of persons who had experienced that paradox not so much in cosmic terms as much as in their daily lives, natural movements, and inner being—the paradoxes of human existence. It is true, of course, that the Śākta "duality-in-unity",[88] itself, probably, constitutes another philosophical enigma to persons rather than an intellectually satisfying solution.[89] But the answer to that also tends to be understood on the level of *religious experience* [90] and is therefore as translogical (Woodroffe: "alogical") as that Whole (Brahman = Śakti-Svarūpa) which, apart from the initiated (Sādhakas), "none know"(s).[91]

Secondly, following our earlier statements, the Śiva-Śakti symbolism provides a prototypical basis for the structural homologation of man and cosmos. To be sure, the relation between man and cosmos in Hindu religious thought has its possible intravarieties. A synthetic reduction of philosophic options, however, takes the form of the following three important "causational" variations: (1) "that which gives birth to an effect is a different entity ... [2] that which evolves an effect but of itself is one with it ..., [and 3] that which gives rise to illusory phenomena in appearances without undergoing any esssential change is the Para Brahman".[92] In the first case, man might differ

---

Purusha ... The One Secondless Eternal ever-lasting Brahma substance becomes dual at the time of creation. As ... a face, though one, becomes two, as reflected in a *mirror* ... we become reflected into many [italics mine] ...". Cf. Arabinda Basu, "Kashmir Śaivism", pp. 84f. and also p. 255.

87 I.e., Potter, *Presuppositions of India's Philosophies*, p. 151: "... there is heavy pressure on Sāṃkhya to combine into one its two basic metaphysical entities—*puruṣa* and *prakṛti*—since the Sāṃkhya philosopher cannot intelligibly say how they come together into relation with one another".

88 Woodroffe and Mukhyopadhyaya, *Mahāmāyā*, p. 12: "Reality is a concrete unity in duality and duality in unity"; *vide* Kāma-Kalā-Vilāsa 11.

89 E.g., Woodroffe, *The World As Power*, p. 49: "Doubtless this doctrine does not explain how logically God can be changeless and yet change".

90 *Ibid.*, pp. 42f. The cosmological paradox is religiously experienced as spiritual integration or unification.

91 *Supra*, p. 151.

92 Cf. T. C. Rajan Iyengar, *The Hindu-Aryan Theory on Evolution and Involution* (New York and London: Funk and Wagnalls Co., 1908), pp. 1-7; *vide* also R. C. Zaehner, *The Comparison of Religions* (Paperback ed.; Beacon Press, 1962), p. 58, for a synthesis of the relation between cosmology and anthropology in the Upaniṣads *Supra* and *infra*:

in form, nature, and activity from his Ultimate Source or Being; although, if not in all these specifics, he might nonetheless differ in the quality of his ontological substance. He would, therefore, remain but a "creature" among creatures vis-à-vis his conception of Ultimate Reality as, perhaps, "Wholly Other".

In the second case, the individual might be conceived as having not only an identical substance (substrate) as his Ultimate Cause, but, because of that homo-substantiality, such a being could probably attain a quality of conscious communion with the Source of his origin, which would mark the transcendence of his own apparent phenomenal existence—in or beyond the world. At any rate, "the All-Pervading character [i.e., the imperishable substantiality] would not then be the exclusive property of Para Brahman or God alone; but it would be the common property of God and Man".[93]

In the third case, the human being might be regarded as having no fundamental and distinct reality apart from the Ground of his being (i.e., the Parambrahman). Hence man's self (*ātman*), when recognized, finally, as essentially and indistinctively the Ultimate under the form of *māyā* ("illusion" = delusion) would achieve its supreme Self-Realization: the mutual identification of the world, himself, and Ultimate Reality.[94]

Combining the latter two of the foregoing perspectives in its application of the principle of "duality-in-unity", the Sakta anthropology understands man to be a theophany of the goddess as incarnate Consciousness. Man, however, is a being of identical reality with the goddess but only as a potentially liberated Consciousness. The phenomenon of Śākta worship is in large part the story of that being's soteriological endeavour to elevate his (ordinary) consciousness to the level of a supra-conscious awareness of Being: both *in* and *with*, and *as* the goddess. This means again that man's phenomenal existence continues to have an ontological structural relation to the Śiva-Śakti

---

it will be seen that the Śākta viewpoint envelops basically all of these viewpoints (Zaehner) except that the universe is not illusory in the sense of "not-real"; and the affirmation of spiritual liberation, *Sa'ham* (She I am), it appears, confirms no "substantial" cosmological-anthropological heterogeneity but, rather, reflects our earlier appropriate use of the term "cosmic anthropomonism" (or else "anthropocosmos" and "makranthropy" via Tucci); *vide* Eliade, *Yoga*, pp. 235f. For anthropocosmic images, *vide*, e.g., Kāma-Kalā-Vilāsa 18, 36-38, and commentary, pp. 36, 70, 72f.; Saundaryalahari 19, 34; Devībhāgavata Purāṇa V.8.47-74, IX.2.1ff.; Brahmavaivartapurāṇa II.2.f.

93 Rajan Iyengar, *The Hindu-Aryan Theory* ..., pp. 4-5.

94 Woodroffe, *The World As Power*, pp. 65, 153.

diad. For inasmuch as his lack of Cosmic Consciousness (= supra-consciousness) tends to be typified, granting multiple levels of spirituality,[95] by the perennial delusion of "I"-"This"-ness he is virtually caught between two *realities* : the world as *nāma-rūpa* and his inner being as *cit-Śakti*. Only the goddess knows that they are the *same* Reality.

Man, therefore, on the level of unliberated consciousness, remains a theophany of the goddess, but he appears to be an ambivalent entity : a being caught between the "fact" of Being and the "expression" of Becoming, the Cause (his "Creator") and the Effect (the individual as "creation"), being Power-held and a Power Holder (*Śaktiman*). Ideally and phenomenally, at any rate, just as

> to the Śākta ... the Mother of the world is a Divine Person, the Supreme "I" (*Pūrṇāham*) in which all other *limited* Egos are ...[96] Man is threefold as Spirit, Mind, Body.[97] As Spirit he is Śiva who, in Himself, is pure Consciousness. As Mind and Body he is Śiva as Power, or "God in Action" or Śakti. That Power contracts consciousness in those subject to it.[98] The same Power in the liberating aspect expands man's consciousness until it becomes infinite and one with Hers. *Māyā-Śakti* is the Mother Herself as the World-Creatrix. *Avidyā-Śakti* is the Mother in the form of man and all other beings and things. (Italics mine).[99]

The goddess is, moreover, specially and archetypically related to the female sex in essence and manifestation. "She is the Gem amongst women. ... Every female in every Universe is sprung from a part of Śrī Radha or part of a part";[100] that is,

> the women of the world are descended from her digits. Insult to women is indignity to Nature [= Prakṛti = Goddess] ... Her digits are worshipped, particularly in the sacred land of India.[101]
>
> Each mother, whether of plants, animals, or men is the type of the archetypal Mother Goddess, Mahā Devī, Mahā-Mātā.[102]

---

95 Woodroffe and Mukhyopadhyaya, *Mahāmāyā*, pp. 149f. A diminutive level of human spirituality might, of course, be equivalent to the "first case" (*supra*, pp. 166), i.e., perception of the goddess as "Wholly Other" (whom "none knows").

96 Woodroffe and Mukhyopadhyaya, *Mahāmāyā*, pp. 147f. *et passim*.

97 Woodroffe, *The World As Power*, pp. 137f., 151f., 155ff., 167ff. (cf. Kāma-Kalā-Vilāsa 5); Woodroffe, *Introduction to Tantra Śāstra*, pp. 43-58; J. Sinha, *Shakta Monism*, pp. 9-12.

98 *Vide* Woodroffe, *The World As Power*, pp. 190-191.

99 *Ibid.*

100 Devīghāgavata Purāṇa IX.1.

101 Brahmavaivartapurāṇa II.1.139f.; cf. vs. 138 : "The village goddesses are likewise her digits"; Devībhāgavata Purāṇa IX.1; *vide* also Brahmavaivartapurāṇa XLIII.79ff. ("Krisna Janma Kandha").

102 V. S. Agrawala, *The Glorification ...*, p. 25.

On the whole, it is the foregoing cosmological and theological macranthropy combined with a tantric vision of the theandrous possibilities in human nature which provides the soteriological background for Śākta convictions about "the transformation of the human body into a microcosmos".[103] Upon entering the next chapter we shall have occasion to re-encounter such a vision in the context of Śākta worship and adoration of the goddess. For now, we merely note that the new phenomenological possibility to which we referred earlier concerns a cosmogonic intentionality hidden in the Being and Becoming of the goddess. Its "Factuality" would seem to have been the discovery of the human spirit rather than the rational pre-fabrication of the intellect. Sir John Woodroffe invites us to contemplate that *Saccidānanda-mayī* as Creation is Love, i.e.,

> the production of the Universe is according to the Śākta *an act of love*, illustrated by the so-called erotic imagery of the Śāstra.[104] The Self loves itself whether before, or in creation. The thrill of human love, which continues the life of humanity is an infinitesimally small fragment of and faint reflection of the creative act in which Śiva and Śakti join to produce the Bindu which is the seed of the Universe. (Italics mine)[105].

This *raison de créer* regarding the Cosmos and man, alike, raises our sights beyond the enigmatic question of the original "imperturbability" of the Infinite. It suggests that there has persisted in the Śākta *Weltanschauung* an anthropocosmic teleology which, though itself a great mystery, seems to bypass that "classic problem of metaphysics" (Zimmer), as well as "the question as to how or why the original ignorance [*Avidyā-Śakti*] becomes operative", thereby making such an enigmatic question "by its very nature philosophically inadmissable".[106] For in keeping with the *sādhanic*[107] quality of Śākta ontology, what remains incomprehensible at the level of discursive thought becomes an *experience* of the Ultimately Real in the union of Śakti and Śākta.

---

[103] Eliade, *Yoga*, p. 235.

[104] *Vide* also Brahmavaivartapurāṇa XLIII.68-XLIV.1-59, esp. vss. 11-54.

[105] Woodroffe, *Śakti and Śākta*, p. 182.

[106] R. N. Dandekar, "The Role of Man in Hinduism", in Kenneth W. Morgan, ed., *The Religion of the Hindus* (New York : The Ronald Press Company, 1953), p. 122.

[107] *Supra*, pp. 131; Woodroffe, *The World As Power*, p. 207.

Devigenesis

The Nature of the Goddess : Durgā-Kālī

The goddess who is the eternal, pervasive, and personal Ground of *Saccidānanda* as Love is also capable of multi-modal births in further testimony of her unlimited cosmic creativity. This creativity has to do with the goddess as manifestation or emanation. For "I do whatever I wish [108] ... What is real can only be born. ... Thus ... there does not arise any inconsistency in My being everything".[109] That is to say,

> When she reveals herself in order to accomplish the purposes of the gods, it is then said in the world that she is born; [yet] she is also named the Eternal One.[110]

"Birth" for this deity, then, is not birth but manifestation: tendentious and responsive (i.e., invocational); "Creation" for this Being is not creation but emanation : purposive and (seemingly) "involuntary". In each case, there is no absolute discontinuity between emanation-manifestation [111] and responsive, Divine Self-disclosure. For the student of Hinduism who underestimates the Power (Śakti) of (and which *is*) the goddess as Play (*Līlā*) has not begun to understand the paradoxical coherence of Cosmogenesis and Devigenesis. Let us step further into this maze of Self-disguised and Self-disclosed wonder.

The Goddess as Tendentious Manifestation

This manifestation of the goddess occurs as a dramatic literary-historical prelude to other manifestations, under the form of that divinity who is both Brahmavidyā and Mystagogue of the gods—Umā.[112] The "fourth" of Śaṇkara's historical-religious "explanations"[113] for the introduction of the goddess into the presence of the gods requires an additional hermeneutical perception; that is, the goddess

---

[108] One of the marks of genuine theological *aseity*; likewise, Exodus 33:19; Romans, 9:15ff.; cf. Walter Harrelson, *Interpreting the Old Testament* (New York : Holt, Renihart and Winston, Inc., 1964), p. 78 : "I cause to be what I cause to be", and "I cause to be what occurs". Notwithstanding the respective distinctness of context, there is a comparable quality of ontological independence.

[109] Devībhāgavata Purāṇa III.6.14-27.

[110] Mārkaṇḍeya Purāṇa LXXXI. 48.

[111] Preferred and suggested by Bharati, *The Tantric Tradition*, p. 212; cf. Eliade, *Yoga*, pp. 21f.

[112] *Supra*, pp. 116f.

[113] Cf. Mahadevan's commentary in *Kena Upanishad*, pp. 13-14.

as the "transcendentally beautiful", or "exceedingly resplendent" Woman is *intentionally* possessed of a knowledge and wisdom of the Truth. In phenomenological terms, then, that Truth or Essence of Śākta philosophy diminishes with its light the other reasons rendered for her mystagogic theophany before the gods.

Thus, in expulsive relation to other attendant *non*-phenomenological descriptions (1) the gods, assuming that they possessed Brahmavidyā, knew "It" not, because they did not know the Divine Pedagogue par excellence, for Who or What she is—the one, extremely "near"[114] the Essence (the Self) that is Ultimate Knowledge—Permanent Salvation. Hence (2) the self-sufficiency of the gods was found to be "not real" (*asat*), did not exist, and was not indeed the Knowledge (*Vidyā*) which is the Essence of Brahman.[115] The gods, then, had acquired majestic superiority because of austere praise of Brahman (Indra excelling: IV.3); however, they did not fully realize that the purpose of their possession of Power lay not in the mere enjoyment of the fruits of their actions. It lay rather in the performance of even their "epic function's' in perpetual homage to the Source of Power, Truth, and Knowledge— "the Intelligence-Self which is their substrate";[116] (3) beings, again, whether men *or* gods, have no *sui generis* power to perpetuate their *knowledge* of Brahman even after an initial realization of "It"; for the eventual cosmic degeneration of Time (i.e., Yugic fatigue) as well as the recurrence of Asuric ascendancy which threatens Deva-hood attests to the same.

---

[114] Cf. *ibid.*, p. 36 : "A being's excellence is to be measured by its nearness to God ..."; "Brahman is superior even to the gods ... it is the God of the gods" (*ibid.*, p. 29). The Upanishad is probably not a Śākta Upanishad in literary intention (even if there were admitted any Śākta influence). The goddess is not explicitly but only implicitly identified with the Brahman; nonetheless, her appearance "in that very space" (Kena Upanishad III.12; III.2) and her mystagogy suggests, strongly, a tendentious mythic phenomenology. Cf. *supra*, pp. 116, 120. *Vide* also S. Radhakrishnan, ed., *The Principal Upanishads* (New York : Harper and Row, 1953), p. 589.

[115] In the context it is not that the victorious Power of the gods was not due to Brahman; but that they began to take for granted, proudly, the effective continuity of their epic might from the glory of the event (*Devāsuram*) as conquest. In a word, their Power was not any longer' "real". For "The Flash of lightning does not stay for a long time. It appears for a moment and then vanishes ... Yet it reveals itself on occasions to those who have prepared themselves for its revelation" : Mahadevan, *Kena Upanishad*, p. 38; cf. Radhakrishnan, *The Principal Upanishads*, p. 591 : "... the sudden glimpse ... into Reality ... has to be transformed into permanent realization". Cf. *supra*, p. 117, n. 409.

[116] Mahadevan, *Kena Upanishad*, pp. 8, 10f.; Devībhāgavata Purāṇa III.7.15a.

Finally, (4) the hidden cosmic intentionality of the goddess' presence near Brahman thus brings together the phenomenology of myth and the history of religious valorization, insofar as there is in this eventful theophany an implicit, therefore, unrevealed motif of grace (*anugraha*), "the grace of Umā",[117] the goddess. Her presence is a revelation to both the gods and men (who study the acts of the gods) that they are to look to her [118] for the *sustaining* Knowledge of Brahma (*Brahmadidyā*). The element of "conceit",[119] then, reminds the contemplative mind of the need to accept the truth that all beings are to assume an attitude of humility on *all* planes of existence in the face of the supreme *yakṣa* (i.e., Brahman).[120]

The Goddess as Invocative Manifestation

The mytho-phenomenological correlate to the former manifestation of the goddess appears in that primary text which bears her name—the Devībhāgavata Purāṇa. It presents us with an occasion for another "Birth", or "invocative" manifestation of our divinity; again, it calls to mind the proper attitude which the gods are to assume towards this goddess as the Incomparable Being.

The narrative constitutes a striking variation on goddess-manifestation; for, here,[121] the gods are counselled by the ever-Preserving Viṣṇu to recall the chaotic world [122] to Order through "the sincerest devotion". The divine milieu follows upon the grief of Śiva over Satī's demise. Turning their minds, however, to the crisis at hand (symbolized by Taraka, the Asura), the gods give themselves over to sundry sacrificial rites and gestures; they dedicate themselves in the main to the Devī through the Puraścaraṇa Karma ceremony.[123] By

117 Mahadevan, *Kena Upanishad*, p. 13; Radhakrishnan, *The Principal Upanishads*, p. 590 (bottom).

118 Devībhāgavata Purāṇa I.1.1.

119 Kena Upanishad III.2.

120 Vide *infra*, p. 205 and n. 149.

121 Devībhāgavata Purāṇa VII.31.3-54.

122 Cf. *ibid.*, VII.31.3ff., for the reversal of the harmony of Creation : nature (including planets), gods, kings, and other beings.

123 *Ibid.*; literally, "'the act of placing in front'. By repetition of the name or Mantra of the Deity, His or Her presence is *invoked* before the worshipper [italics mine]" : Arthur Avalon (John Woodroffe), trans., *The Great Liberation* (4th ed.; Madras : Ganesh and Co. Private, Ltd., 1963), p. 200. For more on this ceremony—its meaning, method, and relation to the Brahma Puraścaraṇa, *vide* Mahanirvāṇa Tantra III.114-119; VII.69, 75-85, 86-94, in *The Great Liberation*.

this and other attendant rites they sought to invoke the goddess into their midst.[124]

After many (divine) years of being implored, the goddess, who is "the Highest Light of the Supreme Powers", appeared at once before them "in the form of an exceedingly beautiful Divine Woman"; "the Mother Goddess, the Incarnate of unpretended mercy ... ready the offer Her Grace, the Mother of the Whole Universe". The gods state their collective requests, but not before they have been inspired to tears by her, "the Enchantress of All".[125]

The Goddess as "Involuntary Creation"

Another account of the "birth" of the goddess, which one scholar has called an "involunraty creation",[126] is told in a text devoted to her: the Kālikā Purāṇa. Without attempting to cite the myth *in extensu*, we are in this text brought face to face with a stirring mythic mode of the divine manifestation. Here the goddess appears under the form of Uṣa (Dawn)[127] as Erotic Entrancement. She assumes the form of a divine being of irresistible beauty before the gods. Her enchanting loveliness subjects even the gods themselves to the cosmic Illusion (Mahāmāyā).

The creative event is the first phase of what is a cosmo-romantic biography of the goddess as Kālī, "The Dark Lady". Set against a cosmological background of the incipient "Creation" of the universe at the hands of Brahmā, the event reveals a dimension of "surprise" in Hindu theogony because of the goddess.[128] During the creative rehearsal of the Great Cosmogonic Tradition, various and sundry beings and creatures pour forth from Brahmā's abysmal yogic trance as multitudinous embodiments, including other secondary Creators (the "Lords of Creatures").

But, then, as if "Brahma does not know the depths of his own

---

[124] Cf. Mārkaṇḍeya Purāṇa LXXXV.4ff., 37f., 42; for other "theophanies", *vide* Harivaṃśa CCLIV.1-18, esp. vss. 14 and 18; CCLXVII.1-15 (ed. and trans. M. N. Dutt [Calcutta: n.p., 1897]); Harivaṃśa LVIII (*O.S.T.*, IV, 435).

[125] Devībhāgavata Purāṇa VII.31.

[126] The term "Involuntary Creation" is used by Heinrich Zimmer, *The King and the Corpse*, ed. Joseph Campbell (New York: Meridian Books, Inc., 1960), pp. 239-316, which contains a partial textual translation and narration of the Kālikā Purāṇa.

[127] *Supra*, pp. 105-106.

[128] Zimmer, *The King and the Corpse*, pp. 241, 261, 262.

being",[129] *a new thing* happens. Before the god appears "the most beautiful dark woman", stark naked, radiant, and vivacious. She is Dawn, but she is erotic, entrancing Dawn, the Dawn of a New and Incomparable Reality and Experience for those who gaze upon her. She laughs; for she knows who she is—the Creatrix Incognito—yet the Greatest Vision of Reality.[130]

The event moves along until it centers around "the most important couple in the Indian pantheon, Śiva-Kālī"[131] (the goddess now as "Pārvatī"). The other gods have consorts (or *Śaktis*, i.e., Brahmā, his Sarasvatī; Viṣṇu, his Lakṣmī). However, there is much concern that Śiva has taken no wife (i.e., Kālī/Uṣa/Satī/Pārvatī), for such a union has crucial implications for the nature and destiny of the cosmos as Chronic Rotation. The inducements of the god Kāma ("Love", "Desire")[132] having failed, the austerities of the goddess under the re-incarnate form of Sati [133] provide the final attraction of Śiva to herself.

The cosmogonic significance of these portions of the myth (Kālikā Purāṇa I.1-5.10; V.11-13.53) is not grasped unless it is understood that (1) the Trimūrtian government of the universe (under Creation, Preservation, and Destruction) lies in the interdependent performances of each of these three Great Gods : Brahmā, Viṣṇu, and Śiva, without which there can be no world or world-process; (2) there remains and always will be an anti-cosmic (i.e., chaotic, disruptive) threat from titans and anti-gods (Asuras) whom each member of the Trimurti (including the goddess [Mahāmāyā]) will have to kill for the sake of the Supernal Order; and (3) each goddess : Savṛti (Sarasvatī), Lakṣmī, Dawn (e.g., Durgā-Kālī) must play the role of "the godly force" (*Śakti*)[134] that both interpenetrates the Trimūrti during cosmogonic activity and inspires the integration of opposites (*coincidentia oppo-*

---

129 *Ibid.*, p. 258, n. 2.

130 *Ibid.*, pp. 241-242.

131 Eliade, *Patterns in Comparative Religion*, p. 421. Despite her option to remain "Alone" after *Pralaya*, Śiva remains her preferred husband and lover. She chooses him—"again"—for instance, when Mahiṣāsura first tries romantic wooing instead of martial confrontation : Devībhāgavata Purāṇa V.16ff., esp. V.16.35ff.; elsewhere the goddess displays some interesting and alluring "femininity" : Mārkaṇḍeya Purāṇa LXXXV.42-76, esp. vss. 66-70; Devībhāgavata Purāṇa V.24.

132 Here he is "the incarnation of her spell" : Zimmer, *The King and the Corpse*, p. 261, the myth.

133 *Ibid.*, pp. 269-271.

134 Cf. *supra*, pp. 155-156; also *vide* Devībhāgavata Purāṇa III.6.28-85; VII.31.44-54.

sitorum)[135] in an eternal Cosmic Romance. In behalf of this cycle of eternal return and responsibility for gods and men, Brahma bids Śiva to take to himself "a glorious woman".[136]

The Goddess as Purposive "Creation"

The distinctively purposive "Creation" of the goddess is portrayed, finally, as under the ontological conditions of a Cosmos turned once again to Chaos. In a remarkable account in the Devī-Māhātmya section of the Mārkaṇḍeya Purāṇa, and which is paralleled in the Devībhāgavata Purāṇa,[137] the cosmos has been threatened by the dominance of Asuric Powers who have confiscated "the Yajñas performed by the Brahmans". Indeed, the demonic forces have made the Devas "terror-stricken ... and wandering in mountains and fastnesses".[138]

Following an initial emanative gesture by Viṣṇu, the Preserver-of-Cosmos, however, the other gods repeat his act in a concerted effort to transform Chaos into Cosmos. Unlike the Devī-Māhātmya account which makes their collective emanative activity [139] appear as a spontaneous response to universal danger, the Devībhāgavata Purāṇa renders an explicit account of this Devigenetic phenomenon as a *purposive* "creation" :

> Viṣṇu ... spoke smiling "we fought before; but this Asura [Mahiṣa] could not at that time be killed. Hence if some beautiful female Deity be now created out of the collected energy and form of the Śaktis of each of the Devas, then that Lady would be able easily to destroy that Demon by sheer force.[140]

Although the account of her effulgent "creation" is not radically different in either text in a comparative sense, the Devī-Māhātmya's

---

[135] E.g., *infra*, pp. 180 and Chap. IV.

[136] Zimmer, *The King and the Corpse*, pp. 271-273. For cosmogonic-erotic legends in the popular vogue, *vide* the goddesses "Ellamma", "Māriyamma" ("Peddamma", *et al.*), in Oppert, *On the Original Inhabitants* ..., pp. 465n-467n; 471n-474n.

[137] Devībhāgavata Purāṇa V.8.1-75; Mārkaṇḍeya Purāṇa LXXXII-LXXXIV.

[138] Devībhāgavata Purāṇa V.8.14ff.; cf. Mārkaṇḍeya Purāṇa LXXXII. 6f., "al the hosts of the gods ('Immortals') wander on earth like mortals.

[139] *Vide* an iconographic "Origin of the Goddess ... from a late XVIII century manuscript of the Devī-Māhātmya ...", in Zimmer, *Myths and Symbols* ..., p. xiii, Plate 56.

[140] Devībhāgavata Purāṇa V.8. Cf. *ibid.*, "Śaktis of each of the Devas", i.e., "Therefore ask ye now all, with your wives respectively, boons from that portion which resides in you all in the form of Fiery Energy [*tejas*] that [it] thus manifested may assume the form of a Lady". Cf. *ibid.*, VII.29.20-44 : Mārkaṇḍeya Purāṇa LXXXVIII.11-21, 32-61.

version of the anthropomorphization of "The Lady Deity"[141] seems to capture the imagination quite vividly :

> The gods beheld the mass of intense energy there like a burning mountain, pervading the other regions of the sky with its blaze; and that unparalleled energy borne of the bodies of all the gods which pervaded the three worlds with its light, gathering into one *became* a female ... the auspicious *goddess*.[142]

COSMO-REDEMPTION

The Restoration of the Cosmos : Caṇḍīkālī

It is in her role as Redemptrix of the Cosmos that the goddess becomes the focus of the *Devāsuram* motif "revisited".[143] Earlier indications were that by the time of the Purāṇas the meaning of the term *asura* (vis-à-vis *deva*) had become a symbol of the ontological polarization of the universe. That is, "the universe is in the visible form of a *Daivāsuram* conflict in which the Devas and the Asuras are locked in a trial of strength every moment and everywhere".[144] It is this cosmic-chaotic milieu which provides the background for, and which is symbolized by, the ultimate epic confrontation between the goddess Durgā-Kālī and the asura-of-asuras—Mahiṣāsura, i.e., the Buffalo-Demon.[145]

The Battle Myth

In the two primary sources for this epic confrontation, the Devī-Māhātmya and the Devībhāgavata Purāṇa,[146] we seem to be witnessing a magnificent, perhaps, incomparable portrayal of the Indian mythological imagination at the crossroads; that is, so much of the various and sundry mythological traffic of her religious past is brought

---

141 Devībhāgavata Purāṇa V.8.

142 Mārkaṇḍeya Purāṇa LXXXII.11-12, 17b (Pargiter's text used subsequently). Cf. Devībhāgavata Purāṇa V.8.33-46 for an elongated "dazzling" account.

143 *Supra*, pp. 94-98.

144 Cf. V. S. Agrawala, *The Glorification ...*: p. 5.

145 Cf. Marshall, *Mohenjo-Daro and the Indus Civilization*, p. 72 : on the negative symbolism of the "buffalo"; for the mythical nativity and other notes on "Mahiṣāsura", *vide* Devībhāgavata Purāṇa V.2; cf. Quackenbos, "Bana's Caṇḍīśataka", p. 256 and n. 7 (we agree with the author); also *ibid.*, p. 312. Cf. V. S. Agrawala, *The Glorification ...*, pp. 18, 190 ("Mahiṣa").

146 Mārkaṇḍeya Purāṇa LXXXI-XCIII; Devībhāgavata Purāṇa V.3-18. On comparative literary presentations, *vide* D. Sharma, "Verbal Similarities ...", p. 104 *et passim*.

together in a dramatic symbolization, to be sure, of the ambiguities that have characterized the spirit of prehistoric, ancient, and modern man.

The Vedo-Brāhmaṇic-Purāṇic continuity is specifically highlighted with the divine rehearsal of the "prototypical" Indra-Vṛtra episode, which, now, has become transformed into the Devī-Mahiṣa encounter.[147] Now with the goddess as the central theistic symbol of cosmic unity or unification, the "gifts of the gods" to her as weapons [148] have a meaning beyond their individual significance; their act of "creation" and donation is thus a testimony both to recollection (*smṛti*) of an original revelation (*ādi-śruti*) and the advent of something new. "Creation" and "donation", therefore, are superseded by cosmic *innovation*, if not, indeed, the re-discovery of a theretofore unrealized secret : the essence [149] of a *śruti* which has remained unchanged from the beginning.[150]

The phenomenon of "cosmic combat" or "ritual contest", though not confined to Hindu mythology,[151] receives, perhaps, its most mind-boggling representations in India. In the case of the two foregoing texts India's capacity for tortuous metaphysical and paradoxical symbolism is fully evident. For example, there is the presence of interspersed combative episodes in apparent cyclical relation to the main event—the cosmo-redemptive action of the goddess as Durgā-

---

[147] Cf. V. S. Agrawala, *The Glorification ...*, pp. 160f.; *vide* Ṛg-Veda I.32; cf. in Sacred Books of the East, Vols. XII and XIII. Śatapatha Brāhmaṇa I.1.3.4ff., I.6.3.1-17; Ṛg-Veda X.48.3.11; Taittirīya Brāhmaṇa II.2.3.3 (*O.S.T.*, V, 80, n. 152); Mahābhārata XVII-XIX (Adi Parvan); esp. Devībhāgavata Purāṇa VI.1-5.

[148] Mārkaṇḍeya Purāṇa LXXXII.18-31; Devībhāgavata Purāṇa V.9.1-22; cf. Śatapatha Brāhmaṇa I.2.4.1-7.

[149] I.e., the goddess, *supra*, p. 170.

[150] Devībhāgavata Purāṇa I.1.3, 6ff.; Mārkaṇḍeya Purāṇa XLV.20-23. Cf. Pargiter, *Ancient Indian Historical Tradition*, pp. 30-31. Mythic episodes or cycles (e.g., Devī versus Mahiṣa) might be regarded (minus the metaphysical Śākta cosmology) as "non-cosmogonic"; cf., e.g., S. N. Kramer, ed., *Mythologies of the Ancient World* (Anchor Books; New York: Doubleday and Co., Inc., 1961), p. 124. Cf. Eliade, "Cosmogonic Myth and 'Sacred History'", p. 75 : "... the myth of the creation of the world does not always look like a cosmogonic myth *stricto sensu* ..."; however, *vide ibid.*, pp. 75f., and also *Patterns in Comparative Religion*, pp. 412-413, 416.

[151] Cf. T. H. Gaster, *Thespis* : *Ritual, Myth, and Drama in the Ancient Near East* (Torchbook ed.; New York: Harper and Brothers, Publishers, 1966), pp. 93, 137ff., 245ff. *et passim*.

Mahiṣāsura-mardini.[152] Such episodes are (1) "The Slaying of Caṇḍa and Muṇḍa", and (2) "The Slaying of Śumbha and Niśumbha".[153] As cyclical phenomena, however, their relevance to the repetition of the cosmogony is suggested in the Skanda Purāṇa by Caṇḍi's words to Shiva : "O god of gods ! formerly I slew Chaṇḍa and Muṇḍa in battle, but they have been born again as mighty Asuras. ..."[154] Combative episodes such as the foregoing constitute recurrent "restorational" events that are in keeping with the larger Hindu cosmological pattern of creation, dissolution, and re-creation of the universe; for the universe "is only one of an infinite series in which there is no absolutely first Universe".[155] The goddess Durgā-Kālī, therefore, restores the Cosmos into the hands of the gods as an act of eternal return as well as the redemption of Time. She bids them to call upon her at liberty whenever the universe is again threatened or overwhelmed by the demonic foes of harmony and order, the bringers of evil and death.[156]

The Triumph of the "Warrior" Goddess

Inside the "Battle Myth", and behind and beyond the bizarre and bloody content of the cosmic conflict, there lies the phenomenon of Durgā-Kālī as the *martial* deity. In the latter half of the last century, while noticing that the goddess was called Prakṛti (or Nature), Ādya Śakti, or Māyā, a writer posed the inevitable question, which is : "... why should Nature, our common mother ... be portrayed as waging war with demons and not nursing her children with fostering care ?"[157] Although we shall make no attempt to answer such a question here,[158] there are certain structural observations to be made with reference to the general Śākta cosmology.

---

152 Cf. Zimmer, *The Art of Indian Asia*, I, 91 : "The Unconquerable Goddess (*durgā*), Crushing (*mardinī*) the Demon (*asura*) Buffalo (*mahiṣa*)"; *ibid.*, Vol. II, Plates 234, 284-285, 288, and also Plates 117, 210, 326, 434. A special emphasis upon this motif appears in *Marg* : *A Magazine of the Arts*, XXIII, No. 4 (September, 1970), 66ff,. 71, 75, 77-78, 102-104, 107f., and Figs. (*passim*).

153 Mārkaṇḍeya Purāṇa LXXXV-XC (Caṇḍa and Muṇḍa = LXXXVI.17-LXXXVII. 23).

154 Quoted in Vans Kennedy, *Researches into the Nature and Affinity of Ancient and Hindu Mythology* (London : Longman, Rees, Orme, Brown, and Green, 1831), p. 339.

155 Woodroffe, *Śakti and Śākta*, p. 429. *Vide infra*, Chap. V.

156 Mārkaṇḍeya Purāṇa LXXXIV.31-32.

157 Ghosha, *Durgā-Pūjā*, pp. iv, v.

158 *Vide infra*, Chap. VI.

It is, first of all, evident that we are witnessing in the battle imagery of the Candika/Mahiṣa Episode a representation of the theological ambivalence of the goddess on the epic-cosmic plane.[159] Let us recall with Eliade the pan-Indian vogue of this mythological bi-characterization.[160] To be sure,

> It is in India that the experience of the Terrible Mother has been given its most grandiose form as Kali, "dark, all-devouring time, the bone-wreathed Lady of the place of skulls". ... In her "hideous aspect' (*ghora-rupa*) the Goddess, as Kali ... raises the skull full of seething blood to her lips;[161] her devotional images hows her dressed in blood red, standing in a boat floating on a sea of blood: in the midst of the life flood, the sacrificial sap, which she requires that she may, in her gracious manifestation (*sundara-murti*) as the World Mother (*jagad-amba*), bestow existence upon new living forms in a process of unceasing generation ...[162].

This paradoxical iconographic symbolization of the goddess (Durgā-) Kālī is the analogue to the goddess as an evolving (i.e., devolving) polarity in the Cosmic Diad (Śiva-Śakti) as well as the ambiguities that characterize all phenomenal existence. On the terrific side of her restorational activity she, therefore, has both "the visage of a fiend"[163] and performs her deeds with intermittent shouts that reverberate throughout the worlds and all of nature.[164] Moreover, in an historico-phenomenological prespective, she appears to be the mythic magnification of the chthonian "Yakṣinī of the Battlefield"—*Raṇa-yakṣinī*.[165]

Secondly, the goddess as Epic Stentoria reveals a structure of mythological activity which seems to correspond in its dynamic elusiveness to the variegated forms of her cosmic creativity. If in her "Self" as anthropomorphic Warrior-Goddess she has a peculiar diamorphic disposition, she also has the capacity for *paramorphosis* as well as *infra-dynamic manifestation*. Her activity is characterized by paramorphosis[166] in her encounter with the Asuras: Caṇḍa

---

159 Cf. *supra*, p. 163.

160 Eliade, *Patterns in Comparative Religion*, p. 419; Mārkaṇḍeya Purāṇa LXXXIV.25 (cf. XCI.36-40. 25-46); Harivamśa LVIII.12 (trans. Dutt).

161 *Vide* Neumann, *The Great Mother*, Plate 65; cf. Ajit Mookerjee, *Tantra Art: Its Philosophy and Physics* (New Delhi: n.p., 1966), Plate 65, pp. 102, 110.

162 Neumann, *The Great Mother*, pp. 150, 152.

163 Otto, *The Idea of the Holy*, p. 62.

164 Mārkaṇḍeya Purāṇa LXXXII.31b-33a.

165 *Supra*, p. 51 and n. 53.

166 The Mahiṣāsura reveals a capacity for epic *metamorphosis*: *vide* Mārkaṇḍeya Purāṇa LXXXIII.20, buffalo-shape; vss. 28-30, lion, man-like, elephant; cf. Devībhā-

and Muṇḍa, i.e., "Ambikā uttered her wrath aloud against those foes, and her countenance then grew dark as ink. ... Out from the surface of her forehead, which was rugged with frowns, issued Kālī of the terrible countenance. ..."[167]

Her capacity for infra-dynamic manifestation occurs during the entrance of the Śaktis of the gods into the cosmic combat. It represents a unique development within the mythic narrative; for after the various Śaktis "went in the forms of those gods to Candika", she *herself* as a unique (collective) Śakti "born" of the gods, *emanates her own Śakti*! "Thereupon from the goddess' body there came forth *Candika's Energy*, most terrific, exceedingly fierce howling like a hundred jackals [italics mine]".[168]

The triumphal advent of the Warrior-Goddess is a three-fold phenomenon,[169] but which is paradigmatized in the Candika/Mahiṣasura conflict. Those triumphs are the following: (1) the "Battle against Śumbha and Niśumbha", (2) the "Battle against Chaṇḍa and Muṇḍa", and (3) the "Battle against Raktabīja".[170] It is the struggle between the goddess Durgā-Kālī and the Buffalo-Demon Mahiṣāsura[171] that has tended to symbolize the ultimate Reality and Supremacy of the goddess. Of the "Devī-Charitas" the Madhyama Charita[172] is, then, most significant in that the conquest of Indra by Mahiṣāsura means both (a) the dethronement of the traditional martial prince among the gods, which symbolizes the supersession of

---

gavata Purāṇa V.18. A Javanese art piece shows Mahiṣāsura (or Asura-Mahiṣa) "stricken to death by the goddess brandishing her weapons ... the demon who had turned himself into a bull, but then is seen emerging from the beast's neck to resume his demon shape": J. Hackin *et al.*, *Asiatic Mythology* (New York: Thomas Y. Crowell Co., n.d.), p. 232. Cf. Zimmer, *The Art of Indian Asia*, Vol. II, Plate 503, but esp. I, 102 and Text Plate B4a. The unlimited metamorphic power of the *Goddess* is strikingly dramatized by her capacity to assume even the form of "innumerable Bees" for the restoration of the Cosmos from Asuric Powers: Mārkaṇḍeya Purāṇa XCI.47-48; see esp. Devībhāgavata Purāṇa X. XIII: 97-120.

[167] Mārkaṇḍeya Purāṇa LXXXVI.4, 5; cf. vss. 6, 7; Neumann, *The Great Mother*, Plates 66, 67; p. 153; Zimmer, *The Art of Indian Asia*, Vol. II, Plate 424.

[168] Mārkaṇḍeya Purāṇa LXXXVIII.12b-13, 22-23a.

[169] Excluding the Viṣṇu (Māyā)/Madhu-Kaitabha Epidose, *ibid.*, LXXXI.49-77, esp. vss. 68-69; LXXV.37-41, a "*Voluntary* Creation".

[170] *Supra*, p. 177, n. 153; Mārkaṇḍeya Purāṇa LXXXVIII.39ff. Cf. V. S. Agrawala, *The Glorification ...*, pp. 5-21, esp. pp. 19ff.

[171] For an interesting episodic variation, *vide* Oppert, *On the Original Inhabitants ...*, pp. 473n-474n.

[172] V. S. Agrawala, *The Glorification ...*, pp. 16ff.

the "Old Order";[173] and (b) the birth of a new reverence, power, and harmony now in the hands of the Eternal Goddess. Perhaps the most decisive (almost inconspicuous) illustration of her sovereign incomparability is the fact that the *coup de grâce* to Mahiṣāsura is *preceded* by a nonchalant[174] kick of her foot;[175] for, in trans-epic, transcendental terms, she is no one "power" but Absolute Power (Para-Śakti) tending to carouse with itself under the form of (re-) Creation.

The final testimony of the all-encompassing, cosmological majesty of the goddess Durgā-Kālī (though we shall say more of the "integration of structures" in our Conclusion) takes us back to the wonder of this divinity as Mahāmāyā. For in this capacity it becomes clear, once more, that the goddess, in whom both "compassion in mind and relentlessness in battle are seen",[176] turns out to be both "Mahādevī *and* Mahāsurī i.e., Supreme Power of the Devas and of the Asuras. ... In the Universal both exist together".[177] The phenomena of cosmogenesis, devigenesis, and cosmo-redemption are ultimately "creations" of her-"Self", the Absolute Noumenon, whose Para-Form "none knows". However, she has revealed this Reality to us in the shape of the universe, gods, men, and things, which, therefore, are *all* alive. Let us accept in the next chapter the only recourse left to us in the face of all this majesty—her worship.

---

173 Cf. Devībhāgavata Purāṇa I.1.19-25.

174 Cf. Zimmer, *The Art of Indian Asia*, I, 106f.

175 The "Foot-Motif" plays a prominent role in Bana's "Caṇḍīśataka": *vide* Quackenbos, "Bana's Caṇḍīśataka", pp. 247, 251ff., 267ff.

176 Mārkaṇḍeya Purāṇa LXXXIV.21b; cf. Brahmavaivartapurāṇa II.1.91: "Fight with the demons for the preservation of the world is mere child's play to her".Likewise, vis-à-vis the Mārkaṇḍeya Purāṇa, wherein the goddess has an army (e.g., LXXXIII.20ff.), the Devībhāgavata Purāṇa (V.10.1ff.) depicts her as one who can destroy the Arch-Demon "without any army".

177 V. S. Agrawala, *The Glorification* ..., pp. 181, 182; *supra*, p. 97.

CHAPTER FOUR

THE STRUCTURAL PHENOMENOLOGY OF RITUAL TIME : KĀLĪ-PŪJĀ

Cosmic Time and Ritual Time

The cosmogonic creativity and the ritual worship of the goddess are also inseparable [1] just as she (Mahākālī) is metaphysically inseparable from the god Śiva (Mahākāla). For the time af man and the Great Time, or, indeed, the "Eternal" time of the goddess are never continuous or identical for man except in "ritual time", which enhances his participation in the Ultimately Real. By this, to be sure, we do not mean that all of time is not actually sacred, but that for man, soteriologically *en route*, if not outside of the ritual milieu, the omni-sacral consciousness remains only potentially realized, or partial, yet enduringly "Factual" (Guenther) only to the Great Goddess Durgā-Kālī. It is thus in the rituological context of her devotees' response to her factual *and* expressive glory that the former "inseparability" receives multiple confirmation.

To begin with, we acknowledge that, on the face of things, this ritual devotion and festive celebration would seem to be intelligible in purely "profane" calendrical terms. However, they are to be understood here within the perspective of the real omni-sacrality which, we said before, characterizes the world because of the qualitatively non-diminished (i.e., "unlimited") *pleroma* of the goddess as Creatrix.[2] There is, then, no dimension of Being, Time, or Space, which the goddess does not fill with her presence (*supra*) : the universe, gods, men, and things are all alive to her. This point cannot be overstressed in our present context (*vide* also Chapter V), for "there cannot be Sādhanā in an unreal world by an unreal Sādhaka of an unreal Lord" (= goddess).[3] Nonetheless, as the Source, Dynamics, and Embodiment of the World-Reality, the goddess must, therefore, be Time as well as *something other* [4] than Time as mere chronic duration. In a word, the

---

1 *Supra*, pp. 159, 163f.

2 For this vision in "cosmogonic art", *vide* A. Mookerjee, *Tantra Art*, p. 53, Plate 16.

3 Woodroffe, *Śakti and Śākta*, p. 250.

4 Cf. Eliade, *Patterns in Comparative Religion*, p. 452.

goddess Durgā-Kālī symbolizes at least three principles of Time-Consciousness : (a) the para-chronic (i.e., *Parākāla*, which is ultimately the dimension of depth in time as an "Eternal" continuum);[5] this is analogous to the continuity between the form of the goddess as ontological abstraction and her creativity as cosmogonic manifestation. Moreover, the para-chronic dimension of Reality-experience is reserved to those who have attained the ultimate transformation of spiritual consciousness, which is correlative to the vision of the goddess as Para-form (*Parambrahman*); (b) the macrochronic (i.e., the fact of the goddess (Mahākālī) as not herself being subject to time yet being, as it were, a cosmic river of time, which is itself sourceless, fractionless, and inexhaustible. In the Śākta world-view the goddess thus becomes an astrologico-symbolic [6] reality which encompasses and personifies the traditional Great Year [7] of Brahman (the Mahā-Kalpa); (c) the micro-chronic, that is, the phenomenon of time as duration (*kāla-kāla*) and/or the "digits" of Time. These are the "moments"of the goddess when, though she remains temporally and trans-temporally One Reality, the special utterances of myth, doings of cult, and thinking upon symbols redintegrate to enhance the realization of her devotees of both the Presence of the Ultimate and the sacrality of the Intimate. It has already been recognized regarding the foregoing macro-chronic and micro-chronic aspects that

> the Indian peoples have for at least two millenniums (i.e. since astrology based on the zodiacal signs was current in India) related the day to the year, and with a relation which the *Sūryasiddhānta* [8] implies to be the one existing between gods and men ... In short, man superimposes the day of the gods on the human year by proper religious observances at important times of the day and year.[9]

The Śākta phenomenology of "ritual time" has both a solar and a lunar structure (especially the latter). In the former structure the goddess, besides being an astronomical representation of the year,

---

[5] *Supra*, p. 161; cf. A. Mookerjee, *Tantra Art*, p. 53, Plate 13.

[6] In this respect we are making use of a most helpful source : B. S. K. Yogatrayanand Ji's "The Nature of Time" (original in Bengali), trans. with notes and extracts from the Hindi version by Siva Saram (Alain Danielou ?) in *Journal of the Indian Society of Oriental Art*, XI (1943), 75-102; *vide infra*, p. 193, n. 76.

[7] *Vide infra*, Chap. V.

[8] Cf. Sūrya-siddhānta I.13 : "Twelve months make a year, this is called a day of the gods"; cf. Śatapatha Brāhmaṇa XII.3.2.1.

[9] Cf. Alex Wayman, "Climactic Times in Indian Mythology and Religion", *History of Religions*, IV, No. 2 (Winter, 1965), 301.

is also, as the wife of Śiva, a representation of the Eliptic.[10] Moreover, within a solar structure, just as Time "associated to a particular form of action ... becomes day", Time, again, "associated to another form of action becomes ... month".[11] It is *a propos* that the latter associative symbolic action is homologatively understood within a lunar rituological structure.

The Durgā (-Kālī) Pūjā festival of Bengal occurs within a religious framework of astrological-cultic correspondences which reflect a lunar rituological structure. It is in this way that the participants are able to discern the (natural) signs and astroreligious symbols which, respectively, govern and determine [12] the eventuality and auspiciousness of times and seasons.[13] The Pūjīc Festival is traditionally held as a celebration of the autumnal equinox during the second quarter of the moon, September 15 to October 15 in the sixth month of Bengal (i.e., Aśvina).[14]

The time of the celebration is intimately related to the multivalent symbolic significance of the goddess as both a deity in whom there co-inhere natural and existential opposites, but also in whose name itself there are persistently symbolized various aesthetic and theological apprehensions which have converged to make (Durgā-) Kālī such a composite Hindu divinity. We recall Jean Przyluski's insights concerning the relations between cultural-linguistic borrowing and religio-symbolic nuance (e.g., Kālī, Kāla, Kalki).[15] It is, moreover, significant in our present context to contemplate another scholar's attempt to connect "with the moon the Skt. words *kāla, kalā, kalpa*", and to explain "the sense of *kāla* 'dark, black, god of death' in connection with the Dravidian name of the new moon".[16] Przyluski could, therefore, notice that the goddess Kālī is a kind of theistic nodus to which a range of aesthetic, moral, astronomical, and metaphysical polarities

---

10 W. Brennand, *Hindu Astronomy* (London : Charles Straker and Sons, Ltd., 1896), p. 140.

11 Yogatrayanand Ji, "The Nature of Time", pp. 81-82.

12 Cf. *ibid.*, pp. 101ff., 93f.; cf. Mārkaṇḍeya Purāṇa LVIII. 55-81.

13 Cf. Brennand, *Hindu Astronomy*, pp. 25, 26.

14 Cf. *ibid.*, p. 61 : the astrological nativity of the goddess; cf. Devībhāgavata Purāṇa VII.28.1-80; and *supra*, pp. 113-114, esp. p. 57, n. 91.

15 *Supra*, p. 83; also Jean Przyluski, "La Croyance au Messie dans l'Inde et l'Iran", *Revue de l'Histoire des Religions*, C (1929), 1-12.

16 *Vide* Marc Collins, in Przyluski, "From the Great Goddess to Kāla", p. 269.

gravitate as aspects of "a dualistic system where two series of notions oppose each other" :[17]

white	pure	auspicious	bright fortnight	propitious god
black	impure	inauspicious	dark fortnight	terrible god[18]

Cosmic Time and Ritual Time, therefore, come meaningfully together particularly when the matter concerns the proper consideration of the previous phenomena. The author of the invaluable source, *Durgā-Pūjā*, can thus tell us that

> The Daksninayana is the night of the gods and the Uttarayana their day. The equinoxes, therefore, are the Dawning and Gloaming of the gods, the proper moments for worshipping Durga, the Dawn of the Puranas. The Morning of the Equinoxes is the Dawn of Dawns, and hence held sacred to the worship of Durga the goddess Dawn. ... The dark fortnight of a lunar month is the period when darkness predominates and is therefore considered unfit, i.e., inauspicious for certain ceremonies.[19]

Rituo-structurally, in keeping with both the symbolic multivalence and the dispositional ambivalence of the goddess,[20] it is reported that between October 15 and November 15 the celebration of a *Kālī*-Pūjā can take place during "the *darkest* night, the night of no moon, of the seventh Bengali month of Kartik [italics mine]".[21] In general, the celebration of *pūjās* of "Durgā" *and* "Kālī" correspond as sacred events to the periods of the approaching Full Moon and the next

---

17 *Ibid.*

18 I.e., especially the divinity as a symbol of death. Cf. Mārkaṇḍeya Purāṇa XCII.35 ("Mahākālī") and asterisk; *vide* also Mahākāla and Mahākālī at Benares, in Przyluski, "From the Great Goddess to Kāla", p. 273.

19 Ghosha, *Durgā-Pūjā*, pp. xix-xx, xxi; Yogatrayanand Ji, "The Nature of Time", p. 88; M. Underhill, *The Hindu Religious Year* (Calcutta : Association Press, 1921), pp. 30ff. *et passim*. For "inauspicious" action, *vide*, e.g., Carl Gustav Diehl, *Instrument and Purpose : Studies in Rites and Rituals in South India* (Lund : C. W. K. Gleerup, 1956), p. 204.

20 E.g., Durgā-Kalī-Umā-Parvatī-Uṣas-Satī-Mariyamma, etc.; Durgā/Kālī, Gaurī/Kālī, Saundarya-devī/Bhairavī, Bhadrakālī/Bhairavī-kālī, etc.

21 *Encyclopedia of Religion and Ethics*, 1924, VII, 643; *vide* Collins (*supra*). For separate treatments of "Kālī" and "Durgā", *vide* C. Chakravarti, *The Tantras*, pp. 89-93, 94-103. Such distinctions are more feasible on the level of cult compared to "cosmology", although the goddess as Multiform marks the integration of symbols (hence, *ibid.*, p. 99 : "Kālī" as a "form" of Durgā). Nonetheless, the phenomenon of variant "time"-celebration is also mentionable (e.g., *ibid.*, pp. 92, 96, 97, 99f.; cf. *ibid.*, p. 98, n. 10); cf. Marriott, "Little Communities ...", pp. 192, 194; according to *mūrtis* : C. Chakravarti, *The Tantras*, p. 94, n. 4.

New Moon, respectively.[22] Moreover, in terms of Przyluski's "dualistic system where two series of notions oppose each other" (*supra*), the pujic celebration of the goddess both as "Durgā" and "Kālī" points to their symbolic co-inherence as part of a single ritual-complex. Indeed, their lunar contrariety not only corresponds to the potential ambivalence of reality on the level of the cosmogony, but it also represents the paradox of existence (acutely expressed in the Devī-Māhātmya on the plane of human history.

Following the Kāma-Kalā-Vilāsa's astral-erotic symbolism,[23] the undulating movement of Śiva-Śakti in solar-lunar continuum gives rise to "different shapes",[24] which are themselves correlated with world-phenomena within the tri-phasal cosmology;[25] but it is now capable of being dynamically infra-structured into a sexa-phasal process: taking birth, enduring, evolving, growing, declining, and being destroyed.[26] Furthermore, the goddess, albeit she as "Time (*Kāla*) is eternal", and the Ground of a "Time principle", which is essentially an "eternal ... Time energy",[27] gives chronic reality to an additional devolving process. For this goddess of inexhaustible cosmic Time, who is conceived as indivisible, unconcentrated Being (i.e., "partless duration"), also brings about through her Supreme Will (*Para-Icchā-Śakti*) the temporal *fractionalization* of her Self; so that

> instants, moments, days, fortnights, seasons, equinoctial half-years, years ages, periods of one Manu (manvantāras), aeons (kalpa), and universal destructions, in the view of the Primordial Knowledge,[28] are but particular conditions, particular moments of divisible time.[29]

---

22 Cf. R. Basak, "The Hindu Concept of the Natural World", in Morgan, *The Religion of the Hindus*, pp. 96f.; Yogatrayanand Ji, "The Nature of Time", p. 99. *Vide* also Durgā and "Sandhyā' (*infra*).

23 Kāma-Kalā-Vilāsa 6, 7, 17 (and Avalon's commentary, pp. 17, 34f.). For esoteric sun-moon symbolism, *vide* Woodroffe, *Varṇamālā*, pp. 227-230.

24 Yogatrayanand Ji, "The Nature of Time", pp. 81, 79-80; cf. *ibid.*, p. 83: "The world cannot for one instant even remain without transforming itself; without changing it cannot exist, transformation is the world's nature, transformation its intrinsic form". *Vide* also Eliade, *Patterns in Comparative Religion*, p. 183.

25 I.e., Creation (*sṛṣṭi*), Preservation (*Sthiti*), and Dissolution (*Saṃhāra*).

26 Yogatrayanand Ji, "The Nature of Time", p. 79.

27 *Ibid.*, pp. 81, 92, 79, and also 75.

28 *Nota Bene*: the goddess is the "Mother of the Vedas" (= Primordial Knowledge); *vide supra*, p. 120.

29 Yogatrayanand Ji, "The Nature of Time", p. 89; cf. *ibid.*, p. 86; also *supra*, p. 161, n. 70; Mārkaṇḍeya Purāṇa XCI.8a.

Accordingly, within a specifically lunar structural microcosm such as suggested by the Skanda Purāṇa, the goddess is understood, to be sure, as "the Arch-portion (*Mahā-kalā*)", which "knows no rise nor decline ... the eternal day".[30] Yet as the moon itself is but a particular manifestation or *embodiment*[31] of the goddess' Time-energy (*Kāla-Śakti*), the phases of the moon represent another dynamic confirmation of her capacity to be a symbol of both the Absolutely Ultimate *and* the Relatively Intimate. For the intimate side of her astrologico-symbolic Presence corresponds to the temporal "lunar day" (*tithi*) : "the particular extension of time in which the moon increases or decreases by one portion (kalā = 1/16th ..."[32]

The Lunar-Goddess : Art, Gesture, and Incarnation

As the Goddess-in-the-Moon, Durgā Kālī is a symbol of the astro-cosmic totality, for the sixteen digits of the moon correspond, structurally, to the (Vedic) contemplation of the universe as having sixteen parts.[33] The goddess herself, in the realm of religious iconography, may (with variations)[34] be "represented with 16 arms, connected with the 16 fractions (*kalā*) of the moon".[35] Whether with ten, sixteen, or even the phenomenal presence of thirty-two arms,[36] it is probable,

---

30 Yogatrayanand Ji, "The Nature of Time", p. 98. Cf. Woodroffe, *Śakti and Śākta*, p. 413 : "The Mother is both the Whole and, as Samvid Kalā, is the Cause and archetype of all Partials (*Kalā*). She is Herself the Supreme Partial as She is also the Whole"; cf. his *Varṇamālā*, pp. 185-192.

31 The Lalitāsahasranāma ("One Thousand Names of Lalitā"), a tantric text, envisions the goddess (Tripurasundarī) "as actually being *in* the moon" : Eliade, *Patterns in Comparative Religion*, p. 177. In Devībhāgavata Purāṇa VII.4, the Aśvins refer to a paragonic bhaktadigit of the goddess as" ... One with a face lovely like the Moon!" *Vide ibid.*, VII.4.12-58, esp. vss. 31-40.

32 Yogatrayanand Ji' "The Nature of Time", p. 98; Devībhāgavata Purāṇa VIII.24.1-41, 42ff. Cf. Bṛhad Āraṇyaka Upaniṣad 1.5.14f.; Chāndogya Upaniṣad VI.7.1ff.

33 Cf. Gonda, *Change and Continuity in Indian Religion*, p. 121; the author's Chap. IV, pp. 115-130 deals with this correspondential numerology in its fixation, flexibility, and variation.

34 Cf. Banerjea, *The Development of Hindu Iconography*, pp. 497ff.

35 Mircea Eliade, "Cosmical Homology and Yoga", *Journal of the Indian Society of Oriental Art*, V (1937), 200.

36 Banerjea, *The Development of Hindu Iconography*, p. 500. This author does not know the maximum number of *arms* ever represented iconographically; nonetheless, *vide* A. Mookerjee, *Tantra Art*, p. 31, Palte 10; p. 30n.

in the face of less positive evaluations,[37] that those arms "are meant to emphasize ... the all-powerful and all-embracing character of the Divine Shakti".[38]

> Now hear ... of the Moon. The Moon ... shares with the motion of the Sun [39] for one year; and She enjoys as well every month with the Sun in the shape of the dark and bright fortnights. ... During the bright fortnight, the Moon becomes more and more visible and gives pleasure to the Immortals by Her increasing phases; and during the dark ... phases, She delights the Pitris.[40] [Thus] by Her ... phases ... She becomes the Life and Soul of all the living beings. ... She is Full and the Soul without any beginning. She fructifies the desires [41] (Sankalaps) [*sic*] and resolves all; hence She is called Manomaya. She is the Lord of all medicinal plants (Oṣadhis); hence She is called Annanaya. She is filled with nectar; hence She is called the Abode of Immortality and She gives Nirvāṇa (the final liberation) to all.[42]

When Durgā-Kālī, the Moon-Goddess, is portrayed with her consort Śiva in the "Island of Jewels" (*maṇi-dvīpa*),[43] once again the lunar symbolism points to their significance as the "totalization" of all life's vicissitudes. Here Śiva appears in a double anthropomorphic representation (one form upon the other). "The upper figure ... is Sakala Shiva; the figure beneath is Nishkala Shiva";[44] the former is a symbol of immanent and energetic Actuality; the latter is a symbol of transcendental and imperturbed Potentiality; "*sakala* is the moon possessed of all its digits 'whole, entire, complete, all'—the Full Moon. The opposite of *sakala* is *niṣkala*, 'devoid of digits or of constituent parts'; the New Moon, which, though virtually existent, is imperceptible, intangible, apparently non-existent".[45] This Śaivite-Tantric philosophic representation of the goddess as Māyā, Zimmer remarks, is a revelation of the vicissitudes of life, the perturbableness of the

---

37 Cf. A. K. Coomaraswamy, *The Dance of Shiva* (rev. ed.; New York : The Noonday Press, 1957), pp. 79ff.

38 Banerjea, *The Development of Hindu Iconography*, p. 500.

39 Cf. Yogatrayanand Ji, "The Nature of Time", pp. 98f.; *supra*, p. 185, n. 23.

40 Cf., e.g., Mārkaṇḍeya Purāṇa XXXIII.8.

41 Cf. Mahānirvāṇa Tantra VI.32-37a.

42 Devībhāgavata Purāṇa VIII.15.

43 Cf. Zimmer, *Myths and Symbols ...*, Plate 66 (a Rajput painting around the eighteenth century).

44 *Ibid.*, p. 204. "*Sakala* is the compound, *sa-kala*; *kalā* meaning 'a small part of anything, a bit, a jot, an atom', especially 'a digit of the moon'; *sa* meaning 'with'" (*ibid.*). *Vide* "Nishkala Shiva", *ibid.*, p. 206; cf. *ibid.*, pp. 214f.

45 *Ibid.*

universe, as well as the holiness and divinity of the Ātman within man. Yet

> just beneath the veil of Māyā ... dwells tha Absolute. And the energy of Māyā is precisely the energy of that Absolute, under its dynamic aspect. Shakti, the Goddess, emerges from Nishkala Shiva, so that he may show forth the totality of his potentialities, as the moon its total orb.[46]

In the endeavour to "punctuate" the sacred continuum of the Cosmic Time of the goddess and the ritual time of man, the devotees of Durgā-Kālī contemplate a remarkable thing. That is to say, that the possibility exists of seizing upon a critical "moment" of chronic sacredness for *the most intensely auspicious worship of the goddess.* Following the injunctions of the Śāstras, stress was laid upon paying homage to her during the morning-time of the bright fortnight—under the form of "Dawn". The Purāṇas refer to this auspicious time-of-times as Sandhyā: a junction between (or which includes both) the Dawn (Uttarayana) and the Gloaming (Daksinayana). Seeking, then, the most intensely auspicious *and precisely momentous* "times" of worship amidst the Universal Sacral Continuum, the Tantric vision extols

> the Gloaming, evening, *the* Sandhya *par excellence*, and the worship of Sandhya therefore has superseded that of Dawn. The principal puja of Durga is accordingly held at the great Sandhya of Ashtami and Navami Tithis, a moment very near the center of the bright fortnight. From the Navami tithi of the bright fortnight the reign fo Light may be said to prevail.[47]

The lunar structure of the worship of the goddess Durgā-Kālī is also present in terms of "numerical participation", and what we shall call "paradoxical gestures of festivity". With regard to the latter, however, what appears as contradictory (or socially anomalous) behaviour turns out to be structurally coherent in the overall rituological context. In the former case we call attention to a list of lunar associative symbols noticed by a scholar [48] who has examined numerous ritual-structural patterns in their unity and diversity) Thus we learn that in accordance with lunar-digital symbolism (1. the Tantric *pūjā* (as suggested above) may ceremonially "re-enact the phases of the moon as a whole";[49] (2) the *pūjā* may require

---

[46] *Ibid.*, p. 209.

[47] Ghosha, *Durgā-Pūjā*, p. xx; for "times" and rites of "Sandhyās", *vide* Devībhāgavata Purāṇa XI.16.

[48] Cf. Eliade, *Patterns in Comparative Religion*, pp. 177f.

[49] *Ibid.*, p. 177.

sixteen participating Brahmins (each one moon-tithi) who represent the totality of the goddess (the Moon); (3) the *kumārī-pūjā* (i.e., "the adoration of a maiden")[50] began, traditionally, "at the new moon and lasted fifteen nights", requiring, instead, "sixteen *kumarī* to represent the sixteen *tithi* of the moon" (the goddess).[51] There are, again, sixteen *Upacāra* (material elements used and actions performed) in the *pūjā* of the goddess.[52] Moreover, besides the notion that there are portions of Śakti [53] that are manifested in women, goddesses, and mortals, "the wives of eminent personages are mostly endowed with a sixteenth portion of Śakti".[54] It is interesting to notice another homologation of this time-numeral and the Moon-Goddess in the Devībhāgavata Purāṇa. There a potential worshipper of Ādya Śakti Bhagavatī is informed of certain proper "times" and "forms" of the goddess, among which is mentioned the need to worship "for sixteen years consecutively without any break" as a vow to Mahā-Lakṣmī.[55]

The element of paradoxical gestures of festivity comes to light, insofar as during the Durgā-Pūjā celebrations it has been found that participants are called to indulge in sundry "vulgar songs", "vulgar acts", and "ill-speaking",[56] contrary to normative social behaviour patterns. Hence "the injunction ... is that everyone shall join the Śavaras and sing their songs and even do things revolting to the

---

[50] Cf. Devībhāgavata Purāṇa III.2; note also *ibid.*, III.27.1-5. *Vide* Gonda, *infra*, Chap. V, p. 244, n. 90.

[51] Eliade, *Patterns in Comparative Religion*, p. 177; cf. Devībhāgavata Purāṇa VII.38.47; *vide* also Tucci, "Earth in India and Tibet", p. 361.

[52] John Woodroffe, *Śakti and Śākta* (7th ed.; Madras : Ganesh and Co. Private, Ltd., 1969, p. 348 (this edition will be used hereafter). "The sixteen, "allowing variations—*vide* Arthur Avalon, *Principles of Tantra* (2 vols.; London : Luzac and Co., 1914-1916), II, 399ff.—"which include some of the lesser number and are included in the greater are : (1) Āsana (seating of the image), (2) Svāgata (welcoming of the Devatā), (3) Pādya (water for washing the feet), (4) Arghya (offerings which may be general or Sāmānya and special or Viśeṣa) made in the vessel, (5), (6) Ācamana (water for sipping and cleansing the lips—offered twice, (7) Madhuparka (honey, ghee, milk and curd), (8) Snāna (water for bathing), (9) Vasana (cloth for garment), (10) Ābharaṇa (jewels), (11) Gandha (Perfume), (12) Puṣpa (flowers), (13) Dhūpa (incense), (14) Dīpa (lights), (15) Naivedya (food), and (16) Vandana or Namaskṛyā (prayer)". Cf. Woodroffe, *Introduction to Tantra Śāstra*, p. 98.

[53] Cf. Devībhāgavata Purāṇa III.6.14ff., IX.1.71-95.

[54] Oppert, *On the Original Inhabitants* ..., pp. 448, 449.

[55] Devībhāgavata Purāṇa IX.38.80ff.

[56] E.g., "throwing mud and dust at each other, uttering obscene expressions, singing vulgar songs", youthful "revelries" (C. Chakravarti, *The Tantras*, p. 100). *Vide* also traditions of the Kālikā Purāṇa and Bṛhaddharma Purāṇa, in Eliade, *Yoga*, pp. 342-343.

civilized taste. Anyone not doing so out of vanity or a false sense of dignity incurs the wrath of Durgā".[57] These gestures, which tend to have a *prima facie* anomalous character, are not only communal in nature; but, psychologically, they may reflect a kind of positive "paradoxical itention"[58] which ,apart from their cathartic value, is analogous to a cultic tradition found among the Vāmācāras and others in India. That is to say, such apparently anomalous gestures may constitute meaningful sacred acts whereby through seemingly contradictory behaviour what the participants fear most is avoided and what they most desire is by the grace of the goddess realized; or, on the level of advanced Tantric teaching (e.g., Vāmacarya), it may be a mode of indulging in unorthodox acts and elements, perhaps even in traditionally acceptable ones in *unorthodox* fashion, by which one achieves, ultimately, the spiritual transcendence of such things.

That pujic-festive homage paid to the goddess (Durgā-) Kālī, which encompasses (a) a primary emphasis on the sacred language of "gestures" (*mudrās*), (b) mythological event under the rhythmic form of masked pantomimic personations of good and evil forces (e.g., Kālī versus Asuras), (c) the phenomenon of "possession", presumably by the goddess as Śakti, as well as (c) the motif of *śṛṅgāra*, "the sentiment of love", is known as Kathakali.[59]

A testimony to the "nearness" of the goddess to man [60] within a lunar structure is also revealed in that very form of worship, formerly mentioned, the *Kumārī-Pūjā*.[61] For, here, a factor in addition to the the presence of sixteen maidens or virgins is that "the adoration is *vṛddhibhedana*, that is, in order of age, and the sixteen maidens must be aged from one to sixteen".[62] Consistent with the goddess as the Moon

> each participator represents an aspect of the heavenly body. Beginning at new moon the organizers and performers of the rite aim at furthering the growth of the moon

---

[57] Nani Gopal Banerjee, "A New Light on Durgotsava", *Indian Historical Quarterly*, XXI (1945), 231. *Vide* Kālikā Purāṇa 63:12-14, 19-23.

[58] Cf. Viktor Frankl, *Man's Search for Meaning* (Paperback ed.; New York : Washington Square Press, Inc., 1964), pp. 193-204.

[59] Cf. C. A. Menon, "The Histrionic Art of Malabar", *Journal of the Indian Society of Oriental Art*, IX (1941), 105-132. As a type of "sacred performance", *vide* L. P. Vidyarthi, *The Sacred Complex of Hindu Gaya* (Bombay : Asia Publishing Co., 1961), pp. 32, 33.

[60] Cf. *supra*, p. 170 and n. 114 on that page.

[61] *Vide* Mahānirvāṇa Tantra VII.16 (and Avalon's commentary, pp. 187f., and n. 8).

[62] Eliade, *Patterns in Comparative Religion*, p. 177.

and no doubt also of all phenomena which have the same rhythm or are believed to be associated with the celestial body.[63]

It has been noted with some generality that there is an absence of congregational worship in Hinduism: "worship is an individual experience... the orthodox Hindu looks upon both [communal and congregational forms] as poses and artificial elaborations".[64] Furthermore, it is claimed that "the single worshipper, or in South India, only the priest of the temple and the 'pūjārī' ... perform the sacred rites for the worshipper".[65] Notwithstanding the same, however, the actual promotion of a potential for communal fellowship may be occasioned by the "time" of the worship of the goddess; so that in an atmosphere of pūjic festivity there is something of a coincidence of (a) cosmic time and pūjic cult, and (b) the *ethos* of goddess worship and communal festivity.[66]

To be sure, a particular traditional event which (to use Wach's phraseology) tends to have a "fomenting and integrating power"[67] is *Vijayā Daśamī*. This is the "Tenth Day" (of Victory), a day of "the waxing of the moon when the image of the Goddess is consigned to the waters after the performance of prescribed ceremonies".[68] Described by Chakravarti as a time of hope, joy, love, and brotherhood, "a festival for awakening of universal unity, fraternity, peace, and bliss",[69] the author also calls attention to a distinctive and meaning-

---

63 Gonda, *Change and Continuity in Indian Religion*, p. 127.

64 Sivaprasad Bhattacharyya, "Religious Practices of the Hindus", in Morgan, *The Religion of the Hindus*, p. 155.

65 Stella Kramrisch, *The Hindu Temple*, I (Calcutta : University of Calcutta, 1946), 142 and note.

66 Cf. these transitional observations by C. Chakravarti, *The Tantras*, pp. 96, 97 : (1) "worship in private houses has become rare; [2] public worship in public places with the help and co-operation of neighbouring people has become the order of the day; though [3] the worship proper ... is not always a public performance; yet [4] persons may be found worshipping for days together in temples and many houses". Cf. Diehl, *Instrument and Purpose*, pp. 355-357; consider also Kūlārṇava Tantra X, free trans, and readings M. P. Pandit (Madras : Ganesh and Co. Private, Ltd., 1965), p. 73; *infra*, Chap. V.

67 Wach, *Sociology of Religion*, p. 6.

68 *An Alphabetical List of the Feasts and Holidays of the Hindus and Mohamedans* (Calcutta : Indian Imperial Record Dept., 1914), p. 24. Cf. Ghosha, *Durgā-Pūjā*, pp. 79-82; C. Chakravarti, *The Tantras*, p. 100.

69 Swami Sivananda, *Hindu Fasts and Festivals* (Rikhekesh : The Sivananda Publication League, 1947), pp. 54-56. On the other hand, a "Devī Mahā Yajña" aimed at "peace, plenty and prosperity in the country and/or restoration of communal harmony" can be rather expensive. *Vide* Diehl, *Instrument and Purpose*, p. 266, n. 3, and p. 267.

ful custom which we regard as extraordinarily significant in the context of the lunar structure, homology, and theology of the goddess. It so happens that on Vijayā Day

> in the morning, worship is offered on a small scale with offerings which resemble food and other things given formerly to a daughter on the occasion of her leaving her father's house for her husband. Durgā is looked upon as one's daughter, and she comes to the house of the worshipper, her father, annually for three days [she is worshipped] as the Supreme Mother .... Deep paternal care is also reflected in what are called the *āgamanī* songs [70] which hail the deity, the daughter, coming to the house of her father after a year's stay in the house of her husband .... One witnesses really a pathetic scene when the image of the deity is taken away from the place of worship and members of the family of the worshipper gather round with tears in their eyes.[71]

Structurally, first of all, these events occur within the context of a "time" of the Goddess of the Moon, during whose momentous "month" the total myth and ritual complex is developed and consummated. The homologations which emerge as infra-structures thus comprise lunar-digital symbols, human participants and specialists, as well as communal customs. Yet a significant phenomenon which must not escape our attention, secondly, concerns what Eliade indicates as "the meaning of these lunar homologies ..."[72]

> It is not only the well-known relations between the Moon, the Woman, the Sea, the Goddess. We have to do here with a "living Whole" : the lunar cycle. The "life" of the moon symbolizes perfectly the "unity in the beginning"; for, although the moon appears ("is born"), grows, and disappears ("dies"), she is still a "whole" and forms a measure equable for the entire Universe.[73]

Theologically, in the third sense, the visiting-daughter motif is an encompassing testimony of the previous lunar correspondences. For in this singular event (1) Cosmic Time of the Goddess, which has become a lunar microcosm of worship, fellowship, and joviality, is also now the Time of Man; (2) the "nearness" of the goddess is re-

---

[70] "Touching songs, called *vijayā* songs, were composed in Bengali from the eighteenth century onwards, commemorating this occasion"; C. Chakravarti, *The Tantras*, p. 100.

[71] C. Chakravarti, *The Tantras*, p. 100. Mythologically (Ghosha, *Durgā-Pūjā*, Appendix, pp. ix, x), "Devi is supposed to have come to the house of Himavat with her children [*ibid.*] about this time. ..." C. Chakravarti (*The Tantras, ante* p. 101) relates that "the popular belief is that the goddess does not come alone to her father's house and so she is accompanied by her two sons and two daughters" (= Gaṇeśa and Kārttikeya, Sarasvatī and Lakṣmī).

[72] Eliade, "Cosmical Homology and Yoga", p. 200.

[73] *Ibid.*

enacted in anticipated yet spontaneous drama by the thoughtful tradition that the visiting-daughter is *actually* the goddess herself, who has come to bless the home and family with her Presence in the flesh. Iconography, then, becomes theophany, and theophany is understood to be incarnation.

The two motifs, i.e., Kumārī [74] and visiting-daughter, are therefore homologous in that the goddess as the astral-virginal princess (i.e., "Virgo")[75] paradoxically partakes of the phases of man's terrestrial life-in-family : marriage, motherhood, and progeny. Eliade has already shown us that the goddess is both the dynamics *and* the *dynamis* of the moon; likewise, in the festive milieu, the goddess, who might have been conceived as the aloof astral-spiritual divinity, has now come near to her devotees in essence and manifestation. In the words of Danielou, "a deity is truly nearer on the 'day' dedicated to it".[76]

Mythic Event and Sacred Space

The sacred continuum between Cosmic Time and Ritual Time is structurologically analogous to the correlation between mythical event and sacred space. For, as we have seen above (Chapter III),

---

[74] In this regard we recall the Kumārī tradition of the Himālayan kingdom of Kāṭmāṇḍu, Nepal; cf. Briggs, *Gorakhnāth and the Kānphaṭa Yogīs*, p. 79 : "'Kāthmāṇḍu', i.e., 'Kaṭh Mandir', or 'Temple of Wood', a shrine built about 1600 A.D., by Lakṣmi in honour of Gorakhnāth" : (1) "kumaris are chosen around 3 years old (reigning until the onset of puberty" (cf. Devībhāgavata Purāṇa III.27.41-43) or until scratched, perhaps caused to bleed by accident; (2) initiatory eligibility includes separation of girls from mothers and the placing of potential "Kumārīs" in "a dark room filled with the bloody heads of sacrificial buffalo, goats, and chickens", while "huge drums are beaten and horns are blown ... a frightening din". All other girls will panic, the priests claim, except the "new Kumari"; her weeping would mean "a great calamity"; (3) dressed in red, allowed no play or walking in the courtyard, attended by a *guruma* (i.e., a mother-teacher), and confined to the "inner recesses of the temple", this "daughter of the heavens" is said to be a "living goddess"; (4) her mission completed, this unofficial "ex-goddess" is granted gifts (including jewelry) and money, as she returns (we note with interest) "to live with her parents" : Conrad Fink, "A 'Living Goddess' at 6— But Her Life's A Lonely One", in *The Chicago Sun-Times*, August 8, 1965, p. 50. The goddess in Nepal is mentioned (e.g.) in Devībhāgavata Purāṇa VII.38.11.

[75] *Vide* Ghosha, *Durgā-Pūjā*, "Introduction". *Vide* Kālikā Purāṇa 62:6-7, 12, 17, 22 Cf. Bālāmbikā/Kanyā Kumārī", in Agehananda Bharati, "Pilgrimage in the Indian Tradition", *History of Religions*, III, No. 1 (Summer, 1963), 167, n. 86.

[76] Shiva Sharana (Alain Danielou), "The Mystery of the All-Powerful Goddess (Shri Bhagavati", adapted trans., *Journal of the Indian Society of Oriental Art*, XIII (1945), 195. (Single quotation marks added.)

the goddess as Anthropo-monistic Being meant — to use Eliade's terms — that "the cosmos as a whole is an organism at once, *real, living,* and *sacred*".[77] Neither time nor space, then, is essentially "profane", and both of them are ultimately and intimately real.[78] Yet the coincidence of the ultimate and intimate dimensions of the goddess' Self-revelation requires further "punctuation" in the form of specifically sacred *loci.* Thus, on the one hand, we may legitimately speak (within the Śākta cosmological context) of the totalistic Non-Profane, which means that "Life" itself may be understood "as a Ritual".[79] On the other hand, however, in view of the transitional, often ambiguous,[80] quality implied in all soteriologies, *persons* as the "human digits" of the goddess need, spiritually, to identify themselves with, and to find "an inexhaustible source of power and sacredness" in *a particular locus,* i.e., "*There,* in *that* place -[italics mine]"; such a "place" must be one in which the individual (a) can be confident that its "sacredness will continue", but, again, in which the individual (b) can be confident that it is possible "to communicate with the sacred".[81] Thus as far as the cosmological *and* rituological phenomenology of Time is concerned, there are grounds for maintaining, respectively, the integrity (monism) and the ambiguity (dualism) of Śākta Hinduism as a *soteriological* vehicle.[82] In terms of worship, therefore, the coincidence of mythic event and sacred space revolves, principally, around the following two phenomena : (a) the enigmatic figure of the "Passionate Yogī" : Śiva, and (b) the "Spatial-Digits" of the goddess : Pīṭhas. Mytho-phenomenologically, both elements are coordinated by the "Death" of the goddess as Satī.

---

[77] Eliade, *The Sacred and the Profane,* p. 117; Woodroffe and Mukhyopadhyaya, *Mahāmāyā* (*supra,* p. 160); *supra,* pp. 161, 167, 180.

[78] Cf. Woodroffe, *Śakti and Śākta,* p. 208 : "Thus life and consciousness exist throughout. All is living. All is consciousness".

[79] Danielou, *Hindu Polytheism,* p. 374.

[80] *Supra,* pp. 167, and also cf. *supra,* p. 13.

[81] Cf. Eliade, *Patterns in Comparative Religion,* p. 368.

[82] On this integrity and ambiguity, *vide,* e.g., Woodroffe, *Śakti and Śakta,* p. 285 : "In meditation (Dhyāna) there is duality ,namely, the subject who meditates and the object of such meditation, though in fact, the two are (according to the Advaita or non-dualism of Śāktas), both differing aspects of the one Brahman through Its Power". *Vide* also M. P. Pandit, *Studies in the Tantras and the Veda* (Madras : Ganesh and Co. Private, Ltd., 1964), pp. 69f.

The Passionate Yogī : Śiva

I am the greatest of the eleven Rudras, the lord of yoga; how can I take a beautiful wife, a woman who is the very form of illusion? Any yogi ought to regard every woman as if she were his mother; I am a yogi; how can I marry a woman, my mother?[83]

A previous glimpse of the god Śiva found this divinity being pursued by the amourous austerities of the goddess under the form of Satī. Moreover, Śiva was being counselled by Viṣṇu concerning the inseparable relation between Divine Nuptiality and the harmonious eternal return of the Cosmos.[84] It is nonetheless an apparent mystery that Śiva should so be portrayed as one who not only allows himself to be distracted from his yogic meditations as the Great Yogī; but, also, that this divinity should be so contrarily described as having erotically "lost himself in her [the goddess] as a yogī in full self-collection submerges in the Self, there deliquescing totally".[85] While it is true that we are not primarily concerned with this Śiva-Motif (as it is itself a possible mythological distraction of extremely complicated nature), its mytho-paradigmatic value for subsequently developed initiatic motifs warrants that we turn to its brief consideration.

Our task is much facilitated, though not completely undertaken (in the light of our thesis context: the goddess) by the Sanskritic scholar, O'Flaherty, who has rendered a synthetic analysis of the subject as a problem of Indian mythology.[86] To be sure, this scholar has examined a host of myths which suggest not only the sexuality of the god Śiva, but which, again, have enabled her to draw a few interesting and significant conclusions about *how* asceticism and sexuality are *both* integral to the character of Śiva.

The author, first of all, disarms us at once by insisting that the

[83] Bhaviṣya Purana III.4.14.40-43, cited by Wendy D. O'Flaherty, "Asceticism and Sexuality in the Mythology of Śiva, Part II", *History of Relilions*, IX, No. 1 (August, 1969), 30. In the previously mentioned "cosmogonic legends" (*supra*, p. 174, b. 136), Brahma, Viṣṇu, and Śiva, having resisted the demand of the goddess (as Ellammā) for sexual union with their insistence that she is their "mother", the goddess answers: "I am not your mother but only your grandmother, as you were born from an egg, so you need not hesitate": Oppert, *On the Original Inhabitants* ..., p. 466; likewise, Peddammā, *ibid.*, p. 473n.

[84] *Supra*, pp. 173-174, and also cf. *supra*, p. 123.

[85] Zimmer, *The King and the Corpse*, p. 287.

[86] O'Flaherty, in two articles (as portions of a Harvard University doctoral thesis), entitled "Asceticism and Sexuality in the Mythology of Śiva" (Parts I and II).

answer to the enigma "is not ... a kind of 'conjunction of opposites'";[87] although it is also apparent that this notion is not entirely inapplicable to the matter (*infra*). Her critical observations regarding a maze of myths about Śiva *et al.* lead the scholar to assign a key importance to how one conceives of the nature and function of the notion of *tapas*. In essence her remarks are the following : (1) *tapas* (i.e., austerittties) for which performance Śiva, the Mahāyogī, is traditionally renown, is actually a dynamic-bivalent phenomenon. that is, (a) it has a potentially destructive aspect *and* (b) it has a potentially creative aspect.[88] Barring any mutual exclusion of divine attributes (in the sense of absolute ambivalence), (2) the paradoxical nature and function of *tapas* may be stated succinctly :

> Chastity develops into desire, and the fulfillment of desire leads to chastity. ... *Tapas* and *kāma*, interchangeable forms of cosmic heat, replace and limit one another to maintain the balance of the universe.[89]

Again (3), this dynamic paradox reflected in sundry myths, as well as in some measure related to Tantric (soteriological) philosophy, finds its correspondential resolution in Tantric rites; that is, in the relations between *pravṛtti* (i.e., activity, worldly involvement) and *nivṛtti* (i.e., quiescence, withdrawal).[90] For *pravṛtti* encompasses *tapas* and *kāma* as "forces of energy", while *nivṛtti* remains "their true opposite".[91] *Nivṛtti* "in its broadest sense", however, is the "moment" when "the two extremes of chastity and sexuality" (as "episodes of *pravṛtti*") cancel out and become "an apparent calm which is in fact a perfectly balanced tension".[92] Finally, it appears to us that (4) the scholar's remarkable array of mythological episodes lends itself to several *hermeneutical* conclusions, but that she *prefers to emphasize* the phenomenon of dynamic paradox—indeed we have been shown *a more markedly "pendulous" paradox.*[93]

Before pointing out the specific relevance of these remarks for our own study, we would call attention to the following items critical to the historian of religions. First, the author, in pursuing a synthetically

---

[87] *Ibid.*, Part I, p. 301.

[88] *Ibid.*

[89] *Ibid.*, Part II, p. 39.

[90] *Ibid.*, pp. 39, 40.

[91] *Ibid.*, p. 39.

[92] *Ibid.*, p. 40.

[93] *Ibid.*, p. 41 ; cf. *ibid.*, Part I, pp. 318f., Sec. 5, and pp. 313f.

descriptive key to the maze of erotic mythological imagery about Śiva, does not, it seems, take account of the experiential-soteriological implications of the given levels of comprehension which are also integral to those myths. For example, *another thing* about what the Hindu sees as "an opposition in the Indian sense",[94] is the fact that on the level of *ordinary* human experience there *is* (i.e., appears to remain) a logical discrepancy in the nature of the gods (including Śiva) as they are conceived to be related to life's good or ills. The experiential "what isness" of the average Hindu [95] must then be distinguished from the scholar's intellectual comprehension (or even that of the "educated men of the Sweeper and ... other castes"[96] of those "correlative opposites that act as interchangeable identities in the essential sense".[97]

Secondly, the author's hermeneutical preference for a more markedly pendulous paradox of nature and function for Śiva does not necessarily *preclude* the applicability of the notion of *coincidentia oppositorum*. To be sure, it would seem to suggest that such a notion is indeed *among* the varying approaches used by the Indian mythographers themselves toward the ambiguous character of Śiva;[98] although the author is correct in pointing out the earlier absence of other literary possibilities for a more comprehensive consideration of his origin, as well as the discovery of an interpretive resolution of his functional duality (i.e., asceticism and sexuality).[99]

Thirdly, it is appreciable to the historian of religions that the so-called *extra*-religious factor (though, sociologically, the term has

---

94 *Ibid.*, p. 300.

95 For example, Pauline Mahar Kolenda's "Religious Anxiety and Hindu Fate," in Harper, *Religion in South India*, pp. 71-81, shows by her detection of non-traditional approaches by high and low castes (especially the latter) to their situations in the world, that the proper *referent* for the myths of resolution (*supra*) was probably a specific *religious consciousness* : a perception of the world in relation to Ultimate Reality (*vide supra*, pp. 30-34); so that Kolenda's subjects, by their adoption of "a different set of theories", suggest that they do not respond at a level of consciousness which sees the "opposites" of life, or the gods, as *logically* "interchangeable identities".

96 Kolenda, "Religious Anxiety and Hindu Fate", p. 78; *vide* esp. pp. 73, 75-79.

97 O'Flaherty, "Asceticism and Sexuality in the Mythology of Śiva, Part I", pp. 300, 301.

98 Cf. *ibid.*, pp. 306-307; e.g., p. 328 : "The *Śiva Purāṇa* ... : 'He who burns his body with the fire of Śiva and floods it with the elixir of his *śakti* by the path of yoga—he gains immortality".

99 *Ibid.*, pp. 303-304.

limited applicability to Hinduism), i.e., societal ambivalence,[100] has not been ignored by the author. As we noted earlier, the ambivalence has tended to affect more than one area of life in Indian history;[101] but this also leads us to make the following observations concerning all the previous remarks and their relevance for our work.

The "Passionate Yogī" motif may thus — with no deference to Freud — signify an Indian historical-anthropological testimony to the relentless power of *human* sexuality; that is, the phenomenon is as naturally given and integral to the life of *homo sapiens* as much as it is to *homo religiosus,* even when the latter aspires "to achieve the most absolute possible degree of transcendence of any and all the conditions that limit and frustrate man".[102] We recall, for example, O'Flaherty's observation upon the connection of Śiva with the sexual elements in the symbolism of the Vedic (apart from the "non-Vedic") divinities (i.e., Indra, Prajāpati, and Agni).[103] The Sexuality Motif may, in deference to O'Flaherty's comments on *tapas,* represent the mythographic endeavour to arrive at a meaningful and practicable theory of the coincidence of, and the interplay between, the Ultimate and the intimate dimensions of man's apprehensions of the Sacred. Moreover, an historical-traditional emphasis may support the idea that Śiva's complex character reflects that *also* paradoxical problem of Magna-Minor Traditional relations in Indian history and religion; so that such myths aim at the conciliation of Śiva's cosmic *and* rustic aspects.[104]

A final consideration *a propos* Śākta soteriology regards, again, the asceticism *and* sexuality of the god Śiva as consistent with the all-encompassing sovereignty of the goddess—hence the *pansacralization* of the Intimate (i.e., *pravṛtti* : wordly involvement, *including sexual* activity). If we apply—in our phraseology—O'Flaherty's "pendulous paradox" to the mythology of the *goddess,* it occurs to us that the application of the Nuptial Motif (including sexual rapture) to Śiva

---

[100] *Ibid.,* pp. 323f., 327, 328ff.

[101] Cf. *supra,* pp. 62ff, 91f., 93-98; p. 91, n. 250; p. 92, nn. 254-5; p. 138 n. 532; Elwin, *The Religion of an Indian Tribe,* pp. 11-13; esp. *supra,* p. 132 and n. 532 of that page.

[102] King, *Introduction to Religion,* pp. 281-282.

[103] O'Flaherty, "Asceticism and Sexuality in the Mythology of Śiva, Part I", p. 304; cf. *ibid.,* Part II, pp. 11ff.; likewise two intersecting "ascetic-yogic-upaniṣadic" contemplations, *supra,* pp. 116 and n. 398.

[104] Cf. Dimock, *The Thief of Love,* pp. 10-11, 198.

becomes the *will* of the goddess, who is both the "leader of Yogīs" *and* the Passionate Goddess on Mount Himālaya.[105] As a participant in amourous activity, on the one hand, Śiva, in erotic relation to the goddess, symbolizes the fact that "lust remains a threat to religion only until it is answered"; agamically, the goddess says to Śiva, "My lord, having made love with you for many years, I am satisfied, and your mind has withdrawn from these pleasures. I wish to know your true nature, that frees from rebirth".[106] On the other hand, the failure to transcend an extreme state of attachment (i.e., "a static [soteriological] solution")[107] means that one has not performed "the *act* of sexual intercourse without losing one's purity", or kept "the mind ... uninvolved".[108] Hence the participant's consciousness remains for an *indefinite* period at the level of non-liberating entrancement—under the "law of time and death" (Eliade).[109]

The "Spatial-Digits" of the Goddess : Pīṭhas

What appears as the reality of "Death" to the unliberated consciousness under the spell of Time (kāla = kali = Kālī) is but "Deathlessness" to the goddess, who is both Kālamāta, the "Mother of Time", and Kālaharshinī, the "Destroyer of Time".[110] Still in her unlimited capacity for formal manifestation as love or terror, the goddess combines these two dimensions as Devī-Satī : the Ultimate Being, who seems to "die" yet who confirms her inimitable Immortality through recurrent theophany.[111] Śiva, then, in the midst of the most inconsolable grief at the loss of the company (i.e., "Presence") of Devī-Satī can say, "Goddess ... Through your help, one may be a god; but without you, I am godless".[112]

---

105 *Vide supra*, p. 121, n. 428; Zimmer, *The King and the Corpse*, :. 287 (Kālikā Purāṇa).

106 Śiva Purāṇa II.2.23.7-8, cited by O'Flaherty, "Asceticism and Sexuality in the Mythology of Śiva, Part II", pp. 332-333.

107 *Ibid.*, Part I, p. 41.

108 Cf. *ibid.*, Part II, p. 311 (myth : Śiva rescues Viṣṇu); *vide* also Brahmavaivartapurāṇa XLIV.54-XLV.1ff. ("Kṛṣṇa Janma Khanda"), where *Śiva* is bidden to "relent" from passion as the Lord of Yogīs; cf. Bhagavad-Gītā IV.16-20.

109 O'Flaherty, "Asceticism and Sexuality in the Mythology of Śiva, Part II", p. 335; *supra*, p. 167. O'Flaherty's complete work is *Asceticism and Eroticism in the Mythology of Śiva*, London : Oxford University Press, 1973.

110 *Supra*, p. 156.

111 E.g., Brahmavaivartapurāṇa XLIII.91-107 ("Kṛṣṇa Janma Khanda").

112 *Ibid.*

In the most specific sense of mythic event and *sacred space*, it is Śiva's passionate involvement with the goddess, as Satī, which provides the setting for "Death" as pendulously related to "Life"—the Satī-Suicide in the Kālikā Purāṇa (XIV.1-16.70).[113] Moreover, the Satī-Suicide is intimately wrapped up with the legend of *Dakṣa-yajñanāśa*.[114] The story, not without some possible Vedo-Brāhmanic roots (Ṛg-Veda X.61.5-7; Aitareya Brāhmaṇa III.33-34) is found in several literary sources, but it is believed that its "earliest form ... is probably to be traced in the Mahābhārata (XII.282-283) ..."[115]

> In the Mahābhārata version of the story ... the wife of Śiva is only responsible for pointing out, to her husband, Dakṣa's impertinence in disregarding the great god ....[116]

In a later "modified version" (the Purāṇas and Kālīdāsa) the story goes that

> the mother-goddess, who was the wife of Śiva, was in the form of Satī one of the daughters of Dakṣa Prajāpati. Dakṣa was celebrating a great sacrifice for which neither Satī nor Śiva was invited. Satī, however, went to her father's sacrifice uninvited, but was greatly insulted by Dakṣa. As a result of this ill-treatment, Satī is said to have died by yoga or of a broken heart, or as Kālīdāsa says, she put herself into fire and perished.[117]

It is held as probable by Sircar that the early medieval period saw the engraftment of a "new legend" upon the foregoing narrative, as reflected in later goddess-oriented texts. Śiva, driven "mad" by his inconsolable loss of Satī, destroys the *Mahā-yajña* of Dakṣa. Expressing a nemesic "fire of anger" so intense that "the Pralaya seemed to threaten the three worlds", Śiva's mercy prevailed amidst sorrow, nonetheless; and the god destroyed only Dakṣa [118] and his sacrifice. The "Deva of Devas" himself, however, "saw that the body of the Intelligent Satī was being burnt in the fire of the Chita. He cried aloud : Oh, my Satī ! Oh My Satī ! And taking Her body on His neck,

---

113 In Zimmer, *The King and the Corpse*, pp. 285-296; cf. Brahmavaivarta XLII.82-95 ("Kṛṣṇa Janma Khanda"(.

114 Kālikā Purāṇa XVII.1-XIX.13, in Zimmer, *The King and the Corpse*, pp. 296-306.

115 Dines Chandra Sircar, "The Śākta Pīṭhas", *Journal of the Royal Asiatic Society of Bengal*, XIV, Part I (1948), 5.

116 *Ibid.*, pp. 5f.

117 *Ibid.*

118 I.e., Śiva "cut off his head and instead placed the head of a goat, brought him back to life and thus made the Gods free from all fears" (*ibid.*). Cf. the "pravargya" motif, in Coomaraswamy, "Angel and Titan : An Essay in Vedic Ontology", pp. 374ff.

began to roam in different countries, like a mad man".[119] The aftermath of the "Death" of the goddess has two mythological variants: (1) the gods Brahma, Viṣṇu, and Sani enter Satī's body and divide it into fragments, and (2) Viṣṇu, following after the wandering Śiva, dismembers Satī's body with his arrows.[120]

Earlier we alluded to the Digit-Motif of the goddess as having special significance as far as the feminine dimension of life-forms is concerned: "O Goddess ... You have created everything in the garb of a woman and you have wielded the form of a woman through the digits of your digits".[121] Moreover, it was seen that the *Grāmadevatās* throughout the land of India are also divine "digits" or, we might say, "digit-children" of her as Mahākālī, the Personification of Time.[122] Between her reality as the Great Goddess of Time, with her innumerable *mātās* and *ammās*, and the human [123] personifications of her own Being, there stand her sacred "spaces"; these are the *pīṭhas*, i.e., "seats", or "sanctuaries of gods",[124] sacred "places" which are believed to provide for the continuity and intensification of the sacred as well as the opportunity for Divine-human intercourse.

Apart from the glorious capacity of the goddess for re-theophanization, the *prelude* to the "creation" of her various *pīṭhas* through her redemptive "death" occurs still in indirect relation to the goddess; and that prelude involves divinities who have been touched by her presence but now disconsoled by her absence—the "Eclipse" of the goddess. Sacred spaces thus emerge out of the very grief of the gods, particularly Śiva's. Indeed the account in the Brahmavaivartapurāṇa (XLIII.1-107) constitutes an answer to the *apparent* ultimacy of Death, in that sacred spaces of divine Life—the Presence of the goddess—are made available to persons, laymen and specialists alike, who seek after the saving Truth. For even while Viṣṇu seeks to *counsel* the despairing Śiva (who has committed the grave error of "for-

---

119 Devībhāgavata Purāṇa VII.30.39ff.

120 Eliade, *Yoga*, p. 347; Sircar, "The Śākta Pīṭhas", pp. 6f.

121 Brahmavaivartapurāṇa XLIII (p. 294); *supra*, p. 167.

122 *Vide supra*, p. 167, n. 101.

123 Ideally, men and women may share the "mutual reality" (*supra*, p. 164) of Śiva and Śakti as "Univalent Being" (*supra*, p. 163): men = Śivas = women = Śaktis = Devī. *Vice infra*, Chap. V.

124 Bharati, "Pilgrimage in the Indian Tradition", pp. 147f., 159; cf. Banerjea, *The Development of Hindu Iconography*, pp. 298f., 273f.

getting"[125] who he is) through "metaphysical, beneficial, and substantial doctrines"—a discourse "on Ontology"—wonders occur.[126]

Following, then, Śiva's wandering [127] over mountains and valleys, oceans and deserts, lingering at islands and under trees (e.g., the Banyan Tree; the *nyagrodha*)[128], a *tank* [129] (i.e., the "pond of tears") is created out of the god's tears; it is a place where one dip by a man brings absolution and liberation : "the sins of a hundred births" and the power to enter "the land of Hari. Again, a *shrine* is developed out of the tears of Hari and Hara, together (near the nyagrodha), where ascetics may find release.[130]

The *pīṭhas* par excellence of the goddess derive from the fragmentation (or "dismemberment") of Devī Satī after her disconsoling demise. The various parts of her body fall from the realm of the gods and in their scattering became *loci* [131] of hope for millions; these *loci* became the emblematic digits of her "forgiveness ... contentment ... victory ...", as well as her "peace ... wisdom and *memory* [italics mine]" in relation to her devotees.[132] The number of these worship centers varies, to be sure, ranging from four mentioned in the Tantras and Purāṇas [133] to fifty-one, even 108 scared spaces, this last of which may be seen as having a symbolic relation to a

---

[125] Cf. Brahmavaivartapurāṇa XLIII : 34-45, Śiva to Viṣṇu : "O Magnanimous being ... I pray you tell me who you are ... Who is Satī ! Who am I ? ..."; considering Śiva's condition, "Lord Hari ... wept ..." For the "primitive" apprehension of "forgetting", *vide* Adolf E. Jensen, *Myth and Cult Among Primitive Peoples,* trans. M. T. C. Childin and W. Weissleder (Chicago and London : University of Chicago Press, 1963), pp. 198, 201.

[126] Brahmavaivartapurāna XLIII : 46-55. Applying the foregoing analogy : Śiva has "forgotten" the "metaphysical imperative" of the Divine Reality. *Vide* Viṣṇu's "lecture", *ibid, loc cit.*.

[127] *Supra,* p. 122.

[128] *Vide supra,* p. 55, n. 79; p. 56, n. 85.

[129] For this phenomenon in connection with the Mother-Goddess as an ancient "terra-cotta" worship form and the Kumārī-Pūjā, *vide* S. R. Das, "Clay Figurines of the Kumārī-Vratas of Bengal", *Journal of the Indian Society of Oriental Art,* XIV (1946), 91-94.

[130] Brahmavaivartapurāṇa XLIII.1-24, 45-46.

[131] Cf. Devībhāgavata Purāṇa VII.30; Kālikā Purāṇa 64:48-54.

[132] Brahmavaivartapurāṇa XLIII.77, 78.

[133] Cf. Bharati, "Pilgrimage in the Indian Tradition", pp. 166f.

like number of the goddess' epithets.[134] Among the *pīṭhas*, as examples of symbolic-somatic correlation, are the following :[135]

Devī Pātan, where her right hand fell.
Valley of Jawālamukhi, where her tongue fell.
Sugandha in South Bengal, her nose fell.
Labhpur, her lips fell.
Janasthāna in the Deccan, her cheeks fell.
Hiṅg Lāj in the West, her forehead (crown of her head) fell.
Benares, her ear drops fell.
Ujjāin, her elbow fell.
Kāmākhyā in Assam, her organs of generation fell.[136]
Calcutta (Kālighāt), her great toe (left foot) fell.
Faljur (Jaintia Parganas), her left leg fell.
Somewhere in "Sylhet (or Kashmir ?)" her neck fell
Ukule Ghāt (or Kālīghāt ?), her fingers fell.

Especially symbolic of the phenomenology of the *pīṭha* as an abode of the goddess is the shrine called Kālīghāt.[137] It is significant because this *pīṭha* enables us to bring together the elements of myth, cult, and symbols in a remarkable way. To this within the perspective of cultural change one should add an historical, perhaps a semi-legendary, factor. The name, of course, signifies the goddess (Kālī) and *ghāt*, the steps (of Kālī) "by which the worshippers from the temple descended to the stream for their ablutions".[138]

Besides the Satī Myth which accounts for the shrine's origin, it is also a place known for sacred rite, which once included the bloody sacrifices of numerous animals,[139] just as the tendency has recently been to use substitute elements (i.e., *pratinidhi*) in the *Dakṣiṇāyana-pūjā*.[140] Sacred trees grow in a garden associated with the Kālī *temple*,

---

134 Eliade, *Yoga*, p. 346; *vide* Devībhāgavatapuraṇa VII.31; note *ibid.*, VII.38.34; cf. Mahānirvāṇa Tantra VII.12-51 : a hundred goddess epithets all commencing with the letter "K".

135 Briggs, *Gorakhnāth and the Kānphaṭa Yogīs*, p. 90, n. 1.

136 For the temple of Kāmākhyā as a center of worship and pilgrimage, *vide* Muirhead-Thomson, *Assam Valley*, pp. 36-38; Hem Barua and J. D. Baveja, *The Fairs and Festivals of Assam* (Gauhati, Assam : B. N. Dutt Barua, 1956), pp. 26-38 (cf. *supra*, p. 64, n. 128).

137 Cf. *Encyclopedia of Religion and Ethics*, VII, 642, for the historical origins and geography of this shrine.

138 *Ibid.*, pp. 642, 643; cf. Campbell, *The Masks of God*, II, 5. Eliade (*Patterns in Comparative Religion*, p. 419) remarks that "her cult is the bloodiest anywhere in Asia".

139 C. Chakravarti, *The Tantras*, p. 99 (bottom).

140 Bharati, *The Tantric Tradition*, p. 244; *vide* this "substitution", also with regard to animal sacrifices in C. Chakravarti, *The Tantras*, p. 93.

for example, the pipal tree (*ficus Indica religiosa*); and pilgrims from various parts of India and abroad are attracted to a particular, unified cluster of (five) trees, the *pañcabati*. This five-trees-in-one phenomenon has become the place for yogīs in their meditative quest for a more intensified experience of the Sacred.[141] The same author calls attention to the fact that technological change facilitating an "intensified pilgrimization", as much as the association of famous personages with *pīṭhas*—in this case the late Bengali mystic, Ramakrishna Paramhamsa—have been especially influential. This mystic, whose *bhakti* for the goddess reached ecstatic heights,[142] used to sit under the *pañcabati* during his meditations.[143]

In light of the foregoing discussion we would make the following structural observations concerning mythic event and sacred space (which will include some remarks upon other cultic symbols that may be homologized with the religious intention of the *pīṭhas*). For we notice that there is a structural-symbolic coherence in the relation between the goddess as the Living Cosmos, the Tantric-Purāṇic conception of the *pīṭha*, and the Vedo-Brāhmanic meaning of the "creative" place of the Sacrifice.

To the goddess, first of all, the entire Cosmos is a temporal and spatial sacred panoply of her Will, Knowledge, and Action (*Icchā-Jñāna-Kriyā-Śakti*). *Pīṭhas* are thus microcosms of the Macro-cosmic Reality of the goddess. They are symbols of the ritual "cosmicization" of what is essentially sacred space, which would appear to us as a profane terrain *before* the goddess "fell". Though the mythic images, it seems, are merely the "fragments" of divinity, rituologically, every *pīṭha* is the center of the world and, indeed, means "the actual presence of the Great Goddess".[144]

Secondly, the structural homologation of the cosmos, the *pīṭha*, and the devotee are startingly effected by what seems a tragic act—the apparent "Death" of the goddess. This mythic act of self-inhumation, however, is implicitly ironical, yet quite consistent with the unending Sport or Play (Līlā) of the goddess; it is so whether she plays with her spouse (Śiva) in the thousand-petalled lotus (*sahasrāra*)

---

141 Bharati, "Pilgrimage in the Indian Tradition", p. 150.

142 Cf. Christopher Isherwood, *Ramakrishna and His Disciples* (New York: Simon and Schuster, 1965), pp. 58-68 (cf. pp. 50-57); and *ibid.*, p. 267 *et passim*.

143 Bharati, "Pilgrimage in the Indian Tradition', p. 150.

144 Eliade, *Yoga*, p. 346.

or plays through the medium of the cosmogony.[145] Her dramatic self-withdrawal and subsequent "dismemberment", therefore, are events which suggest two further rituo-structural homologations that recall the Hindu past but yet point to a new religious valorization.

To begin with, the voluntary dismemberment of the Devī-Satī reminds us of the ancient[146] Vedo-Brahmanic *puruṣa/prajāpati* symbolism of the creative sacrifice by the gods.[147] Here with the goddess, however, there appears to be a *mythic reversal* of the original structure of the event, in that (1) not only does the goddess-with-aseity allow herself to be created out of the united energies (*tejas*) of the gods; but (2) the Vedo-Brāhmanic "primeval sacrifice", though it becomes with the goddess a similar event wherein "'her' members fall from 'her'",[148] the significance of her act differs at least in these two specific respects: (a) her non-tendentious reappearance on the cosmic scene constitutes a radically new beginning, because "She" is now *revealed* as *the* Ultimate Reality,[149] which also lies permanently behind, within, and beyond even the recurrency of the "creation" when understood within the tradition of Trimūrti.[150]

The redemptive "activity" of the goddess,[151] then, though it constitutes a "return to the primordial unity", to the *Samvit* of the goddess "before the creation", is *her* Self-disclosure—and it is new. She is the *Magna Creatrix.* To be sure, she is the most Genuine Surprise in the history of Indian revelation and theogony; (b) her creation of the *pīṭhas*, therefore, as sacred places of pilgrimage for her worship represents the birth of a "universe"[152] of sacred monuments through which *devotion* to her "is prolonged ... continued ... prevented from

---

[145] *Vide* Saundaryalaharī 9b; *supra*, p. 156, and also cf. *supra*, p. 180 and n. 176.

[146] Eliade alludes to the extra-Indian antiquity of this "dismemberment" motif; *vide Yoga*, p. 347.

[147] Rig-Veda X.90.

[148] Cf. Eliade, *Yoga*, p. 109: "... when Prajāpati created the world, his members fell from him ...".

[149] Devībhāgavata Purāṇa XII.8.8-93; cf. *supra*, pp. 169-171.

[150] *Supra*, pp. 155-156.

[151] *Supra*, p. 175.

[152] The idea is suggested by the presence of the great goddess at *each* and *all* the *pīṭhas*—together; but also by a most "interesting phenomenon", a peculiar "iconographical pattern" noticed by Bharati in "Pilgrimage in the Indian Tradition", pp. 160-161.

ceasing to be".[153] These sacred places (= spaces) thus have the exalted function of assuring the "second birth" or spiritual renewal. The moral of the *Śāktapīṭha* mythology is, ultimately,

> the broad-based apotheosis of the motherland conceived in the form of energised centres for *tantric and yogic sādhanā* or for practising special meditation and spiritual discipline.[154]

What is finally remarkable about the relation between the mythic event (the Satī-Suicide) and the Birth of Sacred Space (*Śāktapīṭhas*) is another thing; that is, the Puruṣa/Prajapati "dismemberment" in the Vedo-Brāhmanic tradition is now capable of being structurally understood within the aetiology of the *pīṭha-motif*, so that there is essentially the transformation of anthropocosmic reality into *topocosmic* reality.[155]

Within the cultic realm there are, we stated, certain symbols which may be assimilated to the *pīṭha-motif*. We shall comment, briefly, upon three of them which may be regarded, too, as symbolic "extensions" of the *pīṭhas* and "spatial-digits" of the goddess.

A "primitive" example of the "externalization" (*infra*) of cultic acts in sacred space takes the form of the *Ālpanā*,[156] which is a part of the folk art and festival songs of Bengal. As a religious art-form it is found among such peoples as the Oraons of Chota Nagpur, including the Birhors, Kharias, and among the Mundas. The phenomenon involves drawings or paintings that are made *on the ground* by girls and women during festive occasions. Ranging in configuration from four to five circles, etc., there are some that make "a square (room) with the representation of two human figures [anthropomorphic divinities ?] inside it with the Sun and the Moon above and below ..."[157]

Conceived as a type of sacred altar before which the "Kumārīs" perform, and prayers and chanting occur, the Kumārī Vratas last five

153 Eliade, *Yoga*, p. 109.

154 Vasudeva S. Agrawala, *Śiva Mahādeva : The Great God* (Varanasi, India : Veda Academy, 1966), p. 11.

155 Gaster, *Thespis* ..., p. 24.

156 Cf. S. R. Das, "Ālpanā of the Kumārī-Vratas of Bengal", *Journal of the Indian Society of Oriental Art*, XI (1943), 126-132. Ālpanā (or Ālipanā) have two classes : (1) one in which different kinds of colour are used for making a "dry painting"; (2) one in which Piṭhali is used, a white liquid (*ibid.*, p. 126). The magico-religious "externalization" (*infra*, p. 137) in this "art means that something to their hearts desire [the performing "young unmarried girls"] must be achieved by the representation of the desired object" (Das, "Ālpanā ...", p. 132).

157 *Ibid.*, p. 128.

years, and the Ālpanā aims at (1) the prevention of evils and the "distraction of ... malignant spirits", and (2) the "fulfillment of desires", such as "wealth and plenty".[158] Most significantly, the Vrata-Ālpanā is associated with the goddess as Lakṣmī. The proper "images", therefore, include her renown symbol, the lotus, as well as other "lotus creepers". In addition to the astrological symbols already mentioned, "the circles of the Ālpanā represent the Universe with its luminaries ... and their presiding deities, givers of light and life".[159]

Another cultic-symbolic miniaturization of the living Cosmos (= Devī) may take the form of the *maṇḍala* (i.e., circle).[160] Its assimilation to the topocosmic *pīṭha* begins with its very construction *on the ground*, as well as its quare shape with internal circles (concentric or not), the former symbolizing the unity and integrity of the cosmic zones and their "centre" of gravity (i.e., maṇḍala = *imago mundi* and *axis mundi*); the latter representing the "dimensionalization"[161] of the universe with its "'heavens' or levels" as well as a pantheon : divinities themselves represented in a certain order by images [162] from among whom the *sādhakā* receives or finds his *iśtadevatā* (his chosen deity). Eliade understands the *maṇḍala* to have, basically, two functions : (1) like the labyrinth [163] it "is equivalent to an initiation ritual"; (2) it "protects", warding off all dangers, enhancing concentration, and the individual "to find his own centre." [164] Importantly, the cultic utilization of the *maṇḍala* allows for both its "external" and "internal" contemplation.[165] Since the individual's "discovery of the *maṇḍala* in his own body indicates a desire to identify his 'mystical body' with a microcosm", that "place"[166] is, here, in its

---

158 *Ibid.*, pp. 126, 127, 131.

159 *Ibid.*, p. 129. A ritual diagram used among families of one group (the Khāriās) "represents the points of the compass and over the diagram a light is placed" (*ibid.*, p. 130). Cf. Stella Kramrisch, "Indian Varieties of Art Ritual", Kitagawa and Long, eds., *Myths and Symbols*, pp. 23-45, esp. pp. 38ff.

160 Eliade, *Yoga*, pp. 219ff. Cf. John Blofeld, *The Tantric Mysticism of Tibet* (New-York : E. P. Dutton and Company, Inc., 1970), pp. 94-99, 102-117.

161 *Supra*, p. 161.

162 Eliade, *Patterns in Comparative Religion*, pp. 372f.

163 *Ibid.*, pp. 381ff.

164 Eliade, *Images and Symbols*, p. 53.

165 *Ibid.* Cf. Blofeld, *The Tantric Mysticism of Tibet*, p. 96; *vide* Devībhāgavata Purāṇa VII.40.1-31 ("external"); *ibid.*, VII.39.1 ("internal").

166 Eliade, *Images and Symbols*, p. 53.

initiatic-cosmic totality, "the realm of the Great Goddess" as the Macro-anthropocosm.

It is interesting to notice that the "Passionate Yogī" (Śiva) and the Entrancing Goddess (Kālī-Satī) in the myths may be brought into interstructural relation with the cultic quest for spiritual liberation through another symbol : the *Yantra*. Structurally, it is referred to as a "linear paradigm of the *maṇḍala*".[167] According to our specific interest here—its rituo-structural phenomenology vis-à-vis the Ultimate Reality—the meaning, particularly of its inverse and observe triangles, is clearly stated.

> The triangle pointing down symbolizes the *yoni*—that is, the Śakti; the triangle pointing up designates the male principle, Śiva; the central point (*bindu*) signifies the undifferentiated Brahman. In other words, the *yantra* is an expression, in terms of linear symbolism, of the cosmic manifestations, beginning with the primordial unity.[168]

This implicitly erotic imagery has its place in the triphasal *sādhanic* perception of "Form", ranging from the "anthropomorphic" (*sthūla*) to the mental (*sūkṣma*) and the spiritual (tha para-formal); this last, as the highest contemplation of "the primordial unity", does not perceive the Yoni to be "the generative organ of a woman but ... Kāraṇam or Cause, the Womb of the Universe".[169]

The unity of mythic event and sacred space is, finally, affirmed in the idea that the *Maṇḍala/Yantra* symbolic structure represents an attempt on the part of the devotee of the goddess to achieve both (a) the assimilation of his (somatic) Self to the Universe through the externalization and/or internalization of such objects; and (b) the ultimate, supraconscious realization that, as the *Maṇḍala/Yantra* is the symbolic manifestation of the true form (*Sva-Rūpa*) of the Universal Goddess, the *sādhaka*, too, is one with his Self (*Ātman*), the Universe (*Viśvarūpa*), and the goddess (*Viśvātmā*)—that All is Devī—in a state of *Saccidānanda*.[170]

---

[167] Eliade, *Yoga*, p. 219.

[168] *Ibid. Vide* also A. Mookerjee, *Tantra Art*, p. 79, Plate 52; p. 80; cf. *ibid.*, p. 23, Plate 8. For the *sādhanic* integration of *pīṭha* and *maṇḍala*, *vide* Bharati, *The Tantric Tradition*, p. 254.

[169] Woodroffe, *Tantrarāja Tantra*, pp. 3, 6; *supra*, pp. 162; 162, n. 75.

[170] Woodroffe, *Tantrarāja Tantra*, p. 4.

SACRED REALITY AND SACRED ACTION

The continuity between Cosmic Time and Ritual Time, the correlation between Mythic Event and Sacred Space, cultimates in the practical cultic milieu. It is here that the ultimacy of sacred reality and the intimacy of sacred action combine and create an atmosphere in which myth, cult, and symbols are structured, so that there are accommodated a variety of experiences and expressions of homage to the goddess Durgā-Kālī. On the one hand, the phenomenon of her worship—*pūjā*—may be broadly defined and interpreted to include their historically "primitive" elements; on the other hand, there is structural continuity between *pūjā* and another more sophisticated mode of worship (i.e., Yoga), which, of course, is also of antiquitious origin.[171]

First, as regards the origin of the word *pūjā* itself, it has been accounted for in several ways: (1) a Dravidian compound word *pu-gey* (hence *puṣpa-karma*),[172] i.e., *pu* ("flower") and a root, *cey* (*gey*), which means "to do"; (2) a Dravidian root, *pūsu* (otherwise *pūçu*), meaning "to smear", in the sense of doing so with blood, if not, a type of sandal paste or vermillion, which is assumed to be fundamental to *pūjā* as a rite;[173] (3) a Sanskrit root (which includes other meanings, i.e., positive and negative magic) signifying "to pay homage", a phenomenon taken to be ultimately related to vegetal-oriented cult.[174] This view which suggests a type of man/plant mysticism, says that the typical ingredients of *pūjā* are related to the early Indian veneration of trees, more or less "unshapely" or having "roughly the form of tree trunks"; men vis-à-vis the sacred tree would thus

> paint it with beautiful colours ... rub it with unctious pastes ... water it with nourishing and refreshing liquids ... having garlands on it whose fragrance will

---

[171] Cf. Eliade, *Yoga*, p. 360: "From the beginning, Yoga marked the reaction against metaphysical speculation and the excesses of a fossilized ritualism; it represented the same *tendency toward the concrete*, toward personal experience, that we find again in the popular devotion expressed in *pūjā* and *bhakti*. We always find some form of Yoga whenever the goal is *experience of the sacred* or the attainment of a perfect *self-mastery*, which is itself the first step toward magical mastery of the world". *Vide ibid.*, pp. 359-361.

[172] *Supra*, p. 87.

[173] Cf. Charpentier, "The Meaning and Etymology of Pūjā", pp. 98f., esp. pp. 130-133.

[174] Cf. Jean Przyluski, "Totémisme et végétalisme dans l'Inde", *Revue de l'Histoire des Religions*, XCVI (1927), 352, 353; *supra*, pp. 55, 57, and 60, n. 106.

have the effect of drawing away pernicious influences. This, in short, is the Indian *pūjā*.[175]

Another view (4) which declines the emphasis given by Charpentier, particularly, draws attention to a factor which raises the question of the Hindu religious conception of the relation between *icon* and *devotee* in the *act* of *pūjā*. Here the Sanskrit verbal root *pūj-* (*pūjáyati* : "to honour") is correlated with an *attitude* on the part of the worshipper. The devotee's *pūjā*, then, consists essentially in his treatment of the *iconic devatā* as a Divine "guest".[176] One thus offers this "guest" tumeric paste and does other elemental gestures which are aimed at showing *honour* and "reverence" (or "respect") to "the invited deity"—the utmost hospitality.[177]

It is readily apparent that none of the above definitions and meanings is necessarily erroneous in a diachronic historical perspective. In fact it has been pointed out, for instance, that Thieme, too, seems to include an aspect of Charpentier's account.[178] Accordingly, we shall be using the term *pūjā* in an all-inclusive sense. It will, therefore, encompass the totality of modes and structures involved in the rituological perspective of Time as the medium of Sacred Reality and Sacred Action. *Pūjā*, then, which "is the common term for ritual worship", not only has its functional synonyms but may broadly apply to homage to the goddess even when classified itself into (a) Bāhyapūjā, "objective ritual worship", (b) Mānasa-Pūjā (or Antarpūjā), "inner or mental worship",[179] and (c) parā-pūjā, the transformal worship of the goddess, i.e., "without offerings of flowers and other articles ... the contem-

---

175 Przyluski, "Totémisme et végétalisme dans l'Inde", p. 360.

176 Cf. Paul Thieme, "Pūjā", *Journal of Oriental Research*, XXVII (1957-1958), p. 9; as a complex phenomenon the author would "call the 'root' *pūj* : 1. 'To honour (a guest or a newcomer) with a hospitable reception (greeting, offering a seat, washing the feet, bath, ornamentation, refreshments), to receive with respects, to entertain'. 2. 'To honour (a god) as guest (in a manner customary for the arriving guest)'. 3. 'To honour (objects like weapons, utensils of sacrifice or also the means of magic which are worshipped as divine beings) with flowers, scents, ornaments, etc. (as gods)". *Vide infra*, pp. 223-224.

177 Thieme, "Pūjā", p. 16; cf. *ibid.*, p. 4 : "... at the bottom of the different parts of the procedure lies a common idea which turns it into a meaningful whole from which one cannot easily take out a single element : the *pūjā* ... is the honour which is given to [a] god in his quality as a guest to be entertained".

178 Cf. Diehl, *Instrument and Purpose*, pp. 66f., n. 2.

179 Woodroffe, *Śakti and Śākta*, pp. 344, 345, 349; J. Sinha, *Shakta Monism*, p. 22. The latter author's "para-para" and "apara" categories (*ibid.*) correspond to those of Woodroffe (*supra*).

plation of the Divine Mother as undifferentiated power of pure consciousness and bliss".[180] Again, however, as a Vrata, among others in Bengal, Durgā-Pūjā is the *mahā-vrata* celebrated "in honour of the Devī as Durgā which will continue as long as the sun and moon endure, and which, if once commenced, must always be continued".[181]

This scope of meaning for *pūjā* requires that the following observations be taken into account before we proceed further. First, there is the recognition that, as the goddess herself allows for varying religious perceptions of her "form", there are also corresponding levels of spiritual *consciousness* potential in the human beings who seek her presence.[182] Secondly, with regard to such beings, they are considered to reflect different states of wordly entrancement (*māyā*) or temperament (*bhāva*), so that following the theory of potential *guṇa* interpenetration and predominance, there are comparative *sādhanic* depths or heights of spirituality available to men and women.[183] Thirdly, in the case of every form (*mūrti*) and mode of worship (*ācāra*) there remains the opportunity of approaching such a phenomenon (granting the meta-formal *possibility*) grossly or subtlely but, in either case, according to one's readiness for the same.[184] This is a crucial observation which underlies all the previous points and the modal principle of all worship within the Śākta philosophy as well as Hinduism as a whole. It is the principle of *adhikārabheda*, i.e., the "difference in rights, duties, ceremonies and worship dependent on difference in intellectual, emotional and spiritual equipment".[185] It is nonetheless the *sādhaka* or *sādhika* who becomes *adhikari*, that is, "qualified for all forms of yoga".[186]

---

180 J. Sinha, *Shakta Monism*, p. 22.

181 Woodroffe, *Introduction to Tantra Śāstra*, p. 101; cf. *supra*, p. 205f.

182 Cf. Woodroffe, *Śakti and Śākta*, pp. 205-208; *supra*, pp. 150f.

183 Woodroffe, *Śakti and Śākta*, pp. 337ff.

184 *Vide ibid.*, pp. 285ff., 369; thus there are (*ibid.*, pp. 370f.) ordinary flowers and "flowers of feeling" (*Bhāvapuṣpa*) "to the Divinity ..."; or, in the case of "sound (*śabda*)" (*ibid.*, pp. 322-326). For "forms of *ācāra*", *vide* Woodroffe, *Introduction to Tantra Śāstra*, pp. 76ff.; even within the Kaulācāra there are degrees of perfection: *vide* Woodroffe, *Śakti and Śākta*, p. 334.

185 P. V. Kane, *History of Dharmaśāstra*, II, Part II (Poona: Bhandarkar Oriental Research Institute, 1941), 714. Cf. Bharati, *The Tantric Tradition*, pp. 291, 295, 189; Woodroffe, *Śakti and Śākta*, p. 344; Devībhāgavata Purāṇa VII.40.32; *supra*, pp. 62-64 and p. 62, n. 118.

186 Woodroffe, *Introduction to Tantra Śāstra*, p. 73; and, *Śakti and Śākta*, pp. 280, 337.

Granting these factors, however, the need for some semblance of order or a pattern of devotional development amidst what seems an unmanageable conglomeration of modes and activities still remains. Notwithstanding variations in presentation and process, a four-fold typology of worship among the Śāktas is indicated by Farquhar:[187] (1) the public temple worship of the goddess, which includes the system of vegetarian offerings and animal sacrifices; (2) the form of worship known as Cakra-pūjā (or "circle-worship"), which may include, among other items, the use of *yantra*, *mantra*, and the *pañcatattva* (i.e., the "five elements" of wine, meat, fish, parched grain, and sexual union); (3) the process of *sādhana* which (too, incidentally) may be understood broadly, e.g., *sādhana* as any homage paid to the goddess and, apart from its apparent "secular" significance,[188] refers to the yogic transformation of the initiate into a state of spiritual perfection; and (4) the form of sorcery positive or negative (i.e., for "black" or "white" purposes),[189] the Tantras making room for all these forms mentioned. In our own consideration of most of these elements, however, though we shall certainly point out their major features and significance in the quest for salvation (especially the sacrificial and the initiatic), no attempt will be made to develop a pattern of progressive *minutiae* regarding the worship of the goddess. For our own purposes, at any rate, there are two further remarks that should be made.

First, we find that the adoption of a materialist *contra* immaterialist distinction[190] among *sādhanic* media is not as helpful to us as determining the rationale of the religious perspective underlying any given mode (concrete or discrete) of spiritual transformation.[191] This consideration would then override the sometimes doubtful determination of the concrete or allegorical interpretation of "elements" employed by either the Kaulās or the Samayins, or as *acaryas*, the

---

[187] Farquhar, *An Outline of the Religious Literature of India*, p. 203. Cf. Woodroffe, *Śakti and Śākta*, p. 343.

[188] Woodroffe, *Śakti and Śākta*, pp. 280, 337.

[189] Cf. "Black Sādhana", *ibid.*, pp. 360f.; *vide* also *ibid.*, pp. 330ff.

[190] I.e., use or non-use of formal elements in worship.

[191] Although, for example, Eliade and Bharati take account of the materialist/immaterialist tradition, both scholars also recognize that "it is not always easy to be perfectly sure how far a ritual is to be understood literally" (Eliade, *Yoga*, p. 262); or "there is no hard and fast rule which would apply without any possible modification" regarding such matters in the Tantric tradition (Bharati, *The Tantric Tradition*, p. 229).

Dakṣiṇācāra [192] or the *Vāmācāra*. For there is a real sense in which the "presence" of the human body as a "form", even in Kuṇḍalinīc "interiorization" in *Dakṣiṇācāra*, still constitutes no total abandonment of "form" (= body) as a concrete ingredient.[193] Perhaps the soteriological possibility of the contemplation of the "formless" Ultimate amounts to a more *radical* distinction of means than any other.

The second point concerns the object of our use of the previous ritual phenomena (Farquhar). For us they will tend to have primarily a phenomenological-structural significance. The ongoing relevance of our emphasis upon Time, nonetheless, bears relation to *what can happen in sacred time as sacred event in the presence of Sacred Reality* (= Devī Durgā-Kālī). Toward this end we shall present in the following portion of this chapter what we call "the advent of the honourable Goddess". It illustrates and confirms, further the unity of myth, cult, and symbols within the realm of the great goddess par excellence—Durgā-Kālī.

The Advent of the Honourable Goddess

Although it remains true to say that "*the chief* temple of the Hindu is the universe",[194] the act of individual ritual worship commences in separation and ambiguity. There is a psycho-chronic discontinuum in the mind of the *sādhaka* as *anthropos* initially seeking to be transformed into anthropocosmos (= Durgā-Kālī). For transformation is the ultimate goal of the worship of the goddess, "transformation of thought", that is, "transformation of being"—*cittaśuddhi*.[195] In the beginning, the individual consciousness is not prepared to realize the wonder of the goddess' universe as Pan-Consciousness. He must prepare himself. For the goddess remains a stranger to the one who has not taken the proper steps to sacralize his mind and body, in order that he may become the goddess, or that the godddss may come to him.

> ... when the worshipper enters into the Ritual, he must realize and come into a state of consciousness that feels divine. To truly commune with the Divine and to

---

[192] Bharati (*The Tantric Tradition*, pp. 228f.) emphasizes a "discrepancy" and the "lack of terminological precision", as well as suggests that, consequently, the *Dakṣiṇācāra* might well be "a wider term", including (a) non-use of physical ingredients, and subsuming (b) "substitute" *sādhanas*.

[193] An illustration, though "left-handed", shows this possibility in Woodroffe, *Karpūrādi Stotra*, pp. 92, 93.

[194] Danielou, *Hindu Polytheism*, p. 376.

[195] Woodroffe, *Śakti and Śākta*, p. 354; also *ibid.*, pp. 282f.

offer oneself to the Divine, one must become aware of one's own state of divinity. Such a worshipper attains Fulfilment as well as Release.[196]

To this end, during the sacred time of the autumnal Durgā-Pūjā in Bengal, the individual devotee undergoes several "preliminary" *pūjās*. These *pūjās* are part of a complex process of enhancing the commitment of the mind toward the reception of the goddess, who is to come as a Divine Guest. Following the Kulārṇava Tantra, the process of purification for both the worshipper and the accessories of worship is presented by Danielou.[197]

1. The purification of the person of the worshipper consists in bathing. The purification-of-the-subtle-elements (*bhūta śuddhi*) of the body is done through breath control and through the dedication of the six main parts of the body to the six deities to which they correspond. After this the other forms of dedication are performed.

2. The purification of the place of worship is done by cleaning it carefully, adorning it with an auspicious ornamentation made of powders of five colours, placing a seat and a canopy, using incense, lights, flowers, garlands, etc. All this must be done by the worshipper himself.

3. Purification of the ritual utterances, the *mantras*, is done by repeating the syllables which compose them in the regular order and then in the reverse order.

4. Purification of the accessories is done by sprinkling water consecrated with the basic *mantra* and the weapon-*mantra* (*astra-mantra*, i.e., the sound *phaṭ*) and then displaying the cow-gesture (*dhenu-mudrā*).

5. Purification of the deity is done by placing the image on an altar, invoking the presence of the deity through its secret *mantra* and the life-giving breathing-*mantra* (*prāṇa-mantra*), bathing the image three times while reciting the basic *mantra*, then adorning it with garments and jewels. After this an offering of incense and light should be made.

Presently, we shall proceed to point out the interrelatedness of a few specific rituo-structural elements (including their *mantras*). But, first, we should like to emphasize that an aspect of the last "purification" above, the *Mahāsnāna* ("the great bathing of the deity"), constitutes, as a sacred action, one of the principle acts in the worship of the goddess Durgā-Kālī. The rite calls to mind the earlier cosmological "mirror-motif"[198] in which, as a manner of conceiving the incomprehensible Śiva-Śakti Diad, the goddess Śakti was understood

---

[196] Kulārṇava Tantra VI (commentary by Woodroffe and Pandit, p. 56); cf. the Gāndharva Tantra, cited in Danielou, *Hindu Polytheism*, p. 377; *vide* also Woodroffe, *Śakti and Śākta*, pp. 287, 362.

[197] Danielou, *Hindu Polytheism*, pp. 377-378.

[198] *Supra*, p. 164f and n. 86 of that page.

to be Śiva's own reflection in the Mirror of Mahāmāyā. In the present context, where Creation and Rite-as-Re-creation are conterminous, the actual bathing of the goddess "is performed on the reflected image of the deity in a mirror placed on a pot [199] in front of the priest. Various articles are required for the purpose of this bathing ..."[200] Mantric utterances such as the following are made during this sacred action with sundry-tempered waters :

> Dost thou as Durgā give us success
> Everywhere in virtue of this bathing ...
> Oṃ Jayantī, thou art the Goddess of Victory
> Dispenser of victories all the world over
> Dost thou give victory in my house ...
> May thou inspire me with good intentions ...
>
> Oṃ Dadmī, thou destroyest ... sins ...
> Appeasest the hunger of the world ...
> Dost thou destroy our sorrows,
> Oh Durgā, thou art worshipped by me ...
>
> With warm water
> Oṃ water that is purified,
> Superior and warm,
> Filled with the force
> Of fire and life,
> Destroyer of all sins,
> I anoint you.[201]

Samkalpa : *āsana* : *bhūtaśuddhi* : *nyāsa*

The structural and *inter*-structural significance of these sacred actions lies in their symbolic capacity to establish a rituological context of sacred orientation in preparation for the eventful experience of the advent (i.e., presence) of the goddess.[202] This advent of the goddess, however, is decisively dependent upon the "resolution" (*samkalpa*) of the worshipper; that is, his definite desire and intention to communicate with the goddess with singleness of mind, will, and

---

199 The pot as sacred object of the goddess has great antiquity and vast presence. Cf. Neumann, *The Great Mother*, pp. 132ff.; cf. Eliade, *Yoga*, pp. 349f. : "... one of the favorite images of the Grāmadevatās is the pot, and sometimes a pot even incarnates the Goddess", although she "may be venerated under any form ..."

200 C. Chakravarti, *The Tantras*, p. 99.

201 Ghosha, *Durgā-Pūjā*, pp. 45-46, 48. (liturgical accents added here *et. seq.*

202 *Supra*, pp. 171f.

purpose.[203] This act, otherwise called the *Kalparambha*, is an indispensable part of ceremonial preparation for the fullest devotion to Durgā-Kālī; and it takes place at "the first tithi (lunation) immediately following the new moon of Aśvina".[204] *Āsana*, or a bodily posture, which includes a certain *attitude*,[205] is in the external sense a sacred action most indicative of the seeker's desire to bring the motives and movements of his ordinary, conscious world to a standstill. It is the devotee's *most signal act of sacred inaction* for the sake of entering the world of the goddess and vice versa. Ultimately, this "refusal to move (*āsana*), to let oneself be carried along on the rushing stream of states of consciousness (*ekāgratā*)", involves "a long series of refusals of every kind", in the attempt to become homologized with the sacred image (*pratimā*) of the goddess.[206]

It is in such a spirit of sincerity that the devotee undertakes to purify the gross and subtle elements that compose the body. The *bhūtaśuddhi*, a tantric rite, commences with an act of bathing as a mark of the devotee's willingness to commit the most elementary forms of his being to the quest for the Sacred; specifically it is his search to orientate himself (via *prāṇāyāma*) to Nature's inner forces (*tattvas*), the *acaryas*, and, ultimately, the goddess. The Śāstras thus direct the devotee to do the following:[207]

> Holding an anointed and scented flower on the left temple, one should repeat
> Oṃ obeisance to the teachers ...
> Oṃ to Durgā.
> Then with Oṃ phaṭ rub the palms with flowers, and clap thrice over the head, and by snapping the fingers at ten different directions secure immunity from them ...[208]
>
> Then meditate the 24 essences in nature as concentrated in the amalgam, viz., the five cardinal elements, earth, water, fire, air, and space, the five external organs of sense the nose, the tongue, the eyes, the skin and the ears, with their

---

203 Cf. *An Alphabetical List* ..., p. 24.

204 Ghosha, *Durgā-Pūjā*, Appendix, pp. xiv, xxiiif.; 19ff.

205 Eliade, *Yoga*, p. 48; *vide* also *ibid.*, pp. 53ff.

206 *Ibid.*, pp. 54, 55. Through this act (*āsana*), often begun in pain and discomfort, the mind-body complex is made "*sthirasukham*, 'stable and agreeable'", "absolute cessation of trouble from pairs of opposites' (*dvandvānabhighātaḥ*)", is achieved, and "'the mind is transformed into infinity (*anantasamāpattibhyām*)—that is, when it makes the idea of its infinity its own content'". *Vide ibid.*, pp. 53, 54.

207 Ghosha, *Durgā-Pūjā*, pp. 27-30.

208 *Phaṭ*: a *bīja* with several meanings (*vide ibid.*, Appendix, pp. xxxivff.); on "directions", *vide* Diehl, *Instrument and Purpose*, p. 72 and n. 2 of that page.

objects, i.e. scent, taste, form, and sound, the five organs of action viz., the mouth, the feet and hands, the pudendum, and the organ, and all forms, whether material, mental, or intellectual, with those of self-consciousness, self-cogitation, or egoism ...[209]

Conceive in the right nostril the red mantra, Raṃ the root of fire, and fill the body with air, while repeating the mantra sixteen times. Purify the body by burning the male form of sin with the fire arising from the lower parts of the body.[210]

Then close the nose and hold the breath while repeating sixty-four times the mantra. Exhale the ashes with the breath through the left nostril accompanied with 32 recitals of the mantra ...

The cleansing of the inner and outer body finds its structural extension in the rite of *Nyāsa*,[211] i.e., "the 'placing' of the hands of the worshipper on different parts of his body, imagining at the same time that thereby the corresponding parts of the body of his *Iṣṭadevatā* [Durgā-Kālī] are being there placed..'[212] The *nyāsas* are diverse and will thus be exemplified here with the *Jiva-nyāsa*, whereby "the sādhaka proceeds ... to infuse the body with the life of the Devī".[213]

Placing his hand on his heart, he says the "soham" mantra ("I am He"), thereby identifying himself the Devī. Then, placing the eight Kula-kuṇḍalinīs in their several places, he says the following mantras :

Āiṃ, Krīṃ, Klīṃ, Yaṃ, Raṃ, Laṃ, Vaṃ, Saṃ, Hoṃ, Saṃ, Saṃ, Hauṃ, Haṃsah : the vital airs of the highly blessed and auspicious Primordial Kālikā are here. "Āiṃ, etc., the embodied spirit of the highly blessed and auspicious Kālikā is placed here". "Āiṃ, etc., here are all the senses of the highly auspicious and blessed Kālikā;

and lastly,

Āiṃ, etc., may the speech, mind, sight, hearing, smell, and vital airs of the highly blessed and auspicious Kālikā coming here always abide here in peace and happiness Svāhā.[214]

The ritual acts of *Āsana*, *Bhūtaśuddhi*, and *Nyāsa* are structurally homologous, in that, on the one hand, the devotees' consecrated

---

209 Cf. *supra*, p. 158, nn. 46-7; also A. Mookerjee, *Tantra Art*, Plate 8, pp. 23, 53.

210 Cf. Woodroffe, *Śakti and Śākta*, p. 291 : "Kundalinī"; *vide infra*, Chap. V.

211 From the Sanskrit root *nyas*, "to set or put down". The term's broader (pluralistic) application refers to—cf. Danielou, *Hindu Polytheism*, p. 377 : "the consecration of the different parts of the body to distinct *deities* with the help of seed-*mantras* [italics mine] ..." (e.g., *supra*); "deities", besides one's *iṣṭadevatā*, who, to be sure, remains *decisive*. Cf. Diehl, *Instrument and Purpose*, pp. 75-80, esp. p. 76.

212 Woodroffe, *Śakti and Śākta*, p. 291.

213 Woodroffe, *Introduction to Tantra Śāstra*, p. 109.

214 *Ibid.*

"seat" and body become types of *pīṭha*, the latter a living anthropomorphic *maṇḍala* in and upon which other deities may be given "place" and homage for their roles in the polytheistic, poly-functional, and poly-directional cosmos; while, on the other hand, the structural intention of *nyāsa* is that the body in its totality [215] is a symbol of the goddess (her "Self"), who encircles and infuses it. All these rites together, therefore, accomplish the goal of "transcending the human condition",[216] warding off distractions and "all obstructive spirits",[217] as well as enabling the *sādhaka* to "spread" (i.e., extend) his awareness of "the All-spreading Immense".[218]

Bodhana : prāṇa-pratiṣṭhā : yajña : śaktiman

In Chapter II we caught a glimpse of the goddess in her capacity as a concrete articulation of the Sacred within the realm of the Earth-Cultus. On the one hand, there was the goddess Kālijai in Orissa, whose mode of legendary concretion was a stone—the Numinous Lithos—in the capricious waters of Chilka Lake.[219] On the other hand, we saw the goddess under the form of *Navapatrikā*, the "Nine Leaves", in which she might lodge so completely that the disengagement of a single twig meant to touch the goddess directly.[220]

The further advent of the goddess in the cultic milieu occurs, again, in the form of vegetation symbolism. In the aftermath of preparatory worship, according to the Linga Purāṇa, "on the ninth [221] day of the dark fortnight of Asvina the Devi is to be awakened with great pomp and eclat. This is called the Bodhana or the arousing [i.e., awakening]".[222] At any rate, the Kālikā Purāṇa enjoins that the goddess

---

215 *Vide* Woodroffe, *Śakti and Śākta*, pp. 282-283; *supra*, p. 167 and n. 97 of that page.

216 Eliade, *Yoga*, p. 54.

217 Woodroffe, *Introduction to Tantra Śāstra*, p. 98.

218 Woodroffe, *Śakti and Śākta*, p. 291.

219 *Supra*, p. 49.

220 *Supra*, p. 57. Moreover, "at the time of worship, each sprout is supposed to stand for a particular form of the goddess : Brahmāṇī is the presiding deity of the plantain, Kālī of *kacvī*, Durgā of *haridrā*, Kārtikī of *jayantī*, Śiva of *bilva*, Raktadantikā of *dādima*, Śokarahita of *asoka*, Cāmuṇḍa of *māna*, Lakṣmī of *paddy, and Durgā again, of navapatrika as a whole* [italics mine]" (C. Chakravarti, *The Tantras*, p. 99). *Vide* Ghosha, *Durgā-Pūjā*, pp. 66-88.

221 The time varies : it may occur on "the sixth day of the waxing moon of Asvina" (Ghosha, *infra*), or "the fifth day ... in the evening" (C. Chakravarti, *The Tantras*, p. 99; Shri Ashokanath Shastri, "Durgā-Pūjā", *Bhāratīya-Vidyā*, X [1949], 259).

222 Ghosha, *Durgā-Pūjā*, pp. 17-18.

"is to be awakened on a branch of the Vel [Bel] tree and on a pair of of its fruits".[223] Said to be "a great favourite" of the goddess and, according to *mantras*, the tree upon which the goddess was formerly invoked "by Brahma for the good of Rama and for killing Ravanna",[224] the ceremonial continues:

> Oṃ on the Vel tree as a part of the annual autumnal Durgā-Pūjā, I having worshipped the ganapati and other devas invoke and invite Durgā ...
>
> Aim for the destruction of Rāvanna and for the success of Rāma, Brahma had in earlier days at an unseasonable time awakened thee; I also on the even of the sixth lunar day of Asvina, do arouse thee. Indra having so aroused thee gained dominion and the heavens;[225] therefore do I arouse thee with a view to obtain superhuman dominion and transcendental power. As the ten-faced was destroyed by Rāma so may I have might to destroy my enemies ...
>
> Oṃ Śrī fruit-tree, thou art always gratifying to Amvikā, thou art born on the top of mounts Meru, Mandāra, Kailās, and Himavat, thou art born on the top of Śrī mountain, thou art prosperous fruit, thou art the dwelling place of health and prosperity, thou art by me deputed, oh! dost thou go, thou art the likeness of Durgā! ... oh Śrī tree thou art gratifying to Chaṇḍikā, I am inviting her for worship, dost thou give me thy twig.[226]

It is with the *prāṇa-pratiṣṭhā* [227] that the advent or presence of the goddess receives a fascinating and beautiful mantric portrayal. Speaking of two other cultically related words, a scholar thus tells us succinctly that "the Hindu term ... *Pratika* or *Pratimā* indicat[es] that which is *placed before* one as the immediate and apparent object of worship, *representative* of the Invisible Supreme".[228] In this cultic act, therefore, the priest begins to implore the goddess to make her residence within the image dedicated to her. He does this, first, "by placing the right hand on her breast", invoking her with the *mantra*:

> Oṃ [229]
> Welcome Devī to my house

---

223 *Ibid.*; *vide* Devībhāgavata Purāṇa III.27.22.

224 C. Chakravarti, *The Tantras*, p. 99; *vide* Devībhāgavata Purāṇa III.28-30, esp. III.28.1; 30.18-20, 28, 41-46, 57, 59-61; cf. *ibid.*, III.27.49-52; Kālikā Purāṇa 62: 24-34; 39-40.

225 We are not aware of a specific tradition; nonetheless *vide* Ṛg-Veda X.134.1-6.

226 Ghosha, *Durgā-Pūjā*, pp. 40, 41.

227 I.e., *prāṇa*: life; *pratiṣṭhā*: installation; that is, "the installing of life into the image" (*An Alphabetical List* ..., p. 24). Cf. A. K. Coomaraswamy, *The Transformation of Nature in Art* (Cambridge: Harvard University Press, 1934), Chap. VII, esp. pp. 157ff., 163ff., Rao, *Elements of Hindu Iconography*, I, Part I, 26ff.

228 Woodroffe, *Śakti and Śākta*, p. 288; cf. *ibid.*, pp. 346ff., 303f.

229 Cf. Mahānirvāṇa Tantra IX.9, 10; cf. Gonda, *Change and Continuity in Indian Religion*, p. 436; it is perhaps a specific injunction but without universal application. *Vide* "Om Hrīṃ" (*infra*, p. 223); *supra*, p. 217, n. 212.

With thy eights Śaktis [230]
Annihilator of all transgressions
In this unfordable ocean of the world,
Save me blessed goddess ...
Devī Durgā approach and will
Presence in this vicinity ...
Advance, oh goddess ...

Then, touching the breast of the idol, the priest effects the vivification of the idol with the recitation of five Vedic mantras including, for example, such words as

... the voice, the mind, the eyes,
The ears, the nose, the heart
Take possession of this idol forever ...

The priest next recites another hymn by touching the cheeks:

Oṃ the lives of these
Be here established,
Oṃ the lives of these
Be here moving,
Oṃ let these be deified ...[231]

The pervasive dynamism which characterizes Hindu cosmology, anthropology, and, now, rituology—in terms of forms of worship, stages of preparation, and levels of spiritual attunement to the goddess—applies, again, to the kinds of objects offered to her in sacrifice. It has already been pointed out (in Chapter II) that human sacrifice was indeed a part of her worship;[232] moreover, according to the Rudhirādhyāya [233] portion (i.e., Sanguinary Chapter) of the Kālikā Purāṇa, among the over fifteen types of eligible sacrificial objects, human heads and human blood are considered to bring the greatest pleasure to the goddess.[234] Apart from this phenomenon, however, there is the surpassing desirability of "the meat of buffalo and kid as

---

[230] Cf. Ghosha, *Durgā-Pūjā*, Appendix, pp. lxiii, lxiv.

[231] *Ibid.*, pp. 53, 54, 55. For the structural coinherence of *Prāṇa-pratiṣṭhā* and *yantra* as an esoteric-yogic ritual extension, *vide* Pieter Hendrik Pott, *Yoga and Yantra: Their Interrelation and Their Significance for Indian Archaeology* (The Hague: Martinus Nijhoff, 1966), p. 20.

[232] Cf. *infra*, n. 234; p. 223, n. 245.

[233] Cf. W. C. Blaquiere's translation of the Rudhirādhyayā in *Asiatic Researches* (London), V (1807), 371-391.

[234] *Supra*, p. 59. Cf. J. Ph. Vogel, "The Head-offering to the Goddess in Pallava Sculpture", *Bulletin of the School of Oriental and African Studies*, VI (1932), 539-543, Plates 5-8.

sacrifice" to her.[235] The following selected *yajña-mantras* (via Ghosha)[236] are uttered in the ritual, which ranges from the act of homage to the *devas* to the decapitation of the animal with the *sacred sword* and, finally, a *homa* in honour of the goddess.

Observe the animal and recite ...

Om Agni was an animal, of whom a sacrifice was made ...
  the same will be thine where Agni is ...
  now drink this water
Om Vāyu ... Om Sūrya ...[237]

then rivers ("Oṃ Vahārī, Yamunā, Gangā ...") and seas ("... Kausikī and Maheṣa") are invoked to

Approach for the *ablution* of the goat

Oṃ ... I purify thy life ...
Oṃ I purify thy jaws ...
Oṃ thy life be purified ...
Oṃ purified be what malignant
  in thee

Oṃ be thee same blessed,
Oṃ be thee same pure,
Oṃ pure art thou ...

Sprinkle *water* [238] over the goat ... tie the animal, fix the animal between pillars as dark as the clouds.

Oṃ *be the animal*
With horns and other limbs
Om secure the animal to the pillar
Which divides life from death,
Creation from chaos.
Om secure, fix the animal
Which *represents in part the universe.*[239]

---

[235] Ghosha, *Durgā-Pūjā*, Appendix, p. liv; cf. Mahānirvāṇa Tantra VI.104-106; *vide* Ghosha, *Durgā-Pūjā*, Appendix, pp. liv-lvii.

[236] Ghosha, *Durgā-Pūjā*, pp. 60-66. (All italics mine). For "Yajña", *vide* Woodroffe, *Introduction to Tantra Śāstra*, pp. 99f.

[237] Cf. Henri Hubert and Manuel Mauss, *Sacrifice : Its Nature and Function*, trans. W. D. Halls (Chicago : University of Chicago Press, 1963), pp. 26f., 31.

[238] For the inner significance of this and other accessories, *vide* Danielou, *Hindu Polytheism*, pp. 380-381.

[239] Cf. Mārkaṇḍeya Purāṇa XCI.32.

... loosen the animal with its horns and-other limbs, *set free the animal. Om pardon me* ![240] Apply *vermillion* paste on its forehead ... offer other edibles ...

Then after throwing some *flowers* on the goat, worship the gods residing in its several limbs ...

Oṃ
to the name of the divinity

... in the head ...
... in the forehead
... between the eye-brows
... in the eyes
... in the ears
... in the nostrils
... in the chin
... in the sets of teeth
... in the tongue
... in the mouth
... in the neck
... in the back

Oṃ to the other Gods
in the other parts of the body

Once more observe the animal and address it thus :

Oṃ goat ... thou has appeared as a sacrificial animal ...
Oṃ salution to thou object of sacrifice.
Oṃ all misfortunes of the donor are removed
by the gratification of Chaṇḍikā ...

Oṃ the animals are created by the Self-born Himself
of sacrifice [241]
and therefore do *I kill thee* in this yajña
though thou art unkillable.[242]

Oṃ thou art born in the womb of animal for the
sacred purposes of pūjā, homa ...
Be the goddess propitiated
with thy flesh mixed with blood

---

[240] These words have been of continued interest to us. Do they signify an implicit "ritual humour" in the context of the *līlā* of the goddess ? *Vide* "unkillable", *infra.*

[241] Cf. Hubert and Mauss, *Sacrifice*, pp. 30; 124, n. 171.

[242] Devībhāgavata Purāṇa III.26.34; cf. Bhagavad-Gītā II.18-21, 23, 30.

Then place flowers on the head of the sacrifice with Āiṃ Hrīṃ
Śrīṃ ... To the ear of the animal address the following,

Oṃ ... this goat animal, *may salvation be granted to it*, Svāhā.[243]
... repeat the animal gāyatrī to the ear of the beast.[244]

Bring out the sword and upon it describe with vermillion paste
Hrīṃ, and contemplating it, *adore the sword god*,

Oṃ sombre, spear-handed, the very self of kālarātrī,
excited
red-eyed
red-faced,
red-wreathed,
red-clothed,
noose-handed,
blood-thirsty sword, I salute thee

Thou art the tongue of Chaṇḍikā
and the gratifier of the gods

Then offer ... flowers ... to the sword, and worship the several gods presiding over several parts of the sword.[245]

Oṃ to Mahādeva in the handle
Oṃ to Yama in the edge ...
thy *teeth* are sharp,[246]
and thy waist is narrow.
Thy form is a graceful curve ... —
thou art furious and most mighty ...

Then hold the sword with the following mantra,

Oṃ salutation to Kālī, Kālī, Devī ,the goddess
of thunderbolt,
and the holder of iron club.
Oṃ Hrīṃ Kālī Kālī
oh terrible-teethed ...
devour, swallow, sever
kill,[247]

---

243 *Infra*, p. 226.

244 *Ibid.*

245 *Vide* a representation of the sword in Ghosha, *Durgā-Pūjā*, Appendix, p. lviii. Cf the veneration of the "pickaxe" by the Thagi (= Thuggee) of India in George Bruce, *The Stranglers* (New York : Harcourt, Brace, and World, Inc., 1969), pp. 58-62.

246 Cf. a *devotee's* use of his *teeth* to kill the victim in the festival of the goddess as Māriamma in Oppert, *On the Original Inhabitants* ..., p. 476n; cf. *ibid.*, pp. 497n-498n.

247 Cf. A. E. Jensen, *Myth and Cult Among Primitive Peoples*, pp. 162f., 164-166; for a military orientation in Nepal, *vide* Renou, *The Nature of Hinduism*, pp. 87-88; *supra*, p. 53f.

destroy all the evil-doers,
dispatch this beast,
cut him up by the sword,
cut, cut, kili, kili, chiki, chiki,
drink up, drink the blood ...
Oṃ salutation to Durgā

Having with this mantra *inspired* the sword, give a handful of flowers,

Oṃ sword ... I bow to thee, Mother Prosperity,
I bow to Victoria and to
the Defender of the Faith.

With Oṃ Hrīm Phaṭ take up the shining sword in hand and apply it on the shoulders of the beast.[248]

... and

the
animal
is then
despatched
with one blow.[249]

Then [150] the sankalpa for presenting this blood is made :

Oṃ Āiṃ Hrīṃ Śrīṃ Kauśikī be satiated with blood.
Oṃ salutation to this blood of goat
Oṃ this blood of a goat to prosperous Durgā

On the head of the animal a light is placed and the head with the light is offered to the goddess.

Oṃ salutation to this head of a goat with a light on it.

A sankalpa is again made for offering this head to the goddess.

Oṃ this head with the light I offer to Durgā ...[251]

[248] Cf. Ghosha, *Durgā-Pūjā*, p. 65 : "The sacrifice is taken to the courtyard of the house, where a Y-shaped post is fixed. Between the sacrificial post and the Devī is placed on a cleaned spot an entire left of plantain under which the root Hrīṃ and the triangular Yantra are described".

[249] *Vide* Mahānirvāṇa Tantra VI.116; cf. Oppert, *On the Original Inhabitants ...*, p. 480.

[250] Before this "a small quantity of the blood from the sacrifice ... and a bit of flesh from the trunk of the beast [are placed in a pot] care being taken that no bits of hair be present" (Ghosha, *Durgā Pūjā*, p. 65).

[251] *Vide* Mahānirvāṇa Tantra VI.117.

Following a division of "the blood in the earthen dish into four parts" and its dedication to deities of the four quarters of the world, a prayer to the goddess ensues which has the appearance of comprehending many of the preceding, central aspects of the worship : mythology, expiation, supplication, vindication, and exultation.

> Oṃ three-eyed, terrible-faced, and skull-wreathed goddess, thou art the destroyer of all asuras, thou holder of sword and club, oh, destroyer of the buffalo demon,[252] oh Mahāmāyā, oh suppressor of the pride of all daityas, I give this sacrifice of goat, accept it, oh beloved of Hara. Oh Kālarātrī having received this sacrifice be satisfied, oh Mahākālī protect me Devī Chaṇḍikā.
>
> Om Kālī Kālī and Mahākālī, the destroyer of our sins[253] accept this sacrifice with its blood and confer blessing on us ...[254]

The sacrifice is followed by another ceremony designated as the *Homa* "or the oblation of liquified butter to fire".[255] It is described as being performed

> by a separate priest, sitting on the west of the Homa firepit, and anointing the place with cow-dung and drawing three lines from north to the south by kusa half a cubit long, and taking up by the thumb and the fourth finger the earth scraped out, he throws it towards the north-east corner.[256]

Among other ceremonial features are (1) the recitation of "firebrand" mantras of invocation (or Agni) and solicitude for protection; (2) meditative salutation; (3) circumambulations of the firepit;[257] (4) the Caṇḍī reading;[258] (5) the offering of presents to the priest, and (6) "puṣpanjali" or offerings of flowers to the goddess Durgā.[259]

The festivity of *Ārati* is said to take place every evening, but especially at the time (Daśamī) when the goddess "is prayed to

---

252 Cf. "Mahiṣa-Mardinī-Stotra", in *Kulacūdāmaṇī Nigama*, ed. Arthur Avalon (Madras : Ganesh and Co. Private, Ltd., 1956), Introduction, pp. 24-29; cf. Devībhāgavata Purāṇa III.26.58.

253 Mahānirvāṇa XCI.12; *vide* esp. Devībhāgavata Purāṇa III.27.29.

254 Ghosha, *Durgā-Pūjā*, p. 66.

255 *An Alphabetical List* ..., p. 24; cf. Devībhāgavata Purāṇa III.26.35; Mahānirvāṇa Tantra VI.119-164.

256 Ghosha, *Durgā-Pūjā*, pp. 72-73; the north-east corner is dedicated to the goddess as Kālikā (*ibid.*, p. 66); Kālikā Purāṇa 55:6-8.

257 Cf. Hubert and Mauss, *Sacrifice*, p. 125, n. 177.

258 Mārkaṇḍeya Purāṇa XCII.1-28; Devībhāgavata Purāṇa III: XXVI. 12-17; esp. VIII.24 and VII.XL.30-31.

259 Ghosha, *Durgā-Pujā*, pp. 72-74; *An Alphabetical List* ..., p. 24.

retire".[260] As a means of *invoking* the goddess, nonetheless, the sacred action is

> performed with lighted lamps, with lighted camphor, with white clothes, with flowers, which are gracefully moved up and down before the image; the conch-shell, which is indispensable in almost all ceremonies is sounded, bells[261] are rung and incense is burnt. After the conclusion of this ceremony the whole family of the worshipper and others who are present, prostrate themselves before the goddess.[262]

In advance of the concluding exemplification of the advent of the goddess in worship, we would make the following remarks about the rituo-structural homologation of the goddess and the sacrifice (i.e., the animal). That homologation is, first, confirmed in that the sacrifice of a buffalo or a goat calls for utterances (*supra*, pp. 221f.) which indicate that the goddess not only resides *within*, but—in a rituological sense—*is* the animal who in turn becomes a living synecdoche of the Universe, which is the goddess. It is further significant that, actually, the *Paśu-Gāyatrī* with its *mantra* "severs the bond of its life as a beast", and "liberates a beast from its life of a beast".[263] That is to say,

> the sacrifice is as much for the benefit of the beast sacrificed as for the benefit of the sacrificer, since the beast, though sacrificed, attains after death a higher state of existence.[264]

Finally, there is an important structural correlation between the ritual particularity of the sacrificial victim and the cosmological singularity of the Absolutely Ultimate. For in the Kālikā Purāṇa the he-goat is expressly named in the list of animals eligible for sacrifice to the goddess; and "the word *ajā* means both 'she-goat' and 'the unborn'. The she-goat is taken as the symbol of Unmanifest Nature (*avyakta*)".[265] Furthermore, the prohibition with regard to the sacrifice of the female of any species, especially a woman, suggests a structure of duality *and* dominance concerning, respectively, (1) the relationship of the goddess to the male principle (Śiva) including its derivative "male" manifestations, and (2) the implications of the morphological priority shared by the temporal woman for the absolute ultimacy of the Cosmic Woman. Indeed, not only is it said that "every

---

260 Ghosha, *Durgā-Pūjā*, Appendix, p. xlv.

261 Mārkaṇḍeya Purāṇa XCI.27.

262 Ghosha, *Durgā-Pūjā*, Appendix, p. xlv.

263 Mahānirvāṇa Tantra VI.107-110.

264 Avalon, *Mahānirvāṇa Tantra*, p. 162, n. 7; *vide* also Devībhāgavata Purāṇa III.26.33-34.

265 Danielou, *Hindu Polytheism*, , 286.

naked woman incarnates *prakṛti*",[266] but, according to another Tantric vision,

> Woman is the creator of the universe.
> She is the very body of the universe;
> woman is the support of the three worlds,
> she is the very essence of our body.
> There is no other happiness as that which woman can procure
> There is no other way than that which woman can open to us.
> Never there has been, there is, there will be
> a fortune the like of woman, no kingdom,
> no place of pilgrimage, yoga, prayer,
> mystic formula, asceticism, wealth.[267]

In the milieu of Durgā-Pūjā the phenomenon of *bodhana* finds its exemplification on another level, that is, the advent of the goddess into the body of *man himself* as devotee (= *śaktiman*); it constitutes in essence the rituo-structural correlation of image and man. The goddess, therefore, meets her "Self" again in phenomena which were never inert but already alive and awaiting her *special* "awakening". For we learned earlier [268] that even a stone (e.g., by implication, Kālijai's *lithicon*) is fundamentally filled with her presence; and her presence in man offers the promise of rejuvenation and, ultimately, spiritual liberation (*mukti*). As in the case of Hindu worship generally, however, there are degrees in the presence of the goddess in the lives of her devotees (via "possession").[269] An interesting testimony of the presence of the goddess within a "male" might be not only that he wore the garments of a woman;[270] but also that, while possessed

> he spoke as a woman rather than as a man. The Hindi language has certain forms when a male speaks, and others for a female. When he used the feminine form, it was obvious to everyone that the son had become possessed by the supreme mother goddess.[271]

---

[266] Eliade, *Yoga*, p. 259.

[267] Śaktisaṇgama-Tantra II.52, cited by Tucci, "Earth in India and Tibet", pp. 359-360.

[268] *Supra*, p. 161, n. 70; cf. Woodroffe and Mukhyopadhyaya, *Mahāmāyā*, p. 165: "A block of stone is *Sachchidānanda* or Being-Consciousness-Bliss telling itself in a particular manner, but never so veiling as to make its essential nature completely suppressed. Its Self, its Joy may be *ordinarily* hidden [italics mine] ..."

[269] Cf. Ruth S. Freed and Stanley A. Freed, "Two Mother-Goddess Ceremonies of Delhi State in the Great and Little Traditions", *Southwestern Journal of Anthropology*, XVIII (1962), 255; *vide* also Oppert, *On the Original Inhabitants ...*, p. 487; cf. *ibid.*, pp. 488f., 491.

[270] Briggs, *Gorakhnāth and the Kānphaṭa Yogīs*, p. 97.

[271] Freed and Freed, "Two Mother-Goddess Ceremonies of Delhi State ...", p. 260.

CHAPTER FIVE

THE ESCHATOLOGICAL STRUCTURE OF THE REGENERATION OF TIME : KALI-YUGA

The phenomenon of a "universe of analogies, homologies, and *double meanings* [italics mine]",[1] especially this last phrase, applies well to the relation between the goddess and the Hindu doctrine of the Ages (= Yugas). It is this idea of the chronic orchestration of Time that provides the existential context in which persons live and have their sacred being. The words "eschatological" and "regeneration", therefore, though more often used in Occidental theological studies,[2] have a legitimate application in this study. The eschatological will be understood to have a double sense : (1) the spatio-temporal, and (2) the qualitative-evaluating. Thus

> it points both to the last, the most removed in space and time, and to the highest, the most perfect, the most sublime—but sometimes also the lowest in value, the extreme negative.... Its most primitive immediate as well as most primitive mythological connotation is "the last in the chain of all days".[3]

Such values are also contained in the structuralization of Time in Indian religious thought, except that, there, though we can speak of the "double meaning" of the "End of History", we must also recognize the permanent *absence* of the end as an intrinsic aspect of Hindu cosmology.[4] That other meaning, then, i.e., the "qualitative-evaluating", which must be juxtaposed with the former sense of eschatology, is one which refers to "the 'end' characteristic of every meeting with"[5] the great goddess Durgā-Kālī. This last meaning would apply to those pregnant "moments" of sacred *presence* of the goddess during *Durgā-Pūja*,

---

[1] Eliade, *Yoga*, p. 252.

[2] According to Harrelson (*Interpreting the Old Testament*, p. 496), though the meaning of the word "eschatology" "has a very large place in the biblical literature ... the Bible *does not ... use this particular term* [italics mine]". The term's meaning, therefore, may have extrabiblical, extra-Christian applicability, granting the clarification of its intended use in any given context.

[3] Paul Tillich, *Systematic Theology*, III (Chicago : University of Chicago Press, 1963), 394-395.

[4] *Supra*, p. 177.

[5] Harrelson, *Interpreting the Old Testament*, p. 496.

as well as *each* of those stages or levels of initiation (*dīkṣā*) in which the *sādhaka* encounters the living goddess.[6]

The duo-significance of the term "regeneration" in this context thus comprises both a cosmological and a *soteriological* dimension. On the one hand, there is within the general cosmological framework a more specific *cosmogonic* emphasis, that is, in the sense of the *repetition* of the cosmogony; on the other hand, the soteriological aspect signifies the study or doctrine of salvation. Here the eschatological and the regenerative merge in the milieu of quest-and-attainment : the sādhaka's and/or sādhika's final identification with Devī-Saundarī in paradise. The initiate's achievement of identity with the goddess means (a) that the grace of the goddess enables the devotee to "partake of superearthly delights in an eternal everlasting heavenly world" before the goddess; and (b) that the devotee may also "exercise a sovereign power similar to" the goddess, while she remains the greater Whole.[7]

The Cyclical Traumata of Time

The Kali-Yuga is but one of the Indian four Ages of the World (*infra*). Fundamentally,

> two kinds of chronological systems have been used in India by the Hindus from antiquity. The first requires the year to be reckoned from some historical event (frequently from the consecration or accession of a king or from the beginning of a dynasty). The second starts the reckoning from the position of some heavenly body.[8]

In either case there are, of course, attending difficulties for scholars, such as the limitations implicit in theoretical and speculative astronomy, as well as the problem of historicity mentioned earlier.[9] Thus it was that the Kali-Yuga in Hindu tradition was meaningfully related

---

[6] *Vide infra*, pp. 251-252.

[7] Cf. Helmuth von Glasenapp, *Immortality and Salvation in Indian Religions*, trans. E. F. J. Payne (Calcutta : Susil Gupta India [Private] Ltd., 1963), pp. 92, 93; cf. *infra*, pp. 255-256.

[8] *Encyclopaedia Britannica*, V, 721.

[9] *Supra*, p. 70, n. 151. Nonetheless, *vide* Sri Candra Vidyarnava, "Pauranic Chronology", in the *Matsya Purāṇam*, ed. B. D. Basu (Sacred Books of the Hindus, Vol. XVII; Allahabad : The Panini Office, 1916), Appendix xviii, p. lxxix; cf. Pusalker, *Studies in the Epics and Purāṇas*, p. 13; H. H. Wilson, trans., *The Vishnu Purana*, with Notes (3d ed.; Calcutta : Punthi Pustak, 1961), pp. 389ff., nn. 81-83. *Vide* also K. P. Jayaswal, "Chronological Totals in Puranic Chronicles and the Kaliyuga Era", *Journal of the Bihar and Orissa Research Society*, III, Part 2 (1917), 246-262.

to (1) events of the Mahābhārata war, (2) King Yudhiṣṭhira's accession to the throne, (3) King Parīkṣit's consecration, and (4) Lord Kṛṣṇa's death.[10] In all probability the skepticism will remain concerning the historicity of these traditional events and their details. One quite significant limitation is that, while there may be some ostensible truth in dynastic listings and other events, "in the later Sanskrit puranas [11] ... and later Buddhist and Jain chronicles ... unfortunately, it is not always possible to connect them with any absolute chronology, the precise dates of the reigns given still being usettled".[12]

At any rate, the probability is that as early as the Vedic period there existed the idea of world-destruction (*pralaya*);[13] for example, in the Atharva-Veda we learn that "as between heaven-and-earth Agni went, burning on, all-consuming ... the gods were entered into the seas".[14] The four "yugas" make their first nominal appearance, Eliade [15] informs us, in another text :

> Rohita thinking,
>
> a Brāhman told me to wander, wandered, then a fourth year in the forest. When he was entering a village, after having left the forest, Indra said to him,
>
> The Kali is lying on the ground,
> the Dvāpara is hovering there,
> the Tretā is getting up, but
> the Kṛita happens to walk
> (hither and thither) ...[16]

---

[10] *Encyclopaedia Britannica*, V, 722.

[11] *Vide* (1) "Sarga", (2) "Pratisarga", (3) "Vaṃça", (4) "Manvantara", and (5) "Vaṃçānucharita", in *The Cambridge History of India*, I, 296; cf. Pusalker, *Studies in the Epics and Purāṇas*, p. 23.

[12] *Encyclopaedia Britannica*, V, 721.

[13] Eliade, *Myth and Reality*, p. 60.

[14] Atharva-Veda X.8.39-40.

[15] Eliade, *Myth and Reality*, p. 61, n. 21.

[16] Aitareya Brāhmaṇa VII.(14), 15, trans. Martin Haug (Bombay, 1863); cf. Harivaṃśa VIII.1-12; *vide*, Oppert, *On the Original Inhabitants ...*, p. 330. Cf., however, Pusalker, *Studies in the Epics and Purāṇas*, p. 33 : "The idea of four yugas seems to be an early one. Various theories have been put forth by scholars for explaining the Yugas and Manvantaras. Yuga appears to have meant any unit of time. Yuga has been variously taken to represent a quarter of a day, a month, a period of less than a year, one year, four years, five years, ten years, one hundred years, one thousand years or ten thousand years on the strength of references in Sanskrit works". Cf. D. R. Mankad, "The Yugas", *Poona Orientalist*, V (1942), 206-216. *Vide* also Eliade, *Cosmos and History*, p. 114; Brennand,

Although we are primarily concerned with the Kali-Yuga as an eschatological structure within the totalistic realm of the goddess, the foregoing Brāhmanic chrono-poetic morphology is intimately related to certain other factors which are in nature (a) chronological, (b) socio-religious, and (c) catastrophic.

The chronological aspect of the foregoing yugic paradigm, in the broadest perspective, comprises the essential mythic themes of India's idea of the regeneration of Time : (1) the Ages of the World, and (2) the continuous cycle of creations and destructions.[17] Here with regard to the Kali-Yuga, however, the emphasis falls upon the way in which the cyclical pattern of Creation, Preservation, and Destruction is correlated with the progressive diminution of Time until the nadir approaches during and at the end of the Kali-Yuga. In time-limits which tend to startle the Judaeo-Christian Occidental accustomed to comparatively shorter cosmo-existential calculations, the chronological process leading to the "last age" of a *single* Kalpa (= a day of Brahma = 4,320,000,000 human years) has the following character.[18]

1. Kṛta or Kṛtayuga, the golden age, named after the side of a rectangular ,or long, die marked with four dots, consisting of 1,440,000 human years, plus a dawn and a twilight each of 144,000 human years, giving a total of 1,728,000 years.

2. Tretā or Tretāyuga, the silver age, named after the side of the die marked with three dots, consisting of 1,080,000 human years, plus a dawn and a twilight each of 108,000 human years, giving a total of 1,290,000 years.

3. Dvāpara or Dvāparayuga, the copper age, named after the side of the die marked with two dots, consisting of 720,000 human years, plus a dawn and twilight each of 72,000 human years, giving a total of 864,000 years.

4. Kali or Kaliyuga, the iron age, named after the side of the die marked with one spot, consisting of 360,000 human years, plus a dawn and a twilight each of 36,000 human years, giving a total of 432,000 years.

Perhaps the most significant thing to be noted at this point is the relation between the goddess and the Yugas, especially the "last" yuga (= Kali). Durgā-Kālī has already been portrayed (in Chapter III)

Hindu Astronomy, p. 35. For chronic and infra-chronic tables, *vide* Mukhopadhyaya, *The Kūrma Purāṇa*, p. xxii; D. S. Triveda, *Indian Chronology* (Bombay : Bharatiya Vidya Bhavan, 1963), p. 1; *vide* esp. J. F. Fleet, "Kaliyuga Era of B. C. 3102", *Journal of the Royal Asiatic Society of Great Britain and Ireland*, 1911, pp. 479-496, 675-698.

[17] Eliade, *Myth and Reality*, p. 64.

[18] Cf. W. Norman Brown, *Man in the Universe* : *Some Continuities in Indian Thought* (Berkeley and Los Angeles : University of California Press, 1966), pp. 79-80.

as the *Great* Goddess (Mahādevī), who is beyond Time and Death.[19] She has also been understood to be the symbolic manifestation of the Great (Cosmic) Time (= *Mahākālī*). However, now we see that she has the unique symbolic capacity to integrate several aspects of our previous and present concerns. Structurally, then, the goddess (Durgā-) Kālī unifies (1) the historical-emotive nuances of philology,[20] the nominal-sexual personifications and ambivalences of mythology,[21] and (3) the cyclical schematization and traumatization of sacred chronology.[22] This remarkable historico-phenomenological unification of structures has been epitomized in the most indicative terms :

> The final yuga, that in which we find ourselves now, is ... regarded, more than any other, as the "age of darkness" ; for by a play upon words [23] it has become associated with the goddess Kālī...the "Black". Kālī ... this name of the Great Goddess has naturally been connected with the Sanskrit word *kāla*, "time" : Kālī thus becomes not only "the Black", but also the personification of Time. But etymology apart, the association between *kāla*, "time", the goddess Kālī and *kali-yuga* is structurally justifiable : Time is "black' because it is irrational, hard and pitiless; and Kālī ... is the mistress of Time, of all the destinies that she forges and fulfills.[24]

An important factor, therefore, which underlies the imposing Hindu yugic perspective of the cosmos, as well as the conception of man and his *relation* to the cosmos, is that of *saṃsāra* (i.e., the wandering). Inseparably related, as it is, to the concept of *karma*, that fundamental idea of "wandering" has been variously referred to by Occidentals as transmigration, reincarnation, or metempsychosis. Essentially, *saṃsāra* and *karma* as a "joint doctrine" mean that "death does not terminate one's existence. All it does is to initiate a new existence, the conditions of which are determined by one's actions in previous existences. The number of existences in this repeated continuation is incalcuable".[25] Situated in a universe whose very existence appears (under the guise of *Māyā*) to be the embodiment of Time, the individual experiences a natural ambiguity in the face of a certain harsh realization; although it is a realization which, in the Śākta world-view, is accompanied by a promise of deliverance from suffering

---

[19] *Supra*, pp. 199ff., 201f., 204ff.

[20] *Supra*, pp. 82-85.

[21] *Vide Supra*, pp. 162-164, 183f..

[22] Cf. Devībhāgavata Purāṇa V. XXII: 57; V. 30: 37-64.

[23] *Supra*, p. 83f., n. 207.

[24] Eliade, *Images and Symbols*, pp. 64-65.

[25] Brown, *Man in the Universe*, p. 81.

and sorrow. To be sure, it is basically the fact that, in keeping with his status as an "unenlightened" microcosm (*kṣudrabrahmāṇda*),[26] "the ups and downs of his life are just the same ups and downs as those of the macrocosms beyond him and the microcosms within him";[27] that is, it is so until he comes at last to the feet of the goddess.[28]

The socio-religious aspect of the Kali-Yuga overlaps with the plight of the individual during this period. Yet just as *saṃsāra* remains a key phenomenon in the former cosmic cycles, the change in the attitudes of persons toward *dharma* [29] (or, in case of the individual: his *svadharma* [= one's own merited station and duty in life]) is of crucial importance. For it is the progressive de-orientation of human beings toward the gods, one another, and their respective duties which marks the initial malaise and impending nadir of the Kali-Yuga.

> During *the krita yuga* the moral order of the universe, the *dharma*, is observed in its entirety ... spontaneously and without restraint, by all beings ... the *dharma* is in some sort identified with human existence. The perfect man of *kritayuga* incarnates the cosmic norm, and therefore the moral law. He leads an exemplary archetypal existence.[30]

The intermediate *yugas*, the Tretā and the Dvāpara, mark critical regressions in which, respectively, men's actions are only aligned to the degrees of three-quarters and one-half of the *dharma*. The ominous regression is suggested by the shortening duration of these periods. Accordingly,

> ... in the *kali yuga*, the "evil age", only a quarter of the *dharma* remains. The term *kali* ... the die marked with one pip only ... is also the "losing throw" (personified, moreover, as an evil spirit): *kali* signifies also "dispute, discord" and, in general, the most evil of any groups of beings or objects. In *kali yuga* man and society reach the extreme point of disintegration.[31]

---

26 Cf. *infra*, p. 253.

27 Alan W. Watts, *The Two Hands of God: The Myths of Polarity* (New York: George Braziller, 1963), p. 77. *Vide* "The Parade of Ants", Brahmavaivartapurāṇa XLVII.50-161 ("Kṛiṣṇa Janma Khaṇḍa"), in Zimmer, *Myths and Symbols* ..., pp. 3-11; Devībhāgavata Purāṇa IX.38.

28 *Vide* the words of Devī to Himalaya in the Bhāgavatigītā in Mahābhāgavata, cited by Avalon, *Principles of Tantra*, II, 31-32.

29 Cf. Renou, *Hinduism*, p. 18: "... there is no Hindu term corresponding to what we call 'religion'. There are 'approaches' to the spiritual life; and there is *dharma*, or 'maintenance' (in the right path), which is at once norm or law, virtue and meritorious action, the order of things transformed into moral obligation—a principle which governs all manifestations of India life". *Vide* also *ibid.*, pp. 52-54.

30 Eliade, *Images and Symbols*, p. 63.

31 *Ibid.*

What the *Kali-Yuga* loses in terms of a diminutive chronological duration it gains in the sense of the cumulative diabolical afflictions that have now begun to plague human life.[32] The vision of just a few Purāṇas of the nature of this period becomes a socio-religious analogue of the chronic "death" of a universe about to lie down on the ground of Non-being.

(Maitreya) : Venerable sir, you are able to give me a description of the nature of the Kali age, in which four-footed virtue suffers total extinction.

(Parasara) : Hear, Maitreya, an account of the nature of the Kali age, respecting which you have inquired, and which is now close at hand ...

> In the Kali age, Maitreya, men, corrupted by unbelievers, will refrain from adoring Vishnu, the lord of sacrifice, the creator and lord of all; and will say, "Of what authority are the Vedas ? what are gods or Brahmans" ? ... Men will say, "Who has a father ? who has a mother" ? ... Endowed with little sense, men, subject to *all the infirmities* of *mind, speech, and body,* will daily commit sins; and every thing that is calculated to afflict beings, vicious impure, and wretched, will be generated in the Kali age. (Italics mine).[33]

> In that end of the [Kali] Yuga men will be united with heretical sects; they will strike *friendships for the sake of women.* This is without doubt. (Italics mine).[34]

> In the iron age, there shall occur epidemics, famines, droughts, and *revolutions.* Men shall be devoid of virtue, *possessed of slender powers,* irascible, covetous, and untruthful. ... There shall be a large number of beggars amongst the people; short life, lassitude, disease, and misery shall prevail as consequences of sin and ignorance. ... In the iron age, even Mahādeva the lord of all beings, the god of gods, shall have no divinity to man. (Italics mine).[35]

> The people shall steadily deteriorate *by adopting a contrary course of life.* ... The people will be unholy, unrighteous and oppressed with disease and sorrow; and goaded by failure of rain they will be eager to destroy each other. ... They will subsist on fruits, roots and leaves of trees, and will be clothed in tattered garments,

---

[32] *Vide* Wilson, *The Vishnu Purana,* pp. 499-500, for a presentation of such phenomena. Cf. Woodroffe, *Śakti and Śākta,* p. 276 : "'Identification of the Self with the Non-Whole or Partial (*Apūrnam-maṇyatā*) is Desease and the sole source of every misery'". Cf. Harivamsa IV.1-7.

[33] Viṣṇu Purāṇa VI.1.

[34] Yuga Purāṇa VI, cited in W. W. Tarn, *The Greeks in Bactria and India* (Cambridge : At the University Press, 1951), pp. 452-456; cf. Devīghāgavata Purāṇa IX.8 : "All will be addicted to the Vāmāchāra ritual. ..." *Vide ibid.* for a complete description of the Kali Age.

[35] Mukhopadhyaya, *The Kūrma Puraṇa,* pp. xxix, xxx.

barks and skins, and thus they will wander over the earth in search of livelihood. (Italics mine).[36]

Behold ... the age of destruction is so horrible, that during it the clouds never fall on the surface of the earth as drops of rain for one hundred years. The people then find no food for eating, and being oppressed by hunger, *they are compelled to eat one another*. Being thus overpowered by what is wrought by time, the men gradually lead themselves to utter destruction. (Italics mine).[37]

Thus we catch a glimpse of the traumata of time under the form of social and religious disintegration. It is as if the threatening involution of the Universe were attempting to swallow up in catastrophic prelude the socio-religious world of man, before nature, too, finally, screams in pain and fatigue for a new birth. But for those who have practised *adharma* the end is not yet. Time leads to death, but even death might defer to terror :

Those, who are fallen from an Āśrama (stage of life), fall into the fire and are eaten by black and variegated crows with ironbeaks; and (one who is guilty) of breach (in the performance) of a sacrifice or vow, is cooked in the hell called Samdamsa. ... All those who, out of anger or delight, perform acts contradictory to the (rules of) castes and Āśramas, to go hell.[38]

It is the phenomenon of ultimate world-catastrophe which, finally, unites the chronological and the socio-religious. Catastrophe and adharmic activity are, therefore, in the Kali-Yuga held in cumulative mutual relation. Hence, on the one hand the Harivamśa can tell us that "in the last cycle will take place great wars, great tumults, great showers, and fears; know these to be the signs of sinfulness";[39] but, on the other hand, the text tells that "the stars will not be united with proper planets, the quarters will be contrary".[40] Moreover, apart from the individual's presumed deviation from the cosmic norm by *choice*, the depreciation of the macro-chronic superstructure does present "an inescapable feature", i.e., an "impermanence", which makes it appear that "Doom ... is always just around the corner".[41] Here, however, we refer to the fact that the individual seems to become trapped in the "crepuscular decomposition" of a cosmos whose deca-

---

[36] Matsya Purāṇa CCLXXIII.

[37] Bhāgavata Purāṇa XII.4.

[38] Vāyu Purāṇa CL, cited by Hazra, *Studies in the Purāṇic Record*, p. 236. Cf. Devībhāgavata Purāṇa VIII. 22, 23; IX. 23-36.

[39] Harivamśa IV ("Bhaviṣya Parva") (trans. Dutt, p. 827).

[40] Harivamśa III.5ff.

[41] Cf. Brown, *Man in the Universe*, p. 86.

dence seems to determine the temporal demoralization of human life. We must not defer to catastrophe, nonetheless, for Eliade would have us consider that there is something "invigorating and consoling" in this Indian cosmos; and this means that the yugic theory enables man to develop both a rational understanding of his place in the world, as much as it may challenge him to "understand the precariousness of his human condition and thus facilitate his enfranchisement".[42] Notwithstanding these remarks, which anticipate our consideration of "the soteriological function of the Kali Yuga",[43] one can hardly disagree with the same scholar that this remarkable cyclical cosmology in the Indian tradition marks the "boldest formulation" of the myth-of-the-eternal-return.[44] Though unlike the Iranian conception which "does not repeat itself but will come to an end", both systems share the expectancy that "the world will end by fire and water, *per pyrosim et cataclysmum*".[45]

A consummative glance at this eschatological phenomenon (according to the Mahābhārata and the Purāṇas) tells us that

> the horizon will burst into flame, seven or twelve suns will appear in the heavens and will dry up the seas and burn the Earth. The Samvartaka (the Fire of the Cosmic Conflagration) will destroy the entire Universe. Then rain will fall in floods for twelve years, and the Earth will be submerged and mankind destroyed. ... Sitting on the cosmic snake Śesa on the surface of the Ocean, Visnu is sunk in yogic sleep. ... And then everything will begin over again—*ad infinitum*.[46]

The eschatological affirmation of those who worship the goddess remains, nonetheless, that even "he whose place of moving was the waters" (= Nārāyaṇa = Viṣṇu) is another "name" (*nāma*) and "form" (*rūpa*) of the goddess. The very place of her birth (= manifestation)[47] is the waters upon which Viṣṇu rests. Ultimately, it is "the Goddess [who] is the principle and origin of the gods and the universe".[48] Phenomenologically, as we said before, she compels us to bypass even the traditional creator of the world (i.e., Brahma).[49] Indeed, "'it was I who, in the beginning, created the father of this world' (*aham suve*

---

[42] Eliade, *Cosmos and History*, p. 118.

[43] *Ibid.*

[44] *Ibid.*, p. 112.

[45] *Ibid.*, p. 125.

[46] Eliade, *Myth and Reality*, pp. 61-62.

[47] *Supra*, p. 169.

[48] Eliade, *Yoga*, p. 350; *supra*, p. 55, n. 77.

[49] *Supra*, pp. 149, 150.

pitaram asya mūdhan)".[50] In other words, it is possible to contemplate that there is a real cosmological-rituological homologation not only between the goddess and the Primeval Ocean, but also between Śeṣa and Kundalini. We shall again refer (*infra*, "The Regenerative Power of the Goddess") to this divinity who in essence awakens her "Self" in men who, like Viṣṇu, have fallen asleep. For now, it suffices to add that it is the goddess Durgā-Kālī whom "men worship ... as Nārāyana"; it is she "who saves from the ocean of Hell", as much as it is she who is the "allayer of grief", and the "giver of knowledge".[51]

> ... She it is who maintains the world.
> And she, again, it is who, in the form
> of Fire, destroys the whole universe at
> the end of the ages [Kālāgni-rūpiṇī][52]

THE SOTERIOLOGICAL EXCELLENCE OF THE KALI-YUGA

The de-ontogenetic picture of the cosmos and the human condition in the Purāṇas, doubtless, reaches its nadir during the period of the Kali-Yuga. This yuga, therefore, represents the beginning and the end of the *radical* ontological polarization of the perfect dharmic age (= Kṛta Yuga) and a "time" of rampant spiritual and social evil. It is mythologically appropriate to recognize this "time" as that during which the *Asuric* powers of the universe commence to gain ascendancy over the powers of "right-order" (*ṛta*) and "right action" (*dharma*).[53] Rituologically, however, this age also points to the *reversal* of the preponderance of *tamasic* thought, words, and deeds which govern the dispositions of persons dispersed amidst the phenomenal world. And, eschatologically—particularly at *this* period—the mythic and the cultic converge in this broad "moment" of Time (= Kali Yuga), taking the shape of opportunity for Liberation (*Mukti*) but alongside the disadvantageous fact of the *brevity* of *this* "time" in the broadest perspective (i.e., a caturyuga or *mahā-yuga*, not to mention a Kalpa).

When one considers the apparent chronic megalomania which is reflected in the Hindu cosmological cycles, the question arises concerning the persistent adherence of persons to such a scheme. It would

50 Eliade, *Yoga*, p. 350.

51 Tantrasāra ("Bhairavīstotra"), cited in *H.T.T.G.*, pp. 27-28.

52 *Ibid.*, p. 27; Devībhāgavata Purāṇa IX.1; cf. *supra*, p. 230.

53 S. Radhakrishnan, *The Hindu View of Life* (Paperback ed.; New York: The Macmillan Co., 1964), p. 56.

seem to be a religious contemplation completely heteronomous to the soteriological hunger of the human spirit. To be sure, many religions have recognized the element of threat in the phenomenon of Time; indeed, it tends to be so much a part of man's consciousness, bringing change and mortality, that the association in Hinduism of the theological ambivalence of the goddess Durgā-Kālī (and/or Siva) with phenomenal Time (*Kāla*) constitutes a significant religious evaluation of historical existence.[54] Brandon notices, however, that in the face of Time as Death (i.e., *Mṛtyu* = *Kāla*) the human response may take the form of (a) holding off such an event as long as possible; or (b) seeking to command some form of salvation from its terrors.[55] It is true, of course, that death alone cannot be maintained as the key *raison d'être* for *homo religiosus*. Nonetheless, if death be understood in a complex sense,[56] the threat of death as Time may symbolize the total existential encounter of human beings with the ultimate meaning of all the experiential phenomena of life. It is significant, therefore, that the principal rationale of the Yugic Rotations cannot be separated from that same spiritual quest for ultimate deliverance.

> The important point for us to note is that the Indians, in magnifying ever more audaciously the duration and the numbers of the cosmic cycles, had *a soteriological aim in view*. ... the Indian was in a sense obliged *to seek a way out* of this cosmic rotation and these infinite transmigrations. (Italics mine.)[57]

The mythological confirmation of the soteriological excellence of the Dark Age" occurs in the answer of the Ur-sage, Vyāsa, to his inquirers concerning the possibility of gaining meritorious deliverance at this "time":

> Excellent, is the Kali Age!
>
> The fruit of penance, of continence, of silent prayer, and the like, practised in the Krita age for ten years, in the Treta for one year, in the Dvapara for a month, is obtained in the Kali age in a day and night; therefore did I exclaim, "Excellent, is the Kali age"! ... In the Kali age a man displays the most exalted virtue by every

---

[54] Cf. S. G. F. Brandon, *History, Time, and Deity: A Historical and Comparative Study of the Conception of Time in Religious Thought and Practice* (Manchester: Manchester University Press, 1965), pp. 1-10, 36-37; Zimmer, *Myths and Symbols ...*, p. 211; cf. *ibid.*, p. 22.

[55] Brandon, *History, Time, and Deity*, p. 11.

[56] I.e., Eliade, *Cosmos and History*, p. 117: "... historical catastrophes ... the progressive decadence of humanity, biologically, sociologically, ethically, and spiritually".

[57] Eliade, *Images and Symbols*, p. 73.

little exertion; therefore pious sages, who know what virtue is, I was pleased with the Kali age.[58]

This affirmation of hope (vis-à-vis the Kali-Yuga) is as bold in its soteriological implications as the Hindu contemplation of cosmic cycles is audacious. It reminds us of the creative response that, we saw, might be manifested with the Durgā-Pūjā of the goddess in the face of tragic historical event,[59] if not, the simple need for communal and personal renewal. Essentially, what appears in the proclamation of the Viṣṇu Purāṇa above is seen as well, however, in the Sākta śāstras dedicated more explicitly to the goddess; that is, there is a strain of *bhakti* which underlies even the recurrent recitation of the "name" of the deity.[60] *Bhakti* is doubtless one of the pre-eminent modes of religious response to the impersonalism of the Cosmic Cycles of Time.[61] The *avatāra* tradition of the Vaiṣṇavas is apparently another theological answer to the thirst for a more intimate relation to the Ultimate Sacred.[62] The two phenomena are, to be sure, correlative. Eschatologically, nonetheless, the tradition of *avatāra* culminates in the "incarnation" of Kalki during the Kali-Yuga, a being who is known for his "apocalyptic" martial and redemptive activity. Kalki comes to remove "the dirt of the Kali Age".[63]

The Śākta expression of a more personal divine-human relation does not legitimately consist, it would seem, in the notion that "Mahākālī", "Mahālakṣmī", and "Mahāsarasvatī" (of the Devī-Māhātmya) are either avatars or incarnations of the Supreme Goddess;[64] for these

---

58 Wilson, *The Vishnu Purana* (3d ed.), pp. 491, 492.

59 *Vide*, for example, the festival of the goddess as Ankamma in this regard in Oppert, *On the Original Inhabitants ...*, p. 490. The event also includes several of the ritual elements, gestures, and experiences mentioned in Chap. IV, *supra*.

60 *Vide* Wilson, *The Vishnu Purana* (3d ed.), pp. 491, 492.

61 Cf. David F. Pocock, "The Anthropology of Time-Reckoning", *Contributions to Indian Sociology*, No. 7 (1964, pp. 27f.

62 *Ibid.*, pp. 28f.; cf. Kane, *History of Dharmaśāstra*, II, Part II, 717ff.

63 Hazra, *Studies in the Purāṇic Record*, p. 88. The Vāyu Purāṇa says, "When sacrifices grew rare, lord Vishnu was born again and again for establishing Dharma and destroying Adharma" (cited *ibid.*, p. 233); *vide* also Matsya Purāṇa CCLXXIII.27; cf. Arthur Avalon (John G. Woodroffe), *Tantra of the Great Liberation* (*Mahānirvāṇa Tantra*) (London: Luzac & Co., 1913), Introduction, p. xlviii; Wilson, *The Vishnu Purana* (3d ed.), pp. 388-389. Kalki's name and function are paradoxical: *vide* Przyluski, "From the Great Goddess to Kāla", pp. 268, 273, 274; and esp. his "La Croyance au Messie dans l'Inde et l'Iran", p. 12.

64 Cf. Rai Bahadur Gupte, *Hindu Holidays and Ceremonies* (2d ed. rev.; Calcutta: Thacker, Spinkad and Co., 1919), p. 182. Once again, even acknowledging the static-

hypostatic divinities are not given, for example, the same quality of "historical" contemplation and anticipation as the Vaiṣṇavite avatar, Kalki, or, even, the Buddhist avatar, Maitreya.[65] Mahākālī, Mahālakṣmī, and Mahāsarasvatī, as tri-emanative "processions" of Mahādevī, constitute cosmo-*guṇic* (but still largely, *supra*-historical) pro-ordinations in the birth-process of the universe. Perhaps the most authentic and meaningful symbols of the personal "intervention" (as such) of the goddess (granting that all *devas* and *Iśvaras* are her "instruments"),[66] are her near omnipresent "digits"—the Grāmadevatās (*supra*, p. 37). These are her constant "substitutes" for the traditional *avatāras*. The factor of ambivalence in their dispositions toward persons need not blur one's perception of their redemptive function. For they are, phenomenologically, intentional extensions of the Great (Mother) Goddess,

> Who is the sentiment of Love Incarnate,[67]
> Who feels very much for the mental pain of Her Bhaktas.[68]

The earlier presented symbols of the nearness and presence of the goddess during the Pūjā, then, suggest to some extent a sacred-festive milieu in which persons experience an eschatological encounter with the Living Goddess in the midst of community. Thus in the "qualitative-evaluating" sense

> it is in ourselves to decide whether we should give up the kingdom of the mind to the rule of the Mahisasura or enthrone Mother Durga in our breast. *She can only be brought down to our heart* by concentrating all the Divine graces that are innate in our inner being. (Italics mine).[69]

Yet the pre-eminent mark of the Śākta revalorization of Vedo-Brāhmaṇic tradition and its caste-restrictive "rites of passage" to the Ultimate Sacred is another thing. It has to do with a qualified [70]

---

dynamic reality of the goddess (cf. Shastri, "Durgā-Pūjā", pp. 246-248), the word *emanation* still more properly supersedes the notions of avatāra or incarnation concerning the goddess; they can hardly apply to the above mytho-nominals in the denotative sense. The same author's use of the term "minor incarnations", however, comes closer to that sense (*vide ibid.*, pp. 249f.).

65 Cf. Richard A. Gard, ed., *Buddhism* (New York: George Braziller, 1962), p. 93.

66 *Supra*, pp. 156.

67 I.e., during the ritual; cf. "Creation as Love" (*supra*, p. 168).

68 Devībhāgavata Purāṇa VII.39.

69 Sri Aurobindo, cited in Barua and Baveja, *The Fairs and Festivals of Assam*, p. 46.

70 *Vide infra*, p. 251 and n. 149 of that page.

de-esotericization of certain religious rituals, particularly during the Kali-Yuga. Thus the Mahānirvāṇa Tantra [71] tells us that

> Śrī Devī said:
> ... Do Thou in Thy mercy speak to Me of the ordinances relating to such initiation.[72]
> Śrī Sadāśiva said:
> In the three Ages this rite was a great secret; men then used to perform it in all secrecy, and thus attain Liberation.
> When the Kali Age prevails, the followers of Kula rite should declare themselves as such, and, whether in the night or the day, should openly be initiated.

Beyond the fact that the Tantric path is a "revelation ... addressed to all",[73] however, lies another correlation between "Ritual" and "Time". Eliade calls attention to the proclamation of several Tantric texts which reflect the dynamic convergence of cosmology, anthropology, and soteriology. That is to say, there are correlations that exist between the following phenomena: (1) "the rediscovery of the Goddess" and "the carnal condition" of man in the Kali Age; (2) the advent of "a new relation" and the inadequacy of the Vedo-Brāhmaṇic tradition during "this 'dark age'".[74]

> Man, they held, no longer possessed the spiritual spontaneity and vigor that he enjoyed at the beginning of the cycle; he was incapable of direct access to truth; he must, then, "stem the current", and, to do so, he must set out from the basic and typical experiences of his fallen condition—that is, from the very sources of his life. This is why the "living rite" plays such a decisive role in Tantric *sādhana*; that is why the "heart" and "sexuality" serve as vehicles for attaining transcendence.[75]

Moreover, with regard to Vedo-Brāhmaṇic-Tantric continuity and change the same scholar says the following about the phenomenon of "sexuality" under the form of mystical eroticism: "*Maithuna* was known from Vedic times, but it remained for tantrism to transform it into an instrument of salvation".[76] After referring to (1) conjugal union as a hierogamy and (2) orgiastic sexual union as "two possible values of sexual union" in pre-Tantric India,[77] Eliade adduces that "if the sexual plane is sanctified and homologized to the planes of

---

[71] Mahānirvāṇa Tantra X.109-111 (and Avalon's nn. 2-4).

[72] I.e., "... the fully initiated Kaula" (*ibid.*).

[73] Eliade, *Yoga*, p. 296 (bottom).

[74] *Ibid.*, pp. 203-204; *vide* Mahānirvāṇa Tantra II.14-20, IV.87-91; Woodroffe, *Introduction to Tantra Śāstra*, pp. 41-42.

[75] Eliade, *Yoga*, p. 204.

[76] *Ibid.*, p. 254.

[77] *Ibid.*

ritual and myth, the same symbolism also operates in the opposite direction—the ritual is explained in sexual terms".[78] These observations apply particularly to the Vedo-Brāhmaṇic precedents, but they also have significance for the rituo-structural correspondences which we shall point out presently.

For now, we epitomize the previous discussion upon the soteriological excellence of the Kali-Yuga. The Kali-Yuga, therefore, represents the beginning and the end of the ontological polarization of the Kṛta and the Time of Darkness. Universal plenitude of being has shifted from the first age when men had more immediate access to the Truth, the Real—toward a later universal impoverishment of being in the last age, wherein access to the Sacred requires rites commensurate with the state of human existence. That ontological polarization requires, moreover, a series of spiritual exercises the nature of which is expressed in paradoxical relation to the yugic dichotomy. Thus the *way out* (*supra*, p. 238) of the age (or ages) is contemplated in the form of an ingenious theory of *acceleration* and *route of access* to the Great Time—and Beyond. To be sure, the Rudrayāmala contains the words: "I shall proclaim left-handed practice, the supreme *sādhanā* of Durgā; following which the adept obtains *siddhi* speedily in this *Kali*-age".[79] Hence the movement of accelerated degeneration in the Kali-Yuga requires a peculiarly momentous efficacy of the ritual vehicles of spiritual realization of the Great Self of the goddess.

The Regenerative Power of the Goddess

Like the seemingly abysmal character of the Hindu religion in general, a plethora characterizes those ritual forms of initiation (*dīkṣā*)[80] which are, really, modes of *sādhana* for Self-realization; that is, here: the striving to fulfill a soteriological end which is "some form of Unity with God as ... Mother",[81] in keeping with the orientation of the Śāktas.[82] There has already been recognized in the long

---

[78] *Ibid.*, p. 256.

[79] Bharati, *The Tantric Tradition*, p. 230. Likewise, Eliade, *Yoga*, p. 205: "the aim of the *Guhyasamāja tantra* is rapid arrival at Buddhahood".

[80] No less than twenty-five kinds of *dīkṣā* are mentioned in the Jayadratha Yāmala: *vide*, *The Cultural Heritage of India*, IV, 219; Gonda, *Change and Continuity in Indian Religion*, p. 443, n. 576.

[81] Woodroffe, *Śakti and Śākta*, p. 280.

[82] *Supra*, p. 134.

history of Indian religion a tendency not to dispense completely with ancient symbols both in myth and ritual.[83] In fact, the history of Hindu religion reveals *both* (a) that there have been change and continuity in the matter of initiatic forms with regard to the relation of Vedo-Brāhmaṇic and Purāṇic-Tantric traditions;[84] and (2) that there has been the influence of ancient *extra*-Brāhmaṇic popular rubrics and styles of ritual practice.[85] At any rate, the problem of ritual prolixity, if not complexity, has posed a challenge even outside of Indian studies, for instance, in the case of Hebrew religion. There, too, however, scholars have sought to find some basis of structural synthesis for a variety of potentially overlapping but ordinarily assorted rites.[86]

Thus, according to *darśanic* tradition and Indological scholarship, the term *dīkṣā* has multiple and, often, interrelated meanings.[87] Our present interest in this phenomenon, nonetheless, is not inconsistent with an understanding of its basic intention as an introductory preparation for one's entering upon the performance of a more distinctive sacramental rite (e.g., *soma-yajña*). We would emphasize, however, as fundamental to the *dīkṣā*, soteriologically conceived,[88] the desire on the part of the postulant (*śiṣya*) to have "access to the deepest zones of sacrality ... a more complete participation in the sacred ..."[89] It is, perhaps, the conviction that a profounder religious experience

---

83 *Supra*, pp. 74-76.

84 *Supra*, p. 241f.; *vide* also Gonda, *Change and Continuity in Indian Religion*, pp. 315, 398f., 401f., 411-413, 430ff., 435f.; cf. *ibid.*, pp. 391, 438ff.

85 Gonda, *Change and Continuity in Indian Religion*, pp. 334, 335.

86 Cf. Hubert and Mauss, *Sacrifice*, pp. 16ff., where the rites are structurally reduced to four fundamental types. Using various sources, including Tantric texts (the latter about whose origins and circles of use little is known), D. J. Hoens ("Initiation in Later Hinduism According to Tantric Texts", *International Association for the History of Religions*, Vol. X: *Initiation*, ed. C. J. Bleeker [Leiden: E. J. Brill, 1965], pp. 71-80) suggests variety (*ibid.*, pp. 74f.) and synthetic reduction (*ibid.*, p. 79): "the *samaya-* and *nirvāṇadīkṣā* it is clear ... are a mixture of ... different kinds of *dīkṣā* ..." (*vide ibid.*, pp. 75-79); the complexity of the rituals (*ibid.*, p. 76) does not preclude, however, a list of "four dīkṣās" which correspond to advancing stages of spirituality (*ibid.*, p. 79).

87 Gonda, *Change and Continuity in Indian Religion*, pp. 318f.; on theories of its origin, *vide ibid.*, pp. 340ff.; cf. A. Basu, "Dīkṣā", in Bleeker, *Initiation*, p. 81.

88 Dīkṣā (A. Basu, "Dīkṣā", p. 80) may serve other, more profane, ends, e.g., "to obtain wealth, to gain superiority over enemies", etc.

89 Mircea Eliade, *Rites and Symbols of Initiation: The Mysteries of Birth and Rebirth*, trans. Willard R. Trask (Torchbook ed.; New York: Harper and Row, Publishers, 1965), pp. 104 and also 54ff.

of the goddess was available to certain persons [90] that also encouraged the claim of it as both an indispensable prelude to Liberation (*Mokṣa*)[91] as well as a quest requiring a *guru,* or spiritual teacher.[92] Following Hoens, then, the more significant soteriological conceptions underlying the *dīkṣā* are these : (1) the act or acts of purification (a basic step in all Hindu rites),[93] (2) the idea of a new creation (or new birth), and (3) the hope of attaining the sphere of a deity [94]—here : the goddess.

Before making a few important rituo-structural observations concerning paths of *sādhana* among the Śākta schools, we call attention to these salient elements in the Guru-Śiṣya relation :[95] (a) the act of mutual examination or observation by master and pupil; (b) the guru's establishment of his own self-divinization : that he has *prāṇa-śakti* (= Śaktimān);[96] (c) the giving of the *mantra* of the *Iṣṭadevatā* to the pupil; (d) the guru's transmission of spiritual power to the pupil (= *Śaktipāta*);[97] (e) the pupil's entreating of the master to grant that his *sādhana* will be successful.[98] In a word, one might say that, religiously, *dīkṣā* refers to that *initiatic event* "which gives a knowledge of things divine and destroys all that leads to a fall".[99]

Inherent in these sacred actions (including the foregoing remarks on the "advent of the Goddess") is a pervasive atmosphere of *bhakti* : "mystical devotion", "fervent love", or "deep loving adoration" of the goddess.[100] Moreover, there is present an intense dimension of

---

[90] Gonda, *Change and Continuity in Indian Religion,* p. 435; in the case of the defective, *vide ibid.,* p. 443; cf. *ibid.,* pp. 445f. : the Gautamīya-Tantra's criteria.

[91] Cf. A. Basu, "Dīkṣā", p. 82.

[92] Kulārṇava Tantra XIV (Pandit ed., p. 101); Gonda, *Change and Continuity in Indian Religion,* p. 442 : "Without the dīkṣā, Tantrist authorities hold, japa of the mantra, pūjā and other ritual acts are useless". *Vide* also *ibid.,* p. 444. On the *female* guru, *vide* Avalon, *Principles of Tantra,* II, 73ff.

[93] *Supra,* p. 214.

[94] Hoens, "Initiation in Later Hinduism ...". p. 80.

[95] *Ibid.,* pp. 73-74; Kulārṇava Tantra XIII (Pandit ed., pp. 87-100).

[96] Woodroffe, *Introduction to Tantra Śāstra,* p. 69; cf. *ibid.,* pp. 66f.

[97] Kulārṇava Tantra XIV (Pandit ed., p. 104): "The disciple receives the Grace according to the impact of the Shakti, *saktipāta*; where there is no impact of *śakti,* there is no fulfillment".

[98] Cf. Gonda, *Change and Continuity in Indian Religion,* p. 446.

[99] A. B. Ghosh, "The Spirit and Culture of the Tantras", *The Cultural Heritage of India,* IV, 245. Cf. the "etymological explanation", in Gonda, *Change and Continuity in Indian Rdligion,* p. 319.

[100] Cf. Eliade, *Yoga,* p. 348; J. N. Banerjee, in Morgan, *The Religion of the Hindus,* pp. 49f., 406 (Glossary); cf. Devībhāgavata Purāṇa VII.37.1-37; *vide* also Edward

yoga (e.g., *dhyāna*),[101] which comes into fuller fruition in the course of the *dīkṣita's* endeavours to reach a state of success or perfection (*siddhi*).[102] In this regard Woodroffe says that "when a man is Siddha in Sādhana he becomes qualified for yoga, and when he is Siddha in Yoga he attains Perfect Experience. Yoga is thus the process whereby man is raised from Limited to Perfect Experience".[103]

Ācāra

Dakṣiṇā←kuṇḍalinī→Vāmācāra : sādhaka-sādhika

...the soul struck by *dīkṣā* attain[s] to Shivahood. With all *karma* burnt out by *dīkṣā*, all bonds of Maya severed, attaining to the supreme end of Jnana, seedless, *he becomes Shiva.

*'seeds of *samskāra*'

Gone is the shudrahood of a shudra, the brahmanhood of a *brāhmaṇa*; there obtains no distinction of caste where there is the effect of *dīkṣā* ...

... all japa, puja and like activities by those who are not initiated are fruitless like the seed sown on rock.[104]

It is significantly expressed in these stanzas that there is in the Tantric tradition a radical distinction "between the initiated and the uninitiated", as well as "a sharp division between an esoteric and an exoteric doctrine".[105] This means that the Tantric sectarian democracy mentioned earlier [106] is qualified by the thought that pan-caste eligibility remains inseparable from the need *to experience the process of a different sacralization.* Moreover, as we also indicated, the distinction is more properly one of the specific rationale of the use (rather than the non-use) of concrete elements, insofar as even the *use* of such elements as "japa, puja and like activities" becomes itself, within an

---

C. Dimock, Jr., "Doctrine and Practice Among the Vaiṣṇavas of Bengal", in Singer, *Krishna : Myths Rites and Attitudes*, pp. 46-51. The widening significance and recourse to the path (*mārga*) of *bhakti* in modern Indian urban culture is suggested by Singer, *Traditional India*, pp. 146-148.

101 Cf. Karpūrādi-Stotra 17 and Avalon's n. 3; Kulārṇava Tantra IX (Pandit ed., p. 61) : "And of yoga, *dhyāna*, meditation, is an important limb"; Ghosha, *Durgā-Pūjā*, p. 345.

102 Gonda, *Change and Continuity in Indian Religion*, p. 441; cf. *ibid.*, p. 444; Oppert, *On the Original Inhabitants ...*, p. 542; esp. Avalon, *Karpūrādi Stotra*, p. 14 : "The Siddha-Kaula is beyond all rules".

103 Woodroffe, *Śakti and Śākta*, p. 300. Cf. Eliade, "Cosmical Homology and Yoga", pp. 193f. For "yoga" and its constituent elements, *vide* Eliade, *Yoga*, pp. 47ff.

104 Kulārṇava Tantra XIV (Pandit ed., pp. 108-109).

105 Gonda, *Change and Continuity in Indian Religion*, p. 439; *supra*, pp. 3 and 37f.

106 *Supra*, p. 145.

esoteric frame of reference, something more [107]—indeed—"something other" (*supra*, p. 181) than what they appear to the uninitiated.[108]

The two Śākta *ācāras* [109] which represent two traditional soteriological orientations, granting variation of nominal classification,[110] are, as before (*supra*, p. 139 n.), the "Right-hand" (*Dakṣiṇācāra*) and the "Left-hand" (*Vāmācāra*). We are told, however, that such designations are not precise : *dakṣiṇācāra*, actually meaning "favourable", and *vāmācāra* : a sādhana wherein "woman (*vāmā*) enters" (= latā-sādhana).[111] In the former case it is "that ācāra which is favourable to the accomplishment of the higher sādhana, and whereof Devī is the Dakṣiṇā-Kālikā";[112] in the latter case "there is ... worship of the Vāmā-Devī", but in the sense of *nivṛttimārga* as an "adverse" path of *pravṛttimārga*, the paradoxical objective being to employ the very powers of *pravṛtti itself* in order to "render them self-destructive".[113] It is, of course, this quite intriguing *sādhanic* logic which has aroused the suspicions of many an "outsider" (i.e., non-initiate) both Indian and Occidental.[114]

With regard to the above *ācāras*, however, it would seem, again, that Bharati's remarks about the lack of terminological precision [115] still apply. For the scholar points out that the following factors which have particular significance for the Left-handed tradition :

> the *Rudrayāmala*, one of the most reliable treatises of Hindu tantrism, distinguished three types of tantric *sādhanā*, adding "*kulācāra*" (the practice of the tantric in-group) to right- and left-handed worship ... The *Kulācāra* ... is a more opaque

---

[107] Cf. Kulārṇava Tantra XVII (Pandit ed., pp. 118-128; e.g., pp. 121, 126).

[108] Cf. Eliade, *Yoga*, pp. 249-254; *vide* also Bharati, *The Tantric Tradition*, pp. 164-184 *et passim*. A type of "intentional language" existed also among the *Thagi* of India : *vide* Bruce, *The Stranglers*, pp. 219-224.

[109] I.e., Woodroffe, *Introduction to Tantra Śāstra*, pp. 76f. : "the way, custom and practice of a particular class of sādhakas"; Bharati, *The Tantric Tradition*, p. 65 : "ritualistic and meditative methods".

[110] Cf. Karmakar, *The Religions of India*, I, 114.

[111] Woodroffe, *Introduction to Tantra Śāstra*, pp. 77, 78.

[112] *Ibid.*, p. 77.

[113] *Ibid.*, pp. 78, 79; cf. "reverse" in Kulārṇava Tantra II (Pandit ed., p. 30).

[114] Karmakar, *The Religions of India*, I, 114; cf., however, Woodroffe, *Śakti and Śākta*, pp. 403ff. For the erotic representation of the paradoxical intention of Vāmācāra *maithuna*, *vide* Kanwar Lal, *The Cult of Desire : An Interpretation of Erotic Sculpture of India* (New York : University Books, Inc., 1967), esp. Plates and Notes on Plates, pp. 85-104; cf. the goddess as "Bhuvaneshvarī", of the Tantrasāra, cited in *H.T.T.G.*, pp. 35-39.

[115] *Supra*, p. 213, n. 192.

matter. It seems to unite and transcend both the right- and left-handed traditions in a sort of dialectical synthesis.[116]

Accordingly, following the author's remarks, one might say that we are faced with a dynamic phenomenon of soteriological intention which includes (1) a dakṣiṇācāric non-materialist orientation (i.e., which uses no ingredients); (2) a dakṣiṇācāric materialist orientation (i.e., which uses ingredients but "substitute" ones); (3) a vāmācāric materialist orientation (i.e., which uses the *pañcamakāra*); *and* (4) a kula-vāmācāric materialist-non-materialist orientation,[117] which aspires to achieve a dimension of depth *in* and *beyond* the *pañcamakāras* themselves—an experiential physico-spiritual revalorization. Perhaps we are mistaken,[118] and that we cannot deny this distinctive soteriological possibility: Point (4) to either Points (2) or (3). Nonetheless, insofar as both Eliade and Bharati notice the discrepancy, we might still venture to say the following.

First, it is apparent that a broad distinction made on the basis of the use or non-use of materialist elements may be worthy of a *flexible* retention; secondly, granting the inevitable phenomenon of individual or group variability (*supra*, p. 130) of temperament in the *ritual* practice, we might recognize as the *ideal* structural intention of *all* such variations of *ācāra* "an irresistible human desire to transcend time and history";[119] but that, at the same time, the possibility must be considered that human beings may periodically fall short of the mark, become "arrested" by the sheer enjoyment (*bhukti*) of the elemental media of redemption.[120] Thus, though "the flesh, the living cosmos, and time are the three fundamental elements of tantric *sādhana*",[121] the failure to transcend these phenomena (even in the most advanced state of Vāmācāra: "Sveccācāra")[122] constitutes the most serious violation of the Tantric Ideal.[123]

---

116 Bharati, *The Tantric Tradition*, pp. 230, 231.

117 I.e., Bharati's "dialectical synthesis".

118 That we are not far from correct is suggested by Woodroffe's own distinctions among the Vāmācāra (*Śakti and Śākta*, p. 104).

119 Eliade, "Methodological Remarks ...", p. 88; cf. our Preface, p. vii.

120 Cf. Eliade, *Yoga*, p. 206: "... aberrant interpretations of dogma appear in the history of all mystical cults", e.g., "tantric orgies". Cf. Devībhāgavata Purāṇa V. XVI. 34-45.

121 *Ibid.*, p. 204.

122 *Vide infra*, p. 252.

123 Kulārṇava Tantra II (Pandit ed., pp. 36f.); esp. Mahānirvāṇa Tantra XI.104; cf. *ibid.*, XI.29-30. Cf. Eliade, *Yoga*, pp. 205f.: the author's critical stipulations on the

Thirdly, the concept of *kuṇḍalinī-śakti* [124] is shared by both of the above "wings" of *ācāra*. Our previous emphasis upon the lack of terminological precision (Bharati) in reference to those *ācāras*, therefore, warrants that we recognize the apparent arbitrariness of the Dakṣiṇā-to-Vāmācāra initiatic progression. Suppose that we were to consider the possibility that this is so; that the very use of "substitutive" *pañcamakāras* (or *pañcatattva*) might not automatically preclude the Dakṣiṇācāric experience of a depth of spirituality that is comparable to the Dakṣiṇā-to-Vāmācāra *progressive* pattern?[125] Certainly if this were so, the former's implied lower position in the *sādhanic* scale, or their distinction in contrast to the Vāmācāra, would seem to amount to more than the mere position of the woman in the ritual (Woodroffe), even if we grant the aetiologic of this traditional element. Whatever the case, to say that the "Right-handed" *ācāra* in its use of *pañcatattvic* substitutes (recall that the "woman" *may* be present in this path) is a lower means to a more spiritual end than the Vāmācāra may be, after all, as arbitrary as it appears; and, of course, to say that the Vāmācāra approach itself is characterized by a gross material stagnation is not a necessary conclusion.[126] At any rate, the notion of a Dakṣiṇa-to-Vāmācāra initiatic progression is supported by that remarkable, though "Left-handed", Kulārṇava Tantra.[127]

Finally, although it is probable that there is a dakṣiṇācāric "immaterialist" approach to the ritual,[128] the fifth *makāra* (*maithuna*)

"easiness" of the *Buddhist* tantric path apply also to the *Hindu* tantric path. *Vide* Woodroffe, *Śakti and Śākta*, pp. 393f.; cf. *ibid.*, pp. 379f.

[124] John G. Woodroffe, Introduction to his translation of *The Serpent Power, Being the Ṣaṭ-Cakra-Nirūpaṇa and Pādukā-Pañcaka* (7th ed.; Madras: Ganesh and Co. Private, Ltd., 1964), pp. 1f.: "Kuṇḍala means coiled. The power is the Goddess (Devī) Kuṇḍalinī, or that which is coiled; for Her form is that of a coiled and sleeping serpent [cf. *supra*, p. 237; Eliade, *Yoga*, p. 245] in the lowest bodily center, at the base of the spinal column, until She is aroused in that Yoga which is named after Her. Kuṇḍalinī is the Divine Cosmic Energy in bodies ..." *Vide* also Woodroffe, *The Serpent Power*, Ṣaṭ-Cakra-Nirūpaṇa I-XLI and Plates 1 (Frontispiece)-8; Devībhāgavata Purāṇa VII.35 and XI.8; Mahānirvāṇa Tantra V.93f. Cf. M. P. Pandit, *Lights on the Tantra* (Madras: Ganesh and Co. Private, Ltd., 1968), pp. 13-20.

[125] Cf. Kulārṇava Tantra II (Pandit ed., p. 30): "... Dakshina, the path where karma, bhakti, jnana are *skilfully* harmonised and synthesised. ... Higher than the Dakshina is the Vāma ..."

[126] Cf. P. R. A. Sastri in Woodroffe, *The Serpent Power*, pp. 246-254, esp. pp. 250f.; *vide ibid.*, p. 250, n. 1; p. 251, n. 1.

[127] Kulārṇava Tantra II (Pandit ed., pp. 30-31).

[128] E.g., "The pupil ... having *before his mind's eye* the figure of the Mūrti or God [or Goddess] connoted by the Mantra he chants" (Woodroffe, *The Serpent Power*, p. 247);

could be, and was, also assimilated to the *kuṇḍalinic* structure in both the Vāmācāra and Dakṣiṇācāra traditions.[129] It is the attempt to compromise with the all-engaging nature of *maithuna*,[130] however, which provides a lesson in religious conservatism and religious creativity For, on the one hand, in the "Right-handed Path" the dominant tendency is to require that the male's counterpart should, properly, be "an initiated wife"[131] before the sacred act's (*maithuna's*) occurrence. On the other hand, in the "Left-handed Path" the conservative element is manifested in that the *women* who are present in the Kula-Cakra fall into *categories* (e.g., Pūjyā-śakti; Bhogyā-śakti),[132] which precludes the use of *unlimited* freedom with women. Yet, as it was earlier intimated, even in the most advanced stage of spirituality the mere enjoyment (*bhukti*) that would come so naturally from "other unions", or "carnal relations" was given either secondary value or no ultimate value at all.[133]

---

cf. La Vallée Poussin, in Eliade, *Yoga*, pp. 261f. To be sure, a "materialistic" *non*-maithunic ritual act was also possible (Bharati, *The Tantric Tradition*, p. 235).

129 The assimilation would remain in the case of the Dakṣiṇācāras whether the process were (a) *samayinic*, i.e., seeking "the identity of Śiva and Śakti and ... to awaken the *kuṇḍalinī* by spiritual exercices" (Eliade, *Yoga*, p. 262), *without* sexual union; or (b) *monogamic*, i.e., in the sense of "a ritually consummated marital union" (for the phraseology, *ibid.*, p. 255); *vide* the "compromise" continued *supra et seq.* For the more explicit and well-known Vāmācāra rituo-structural correlation of the "literal" *pañcamakaras* (specifically, *maithuna*) *and Kuṇḍalini-śakti*, *vide* Bharati, *The Tantric Tradition*, pp. 261, 263-265.

130 Muirhead-Thomson (*Assam Valley*, p. 39) delineates four basic representations of Śiva-Śakti union: (1) "The apposition of linga with gauri-patta (yoni) is one," or (2) "mystic diagrams (yantras) may be drawn on the ground to represent the yoni of the goddess, with sacred fire in the center representing the seed of Siva"; (3) "another method is to dip a certain flower in red sandal paste to represent the linga and this is inserted in another flower—Clitoria—which is shaped like the female organ"; (4) "finally, there may be actual union of the male worshipper with a female, representing Sakti, usually his wife. This last method of sexual union (maithuna) as part of the worship, is one of the elements in a ritual important to the Saktas called five elements, the Sanskrit names for all of which begin with the letter M. They are Wine, Meat, Fish, Parched Grain, and Sexual Union". *Pañcamakāra*: *vide* Bharati, *The Tantric Tradition*, p. 232; cf. "Vijayā", *ibid.*, pp. 250-253; *vide* especially the interesting *aṣṭāṅga maithuna* forbidden the *Paśu*, in Avalon, *Karpūrādi-Stotra*, Preface, p. 5; cf. *ibid.*, p. 12.

131 Eliade, *Yoga*, p. 262 (Kālīvilāsa-tantra); *vide* Mahānirvāṇa Tantra VI.14, 17-20; cf. Ramakrishna and Sarada, in Isherwood, *Ramakrishna and His Disciples*, pp. 146f.

132 Cf. Woodroffe, *The Great Liberation* (Text), pp. 231f., n. 3.

133 Bharati, *The Tantric Tradition*, p. 261; cf. Ch. Vaudeville, "Evolution of Love-Symbolism in Bhāgavatism", *Journal of the American Oriental Society*, LXXXII, No. 1 (1962), 31-40, esp. 32.

While in union (*Maithuna*) the mind must be concentrated on *Devī* Kālī and *japa* must be done of Her Mahāmantra. The devotee should not think of aught else.[134]

Accordingly, whatever bliss might be forthcoming is conceived to be derived from "'the true sexual union ... the union of the Parasakti (*kuṇḍalinī*) with Atman ..."[135]

Nonetheless it would seem that out of his fullest spiritual experience the devotee can still say to the goddess: "Thou grantest Bhukti (enjoyment) and Mukti (freedom) to the souls that are cleansed and pure ..."[136] This "rush of Ananda", therefore, which the Kulārṇarva Tantra tells us "is the real *maithuna*, the final *ma*",[137] requires a perspective which may very well be suggested by Bharati's notion of a vision of Kulacara which constitutes a kind of "dialectical synthesis" (*supra*, p. 247); that is, granting the validity of the previous perspective (*supra*, p. 250), it should not be overlooked that the idea of "liberation-enjoyment (Bhukti-mukti)"[138] could represent the experiential transcendence of all the former compromises and sensitivities; for it has been significantly noted that "according to the Bengal Śākta worshippers, Enjoyment ... and Yoga may be one".[139] Perhaps this qualitative-evaluative possibility is confirmed in words that seem to encompass all these concerns: *maithuna*, *bhukti*, and *mukti*:

... O Devī, the signs of the fifth element are that it is the cause of intense pleasure, is the origin of all breathing creatures and the root of the world which is without beginning or end. ... O Beauteous Face! as to the fifth element, know it to be ether, the support of the Universe. O Sovereign Mistress of Kula, he who knows Kula, the five Kula-tattvas, and Kula worship, is liberated whilst yet living![140]

In full view of these critical considerations, then, we present the following *ācāra* chart of the traditional Dakṣiṇa-to-Vāmācāra initiatic progression,[141] which will be supplemented by further remarks.

---

[134] Avalon, *Karpūrādi-Stotra*, p. 75, n. 5; cf. the Kulārṇava Tantra X (Pandit ed., p. 73): "... if desire creeps in then it becomes a sinful act".

[135] Kulārṇava Tantra V.111-112, cited by Eliade, *Yoga*, p. 262; *vide* Kulārṇava Tantra VIII.107ff., cited *ibid.*, p. 205; cf., however, the Nāyikā-sādhana-tīka, *ibid.*, pp. 266-267.

[136] Devībhāgavata Purāṇa VII.5; Woodroffe, *The Serpent Power*, p. 38.

[137] Kulārṇava Tantra V (Pandit ed., p. 52).

[138] Woodroffe, *Śakti and Śākta*, p. 232.

[139] *Ibid.*, p. 306.

[140] Mahānirvāṇa Tantra VII.108, 110-111; cf. "kulāmṛta", in Bharati, *The Tantric Tradition*, pp. 259-269.

[141] Cf. Payne, *The Śāktas*, pp. 27-28; *vide* Pott, *Yoga and Yantra*, pp. 24ff.

Such remarks bear upon the regenerative power of the goddess in the cosmological-rituological-eschatological context.

A.[142] 1. Veda. The *Sādhaka* must carry out the prescriptions of the *Veda.*[143] Fish and meat should not be eaten on certain days. Cohabitation with one's wife must be carefully regulated. The worship is largely of an external character. This has been described as the Path of Action (*kriyāmārga*).[144] It is admitted that many of the Vedic rites cannot now be performed, and even a Paśu must therefore attend to the Agamic ritual in this Kali age.

2. Vaiṣṇava. The injunctions of the *Veda* are still followed but Viṣṇu is worshipped. It is distinguished from the earlier stage by the endurance of great austerities (*tapas*), and by the contemplation of the Supreme everywhere. It is the Path of Devotion (*bhaktimārga*).[145] The worshipper passes from a blind faith to an understanding of the supreme protecting energy of the Brahman.

3. Śaiva. Meditation is now on Śiva. This is the militant (Kṣatriya) stage. To love and mercy are added strenuous effort and the cultivation of power. Entrance is made on the path of Knowledge (*jñānamārga*).

4. Dakṣiṇa. This is the final preparation for passing out of the Paśu state [i.e., akin to animality, in which *tamas* is predominant]. Meditation is of the Devī. Certain rituals are performed at night.[146] Magic power (*siddhi*) is obtained by the use of a rosary [*rudrākṣa*][147] of human bone. If *Pañcatattva* worship takes place, it is only performed with substitutes for the five elements.[148]

B. 5. Vāma. Details of this path are kept secret because revelation destroys the *siddhi* attained hereby.[149] The help of a spiritual director (*guru*) is throughout necessary. Passion, which has hitherto run "downwards and outwards", is now directed "upwards and inwards", and transformed into power.[150] The bands

---

142 "Veda" to "Dakṣiṇā" = Dakṣiṇācāra; *vide infra,* Point C.9, "Kaula" : final stage of "Vāma".

143 Cf. Gonda, *Change and Continuity in Indian Religion,* pp. 443, 423; cf. Woodroffe, *Śakti and Śākta,* p. 103.

144 Cf. B. Bhagavan in *The Cultural Heritage of India,* IV, 24f.; cf. *ibid.,* p. 93.

145 Cf. Gonda, *Change and Continuity in Indian Religion,* pp. 280ff.

146 Cf. Freed and Freed, "Two Mother-Goddess Ceremonies of Delhi State ...", pp. 253ff.

147 Cf. Bharati, *The Tantric Tradition,* p. 256.

148 Cf. Woodroffe, *Śakti and Śākta,* p. 387.

149 Cf. Gonda, *Change and Continuity in Indian Religion,* p. 438. It is apparent that Payne's statement may also be valid, insofar as "the Kula is not to be had by anyone and everyone. There are certain conditions to be ready before the truth of the Kula could be revealed" (Kulārṇava Tantra II [Pandit ed., p. 32]); cf. Devībhāgavata Purāṇa VII.40.32-45, VII.39.38-47. In a sense "secrecy" is related to one's "readiness" *in* the Kali Age; although, generally, the truth of Kulardharma is not to be concealed in that age (*vide* Mahānirvāṇa Tantra VIII. 203); that is, it is to be made *available* to persons. For "dispositional criteria", vide Bharati, *The Tantric Tradition,* p. 323.

150 Cf. H. H. Wilson's account of the Śāktas, especially the Vāmācāra cult, in Devībhāgavata Purāṇa IX.50 (Vijnananda ed., pp. 1008-1021; p. 1013, n.) : "The object

[bonds] which make a man a Paśu have gradually to be cut away; for example, pity, ignorance, fear, shame, family, convention, caste. There is worship with *Pañcatattva* at night.[151]

6. Siddhanta. This is superior to the previous stage, because the *Sādhaka* shows knowledge, freedom from fear of the Paśu,[152] adherence to the truth; and performs *Pañcatattva* openly.[153] Siddhavīras were allowed special liberties with women.[154]

7 and 8. Aghora and Yoga. These are not always made into separate paths. The Aghoras were ascetics who despised everything earthly, and ate human flesh and excrement.[155]

C. 9. Kaula.[156] One can now become a Divya [a divine being in whom Sattva is predominant]. Knowledge of this path unites one with Devī and Śiva.[157] Every *dharma* is lost in the greatness of *Kuladharma*. There are no injunctions, no prohibitions, no restrictions as to time and place, no rules at all. One is beyond good and evil, and may indulge in practices which the general body of Hindus regard as unlawful. This is the "do as you will" *sveccācāra* stage. "At heart a Śākta, outwardly a Śaiva, in gatherings a Vaiṣṇava, in thus many a guise the Kaulas wander on earth".[158] The Kaula or Kulīna is one who "sees the imperishable and all-pervading self in all things, and all things in the self".[159]

The basic forms of Tantric aspiration continue to have their structural homologation in myth, cult, and symbol. Bearing in mind the foregoing esoteric "rites of passage", we shall point out the vital relation between the cosmo-creative and the cosmo-redemptive aspects of the work of the goddess in this age (Kali-Yuga) in which such rites have their special eschatological significance. For this is the Yuga

---

presented to the followers of the left-hand ritual is nothing less than an identification with Śiva and his Śakti after death, and the possession of supernatural powers in this life". Other glimpses are contained in Elizabeth Sharpe, *The Secrets of the Kaula Circle* (London : Luzac and Co., 1936).

151 Mahānirvāṇa Tantra V.21-24 and notes; *ibid.*, VIII.153-204a (Avalon ed., pp. 231f., n. 3); Karpūrādi-Stotra 10, 18; cf. Woodroffe, *Śakti and Śākta*, pp. 389f., ane also p. 384. For a "literal" (*pratyakṣatattva*), "substitutional" (*anukalpa-tattva*), and "symbolic" (*divya-tattva*) listing of the *Pañcamakāra*, *vide* Pandit, *Lights on the Tantra*, pp. 49-50.

152 *Vide* Woodroffe, *Śakti and Śākta*, p. 278.

153 I.e., the distinction is between *initiatic* details and ritual performance in worship; *vide* Mahānirvāṇa Tantra IV.77-80.

154 *Vide* "Mantrasiddhavīra", in Woodroffe, *Śakti and Śākta*, p. 385.

155 Cf. Eliade, *Yoga*, pp. 296ff.; cf. *ibid.*, pp. 294-295.

156 *Vide* Mahānirvāṇa Tantra X.109-199, and esp. X.112.

157 *Vide* "The Divya Pañcatattva ...", in Woodroffe, *Śakti and Śākta*, pp. 385ff.; *vide infra*, pp. 253ff.,

158 Kulārṇava Tantra X, XI (Pandit ed., p. 75).

159 Mahānirvāṇa Tantra VIII.220, XIV.113.

par excellence, wherein the goddess Durgā-Kālī reveals her works in behalf of her *bhaktas*.

First there is the fundamental image of man himself (i.e., the sādhaka and/or sādhika) as a microcosm (*kṣudrabrahmāṇḍa*). The individual thus constitutes an *imago dei* which includes spiritual, mental, and material correlations or dimensions of the goddess herself as the Macrocosm. The spiritual dimension refers to the individual's transcendental (formless) consciousness, while the mental and material dimensions refer to the embodiment of transcendental consciousness under the form of phenomenal human reality.[160] The homologation of the individual and the cosmos resides in the fact that, in addition to the *Tattvas*,

> there is nothing in the universe which is not in the human body. ... it is said in the Viśvasāra Tantra : "What is here is there. What is not here is nowhere". In the body there are the Supreme Śiva-Śakti who pervade all things. In the body is Prakṛti-Śakti and all Her products. In fact the body is a vast magazine of Power (Śakti). The object of the Tantrik rituals is to raise these various forms of power to their full expression. This is the work of Sādhana ....[161]

Nonetheless, it is basic to the soteriological intention of the sādhanic structure that the individual cannot "realize" this universe within his "Self" without the tantrayogic process.[162] For it is through this process that the individual may achieve the perceptual reorientation of his body to the Universal Body (= Devī), as well as his consciousness to the Universal Consciousness. The goddess, then, gives the *sādhaka* the power (*śakti*) to "remember", te "relive", to "'burn up' the *vāsanās* ... to abolish the work of Time".[163] The eternal recurrence of the yugic cycles ceases to have its overwhelming effect upon the individual. He is able to disengage himself from that dynamic jelly in which *human* existence (creation), *human* depreciation (degeneration), and *human* desistance (dissolution) have their determined eventuality.

> The Ācārya, speaking of Kuṇḍalinī, says : "There is a Śakti called Kuṇḍalinī who is ever engaged in the work of creating the universe. He who has known Her never again enters the mother's womb as a child or suffers old age". That is, he no longer enters the Saṁsāra of [the] world of transmigration.[164]

---

160 Woodroffe, *The Serpent Power*, p. 49.

161 *Ibid.*, p. 50. Cf. Woodroffe, *Śakti and Śākta*, pp. 433ff.; Eliade, *Yoga*, pp. 234-236.

162 Eliade, *Yoga*, p. 234 : "Purely psychophysiological mortifications and disciplines are not enough to 'awaken' the *cakras* or to penetrate them; the essential and indispensable factor remains meditation, spiritual 'realization'".

163 Eliade, *Images and Symbols*, p. 89; cf. Eliade, *Yoga*, p. 185.

164 Woodroffe, *The Serpent Power*, p. 167.

Within the eschatological perspective suggested earlier this "ending" of Time in a qualitative-evaluating sense means the introduction of the individual "to the highest, the most perfect, the most sublime ..." life.[165]

Secondly, the eschatological significance of *Kuṇḍalinī/Maithuna* as a paradigmatic sacred action par excellence—whether literal or substitutional—has, potentially, a *double* symbolic character. On the one hand, it represents a type of *imitatio dei.* For the meaning of the *avadhūtīc* freedom which ensues at the most advanced stage of spirituality is that, because of the Śākta's ultimately para-yogic, parapūjic excellence,[166]

> the paradoxical act takes place on several planes at once: through the union of Śakti (= *kuṇḍalinī*) with Śiva in the *sahasrāra,*[167] the yogin brings about inversion of the cosmic process, regression to the undiscriminated state of original Totality.[168]

The phenomenon receives its paradigmatic mythic confirmation, for example, in the cosmic romance of Śiva, "the Passionate Yogi", and the goddess as Satī in the Kālikā Purana and the Brahmavaivarta-purāṇa.[169] For there, on another plane, the *maithuna* motif now makes more intelligible to us much that is mystically contemplated and practically experienced in the Śākta rituals. In the myths themselves we see a recurrent need to affirm the oneness and integrity of the universe. This occurs both under the forms of (a) the mythic presentation of the inner dynamics of the Trimurtian theological structure (i.e., *devas*←→*śaktis*),[170] as yet itself interrelated to an implicit superstructural "duality-in-unity", which is Devī, "the Goddess of the universe, the very universe itself";[171] (b) the mythic dramatization of the erotic conjugality of Śiva and the goddess, as a result of whose deliquescent union (Zimmer) proceeds both the "death" of the goddess as well as the "birth" of an historical universe of "sacred spaces" (= *pīṭhas*). The importance of these mythic events lies in their symbolic

---

165 *Supra,* p. 228.

166 Mahānirvāṇa Tantra XIV.123-125.

167 Ṣaṭ-Cakra-Nirūpaṇa 40, 41; *vide* also Renou, *Hinduism,* pp. 178-180.

168 Eliade, *Yoga,* p. 270.

169 *Supra,* pp. 172-174, 168 and n. 104 of the latter page; cf. the section entitled "Mythic Event and Sacred Space", *supra,* Chap. IV.

170 I.e., Brahmā←→Sarasvatī; Vishu←→Lakṣmī; Śiva←→Pārvatī.

171 Kālikā Purāṇa (specifically Blaquiere, "The Rudhirādhyāya", p. 380). Thus Devī = Mahāsarasvatī (-Mahābrahmā) = Mahālakṣmī (-Mahāhari) = Mahākālī (-Mahādeva); *vide* also *supra,* p. 173f.

capacity to recreate the eschatological "totalization" (= reunification) of the goddess' (i.e., Terra Mater's diversified humanity [172] through the redemption of the world (*sarva-mukti*) and the ritual transcendence of Time.

Moreover, in the highly symbolic bhaktic [173] verse of the Saundarya-laharī, cherished by Dakṣiṇācāra and Vāmācāra, another correspondential process of man-and-cosmos looms. For, there, the goddess, as "the Beautiful One" (Saundarī) in her *ṣaṭcakrabhedic* activity is really *the* Being who *initiates* the Primordial Mystery of the Serpent Power in her "Self".[174] Indeed, the principal significance of this original Sacred Gesture is two-fold. First, as the Power moves along the *cakras* [175] of the Macroanthropocosmos, the goddess not only emanates the universe, but performs *the prototypical sacred act* for those human beings who would strive to have their microcosmic "serpent powers" to wake up, move, and, finally, to establish their being in the All-Powerful Devī. Secondly, the *sādhaka* and/or *sādhika* may seek to achieve the mastery of *cakra*-movement by evolution or involution; but, most importantly, the worshipper, in effecting the return [176] of the Power to the *sahasrāra* of the goddess, accomplishes a symbolically climactic sacred act. This act, therefore, constitutes a re-enactment of the "Activity" of the goddess as Mahākālī, who also devours Time completely in the end of the Kali-Yuga (*Mahāpralaya*).[177] Furthermore, as in the recitation of the myth (Devī-Mahātmya), this sacred re-enactment means the ultimate conquest of the *devasuric* struggle *within man himself*. He can now "survive" in either *Videha-Mukti* (liberation: outside the body) or *Jivan-Mukti* (liberation: while in the body).[178]

---

172 *Supra* (Atharva-Veda XII), p. 102; cf. Kulārṇava Tantra I (Pandit ed., pp. 17-29).

173 Actually the text (Brown, *The Saundaryalaharī*, p. 17) specifies devotion and mantra as vehicles of worship; Brown, however (*ibid.*, p. 18), notes the *kuṇḍalinī-śaktī* as a possible third mode held by modern adherents of Srī-Vidyā.

174 Saundaryalaharī 36, 39, 40, 41, 37; the text, Brown notes, refers in the case of each *cakra* to "your" (i.e., the goddess' own *cakra*). For an interesting discussion on the applicability of the cosmological paradox of staticity-dynamicity to the phenomenon of Kuṇḍalinī-Yoga, *vide* John G. Woodroffe, *Sādhana for Self-Realization* (Madras: Ganesh and Co. Private, Ltd., 1963), pp. 109-121.

175 I.e., *Sahasrāra, ājñā, viśuddha, anāhata, maṇipūra, svādhiṣṭhāna, mūlādharā. Vide* Eliade, *Yoga*, pp. 241-245.

176 *Vide supra*, p. 155, n. 26; cf. *infra*, p. 256.

177 *Supra*, p. 156.

178 Cf. Mahānirvāṇa Tantra VII.111; also Eliade, *Yoga*, p. 363: i.e., "... to live in an

On the other hand, apart from this *imitatio dei* structure (*supra*, p. 254), the eschatological significance of *Kuṇḍalinī-Maithuna* resides in the capacity of the one who has achieved such power (*śakti*); that is, his willingness to "reveal" it secret to others in the "last" of the ages—the Kali-Yuga. For, according to the teaching of the Devī-Purāṇa, "the devotee who has reached the last stage is both *teacher* (guru) and taught (*bhakta*) [italics mine] ..."[179] An individual is, therefore, considered fortunate if he should find a *guru* who is thoroughly prepared and willing to give to another the tantrayogic guidance into the ultimate presence of the goddess. Thus, as part of the *mahāyogic* power and responsibility of the *Jivan-mukta*, there remains the sacred act of "bringing Devī Kuṇḍalinī back to the Mūlādhāra", i.e., *Anutttarayoga*.[180] This *reversal* of the *Kuṇḍalini-śakti* occurs in the esoteric "prāṇapratiṣṭha ceremony through which jīvātman and Iṣṭadevatā are brought out of the body and projected into a yantra, and finally wholly fused together in the central point of this yantra, the bindu".[181]

In keeping with "the double meaning of the 'End of History'", the relation between rituology and eschatology is further qualified by the following considerations. In the first place, the final attainment of the Ultimate Abode of the goddess (i.e., *Sahasrāra*) is usually a *gradual* process. Spiritual (but incomplete) progress made may be lost because "in the earlier stages ... there is a natural tendency [saṃskāra] of the Śakti to return".[182] To be sure, "liberation is gained only when Kuṇḍalī takes up Her permanent abode in the Sahaṣrāra, so that She only returns by the will of the Sādhaka".[183] In such a magnificent state of spirituality the ultimate realization of immortality and freedom by, through, and with (indeed—*within*) the goddess can only mean the conquest of fear, suffering, and death, and the attainment of courage, joy, and life.

'eternal present', out of time. 'Liberated in life', the *jivan-mukta* no longer possesses a personal consciousness—that is, a consciousness, which is pure lucidity and spontaneity".

179 William McCormack, "The Forms of Communication in Viraśaiva Religion", in Singer, *Traditional India*, p. 124.

180 Pott, *Yoga and Yantra*, p. 21.

181 *Ibid.*; *vide* also *ibid.*, pp. 20-21.

182 Woodroffe, *The Serpent Power*, p. 230.

183 *Vide ibid.*, pp. 243-244, and also p. 250.

CHAPTER SIX

CONCLUSION: THE GODDESS DURGĀ-KĀLĪ AS A RELIGIOUS SYMBOL OF MULTI-STRUCTURAL INTEGRATION

In the previous chapters it has been shown that the goddess Durgā-Kālī is indeed a symbol par excellence with the capacity for integrating multiple structures of historico-religious experience, expression, and meaning.

Apart from the historical and traditional origins of this divintiy (already commented upon in Chapter II), there are basically three structures—a cosmic-mythic (Kālī-Śakti), a rituo-cultic (Kālī-Pūjā), and an eschato-symbolic (Kali-Yuga)—which have been explicated and interpreted largely within a Hindu tantric framework. The unification of structures, more formally designated as cosmological, rituological, and eschatological in nature, has been illustrated through the use of literary, liturgical, and linguistic symbols. We shall make a few summary remarks about each of these structures; and then comment further on their remarkable capacity for being integrated around the goddess Durgā-Kālī.

In the case of the cosmological structure (as seen specifically in myth) there tends to be a monistic substratum of reality which corresponds to the Absolute, the *Parambrahman*, the Unknown, or the *Mysterium Tremendum*. This *Urgrund* would seem to linger in the background of all the forms, dispositions, and activities of the many divinities; and it helps to explain how it is possible for *asuras* (e.g., Mahiṣāsura) to gain great powers through the *Iśvaras* (Brahmā, Viṣṇu, Śiva) and, thereby, use such powers *against* the powers of light (*devas*)—indeed the Iśvaras themselves. In the Vāmana Purāṇa, for example, the text tells us that through "a boon granted by Shiva, Mahisa had been rendered *invulnerable* [italics mine]";[1] while in the Skanda Purāṇa it says that Cāṇḍā and Muṇḍa (enemies of the goddess in the Devī-Māhātmya) were Asuras who

---

[1] Kennedy, *Ancient and Hindu Mythology*, p. 336. The mythological tradition thus shows that Mahiṣāsura in fact became invulnerable to Śiva himself.

> became through a boon granted them by the divine mothers, so powerful as to subdue the three worlds. The gods in consequence implored the assistance of Devi ...[2]

Cosmologically, the significant point here is that, though the boons granted have apparently some providential basis, one can hardly avoid the impression that, once attained, such boons of power have some perpetuity of their own even if it is not unlimited.[3] Nonetheless, this means that such power, once achieved, must have some Ground against which the power of the Asuras becomes an irreversible plentitude of being—non-retractable power. Power, however, may be superseded, but it must be met with More Power.[4]

Yet we also discerned a dualistic cosmic structure which looms in the case of the *devasuric* conflict; and it is this structure which corresponds to a distinctly ambivalent quality in the character of the goddess. Because of its radical function in myth, cult, and symbols, it has been called the *mysterium horrendum* (Payne). It is especially pronounced in the bloody and fierce drama (or "Activity") of Durgā-Kālī as the martial Guarantrix of the Cosmos against the recurrent threat of Chaos. At any rate, the sense of mystery as Numinous Power is symbolized and experienced as the source of sacralized sensuous-spatial reality under the form of the topocosm, as well as in the personal and communal cohesion enhanced through acts of worship. This sense of the *mysterium tremendum et fascinans* also appears in some of the religious poetry and prose of devotees to a form of goddess-mysticism. It is a mystic adoration which seems to embrace, if not to transcend, the phenomenon of divine ambiguity. A poetic devotee can thus say to the goddess :

> Though the mother beat the child,
> The child cries mother, mother,
> And clings still tighter to her
> garment.
> True I cannot see thee,
> Yet I am not a lost child.
> I still cry mother, mother.
> All the miseries that I have suffered
> And am suffering, I know
> O mother, to be your mercy alone.[5]

---

[2] *Ibid.*, p. 338.

[3] Cf. *supra*, pp. 169-170; p. 170, n. 115; p. 171.

[4] Cf. *infra*, p. 262.

[5] Eliot, *Hinduism and Buddhism*, II, 287-288. Cf. P. Spratt, *Hindu Culture and Personality: A Psychoanalytic Study* (Bombay: P. G. Mahaktala and Sons Private Ltd., 1966), pp. 226-228, 243, and also pp. 232ff.

In terms of the rituological structure, which finds its focus in the Durgā-Kālī Pūjā, we saw that there exists a chronological-astrological unification that takes the form of an autumnal equinoctial period. This period is homologized with the Great Time. It is a time for the vital coincidence of Sacred Reality and sacred action, when the devotee might be spiritually victorious *in* time; but its ultimate purpose is the transcendence of time itself. In the esoteric dimension of yogic symbolism, there was also the homologation of the human being as microanthropos and the cosmos as Macroanthropos—here, the goddess, the Woman, the Eternal Feminine. This particular aspect served as an important leitmotif in both the phenomenon of "possession' occurring in certain performances of Durgā-Pūjā, and the *kuṇḍalinīc*-yogic conceptualizations of soteriological processes held by the two traditional branches of Hindu Tantrism. Yet, again, this homological imagery was contemplated and applied to the goddess as a worshipful *living image* in the Pūjā. Her iconic body corresponded to the form of the universe, with her many arms signifying her manifold character, as well as her all-inclusive sovereignty. In the case of more distinct gestures, moreover, the vicissitudes of her grace and her judgment were portrayed in the paradoxical gestures of her subjects during *pūjīc* festivity, as much as in the epic re-creations of sacred performance. The fundamentally inexhaustible multi-form of the goddess would continue to have structurally integrative value whether she were represented as Śrīcakra, Mahiṣāsuramardiṇī, or Ardhanārīśvara, or, even, were she the object of a more sophisticated mystical contemplation (= Tantra-yoga).

Furthermore, we alluded to the element of Play (*līlā*) which presented itself, too, as a dispositional substratum in terms of the festive milieu; but it was also fundamental to the cosmic milieu. It is, therefore, possible to understand the occurrence of tragic event (mythic or cultic) as a form of divine play which symbolizes that the storm and stress of cosmic trauma and existential delusion will pass. This *līlā* thus supersedes the tragic vision or sense of life and corresponds in its fundamental status in the character of the goddess to the importance of the ultimate metaphysical Ground which underlies the cosmic rhythms of time and the terrestrial seasons; yet it also bypasses the relativity of all forms and manifestations in Creation, thereby subjecting them to the Ultimate Form (*Sva-Rūpa*) of the goddess.

There is certainly more than one interpretation given to the iconographical posture of a Kālī standing upon her consort Śiva. The interpretations range from the mythological to the mystical or esoteric. One view, often held, is entertained by Sister Nivedita, which is that Śiva's prostration under the goddess Kālī signifies "inertness, the soul unbounded and indifferent to the eternal".[6] But the important thing is to notice that our understanding of the Śiva-Śakti diad (Chapter III) as a phenomenon of "mutual reality" allows us to grasp the fullest paradoxical import of this iconographical symbol. The goddess, then, like Śiva (Naṭarāja) can also be conceived as the Great Feminine Player: in Creation, Preservation, *and* Destruction (*vide infra*). Her movements can thus be seen in structural-symbolic unity with Śiva's; she is to be understood as his dynamic form, the kinetic aspect of Śiva as the static (passive) transcendental principle of the universe; but, then, this passivity of Śiva constitutes *no real or permanent duality*, because in essence the goddess is *his* activity and Śiva's passivity is *her* inactivity.

The eschatological structure in our study of the goddess was disclosed in paradigmatic fashion in the Devī-Māhātmya portion of the Mārkaṇḍeya Purāṇa. There the *Devāsuram* event which occurs in gargantuan violence and disorder seems to take place as if during the final and most intensive phase of the Kali-Yuga. The universe lingered, therefore, in groaning anticipation of another Cosmic Day in the form of Regeneration and another "Beginning of Time". In this age which is a periodic symbolization of the fast approaching Cosmic Night, there was an *eschatologically salvific* revelation of the goddess before the dissolution of the world. That soteriological aspect took the form of directives for the worship of divinity as revealed by Śiva to his Spouse for the sake of men; this occurs in order that persons might attain liberation from death *in* the Kali Age, the death *of* the Kali Age, and, in a *māyic*, *līlic* sense, the "death" of the goddess herself. Thus the "last" age (in an *interminable* series of ages) had both an eschatological aspect in terms of the natural culmination of chronological time (= Kali-Yuga) and an eschatological aspect in terms of the soteriological urgency that obtains but yet is overcome through regenerative rites. It is the time when the goal of personal renewal, freedom, and immortality could be attained through the presence of the goddess; that is, such fulfillment might occur through the infusion of the *Śakti* of the goddess in the pūjic milieu or by yogic meditation on the goddess as an act of interiorized regeneration.

---

[6] Spratt, *Hindu Culture and Personality*, p. 243.

This constituted, on the one hand, the regeneration of guru and initiate, pūjārī and community; and, on the other hand, the facilitation of the process of ultimate deliverance *from* all the delusions of Time and *to* all the glories of the great goddess Durgā-Kālī.

Perhaps the most remarkable thing about the foregoing structures still remains their theoretical and practical *co-inherence*: each of them is contained both explicitly and implicitly in the others; that is, the integration of the cosmological, rituological, and eschatological structures corresponds to the unification of the Trimūrtian functional symbolization as Creation, Preservation, and Destruction. Thus there continues to be in the *comprehensive* Form, Nature, and Activity of the goddess (1) a dimension of preservation-and-destruction in *Creation*; (2) a dimension of creation-and-destruction in *Preservation*; and (3) a dimension of preservation-and-creation in *Destruction*. These structures find a perennial nodus in the *Devāsuram* theme, which, to some degree, testifies to the phenomenon of Vedic-Purāṇic-Tantric continuity.

The dimension of preservation-and-destruction in Creation is present in the paradoxical sense in which one might say that the Primordial Totality (*Samvit*) of the goddess is seemingly "destroyed" by the cosmogonic emanation, concatenation, and fractionalization of the Undifferentiated Essence of the goddess. Yet the paradox tends to be complete, because our understanding is that the ontological depreciation that would seem inevitably to be intrinsic to the *anuttarayogic* cosmogony of the goddess does not occur. Here lies the mystery of the staticity and dynamicity of Ultimate Reality and its translogical realization by the devotee of the goddess; for in soteriological terms it means both the acceptance *and* transformation of perennial sensuous-spatial existence into spiritual existence *as religious experience*. Moreover, the goddess continues to have her own Ultimate Being, Identity, and Power behind, within, and beyond the actions of all divinities of all universes, even such Lords and Sovereigns that make the Trimūrti (i.e., Brahmā, Viṣṇu, and Śiva); this is especially true with regard to her activity in the conflict between the sons of light (*devas*) and the sons of darkness (*asuras*). It is here that it appears that the birth ("creation") of a new Universal Order means the destruction of chaotic powers for the sake of the (re-) established dominance of Cosmic Power. The goddess, therefore, destroys the *apparent* evil (remember *līlā*!) in the universe of divine, human, and natural life, particularly in the Kali-Yuga.

The presence of creation-and-destruction in Preservation is manifest in that the goddess wills her own recurrent "creation" (= emanation = manifestation) through the gods during the course of universal Yugic Rotation. She does this in order to revitalize and guarantee a *qualitative* dimension in their cyclical continuity, i.e., the resurgence of *Śakti, sattva, dharma*. This act is accomplished, again, in magnitudinous cosmic violence against the powers of evil. In one sense, a greater destructive energy, power, and force (*Mahā-Śakti* is launched by the gods (*devas*) against the acosmic powers; but, in another sense, those powers are overcome not by *another*, Greater Power so much as by the very Essence of Ultimate Reality itself—the Power behind all "powers". The "Factuality" of Preservation underlies creation-and-destruction, finally, insofar as the goddess, who is both Mahādevī *and* Mahāsurī, yet finds it Self-pleasing to dramatize in the cosmogony and in the cult the triumph of the dimension of "Mahādevī" *over* "Mahāsurī". It is a testimony to her devotees-en-route that her *experienced* Presence means both personal salvation and the unmitigated pervasion and permanence of Preservation (i.e., Cosmic Order) even *amidst* divine or human chaos.

The presence of preservation-and-creation in Destruction continues to testify to the integration of multiple structures in the symbolic panorama of the goddess. For in the act of cosmic *combat* and *conquest* of Asuric Powers, the goddess reconfirms the preservation of the universe (as "new creation") which, paradoxically, is cleansed of *rajasic* and *tamasic* forces and tendencies (*saṃskāras*). At the same time the goddess also re-establishes and re-affirms the meaning of existence in the cultic realm of myth-and-ritual; and her devotees emerge as "new creations" through the *conquest* of "Self"-delusion (= *Maya*) with the Power to preserve (i.e., perpetuate) their perception of her as the One Ultimate Reality.

It is not surprising, though it is significant, that the mutual coinherence of the foregoing structures was, to be sure, found *in nuce* in the *cosmological* structure alone: that is, under the form of the *cosmogonic event*. For it was here first revealed that not only are cosmogenesis, "Devigenesis", and cosmo-redemption three aspects of one mythic event; but also that Creation, Preservation, and Destruction are three dimensions of one Sacred Reality. This is another testimony to the historical and traditional prestige of the cosmogonic myth as itself a highly useful key to understanding that the meaning and expression of the "End" tends to be already given in one's understanding of the *experience* of the "Beginning".

Interestingly, it is the phenomenon of *destructive* activity in the characterization of the goddess, which makes her one of the most remarkable symbols of the paradox of "Good" and "Evil". "She is alternately hideous and beautiful and alternately terrifying and loving".[7] We need only recall the query of Ghosha,[8] or consider a later inquiry into "The Terrible Mother : [As] A Psychological Study".[9] It is not improbable that none of several perspectives on the *origin* of the ambiguity of the Indian Mother-Goddess may be arbitrarily rejected as possibly a part of a far more complex phenomenon. Nonetheless, there is a certain appeal which the theory of man's experience of nature has for us; however, this appeal depends importantly upon the scope of meaning that is given to the term "nature". We do not adopt the notion, for instance, that the ambivalence of Durga-Kali is completely and ultimately accounted for by man's experience of the "vicissitudes of nature", i.e., its seasons and whims.[10] Nature were better understood to be applicable to the destructive aspect of the goddess, when it is conceived in a broad perspective. We say this for the following two primary reasons.

First, we are cautious to remember that, anthropologically, human beings who are the devotees of the goddess Durgā-Kālī have, themselves an organic and an organismic kinship and interaction with nature-at-large, i.e., nature *as life.* (It is the "primitives'" remarkable testimony to this fact which, in fact, led to earlier methodological reductionisms concerning that "natural" affinity). We are, again, reminded of our previous emphasis upon man's irrepressible sensitivity to "form" (i.e., the forms of natural existence; also, as in our study : his *own* form). Nature, then, may definitively include in its capacity as a life-referent elements which encourage evaluations of its religious effects upon man ranging from the Freudian to the Ottonian; so that both internal and external motivations in human experience (e.g., time-consciousness and spatial orientations, respectively) have contributed to the coincidence of religion and life *as nature.*

A second, more persuasive, reason takes us back to one of the most significant emphases in the History of Religions as a Discipline

---

7 *Ibid.*, p. 226 and Chap. X. Cf. Przyluski, *La Grande Déesse*, p. 28.

8 *Supra*, p. 177.

9 *Vide* G. D. Boaz, "The Terrible Mother : A Psychological Study", *Journal of Madras University*, XVI (1944), 69-74. Cf. Raphael Patai, "Matronit : The Goddess of the Kabbala", *History of Religions*, IV, No. 1 (Summer, 1964), 67-68.

10 Boaz, "The Terrible Mother', p. 64.

(though it is not there, exclusively). It has to do with man's creative response to nature-at-large *as a religiously meaningful event* (*supra*, p. 11). Accordingly, it is phenomenologically a perspective of the paradoxical characterization of Durgā-Kālī, which recognizes that man-in-history has tended to accept the phenomenon of natural existence *as a religious responsibility*; that is, man's tendency has not been solely to "make himself", but, moreover, to understand himself as both the "created" *and* a creator and sustainer of ultimate values through the very forms of natural existence. Acknowledging, also, then, the phenomenon of man's intuition of "over-againstness" vis-à-vis nature-at-large, his religious evaluation of nature as needing an ally, an imitator, or a "re-creator" may be significantly considered "an ancient conception".[11] It is, however, this realization which adds *rationale* to the dimension of "destructivity" in his religious rites, as well as to his ambivalent symbolization of deity, such as Durgā-Kālī.

If we were to add a third, more specifically *philosophical* reason, it would not essentially consist in the recourse to man's fear born of sin or rebellion against the gods.[12] More profound would appear to be the detection of an *ontological thirst* or *malaise* in the human spirit for more first-hand contact with Ultimate Power. This thirst for qualitative being would thus be correlative to the experience of duality which Śākta initiatic philosophy discerns as the initial state of man's encounter with the goddess. This perspective would not necessarily preclude the sense of "sin" or the attitude of rebellion against the gods; yet it seems to be more profoundly originative, if not, influential than the psychoanalytical reduction of mother-goddess worship (including its "ambiguity") to "narcissism, mother fixation, and a weak repression of the infant's anal attachments";[13] or, again, the interpretive vantage points reflected in several traditionally dogmatic ideas of "Paradise Lost" or the "Fall". At any rate, it is at this point that our conclusions about (1) the significance of Time through the application of our method to this study, as well as (2) the status of the former dimension of ambiguity in relation to woman in Hindu tantric religion and Indian traditional society are appropriate.

---

[11] Cf. Heinrich Zimmer, "The Indian World Mother", in Joseph Campbell, ed., *The Mystic Vision*, trans. Ralph Manheim (Papers from the Eranos Yearbooks, Vol. VI; Princeton University Press, 1968), pp. 74f.

[12] Boaz, "The Terrible Mother", pp. 70f.

[13] Spratt, *Hindu Culture and Personality*, p. 352; cf. *ibid.*, pp. 193ff.

Granting the multiplicity and the unicity of such structures (the cosmological, rituological, eschatological), we found it suitable to apply complex criteria in order to grasp the essential context of meaning which unites those structures; although we have not proceeded with the mere assumption that structural multiplicity requires multiple or complex criteria. Our application of complex criteria has, nonetheless, enabled us to understand that the previous host of historical and religious phenomena happens to be adequately comprehended within the context of *Sacred Time.*[14]

It would appear that within the Hindu Śākta-Tantric perspective to which the goddess Durgā-Kālī belongs, Time is both the enemy and the friend of human beings. Time is a phenomenon to be tolerated *and* transcended. Time is also, however, the crucible of existence in which the very media for ultimate liberation from Time have their being; that is, the ideas, institutions, ways (*mārgas*), and, especially in Tantrism, the paradoxical relation between sexuality and spirituality has its expression.

"Meaning" as *Sacred* Time, therefore, is not to be equated with the phenomenon of Time-in-general; although it may be that such time has its secondary value. "Meaning" thus has its *locus* specifically in that Sacred Time when a new conception and attitude toward temporality have at last come into the consciousness of the individual. Sacred Time is Time-under-sanctity as a means to realizing not only Time's own immensity (i.e., the Great Time);[15] but also Time-under-duress when the very attainmənt of a larger vision of the macrocosmic Time is itself superseded in the form of a trans-cyclical realization of the *relativity* of Time as a medium of redemption. The Hindu *yugas* may themselves reflect more than the "astronomical" or the "astrological" sense; they may indeed reflect, more significantly, an ancient historical-religious awareness in the "Indian Mind" of just how long and difficult it appears to have been in man's history for a human being to take a genuine step toward a more lasting and enduring spirituality. Even this, nonetheless, did not entirely arrest the creative contemplation of those with a hunger for the Pan-sacred from seeking

---

[14] It is fitting to recall the incisive judgment of Pathak ("Ancient Historical Biographies and Reconstruction of History", pp. 11, 13-16 and also *supra*, p. 70, n. 151), who calls our attention to the need of the "modern historian" to understand the "idea of history in the *ontological* perspective of the ancient world [italics mine]" (alongside of the need for "its translation according to the current concepts and terminology").

[15] Eliade, *Yoga*, p. 271, for example.

to discover more expeditious paths. And the recourse to salvific expeditiousness did not in turn completely overcome the ambiguous sentiment, which took the form of both a desire to bring about the democratization of Sacred Power and a desire to insist upon the exclusiveness of the Sacred Path.

Consider, for example, the implicit literary-religious tension between the Mahānirvāṇa Tantra and the Kulārṇava Tantra concerning the call to *overt* and *covert* initiatic processes, respectively. This tension may, again, reflect the "qualitative-evaluating" sense of both a trust and a distrust of the "noose of Time" and the openendedness of Time (i.e., Time as "the happy medium" of redemption). It is significant that in the face of this overall continuity of cosmological, anthropological, and soteriological ambiguity, the Śākta-Tantric world-view (especially the *Vāmāmārgic* tradition) presents us with the nuclear possibility that Time need not be merely tolerated but actually embraced and, ultimately, trans-temporalized in a fashion which does not mean the final rejection of Time. It is here that the scholar is confronted by the ever-impending discontinuity between the phenomenological-religious intention of the goddess' cosmogonic activity as Eternal Continuum and the historical-existential actuality of the world as profane routine.

The implications of this observation for the practical (cultic, rituological) dimension of goddess-adoration (the Pūjā) are the following. The status of the *woman* in the *pūjic-sādhanic* milieu undergoes a radical transvaluation, insofar as she becomes a "*real, living,* and *sacred*" symbol of the goddess—the feminanthropic revelation and embodiment of Ultimate and Creative Power. Outside of this cultic milieu, however, what is *soteriologically perceived* inside of the cultic realm of the goddess remains a startling improbability within the realm of the profane (*infra*, p. 267). For in this latter "world" there still remains an inveterate traditional discontinuity between the position in the social structure of the *man* as a symbolic extension of Hindu patrifocal pantheonic beliefs and the subordinate position and value ascribed to the *woman* as the "modest spouse".[16] In this sense the woman symbolizes on but one level of mythological contemplation or interpretation the status of a Lakṣmī, a Pārvatī, or an

[16] We are aware that there must be exceptions to this overall picture; that women's status in Hindu India today is changing. *Vide*, for example, Raphael Patai, ed., *Women in the Modern World* (New York : The Free Press, 1967), pp. 21-41. Political change, however, is still not the *sacral*-social revaluation of woman's status.

Umā, when *sociologically conceived* in deference to the dominant traditional sovereignty of those patrifocal "Male" divinities of the Hindu Pantheon.[17]

> There is ground for reflection that millions and millions of people, not only in India[18] but in many other parts of the world as well, have time and time again succumbed so completely and willingly to the female conception of the deity. Here we encounter something which evidently touches on the depths of human nature. The female element in religion obviously has its positive aspects, *provided it remains in its natural subordinate place.* (Italics mine).[19]

Perhaps, allowing for the interrelation between Hindu religion and society (i.e., the latter's sacral-caste ordination), we might say that the tension between Tantric Woman and patrifocal conceptions of Social Woman is not to be simply understood as that between the Sacred and the profane; but rather, that, just as the tantric *dīkṣā* represents the search for a *more* intense and qualitative sacred experience within the Hindu "socio-religious order" (*supra*, p. 93), the transvaluation of woman (*sādhika* = Devī) in the ritual to a plane of "mutual reality" (here: *socially*, "mutual dignity") with the man (= Śiva) is still conceived within the traditional (non-Tantric) socio-religious *ethos* as too radical an evaluation for that tradition to bear as a practical reality. Moreover, if we recall our allusion to the presence in Hindu Tantrism of structures of duality and *dominance* (i.e., Devī tends to be the All),[20] no profound conscious reflection is required to consider the probable existence, by and large, of a masculine apprehension that what might begin as a creative spiritual thrust for genuine equality of man and woman could become a matter of *socio-religious* dominance (in favour of the latter). In short, the overall contemporary Hindu *paterfamilias* mentality is such that there is little likelihood that the *sacred dignity* ascribed to the woman in the Tantric

---

[17] Cf. A. B. Bharati, *A Functional Analysis of Indian Thought and Its Social Margins* (Chowkhamba Sanskrit Studies Series, Vol. XXXVII; Varanasi, India: Chowkhamba Sanskrit Studies Office, 1964), pp. 157, 161; *vide* esp. *ibid.*, pp. 155-167; Spratt, *Hindu Culture and Personality*, p. 191; *vide* the mythical incident concerning Indra and Uṣas, *supra*, p. 105.

[18] Cf. Renou, *The Nature of Hinduism*, p. 49: "... they account for something like three-quarters of the worship of the country people in the north, and a little more than this in the south (i.e., the *grāmadevatās* alone").

[19] Wilhelm Koppers, "On the Origin of the Mysteries in the Light of Ethnology and Indology", in Campbell, *The Mystic Vision*, p. 66; cf. *ibid.*, p. 68.

[20] Cf. *supra*, p. 134 and nn. 505-7 on that page; also *supra*, p. 227.

"esoteric ceremonial"[21] can without radical reorientation be centrifugally transplanted to the larger Hindu society. This difficulty is, of course, inseparably related to the history of Hindu religion and society. Hidden, therefore, in the historico-religious *memory* of the contemporary society lies a matrifocal-patrifocal schizophrenia whose resolution in mythic language and sacred experience had its recurrent beginnings in ancient and later India, but whose formal re-adaptation-and-change has yet to merge with modern secular constitutional (i.e., political) ideals.

On the whole we have to face a remarkable fact about the nature of the Hindu culture and personality; that is, religious tradition and cultural change have made it possible for that personality to approach the religious Ultimate Reality on several planes of understanding; but, also, that the historical human reality encompasses dispositions which may *and* may not represent the absolute internalization of either the standardized socio-religious tradition or the sacred transformation of statuses as paradigmatized in the Tantric *sādhana*. Hinduism thus appears to us as an unusual phenomenon : having the potential to integrate many modes of religious apprehension, historical adaptation, as well as cultural interrelation inside the subcontinent of India itself. As a religious phenomenon, then, Hinduism continues to embody the tension of all historically persistent faiths between myth and reality, i.e., "myth" as the mode of expressing the *experiential* Reality of the Religious Object; and "reality" as the challenging structures of social history. It is the latter reality which is both sanctified by, but which also partly rejects, a religiously conglomerate world-view which includes the possibility of the transformation (= equalization) of certain of its participants (e.g., *śudras*, *women*) outside of undoubtedly creative cults (Tantric democracy, Tantric womanhood). Perhaps the spirit of the Gandhian nomination of the untouchables as, indeed, *harijans* will yet find its analogous and appropriate transnomination in the case of the "modest spouses" so designated.

A final significance of our study resides in its theoretical and practical implications for others *outside* of India as a *new possibility* for revaluating the theological symbolization of Ultimate Really and the role of human reproductive capacities (i.e., sexuality). It is not necessary to regard this as a romantic summons to encourage an antinomian perspective of religious freedom; although it is doubtful

[21] Cf. Zimmer, "The Indian World Mother", p. 93.

that even the more radical aspects of the Left-handed Tantric tradition are completely gone in India. The important thing is that the worship of the goddess allows for the integration of aspects of human life into a whole, which includes the achievement of a type of *balance* in view of the oft-stated generalization that religious pantheonic structures tend to mirror the socio-political structures of civilizations. In a civilization outside of India this possibility may still become of wholesome consequence. Furthermore, there is some significance here relative to the modern movements toward the liberalization of sexual practices, as much as it has import for the liberation of women themselves from being regarded solely as sexual "objects" instead of persons of value. Individuals might therefore learn from the testimony of the worshippers of the goddess that, even if certain ideas and forms of the Tantric Vogue may be found unsuitable to certain modern milieux, it is essentially the vision of what both man *and* woman can become to one another in mutual respect of one another's identity, influence, and activity *in* the world that matters finally.

APPENDIX

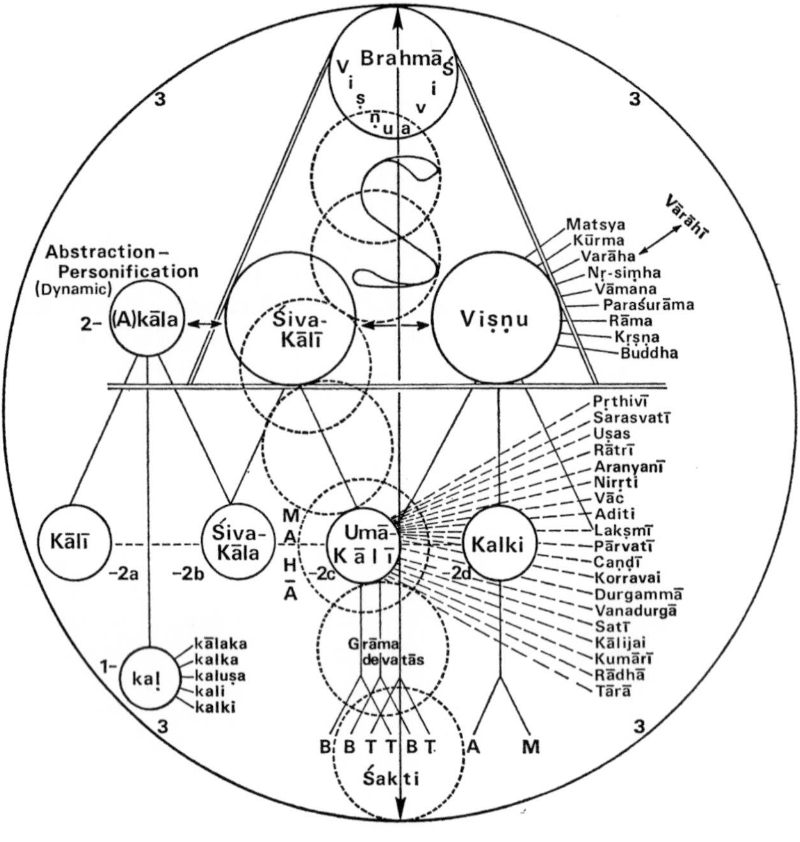

DIAGRAMMATIC NOTES

This diagram, though only partially suggestive, despite our good intentions, has been included and is meant merely to hint at in a very limited way what are really "dynamic" philological-theogonic-philosophical processes which, of course, at this time escape the perfect comprehension of the scholarly community. There is, for example, the ongoing problematic consideration of that often subtle and elusive intercourse between the Great and Little Traditions in Indian culture. The wonder that recurs is that there is, after all, historical validity in such interconnections we have made in this book, and that they are indeed "signs" of religio-cultural continuity and integration. The philological continuity suggested by Przyluski (*vide* pp. 81-84) is so intensely provocative that, in all probability, any further scholarly endeavours to establish an even greater level of historical certainty will require taking account of his ideas.

As we stated in the Preface, we have tried to elaborate and interpret a mythic, cultic, and symbolic unity regarding the prime symbol of the Indian Mother-Goddess world-view, while making use of other kinds of data which seem integral to the achievement of a greater understanding. We are, then, dealing with an extremely complex phenomenon, a composite of remarkably pregnant ideas, whose movements have at sundry times taken paths that are "circular", "circuitous", and even "contradictory". In the final analysis our diagram urges one but to ponder possible implications and dynamics that are not always obvious or specifically indicated. At any rate, the following symbolic breakdown is meant to suggest (1) the philological "nuanciation" of the fundamentally non-Aryan root *k a l*; (2) the process of deomitosis (i.e., nominal, gendric, or dispositional differentiation of a given deity—see infra, 2b); and (3) the capricious yet purposive movement of Kālī, the Black, towards being the object of a monistically-personalistically conceptualized polarity, or the Mistress of all that has been, is, and is to be—all of those varieties of theistic philosophy and mystical experience.

The entire Figure is the Womb of Eternity, or the Abyss of Being, Consciousness, and Bliss (ParaBrahman). The Trimūrti is rather self-evident, however.

The intermittent circles are intimations of Kali's paradoxically static and dynamic movements as Śaivaic polarity and, always, as incipient ("Śaktic") Mistress of a *Cosmic Coincidentia Oppositorum*—e.g., T - B : at center (infra) = "Terrible" - "Benign".

The large "S" in the Trimūrtic Bosom is the Supreme Śaktic essence which they share (i.e., Śiva and Kālī), but, implicitly, The Goddess Kali is always tending to be the Whole, symbolizing that tension which is characteristic of the Devī-Māhātmya, subtily revealed in the Kena Upanisad, yet explicitly drawn in the Saundaryalaharī. Her spectral Self-revelation in the Kena, nonetheless, hints at the inevitable *initiatic* trauma that marks the discovery of who She really is. The lesson is not even that she may have been surreptiously usurping the power of the Universe away from the Gods, but that it has forever been She who is behind *everything*. The birth of her person *from* the Gods, then, turns out to be really *her own* chosen method or mode of Divine Self-disclosure for the sake of cosmic redemption.

2. (A)kāla : the Timeless and Time : philosophical and/or semi-personified abstraction. Time as potentiated being and kinetic energy. Time as creative matrix and the highest god.

2a. Kālī : a mytho-nominal doublet of Kāla, but now as feminine polarity (via deomitosis) of Kāla (2b), both as dynamic personification-abstractions.

2b. Kāla : the mytho-nominal doublet of Kala (2) as Philosophic-Androgynic-Deistic Ultimate Reality, via KĀLA : kāla/kālī, Kāla, as masculine polarity of Kālī (female Time) also notably undergoes Śaivaic absorption : Śiva is superimposed upon Kāla : the black (time)god, probably by a process of sectarian magnification. Śiva as Śiva-Kāla, due to Trimūrtian monism and other attending aesthetic implications, becomes Mahā-kāla (The Great Time), Mahā-Māyā, or even Mahā-

Kāla, the Great Black-Time-God. In the Śiva (kāla)-Kālī diad there is posited also an aesthetic ambiguity, for both Śiva and Kālī, with Umā, perhaps bearing the benign potential.

2c. Kālī; "the Black(One" : Genius of Destruction. While Kāla as the (black)-time-god is absorbed by Śiva, contrariwise Umā ,a traditional consort of Śiva becomes herself absorbed by Kālī, the Black. Kālī : also (The Great Black One; Mahā-Kālī; Nitya Kālī : The Everlasting Black One; Śmaśāna-Kālī : Kali of the Cremation Ground; Rakṣa-Kālī [Goblin Kālī]; and Śyāmā-Kali : Dark Kālī—*Vide* Zimmer, *Philosophies of India*, p. 565), goes on to become not only Mahā-Kālī, the consort of Mahā-Kāla (Siva), but the lingering potential for becoming the Absolute, the Mystagogue of all the gods : vide *red line* : leading from Kali upwards to large "S" — i.e., the Goddess is always the potential World-Śakti and the Essence of Brahman.

2d. Kalki : reveals also a stirring and peculiar ambivalence : (1) he has a mytho-nominal functional duality, and (2) he is again reflective of a purely eschatological ambivalence as apocalyptic and messianic avatar. He is both Vaiṣṇavic Nemesis and Saviour. He is, therefore, a symbol of War and Peace, Violence and Contemplation for the redemption of the world. Kalki, in playing this role symbolizes a problem in Indian Philosophy of the relation between "theo-cosmic providence" and "panentheistic play", the latter of which is the Dance of Śiva. Besides being the source of Śiva's own dynamic play-power, the Goddess is the theogonic relative (i.e., "sister") of Kṛṣṇa. But, ultimately, she is more than a relative; she is the Power in Kalki himself, whether in nemesic play or redemptive providence. A = "Avatar" M = "Messiah".

3. Mahādevī : "She" as the Great Goddess is in absolutely ultimate terms the Para-Brahman, the Source of the Eternal Time-Continuum, Time-Embodiment, and Time-Transcendence; the paradoxical Reality that is *both* Mahādevī *and* Mahāsurī; the Mahāsakti which as Prakṛti is the source of being as Time (Kālī), as Mahāmāyā is the redemptrix of Time as power (Śakti), and as Mahākālī is the destroyer of Time as Śiva (Kāla). The significant truth is that, whether on the human, mythological, or philosophical plane, The Goddess remains the One Sacred Reality in and beyond nature, the Trimūrtian diversity of functions and manifestations, and the metaphysical systems of thought.

BIBLIOGRAPHY

BOOKS

Agrawala, Vasudeva S. The Glorification of the Great Goddess. Varanasi, India : All-India Kashiraj Trust, 1963.

——. Śiva Mahādeva : The Great God. Varanasi, India : Veda Academy, 1966.

Allchin, Bridget and Raymond. The Birth af Indian Civilization. Penguin Books Ltd. Middlesex, England, 1968.

An Alphabetical List of the Feasts and Holidays of the Hindus and Mohammedans. Calcutta : Indian Imperial Record Department, 1914.

Avalon, Arthur and Ellen (Sir John and Lady Woodroffe). Hymns to the Goddess. Madras : Ganesh and Co. Private, Ltd., 1964.

Banerjea, Jitendra N. The Development of Hindu Iconography. Calcutta : University of Calcutta, 1956.

Banton, Michael, ed. Anthropological Approaches to the Study of Religion. London : Frederick A. Praeger, 1966.

Barua, H., and Baveja, J. D. The Fairs and Festivals of Assam. Gauhati, Assam : B. N. Dutt Barua, 1956.

Basham, A. L. The Wonder That Was India. 3d ed. revised. New York : Taplinger Publishing Co., 1968.

Bergaigne, Abel. La Religion védique d'après les hymnes de Ṛgveda. Vol. III. Paris : F. Vieweg, Librairie-Editeur, 1883.

Bhandarkar, R. G. Vaiṣṇavism, Śaivism, and Minor Religious Systems. Strassburg : Karl J. Trubner, 1913.

Bharati, Agehananda. The Tantric Tradition. London : Hillary House Publishers, Ltd., 1965.

Bhattacharji, Sukumari. The Indian Theogony : A Comparative Study of Indian Mythology from the Vedas to the Purāṇas. Cambridge : At the University Press, 1970.

Bhattacharyya, Benotosh. An Introduction to Buddhist Esoterism. London : Oxford University Press, 1932.

Bleeker, C. J., ed. International Association for the History of Religions, Vol. X : *Initiation.* Leiden : E. J. Brill, 1965.

Blofeld, John. The Tantric Mysticism of Tibet. New York : E. P. Dutton and Co., Inc., 1970.

Bloomfield, Maurice, The Religion of the Vedas. New York : AMS Press, Inc., 1969.

Bochenski, J. M. The Methods of Contemporary Thought. Torchbook ed. New York : Harper and Row, Publishers, 1968.

Brandon, S. G. F. History, Time, and Deity : A Historical and Comparative Study of the Conception of Time in Religious Thought and Practice. Manchester : Manchester University Press, 1965.

Brennand, W. Hindu Astronomy. London : Charles Straker and Sons, Ltd., 1896.

Briggs, George W. Gorakhnāth and the Kānphaṭa Yogis. Calcutta : YMCA Publishing House, 1937.

Brown, W. Norman. Man in the Universe : Some Continuities in Indian Thought. Berkeley and Los Angeles : University of California Press, 1966.

Bruce, George. The Stranglers : The Cult of Thuggee and Its Overthrow in British India. New York : Harcourt, Brace and World, Inc., 1968.

Campbell, Joseph. The Masks of God, Vol. II : Oriental Mythology. New York : The Viking Press, Inc., 1962.

——, ed. The Mystic Vision. Translated by Ralph Manheim. (Papers from the Eranos Yearbooks, Vol. VI.) Princeton : Princeton University Press, 1968.

Carpenter, J. Estlin. Theism in Medieval India. London : Williams and Norgate, 1921.

Cassirer, Ernst. The Philosophy of Symbolic Forms, Vol. II : Mythical Thought. Translated by Ralph Manheim. New Haven : Yale University Press, 1955.

Chakravarti, Chintaharan. The Tantras : Studies in Their Religion and Literature. Calcutta : Sankar Bhattacharya, 1963.

Chakravarti, Prabhat C. Doctrine of Śakti in Indian Literature. Calcutta : General Printers Limited, 1940.

Chattopadhyaya, S. The Evolution of Theistic Sects in India. Calcutta : Progressive Publishers, 1962.

Chatterji, Suniti K. The Indian Synthesis, and Racial and Cultural Inter-Mixture in India. Poona : Bhandarkar Oriental Research Institute, 1953.

Cles-Reden, Sybile. The Realm of the Great Goddess. Englewood Cliffs, N. J. : Prentice-Hall, 1962.

Crooke, W. The Popular Religion and Folklore of Northern India. 2 vols. Revised ed. Delhi : Devandra Jain, 1968.

The Cultural Heritage of India, Vol. IV : The Religions. Edited by Haridas Bhattacharyya. 2d. ed. revised and enlarged. Calcutta : The Ramakrishna Mission Institute of Culture, 1956.

Danielou, Alain. Hindu Polytheism. New York : Pantheon Books, Inc., 1964.

Das Gupta, Shashi Bhusan. An Introduction to Tantric Buddhism. Calcutta : University of Calcutta, 1958.

——. Obscure Religious Cults as a Background to Bengali Literature. Calcutta : University of Calcutta, 1946.

Das Gupta, Surendranath. A History of Indian Philosophy. Vols. I and III. Cambridge : At the University Press, 1951, 1952.

De Bary, Wm. Theodore *et al.* Sources of Indian Tradition, Vol. I. Paperback ed. New York and London : Columbia University Press, 1958.

Deussen, Paul. The Philosophy of the Upanishads. Translated by A. S. Geden. Edinburgh : T and T Clark, 1919.

Diehl, Carl G. Instrument and Purpose : Studies in Rites and Rituals in South India. Lund : C. W. K. Gleerup, 1956.

Dikshitar, V. R. Ramachandra. The Lalitā Cult. (Bulletin of the Department of Indian History and Archaeology, No. 8). Mdaras : University of Madras, 1942.

Dimock, Edward C., Jr. The Place of the Hidden Moon. Chicago and London : University of Chicago Press, 1966.

——. The Thief of Love. Chicago : University of Chicago Press, 1963.

Diwakar, R. R. Bihar Through the Ages. Bombay : Orient Longmans, 1959.

Dowson, J. A Classical Dictionary of Hindu Mythology and Religion, Geography, History, Literature. 3d ed. London : Kegan Paul, Trench, Trubner and Co., Ltd., 1891.

Dumont, Louis. Une Sous-Castle de l'Inde du Sud. Paris and The Hague : Mouton and and Co., 1957.
Eliade, Mircea. Cosmos and History (The Myth of the Eternal Return). Translated by Willard R. Trask. New Tork : Harper and Row, Pyblishers, 1959.
——, Mircea. Images and Symbols. Translated by Philip Mairet. London : Harvill Press, 1961.
——. Mephistopheles and the Androgyne. Translated by J. M. Cohen. New York : Sheed and Ward, 1965.
——. Myths, Dreams, and Mysteries. Translated by Philip Mairet. Torchbook ed. New-York : Harper and Row, Publishers, 1967.
——. Myth and Reality. Translated by Willard R. Trask. New York : Harper and Row, Publishers, 1963.
——. Patterns in Comparative Religion. Translated by Rosemary Sheed. Cleveland : The World Publishing Co., 1963.
——. The Quest : History and Meaning in Religion. Chicago : University of Chicago, 1969.
——. Rites and Symbols of Initiation : The Mysteries of Birth and Rebirth. Translated by Willard R. Trask. Torchbook ed. New York : Harper and Row, Publishers, 1965.
——. The Sacred and the Profane. Translated by Willard R. Trask. New York and Evanston : Harper and Row, Publishers, 1961.
——. Shamanism : Archaic Techniques of Ecstasy. New York : Pantheon Books, Inc., 1964.
——. Yoga : Immortality and Freedom. Translated by Willard R. Trask. New York : Pantheon Books, Inc., 1958.
Eliade, Mircea, and Kitagawa, J. M., eds. The History of Religions : Essays on Methodology. Chicago : University of Chicago, 1959.
Eliot, Sir Charles. Hinduism and Buddhism : An Historical Sketch. Vol. II. New York : Barnes and Noble, Inc., 1968.
Elmore, Wilber T. Dravidian Gods in Modern Hinduism. (University Studies of the University of Nebraska, Vol. XV, No. 1.) Lincoln : University of Nebraska, 1915.
Emeneau, M. B. Brahui and Dravidian Comparative Grammar. Berkeley and Los-Angeles : University of California Press, 1962.
Farquhar, J. N. An Outline of the Religious Literature of India. London : Oxford University Press, 1920.
Gaster, T. H. Thespis : Ritual ,Myth, and Drama in the Ancient Near East. Torchbook ed. New York : Harper and Brothers, Publishers, 1966.
Ghosha, P. Durgā-Pūjā. Calcutta : Hindu Patriot Press, 1871.
Glasenapp, Helmuth von. Immortality and Salvation in Indian Religions. Translated by E. F. G. Payne. Calcutta : Susil Gupta India (Private), Ltd., 1963.
Gonda, Jan. Change and Continuity in Indian Religion. The Hague : Mouton and Company, 1965.
Griswold, H. D. The Religion of the Rig Veda. London : Oxford University Press, 1923.
Gupte, Rai Bahadur. Hindu Holidays and Ceremonies. 2d ed. revised. Calcutta : Thacker, Spinkad and Co., 1919.
Harper, Edward, ed. Religion in South Asia. Seattle : University of Washington Press, 1964.
Hazra, H. C. Studies in the Purāṇic Record on Hindu Rites and Customs. Dacca : University of Dacca, 1940.

Hiriyanna, H. Outlines of Indian Philosophy. London : George Allen and Unwin Ltd., 1967.

Hubert, Henri, and Mauss, Manuel. Sacrifice : Its Nature and Function. Translated by W. D. Halls. Chicago : University of Chicago Press, 1963.

Husserl, Edmund. Ideas : General Introduction to Pure Phenomenology. Translated by W. R. Boyce Gibson. 2d ed. London : George Allen and Unwin Ltd., 1967.

Isherwood, Christopher. Ramakrishna and His Disciples. New York : Simon and Schuster, 1965.

Iyengar, T. C. Rajan. The Hindu-Aryan Theory on Evolution and Involution. New York and London : Funk and Wagnalls Co., 1908.

Kane, P. V. History of Dharmaśāstra. Vol. II, Part II. Poona : Bhandarkar Oriental Research Institute, 1941.

Karmakar, A. P. The Religions of India. Vol. I. Lonvala, India : Mira Publishing House, 1950.

King, Winston L. Introduction to Religion : A Phenomenological Approach. 2d ed. revised. New York : Harper and Row, Publishers, 1968.

Kitagawa, Joseph M., ed. The History of Religions : Essays on the Problem of Understanding. ("Essays in Divinity Series", Vol. I.) Chicago : University of Chicago Press, 1967.

——. Religions of the East. Philadelphia : The Westminster Press, 1960.

Kramrisch, Stella. The Hindu Temple. Vol. I. Calcutta : University of Calcutta, 1946.

Lévi-Strauss, Claude. Structural Anthropology. Translated by C. Jacobsen and B. G. Schoeff. New York : Basic Books, Inc., 1963.

Long, Charles H. Alpha, The Myths of Creation. New York : George Braziller, 1963.

Maity, P. K. Historical Studies in the Cult of the Goddess Manasa. Calcutta : Punthi Pustak, 1966.

Malik, S. C. Indian Civilization : The Formative Period. Simla : Indian Institute of Advanced Study, 1968.

Marriott, McKim, ed. Village India : Studies in the Little Community. Chicago and London : University of Chicago Press, 1955.

Merleau-Ponty, M. Signs. Translated by Richard C. McCleary. Evanston : Nortwestern University Press, 1964.

Monier-Williams, M. Brahmanism and Hinduism. 4th ed. enlarged and improved. New York : Macmillan and Co., 1891.

Morgan, Kenneth W., ed. The Religion of the Hindus. New York : The Ronald Press Co., 1953.

Muirhead-Thomson, R. C. Assam Valley : Beliefs and Customs of the Assamese Hindus. London : Luzac and Company, Ltd., 1948.

Neumann, Erich. The Great Mother. Translated by Ralph Manheim. New York : Pantheon Books, Inc., 1955.

New Larousse Encyclopedia of Mythology. Introduction by Robert Graves. Translated by R. Aldington and D. Ames. Revised from the French ed. London : Paul Hamlyn, 1959.

Nilakanta Sastri, K. A. Development of Religion in South India. Bombay : Orient Longmans, 1963.

Oppert, Gustav. On the Original Inhabitants of Bharatavarṣa or India Westminster : Archibald Constable and Company, 1893.

Otto, Rudolf. The Idea of the Holy. Translated by John W. Harvey. 2d ed. revised. London : Oxford University Press, 1952.

Pandit, M. P. Lights on the Tantra. 3d ed. Madras : Ganesh and Co. Private, Ltd., 1968.
——. Studies in the Tantras and the Veda. Madras : Ganesh and Co. Private, Ltd., 1964.
Panikkar, K. M. A Survey of Indian History. Bombay : Asia Publishing House, 1965.
Patai, Raphael, ed. Women in the Modern World. New York : The Free Press, 1967.
Payne, Ernest A. The Śāktas : An Introductory and Comparative Study. Calcutta : Wesley Publishing House, 1933.
Philips, C. H., ed. Historians of India, Pakistan, and Ceylon. London : Oxford University Press, 1961.
Pott, Pieter H. Yoga and Yantra : Their Interrelation and Their Significance for Indian Archaeology. The Hague : Martinus Nijhoff, 1966.
Potter, Karl H. Presuppositions of India's Philosophies. Englewood Cliffs, New Jersey : Prentice-Hall, Inc., 1963.
Prakash, Buddha. Political and Social Movements in Ancient Panjab. Delhi : Motilal Banarsidass, 1964.
Przyluski, Jean. La Grande Déesse. Paris : Payot, 1950.
Pusalker, A. D. Studies in the Epics and Puraāṇs. Bombay : Bharatiya Vidya Bhavan, 1963.
Radhakrishnan, S. The Hindu View of Life. New York : The Macmillan Co., 1964.
——, ed. The Principal Upanishads. New York : Harper and Row, 1953.
Raja, C. K. Survey of Sanskrit Literature. Bombay : Bharatiya Vidya Bhavan, 1962.
Renou, Louis. Hinduism. New York : George Braziller, 1962.
——. The Nature of Hinduism. Translated by Patrick Evans. New York : Walker and Company, 1962.
Sarma, D. S. The Renaissance of Hinduism. Benares : Benares Hindu University, 1944.
Sen, Dinesh C. History of Bengali Language and Literature. Calcutta : University of Calcutta, 1911.
Singer, Milton, ed. Krishna : Myths, Rites, and Attitudes. Honolulu : East-West Center Press, 1966.
——. Traditional India : Structure and Change. Philadelphia : The American Folklore Society, 1959.
Sinha, Jadunath. Shakta Monism : The Cult of Shakti. 1st ed. Calcutta : Sinha Publishing House, 1966.
Spratt, P. Hindu Culture and Personality : A Psychoanalytic Study. Bombay : P. G. Mahaktala and Sons Private, Ltd., 1966.
Sircar, D. C., ed. The Śakti Cult and Tārā. Calcutta : University of Calcutta Press, 1967.
Tarn, W. W. The Greeks in Bactria and India. Cambridge : At the University Press, 1951.
Thompson, E. J., and Spencer, A. M.., trans. Bengali Religious Lyrics : Śākta. Calcutta : Association Press, 1923.
Tillich, Paul. Systematic Theology. Vol. III. Chicago : University of Chicago Press, 1963.
Underhill, M. The Hindu Religious Year. Calcutta : Association Press, 1932.
Upadhyaya, B. S. Women in Rigveda. Benares : Nand Kishore and Brothers, 1941.
Vidyarthi, L. P., ed. Aspects of Religion in Indian Society. Meerut : Kedar Nath Ram Nath, 1961.
Wach, Joachim. Sociology of Religion. Chicago : University of Chicago Press, 1957.
Watts, Alan W. The Two Hands of God : The Myths of Polarity. New York : George Braziller, 1963.

Woodroffe, John. Introduction to Tantra Śāstra. 5th ed. Madras : Ganesh and Co. Private, Ltd., 1969.

——. Śakti and Śākta. 5th and 7th eds. Madras : Ganesh and Co. Private, Ltd., 1959, 1969.

——. The Serpent Power. 7th ed. Madras : Ganesh and Co. Private, Ltd., 1964.

——. Tantrarāja Tantra : A Short Analysis. Madras : Ganesh and Co. Private, Ltd., 1964.

——. The World As Power : Reality, Life, Mind, Matter, Causality and Continuity. 3d ed. Madras : Ganesh and Co. rPivate, Ltd., 1966.

Woodroffe, John, and Mukhyopadhyaya, P. N. Mahāmāyā, The World As Power : Power As Consciousness. Madras : Ganesh and Co. Private, Ltd., 1964.

Zimmer, Heinrich. The King and the Corpse. Edited by Joseph Campbell. New York : Meridian Books, Inc., 1960.

——. Myths and Symbols in Indian Art and Civilization. Edited by Joseph Campbell. New York : Harper and Brothers, 1962.

——. Philosophies of India. Edited by Joseph Campbell. Meridian Book. Cleveland and New York : The World Publishing Co., 1964.

ARTICLES AND PERIODICALS

Agrawala, R. C. "Some Sculptures of Durgā-Mahiṣāsuramardinī from Rajasthana". Adyar Library Bulletin, XIX, Part 2 (1955), 37-46.

Banerjea, J. N. "Some Folk Goddesses of Ancient and Medieval India". The Indian Historical Quaterly, XIV, No. 1 (1938), 101-109.

Banerjee, Nani G. "A New Light on Durgotsava". The Indian Historiocal Quaterly, XXI, No. 3 (1945), 227-231.

Bharati, Agehananda. "Pilgrimage in the Indian Tradition". History of Religions, III, No. 1 (Summer, 1963), 135-167.

Boaz, G. D. "The Terrible Mother : A Psychological Study". Journal of Madras University, XVI (1944), 62-74.

Brown, W. Norman. "The Content of Cultural Continuity in India". The Journal of Asian Studies, XX, No. 4 (August, 1961), 427-434.

——. "Mythology in India". In Mythologies of the Ancient World. Edited by S. N. Kramer. New York : Doubleday and Co., Inc., 1961. Pp. 277-330.

——. "The Name of the Goddess Minakśi, 'Fish-Eye'". Journal of the American Oriental Society, LXVII (1947), 209-214.

——. "Proselyting the Asuras". Journal of the American Oriental Society, XXXIX (1919), 100-103.

Burrow, T. "Dravidic Studies VII : Further Dravidian Words in Sanskrit". Bulletin of the School of Oriental and African Studies, XII (1948), 365-396. (Kraus reprints,1964).

Chakravarti, Chintaharan. "The Cult of Bāro Bhāiyā of Eastern Bengal". Journal of the Royal Asiatic Societyjof Bengal, XXVI (1930), 379-388.

Charpentier, Jarl. "The Meaning and Etymology of Pūjā". Indian Antiquary, LVI (1927), 93-98, 130-135.

Chatterji, S. K. "Purāṇa Legends and the Prakrit Tradition in New Indo-Aryan". Bulletin of the School of Oriental and African Studies, VIII (1936), 457-466.

Chaudhuri, N. M. "The Cult of Vana-Durgā, a Tree-Deity". Journal of the Royal Asiatic Society of Bengal (Letters), XI, No. 2 (1945), 75-84.

Clark, T. W. "Evolution of Hinduism in Medieval Bengali Literature". Bulletin of the School of Oriental and African Studies, XVII (1955), 503-518.

Das, S. R. "Ālpanā of the Kumārī-Vratas of Bengal". Journal of the Indian Society of Oriental Art, XI (1943), 126-132.

——. "Clay Figurines of the Kumārī-Vratas of Bengal". Journal of the Indian Society of Oriental Art, XIV (1946), 91-94.

Dimock, Edward C., Jr. "The Goddess of Snakes in Medieval Bengali Literature I". History of Religions, I, No. 2 (Winter, 1962), 307-321.

——. "The Goddess of Snakes in Medieval Bengali Literature II". History of Religions, III, No. 2 NWinter, 1964), 300-322.

Eliade, Mircea. "Cosmical Homology and Yoga". Journal of the Indian Society of Oriental Art, V (1937), 188-203.

Emeneau, M. B. "India As a Linguistic Area". Language, XXXII (1956), 3-16.

——. "Linguistic Prehistory of India". Proceedings of the American Philosophical Society, XCVIII (1954), 282-292.

Farquhar, J. N. "Temple-and-Image Worship in Hinduism". Journal of the Royal Asiatic Society of Great Britain and Ireland, 1928, pp. 15-23.

Fink, Conrad. "A 'Living Goddess' at 6 — But Her Life's A Lonely One". The Chicago Sun-Times, August 8, 1965.

Fleet, J. F. "Kaliyuga Era of B. C. 3102". Journal of the Royal Asiatic Society of Great Britain and Ireland, 1911, pp. 479-496, 675-689.

Freed, Ruth S., and Freed, S. A. "Two Mother-Goddess Ceremonies of Delhi State in the Great and Little Traditions". Southwestern Journal of Anthropology, XVIII (1962), 246-277.

Gait, E. A. "Human Sacrifice in Ancient Assam". Journal of the Royal Asiatic Society of Bengal, LXVII, Part 3 (1898), 56-65.

Guenther, Herbert V. "Tantra and Revelation". History of Religions, VII, No. 4 (May, 1968), 279-301.

Hornell, James. "The Ancient Village Gods of South India". Antiquity, XVIII (1944), 78-88.

Jayaswal, K. P. "Chronological Totals in Puranic Chronicles and the Kaliyuga Era". Journal of the Bihar and Orissa Research Society, III, Part 2 (1917), 246-262.

Lévi-Strauss, Claude. "Structural Analysis in Linguistics and in Anthropology". In Theory in Anthropology : A Sourcebook. Edited by Robert A. Manners and David Kaplan. Chicago : Aldine Publishing Co., 1968. Pp. 530-540.

Luyster, Robert. "The Study of Myth : Two Approaches". Journal of Bible and Religion XXXIV, No. 3 (July, 1966), 235-243.

Majumdar, B. C. "Durgā : Her Origin and History". Journal of the Royal Asiatic Society of Great Britain and Ireland, 1906, pp. 355-362.

Mankad, D. R. "The Yugas". Poona Orientalist, V (1942), 206-216.

Menon, C. A. "The Histrionic Art of Malabar". Journal of the Indian Society of Oriental Art, IX (1941), 105-132.

Mitra, Rajendrala. "On Human Sacrifices in Ancient India". Journal of the Asiatic Society of Bengal, LXV, No. 1 (1876), 76-118.

Mitra, S. C. "On the Cult of the Tree-Goddess in Eastern Bengal". Man in India, II (1922), 230-241.

——. "The Cult of the Lake-Goddess of Orissa". Journal of the Anthropological Society of Bombay, XII (1920-1924), 190-197.

Morisson, Barrie M. "Social and Cultural History of Bengal : Approach and Methodology". Nalini Kanta Bhattasali Commemorative Volume. Edited by A. B. Habibullah. Dacca : n.p., 1966. Pp. 323-338.

Moti, C. "Studies in the Cult of the Mother Goddess in Ancient India", Bulletin of the Prince of Wales Museum of Western India (No. 12, 1973), pp. 1-47, esp. pp. 28-36.

O'Flaherty, Wendy D. "Asceticism and Sexuality in the Mythology of Siva, Part I". History of Religions, VIII, No. 4 (May, 1969), 300-337.

——. "Asceticism and Sexuality in the Mythology of Siva, Part II". History of Religions, IX, No. 1 (August, 1969), 1-41.

Pocock, David F. "The Anthropology of Time-Reckoning". Contributions to Indian Sociology, No. 7 (1964), pp. 18-29.

Przyluski, Jean. "La Croyance au Messie dans l'Inde et l'Iran". Revue de l'Histoire des Religions, C (1929), 1-12.

——. "From the Great Goddess to Kāla". The Indian Historical Quarterly, XIV (1938), 267-274.

——. "The Great Goddess in India and Iran". The Indian Historical Quarterly, X (1934), 405-430.

Raghavan, V. "Variety and Integration in the Pattern of Indian Culture," *The Far Eastern Quarterly*, XV, No. 4 (August, 1956), 497-505.

Ricoeur, Paul. "The Problem of the Double-Sense as Hermeneutic Problem and as Semantic Problem". In Myths and Symbols : Studies in Honor of Mircea Eliade. Edited by J. M. Kitagawa and C. H. Long. Chicago : University of Chicago Press, 1969. Pp. 63-79.

Sharma, Dasharatha. "Verbal Similarities Between the Durgā-Saptaśāta and the Devī-Bhāgavata-Purāṇa and Other Considerations Bearing on Their Date". Purāṇa, V, No. 1 (January, 1963), 90-113.

Sircar, Dines C. "The Śākta Piṭhas". Journal of the Royal Asiatic Society of Bengal, XIV, Part 1 (1948), 1-108.

Thieme, Paul. "Pūjā". Journal of Oriental Research, XXVII (1957-1958), 1-16.

Tucci, Giuseppe. "Earth in India and Tibet". Eranos Jahrbuch, XXII (1953), 323-364.

Vaudeville, Ch. "Evolution of Love-Symbolism in Bhāgavatism". Journal of the American Oriental Society, LXXXII, No. 1 (1962), 31-40.

Vogel, J. Ph. "The Head-offering to the Goddess in Pallava Sculpture". Bulletin of the School of Oriental and African Studies, VI (1932), 539-543.

Wayman, Alex. "Climactic Times in Indian Mythology and Religion". History of Religions, IN, No. 2 (Winter, 1965), 295-318.

Zimmer, H. "Some Aspects of Time in Indian Art". Journal of the Indian Society of Oriental Art, I, No. 1 (June, 1933), 30-51.

TEXTS

Atharva-Veda. Translated by William Dwight Whitney. 2 vols. (Harvard Oriental Series, Vols. VII and VIII). Cambridge : Harvard University Press, 1904.

The Bhagavad-Gītā. Translated with commentary and notes by Mohini M. Chatterji. New York : The Julian Press, 1960.

Brahma-Vaivarta Puranam. Translated by Rajendra Nath Sen Suddhindra Nath Vasu. (The Sacred Books of the Hindus, Vol. XXIV). Allahabad : The Panini Office Bahadurganj, 1922.

The Devī Upanishad. Translated by Alain Danielou. Adyar Library Bulletin, XIX, Parts 1-2 (1955), 77-84.

Harivamśa. Edited and translated by Manmatha Nath Dutt. Calcutta : n.p., 1897.

The Kālikāpurāṇa (Worship of the Goddess according to), tr. with an Introduction and Notes of Chapters 54-69 by K. R. Van Kooij. Leiden : E. J. Brill, 1972.

Kāma-Kalā-Vilāsa. Translated with commentary by Arthur Avalon (John Woodroffe). Madras : Ganesh and Co. Private, Ltd., 1961.

Karpūrādi-Stotra (Hymn to Kali). Translated by Arthur Avalon (John Woodroffe). Madras : Ganesh and Co. Private, Ltd., 1965.

The Kena Upanishad. Translated by T. M. P. Mahadevan. Madras : Ganesh and Co. Private, Ltd., 1958.

Kulacūdāmaṇi Nigama. Edited by Arthur Avalon (John Woodroffe). Madras : Ganesh and Co. Private, Ltd., 1956.

Kulārṇava Tantra. Free translation and readings by M. P. Pandit. Madras : Ganesh and Co. Private, Ltd., 1965.

Mahānirvāṇa Tantra. Translated with commentary by Arthur Avalon (John Woodroffe). Madras : Ganesh and Co. Private, Ltd., 1963.

The Mārkaṇḍeya Purāṇa. Translated by F. E. Pargiter. Calcutta : The Asiatic Society of Bengal, 1904.

Original Sanskrit Texts. Collected, translated, and illustrated by John Muir. 3d ed. 5 vols. Amsterdam : Oriental Press, 1967.

The Rudhirādhyāya. Translated by W. C. Blaquiere. Asiatic Researches (London), V (1807), 371-391.

The Saundaryalaharī. Edited and translated by W. Norman Brown. (Harvard Oriental Series, Vol. XLIII). Cambridge : Harvard Uhiversity Press, 1958.

The Sita Upanishad. Translated by Alain Danielou. Adyar Library Bulletin, Vol. XIX, Parts 3-4 (1955).

Śrī Mad Devī-Bhāgavatam. Translated by Swami Vijnananda. (The Sacred Books of the Hindus, Vol. XXVI). Allahabad : The Panini Office Bahadurganj, 1921-1923.

The Vishnu Purana. Translated with notes by H. H. Wilson. 3d ed. Calcutta : Punthi Pustak, 1961.

INDEX

A

Aalto, P., 81n
Alekseev, G.V., 81n
Aboriginals/tribals, IX, 39n, 48, 51, 79f., 85-87, 90, 122, 139-140, 147
ācāra(s), 245-249
adhikarabheda, 64
ardhanārīśvara, 143, 259
  theories of, 143-144
Aditi, 109-111
Advaita, 160-161
āgama/nigama, 2, 87, 126n, 163
Agrawala, V.S., XI-XII, 65n, 78n, 93n, 157n, 175, 179-180, 206
Ālpanā, 206f.
anuttarayoga, 256, 261
Āranyaka/Araṇyānī, 103-105, 115-116
āsana, 215f., 217
Asuras/Asur, 3, 4, 91n, 94-98, 117, 175-180
Atharva veda, 82, 101, 102, 255, 230
avatār(s), 239, 240
Ayyangar, T.R.S., 4, 154n

B

Banerjea, J.N., 50n, 52n, 53n, 145n
Basham, A.L., 92n, 103n, 104n, 105n, 106n, 115-116
Beane, W.C., 130n
Bergaigne, A., 95-96, 97n
Bhagavad-Gītā, 87n, 151n, 199n, 222n
bhakta/bhakti, 132, 142, 151, 239, 240
Bharati, A., 2, 131, 211n, 212, 213n, 242n, 246, 247, 248, 249n, 250, 251n, 267n
Bhattacharji, S., 106n, 140n
Bhattacharyya, B., 126, 127n, 128n, 129-131
bhukti, 249-250
bhūtaśuddhi, 215, 216, 217
Boaz, G.D., 263, 264
Bochenski, J.M., 8, 20n
bodhana, 218f.
brahman/Brahman, 109, 150, 151-156
Brāhmaṇa(s), 2
  Aitareya, 108, 230n; Pañcaviṃśa, 108n; Śatapatha, 93n, 107n, 108n; Taittīrya, 101n, 113n
Brāhmans/Brāhmanism, VIII, 40, 62-64, 98-99, 125, 137-139, 141-142
Brandon, S.G.F., 68, 118n, 238
Brown, W.N., 56, 97, 125n, 155n, 231
Buddhism, 1, 82; see Tantrism
Burrow, T., 83n, 84

C

Campbell, J., 42n, 58n, 76, 77n, 78n, 86n, 99, 117, 203n
Chakravarti, C., 51, 127n, 192n, 219
Chandra, M., 78n
Charpentier, J., 49n, 209n, 210
Chatterji, S.K., 80n, 81n, 87-89, 90
Chattopadhyaya, S., 77n, 78n, 92n, 128n, 143, 144
centripetalization, 98ff., 125
  absolute, see Chap. III
Cles-Reden, S., XI, 44n
Coomaraswamy, A., 49n, 50n, 51n, 52n, 97n, 163n, 187n, 200n, 219n
cosmic combat, 40, 175-180, 258, 256-262
cosmogenesis, 150-168, 180, 262
cosmogony/cosmology, see Chap. III; 181-182, 185, 194, 195, 255, 257, 258, 261-262, 265, 266
  and love, 168, 240
cosmoredemption, 175-180
creation/emanation, see Chap. III; 240n, 262
  invocative, 171-172
  involuntary, 172-174
  purposive, 174-175
  tendentious, 169-171
cult(s), see Chap. IV
  goddess, 48n, 49, 51n, 53n, 55-61
Cultural Heritage of India, 4, 53n, 158n, 242n, 244n, 251n

171n, 177n, 181n, 185n, 189n, 194n,